PATROLOGY

VOL. I
THE BEGINNINGS OF PATRISTIC LITERATURE

PATROLOGY

by

JOHANNES QUASTEN

PROFESSOR OF ANCIENT CHURCH HISTORY
AND CHRISTIAN ARCHAEOLOGY
THE CATHOLIC UNIVERSITY OF AMERICA
WASHINGTON D.C.

VOLUME I

The Beginnings of Patristic Literature

CHRISTIAN CLASSICS, INC.
WESTMINSTER, MARYLAND
1983

First Published, 1950
Reprinted by Christian Classics, Inc., 1983

ISBN: 0-87061-084-8
Library of Congress Catalog Card Number: 83-72018
Printed in the United States of America

PREFACE

The present volume is the first of a new Patrology that strives to place at the disposal of the English-reading public a solid introduction to Early Christian literature. So far all the manuals of Patrology in our language are translations. As a result, they do not pay enough attention to versions and studies in English, and have practically gone out of date by the time they reach the reader. Yet, it is especially within recent years that Patrology has taken great strides forward. New finds have been made, new sources opened up. One need but recall the astonishing fact that a sermon preached in the second century by the famous Melito of Sardes turned up among the University of Michigan papyri and was brought out by the American scholar Bonner. It is one publication among many for which we can thank the sands of Egypt. Even more striking was the recent discovery of twelve volumes of Egyptian papyri containing fourty-two Gnostic treatises at the ancient Chénoboskion to the north of Luxor. Many of these writings were known to us from the quotations of Irenaeus and other anti-Gnostic authors but all of them had been lost. This new find is perhaps the greatest ever made in the patristic field. It will cast an entirely new light on the beginnings of Christian theology and the great controversy between Christian doctrine and Hellenistic philosophy. Keeping step with such developments, the philologists have put out new critical editions, while the theologians have by their penetrating studies of the contents of the texts contributed notably to their elucidation and understanding.

For this reason the new Patrology sets great value on presenting a bibliography designed to inform both learner and specialist on the literature of the subject. Therefore, it lists (1) critical editions, (2) translations into modern languages particularly English, and (3) articles and monographs. In order to save time for the scholar and orientate him more readily, it has been thought best to give in full the titles of articles in periodicals instead of merely listing references. Since the reader can thus determine at a glance whether a particular study has anything he needs or not, he is spared considerable trouble and annoyance.

To arouse interest in the works of the Fathers, numerous

excerpts are quoted in English. These are thought of as samples that, by giving the reader a taste of the beauty and sublimity of the Patristic writings, may tempt him to take in hand the original and get his own impression of it, or, if that is too much for him, at least to read it in some good translation. Only this, if achieved, will put the student close to Patristic literature, because only then does he sense the atmosphere of Christian antiquity and begin to penetrate its world. The author's experience as a teacher at the University occasioned his adopting this device. The selections are designed also to show the development of theology in the early centuries and to illustrate the approach of the Fathers to the deposit of faith. May the student share the feeling once expressed by Cardinal Newman: "The vision of the Fathers was always to my imagination, I may say, a paradise of delight."

In conclusion it is my pleasant duty to acknowledge my obligation to Rt. Rev. M. J. Higgins, Ph. D., G. F. Diercks, Ph. D., and C. Bouman for their helpful suggestions. I wish also to thank my colleagues, Rev. J. C. Plumpe, Ph. D., and Rev. Patrick Skehan, S. T. D.

The Catholic University of America
Washington D. C.

JOHANNES QUASTEN

TABLE OF CONTENTS

CHAPTER III

THE BEGINNINGS OF CHRISTIAN ROMANCE, FOLK STORIES AND
LEGENDS

CHAPTER IV

THE BEGINNINGS OF CHRISTIAN POETRY

CHAPTER V

THE FIRST ACTS OF THE MARTYRS 176

CHAPTER VI

CHAPTER VII

CHAPTER VIII

THE BEGINNINGS OF ANTI-HERETICAL LITERATURE

LIST OF ABBREVIATIONS

AAB	Abhandlungen, Berlin Academy.
AAM	Abhandlungen, Munich Academy.
AAWW	Anzeiger der Akademie der Wissenschaften in Wien. Vienna.
AB	Analecta Bollandiana. Brussels.
AC	F. J. Dölger, Antike und Christentum. Münster i.W.
ACL	Antiquité classique. Louvain.
ACW	Ancient Christian Writers, edit. J. Quasten and J. C. Plumpe. Westminster, Md.
AER	American Ecclesiastical Review. Washington, D.C.
AGP	Archiv für Geschichte der Philosophie. Berlin.
AGWG	Abhandlungen der Gesellschaft der Wissenschaften. Göttingen.
AHD	Archives d'histoire doctrinal et littéraire. Paris.
AIPh	Annuaire de l'institut de philologie et d'histoire orientales et slaves. Paris.
AJPh	American Journal of Philology. Baltimore.
AKK	Archiv für katholisches Kirchenrecht. Mainz.
AL	Acta Linguistica. Copenhagen.
ALMA	Archivum latinitatis medii aevi (Bulletin Du Cange). Paris.
ANF	Ante-Nicene Fathers. Buffalo and New York.
Ang	Angelicum. Rome.
ANL	Ante-Nicene Christian Library. Edinburgh.
Ant	Antonianum. Rome.
APF	Archiv für Papyrusforschung. Leipzig.
APh	Archives de philosophie. Paris.
AR	Archivum Romanicum. Florence.
ARW	Archiv für Religionswissenschaft. Berlin and Leipzig.
ASS	Acta Sanctorum, edit. by the Bollandists. Brussels.
AST	Analecta Sacra Tarraconensia. Barcelona.
AT	Année théologique. Paris.
AThR	Anglican Theological Review. New York.
BEHE	Bibliothèque de l'école des hautes études. Paris.
Bess	Bessarione. Rome.
BFC	Bolletino di Filologia classica. Turin.
BFTh	Beiträge zur Förderung der Theologie. Gütersloh.
BHTh	Beiträge zur historischen Theologie. Tübingen.
Bibl	Biblica. Rome.
BiZ	Biblische Zeitschrift. Paderborn.
BJ	Bursians Jahresbericht über die Fortschritte der klassischen Altertumswissenschaft. Leipzig.
BJR	Bulletin of John Rylands Library. Manchester.
BKV	Bibliothek der Kirchenväter, edited by V. Thalhofer. Kempten.
BKV²	Bibliothek der Kirchenväter, ed. by O. Bardenhewer, Th. Schermann, C. Weyman. Kempten and Munich.
BKV³	Bibliothek der Kirchenväter. Zweite Reihe, ed. by O. Bardenhewer, J. Zellinger, J. Martin. Munich.
BLE	Bulletin de littérature ecclésiastique. Toulouse.

BM	Benediktinische Monatsschrift. Beuron.
BNJ	Byzantinisch-Neugriechische Jahrbücher. Athens.
BoZ	Bonner Zeitschrift für Theologie und Seelsorge. Düsseldorf.
BPEZ	Bolletino del Comitato per la preparazione dell'Edizione nazionale dei Classici greci e latini. Rome.
Byz	Byzantion. Paris and Liège.
BZ	Byzantinische Zeitschrift. Leipzig.
CBQ	Catholic Biblical Quarterly. Washington, D.C.
CC	Civiltà Cattolica. Rome.
ChQ	The Church Quarterly Review. London.
CHR	The Catholic Historical Review. Washington, D.C.
CJ	Classical Journal. Chicago.
CPh	Classical Philology. Chicago.
CQ	Classical Quarterly. London.
CR	The Classical Review. London.
CPT	Cambridge Patristic Texts.
CSCO	Corpus scriptorum christianorum orientalium. Paris.
CSEL	Corpus scriptorum ecclesiasticorum latinorum. Vienna.
CTh	Collectanea Theologica. Lwow.
DAL	Dictionnaire d'archéologie chrétienne et de liturgie. Paris.
DAp	Dictionnaire d'apologétique. Paris.
DLZ	Deutsche Literaturzeitung. Leipzig.
DT	Divus Thomas. Fribourg, Switzerland.
DTC	Dictionnaire de théologie catholique. Paris.
DTP	Divus Thomas. Piacenza.
EA	Enchiridion Asceticum, edit. Rouët de Journel-Dutilleul, 4th edit. Barcelona, 1947.
EE	Estudios Ecclesiásticos. Madrid.
EH	Enchiridion Fontium Historiae ecclesiasticae, ed. Ueding-Kirch, 6th ed. Barcelona, 1947.
EHPR	Etudes d'histoire et de philosophie religieuse.
EHR	English Historical Review. London.
EL	Ephemerides Liturgicae. Rome.
EO	Echos d'Orient. Paris.
EP	Enchiridion Patristicum, ed. M. J. Rouët de Journel, 14th ed. Barcelona, 1946
EPh	Ἐκκλησιαστικὸς Φάρος. Alexandria.
ES	Enchiridion Symbolorum, edit. Denzinger-Umberg, 25th ed. Barcelona, 1948.
Et	Etudes. Paris.
ETL	Ephemerides Theologicae Lovanienses. Louvain.
ExpT	The Expository Times. Edinburgh.
FC	The Fathers of the Church. New York.
FLDG	Forschungen zur christl. Literatur- und Dogmengeschichte. Paderborn.
FP	Florilegium Patristicum. Bonn.
FRL	Forschungen zur Religion und Literatur des Alten und Neuen Testamentes. Göttingen.

FThSt	Freiburger Theologische Studien. Freiburg i.B.
GGA	Göttingische Gelehrte Anzeigen. Göttingen.
GCS	Die griechischen christlichen Schriftsteller. Leipzig.
Gno	Gnomon. Berlin.
Greg	Gregorianum. Rome.
GTT	Gereformeerd Theologisch Tijdschrift. Aalten.
HA	Handes Amsorya. Vienna.
HAPhG	Heidelberger Abhandlungen zur Philosophie und ihre Geschichte. Heidelberg.
HJ	The Hibbert Journal. London.
HJG	Historisches Jahrbuch der Görresgesellschaft. Cologne.
HS	Harvard Studies and Notes in phil. and lit. Cambridge, Mass.
HThR	Harvard Theological Review. Cambridge, Mass.
HZ	Historische Zeitschrift. Munich and Berlin.
IER	The Irish Ecclesiastical Record. Dublin.
IKZ	Internationale kirchliche Zeitschrift. Bern.
JA	Journal Asiatique. Paris.
James	The Apocryphal New Testament, transl. M. R. James. Oxford 1924.
JBL	Journal of Biblical Literature. New Haven.
JL	Jahrbuch für Liturgiewissenschaft. Münster i.W.
JQR	Jewish Quarterly Review. Philadelphia.
JR	Journal of Religion. Chicago.
JS	Journal des Savants. Paris.
JSOR	Journal of the Society of Oriental Research. Chicago.
JThSt	Journal of Theological Studies. London.
KA	Kyrkohistorisk Arskrift. Stockholm.
KGA	Kirchengeschtl. Abhandl., edit. M. Sdralek. Breslau.
KT	Kleine Texte, edit. H. Lietzmann. Berlin.
LCL	Loeb Classical Library. London and New York.
LF	Liturgiegeschichtliche Forschungen. Münster i.W.
LNPF	A Select Library of Nicene and Post-Nicene Fathers of the Christian Church, edit. Ph. Schaff and H. Wace. Buffalo and New York.
LQ	Liturgiegeschichtliche Quellen. Münster i.W.
LQF	Liturgiegeschichtliche Quellen und Forschungen. Münster i.W.
LThK	Lexikon für Theologie und Kirche. Freiburg i.B.
LThPh	Laval Théologique et Philosophique. Québec.
LZB	Literarisches Zentralblatt. Leipzig.
MAH	Mélanges d'archéologie et d'histoire. Rome and Paris.
MBTh	Münsterische Beiträge zur Theologie. Münster i.W.
MC	Monumenta Christiana. Bibliotheek van Christelijke Klassieken. Utrecht and Brussels.
MG	Migne, Patrologia Graeca.
ML	Migne, Patrologia Latina.
Mnem	Mnemosyne. Leyden.
MS	Mediaeval Studies. Toronto.
MSCA	Miscellanea Agostiniana. Rome, 1931.
MSCI	Miscellanea Isidoriana. Rome, 1935.

MStHTh	Münchener Studien zur historischen Theologie. Munich.
Mus	Le Muséon. Louvain.
NADG	Neues Archiv der Gesellsch. f. ältere deutsche Geschichtskunde. Hanover.
NGWG	Nachrichten der Gesellschaft der Wissenschaften zu Göttingen.
NKZ	Neue kirchliche Zeitschrift. Erlangen and Leipzig.
NRTh	Nouvelle revue théologique. Tournai.
NTT	Nieuw Theologisch Tijdschrift. Haarlem.
OC	Oriens Christianus. Leipzig.
OCh	Orientalia Christiana. Rome.
OCP	Orientalia Christiana Periodica. Rome.
OLZ	Orientalistische Literaturzeitung. Leipzig.
PB	Pastor Bonus. Trier.
PC	Paraula Cristiana. Barcelona.
Phil	Philologus. Leipzig.
PhJ	Philosophisches Jahrbuch der Görresgesellschaft. Fulda.
PhW	Philologische Wochenschrift. Leipzig.
PO	Patrologia Orientalis. Paris.
PSt	Patristic Studies, edit. R. J. Deferrari, Cath. University of America. Washington, D.C.
PThR	Princeton Theological Review. Princeton.
PWK	Pauly-Wissowa-Kroll, Realencyklopädie der klassischen Altertumswissenschaft. Stuttgart.
QLP	Questions liturgiques et paroissiales. Louvain.
RAC	Rivista di archeologia cristiana. Rome.
RACh	Reallexikon für Antike und Christentum, ed. Th. Klauser. Leipzig.
RAL	Rendiconti della Reale Academia nazionale dei Lincei. Classe di scienze mor., stor. e filol. Rome.
RAM	Revue d'ascétique et de mystique. Toulouse.
RAp	Revue pratique d'apologétique. Paris.
RB	Revue Bénédictine. Maredsous.
RBibl.	Revue biblique. Paris.
RBPh	Revue belge de philologie et d'histoire. Brussels.
RC	Revue critique d'histoire et de littérature. Paris.
RCC	Revue des cours et conférences. Paris.
REA	Revue des études arméniennes. Paris.
REAN	Revue des Etudes Anciennes. Bordeaux.
REG	Revue des Etudes Grecques. Paris.
RELA	Revue des Etudes Latines. Paris.
RelC	Religión y Cultura. Madrid.
Religio	Religio, ed. E. Buonaiuti. Rome.
RES	Revista Española de teología. Madrid.
RF	Razón y Fe. Madrid.
RFE	Revista de filología española. Madrid.
RFIC	Rivista di filologia e istruzione classica. Turin.
RGG	Religion in Geschichte und Gegenwart, ed. Gunkel-Zscharnack. Tübingen.

RH	Revue historique. Paris.
RHE	Revue d'histoire ecclésiastique. Louvain.
RHEF	Revue d'histoire de l'Eglise de France. Paris.
RHL	Revue d'histoire et de littérature religieuses. Paris.
RhM	Rheinisches Museum für Philologie. Frankfurt a.M.
RHPR	Revue d'histoire et de philosophie religieuses. Strasbourg.
RHR	Revue de l'histoire des religions. Paris.
RLM	Revue liturgique et monastique. Maredsous.
ROC	Revue de l'Orient chrétien. Paris.
RPh	Revue de philologie. Paris.
RQ	Römische Quartalschrift. Freiburg i.B.
RQH	Revue des questions historiques. Paris.
RR	Ricerche religiose. Rome.
RSFR	Rivista di studi filosofici e religiosi. Rome.
RSH	Revue de synthèse historique. Paris.
RSPT	Revue des sciences philosophiques et théologiques. Paris.
RSR	Recherches de science religieuse. Paris.
RSRUS	Revue des sciences religieuses. Strasbourg and Paris.
RT	Revue Thomiste. Paris.
RTAM	Recherches de théologie ancienne et médiévale. Louvain.
RTP	Revue de théologie et philosophie. Lausanne.
RTr	Revista trimestrale di studie filosofici e religiosi. Perugia.
SA	Studia Anselmiana. Rome.
SAB	Sitzungsberichte, Berlin Academy.
SAH	Sitzungsberichte, Heidelberg Academy.
SAM	Sitzungsberichte, Munich Academy.
SAW	Sitzungsberichte, Vienna Academy.
SC	La Scuola Cattolica. Milan.
SCA	Studies in Christian Antiquity, edit. J. Quasten. Washington, D.C.
SCH	Sources chrétiennes, ed. H. de Lubac and J. Daniélou. Paris.
Schol	Scholastik. Freiburg-Eupen.
SD	Studies and Documents, edit. K. Lake and S. Lake. London and Philadelphia.
SJMS	Speculum. Journal of Medieval Studies. Cambridge, Mass.
SKGG	Schriften der Königsberger Gelehrtengesellschaft.
SM	Studien und Mitteilungen zur Geschichte des Benediktinerordens und seiner Zweige. Munich.
SO	Symbolae Osloenses. Oslo.
So	Sophia. Milan.
SPCK	Society for Promoting Christian Knowledge. London.
SQ	Sammlung ausgewählter Quellenschriften zur Kirchen- und Dogmengeschichte. Tübingen.
SSL	Specilegium Sacrum Lovaniense. Louvain.
ST	Studi e Testi. Rome.
StC	Studia Catholica. Nijmegen.
StGKA	Studien zur Geschichte und Kultur des Altertums. Paderborn.
ThBl	Theologische Blätter. Leipzig.
ThGl	Theologie und Glaube. Paderborn.

ThJ	Theologische Jahrbücher. Leipzig.
ThLB	Theologisches Literaturblatt. Leipzig.
ThLZ	Theologische Literaturzeitung. Leipzig.
ThQ	Theologische Quartalschrift. Tübingen.
ThR	Theologische Revue. Münster i.W.
ThStKr	Theologische Studien und Kritiken. Gotha.
TJHC	Theology. Journal of Historic Christianity. London.
TP	Transactions and Proceedings of the American Philological Association. Lancaster, Pa.
TS	Theological Studies. Baltimore.
TSt	Texts and Studies, ed. J. A. Robinson. Cambridge, England.
TThZ	Trierer theologische Zeitschrift. Trier.
TU	Texte und Untersuchungen. Leipzig.
TZ	Theologische Zeitschrift. Basel.
VC	Vigiliae Christianae. Amsterdam.
VD	Verbum Domini. Rome.
VS	La vie spirituelle. Paris.
WS	Woodbrooke Studies. Manchester.
WSt	Wiener Studien. Zeitschrift für klass. Philologie. Vienna.
ZAM	Zeitschrift für Aszese und Mystik. Innsbruck-Munich.
ZDMG	Zeitschrift der Deutschen Morgenländischen Gesellschaft. Leipzig.
ZKG	Zeitschrift für Kirchengeschichte. Stuttgart.
ZkTh	Zeitschrift für katholische Theologie. Innsbruck.
ZNW	Zeitschrift für die neutestamentliche Wissenschaft und die Kunde der älteren Kirche. Giessen.
ZST	Zeitschrift für systematische Theologie. Gütersloh.

INTRODUCTION

I. THE CONCEPT AND HISTORY OF PATROLOGY

Patrology is that part of the history of Christian literature which deals with the theological authors of Christian antiquity. It comprises both the orthodox and the heretical writers, although it treats with preference those authors who represent the traditional ecclesiastical doctrine, the so-called Fathers and Doctors of the Church. Thus, Patrology can be defined as the science of the Fathers of the Church. It includes, in the West, all Christian authors up to Gregory the Great (d. 604) or Isidore of Seville (d. 636), and, in the East, it extends usually to John Damascene (d. 749).

The name of this branch of Theology is young; the Lutheran theologian, Joh. Gerhard, was the first to use it as a title of his work, *Patrologia*, published in 1653. The idea, however, of a history of Christian literature in which the theological point of view predominates is old. It begins with Eusebius, for in the introduction to his *Ecclesiastical History* (I, 1, 1), he states that he intends to report about 'the number of those who in each generation were the ambassadors of the word of God either by speech or by pen; the names, the number and the age of those who, driven by the desire of innovation to an extremity of error, have heralded themselves as the introducers of knowledge, falsely so called'. Thus, he lists all writers and writings, so far as he knows them, and gives long quotations from most of them. For this reason, Eusebius is one of the most important sources of Patrology, especially since a great number of the writings which he quotes have been lost. For some ecclesiastical authors he is the only source of information.

The first to compose a history of Christian theological literature was Jerome. In his *De viris illustribus* he intends to answer those pagans who were accustomed to jeer at the intellectual mediocrity of the Christians. For this reason, he enumerates the writers by whom Christian literature was honored. Written at Bethlehem in the year 392 at the request of the Praetorian Prefect Dexter, St. Jerome's work is modeled on the *De viris illustribus* of Suetonius; it extends from Simon Peter to Jerome himself, whose writings prior to 392 are listed. The Jewish authors, Philo and Josephus, the pagan philosopher, Seneca, and the heretical authors of Christian antiquity are incorporated in the list of names, which comprises 135 sections. For the first 78 of these sections, Jerome depends on the *Ecclesiastical History* and the *Chronicle* of Eusebius of Caesarea to such an extent that he reproduces even the mistakes of Eusebius. Each section gives a biographical sketch and evaluates the writings of the author. As soon as the work was published, St. Augustine (*Ep. 40*) expressed his regret to Jerome that he had not taken the trouble to separate the heretical from the orthodox writers. More serious is the fact that *De viris illustribus* suffers to a great extent from incorrectness, and that the whole work betrays the sympathies and antipathies of Jerome, as, for instance, the sections dealing with St. John Chrysostome and St. Ambrose indicate. Nevertheless, the work remains the basic source for the history of ancient Christian literature. For a certain number of ecclesiastical writers, such as Minucius Felix, Tertullian, Cyprian, Novatian, and others, it is the only source of information which we possess. Through more than a thousand years all historians of ancient Christian literature regarded *De viris illustribus* as the basis of all their studies, and their sole endeavor was to write continuations of this great work.

Editions: ML 23, 601–720. — C. A. BERNOULLI, Der Schriftstellerkatalog des Hieronymus. Freiburg i. B., 1895. — E. C. RICHARDSON, TU 14, 1. Leipzig, 1896. — G. HERDING, Leipzig 1924.

Studies: ST. V. SYCHOWSKI, Hieronymus als Literarhistoriker. Eine quellen-kritische Untersuchung der Schrift des hl. Hieronymus De viris illustribus. Münster i. W., 1894. — J. HUEMER, Studien zu den ältesten christlich-lateinischen Literarhistorikern. 1. Hieronymus De viris illustribus: WSt 16 (1894) 121–158. — G. WENTZEL, Die griechische Uebersetzung der Viri illustres des Hieronymus (TU 13, 3). Leipzig, 1895. — A. FEDER, Studien zum Schriftstellerkatalog des hl. Hieronymus. Freiburg i. B., 1927.

About the year 480, Gennadius, a priest of Marseilles, brought out under the same title a very useful continuation and addition, which most of the manuscripts incorporate as a second part of St. Jerome's work. Gennadius was a Semi-Pelagian, a fact which here and there influences his description; otherwise he shows himself to be a man of extensive knowledge and accurate judgment. His work remains of prime importance for the history of ancient Christian literature.

Editions: ML 58, 1059–1120. — A. BERNOULLI, E. C. RICHARDSON and G. HERDING, cf. above.

Studies: E. JUNGMANN, Quaestiones Gennadianae (Progr.). Leipzig, 1881. — B. CZAPLA, Gennadius als Literarhistoriker. Eine quellenkritische Untersuchung der Schrift des Gennadius von Marseille De viris illustribus. Münster i. W., 1898. — J. HUEMER, Studien zu den ältesten christlich-lateinischen Literarhistorikern. 2. Gennadius De viris illustribus: WSt 20 (1898) 141–149. — F. DIEKAMP, Wann hat Gennadius seinen Schriftstellerkatalog verfasst?: RQ 12 (1898) 411–420. — A. FEDER, Der Semipelagianismus im Schriftstellerkatalog des Gennadius von Marseille: Schol 2 (1927) 481–514; *idem*, Die Entstehung und Veröffentlichung des gennadianischen Schriftstellerkatalogs: Schol 8 (1933) 217–232; *idem*, Zusätze des gennadianischen Schriftstellerkatalogs: Schol 8 (1933) 380–399.

Of less value is Isidore of Seville's *De viris illustribus*, written between 615 and 618, which represents another continuation of Jerome's work. It devotes special attention to Spanish theologians.

Editions: F. AREVALO, S. Isidori opp. Rome, 1797 to 1803, vol. 7, 138–178. — ML 83, 1081–1106.

Studies: G. V. DZIALOWSKI, Isidor und Ildefons als Literarhistoriker. Eine quellenkritische Untersuchung der Schriften De Viris illustribus des Isidor von Sevilla und des Ildefons von Toledo. Münster i. W., 1898. — F. SCHÜTTE, Studien über den Schriftstellerkatalog (De viris illustribus) des hl. Isidor von Sevilla, in: M. SDRALEK, Kirchengeschichtliche Abhandlungen. Breslau, 1902, 75–149. — M. IHM, Zu Isidors viri illustres, in: Beiträge zur alten Geschichte und griechisch-römischen Altertumskunde (Festschrift zu O. Hirschfelds 60. Geburtstage). Berlin, 1903, 341–344. – J. DE ALDAMA, Indicaciones sobre la cronología de las obras de S. Isidoro: Miscellanea Isidoriana. Rome, 1936, 57–89. — H. KOEPPLER, De viris illustribus and Isidore of Seville: JThSt 38 (1936) 16–34.

Isidore's disciple, Ildephonsus of Toledo (d. 667), wrote a similar continuation, but his *De viris illustribus* is local and national in character. He intends mainly to glorify his predecessors in the see of Toledo. Only eight of the fourteen biographies deal with authors, and the only non-Spanish author whom he mentions is Gregory the Great.

Editions: F. AREVALO, see above. — ML 96, 195–206.

Studies: G. V. Dzialowski, l.c. — A. Braegelmann, The Life and Writings of St. Ildefonsus of Toledo. Washington, 1942, 32–59.

Not before the end of the eleventh century was a new attempt made to give an up-to-date account of Christian literature. The Benedictine chronicler, Sigebert of Gembloux in Belgium (d. 1112), undertook this task. In his *De viris illustribus* (ML 160, 547–588), he treats first the ancient ecclesiastical writers, closely following Jerome and Gennadius, and then compiles meager biographical and bibliographical notes on Latin theologians of the early Middle Ages; no mention is made of any Byzantine authors. Honorius of Augustodunum, in about 1122, composed a somewhat similar compendium, *De luminaribus ecclesiae* (ML 172, 197–234). A few years later, about 1135, the so-called Anonymus Mellicensis edited his *De scriptoribus ecclesiasticis* (ML 213, 961–984). The place of origin seems to be Pruefening near Ratisbon, and not Melk in Lower Austria, where the first manuscript of this work was found. A far better source of information is *De scriptoribus ecclesiasticis* by the abbot Johannes Trithemius. This work, composed about the year 1494, supplies biographical and bibliographical details about 963 writers, some of whom are not theologians. Even Trithemius receives all his knowledge regarding the Fathers from Jerome and Gennadius.

A complete edition which includes all historians or ecclesiastical literature from Jerome to Trithemius was made by J. A. Fabricius, Bibliotheca ecclesiastica. Hamburg, 1718. For Sigebert of Gembloux see S. Hirsch, De vita et scriptis Sigiberti monachi Gemblacensis. Berlin, 1841. — For the so-called Anonymus Mellicensis see the special edition by E. Ettlinger, Der sogenannte Anonymus Mellicensis De scriptoribus ecclesiasticis. Text und quellenkritische Ausgabe mit einer Einleitung. Karlsruhe, 1896. — For Honorius of Augustodunum cf. J. A. Endres, Honorius Augustodunensis. Kempten, 1906. — For Johannes Trithemius cf. J. Silbernagl, Johannes Trithemius. Ratisbon, 1885. — G. Mentz, Diss. Jena, 1892. — J. J. Hermes, Gymn. Progr. Prüm, 1901. — J. Beckmann, LThK 10 (1938) 296–298.

The time of the humanists brought a period of awakened interest for ancient Christian literature. On the one hand, the contention of the reformers, that the Catholic Church had deteriorated from the Church of the Fathers, and on the other, the decisions reached at the Council of Trent, contributed, to a large degree, to increase this new interest. R. Cardinal Bellarmine's *De scriptoribus ecclesiasticis liber unus*, which extends to 1500, appeared in 1613. Two works of French authors followed: L. S. le Nain de Tillemont, *Mémoires pour servir à l'histoire ecclésiastique des six premiers siècles*, Paris, 1693–1712, 16 volumes, and R. Ceillier, *Histoire générale des auteurs sacrés et ecclésiastiques*, Paris, 1729–1763; this latter work comprises twenty-three volumes, which deal with all ecclesiastical writers prior to 1250.

The new era of a science of ancient Christian literature, however, manifested itself especially in the first great collections and excellent special editions of patristic texts, which originated in the sixteenth and seventeenth centuries. The nineteenth century enriched the field of ancient Christian literature by a great number of new discoveries, especially of Oriental texts. The need of new critical editions was felt. Thus, the Academies of Vienna and Berlin inaugurated critical editions of a Latin and a Greek series of the Fathers, while French scholars began critical editions of two great collections of Oriental Christian literature, and in addition, most universities established chairs for Patrology.

The twentieth century has been predominantly concerned with the history of ideas, concepts, and terms in Christian literature, and the doctrine of the various ecclesiastical authors. Moreover, the newly discovered papyri of Egypt enabled scholars to regain many patristic works which had been lost.

2. GENERAL WORKS ON THE HISTORY OF ANCIENT CHRISTIAN LITERATURE

J. A. Möhler, Patrologie oder christliche Literärgeschichte, edited by F. X. Reithmayr, vol. 1 (the first three centuries). Ratisbon, 1840. The work was not continued.

J. Nirschl, Lehrbuch der Patrologie und Patristik. Mainz, 1881–1885 (3 vols.).

J. Alzog, Grundriss der Patrologie oder der älteren christlichen Literärgeschichte. 4th ed. Freiburg im Breisgau, 1888.

J. Fessler, Institutiones Patrologiae, denuo recensuit, auxit, edidit B. Jungmann. Innsbruck, 1890–1896.

Ch. Th. Cruttwell, A Literary History of Early Christianity, including the Fathers and the Chief Heretical Writers of the Ante-Nicene Period. London, 1893 (2 vols.).

A. Harnack, Geschichte der altchristlichen Literatur bis auf Eusebius. Leipzig, 1893–1904 (3 vols.).

G. Krueger, Geschichte der altchristlichen Literatur in den ersten drei

Jahrhunderten. 2nd edit. Freiburg im Breisgau, 1898. English transl. of the first edit. by C. R. GILLET, History of Early Christian Literature in the First Three Centuries. New York, 1897.

W. N. STEARNS, A Manual of Patrology. New York, 1899.

H. B. SWETE, Patristic Study. London, 1902.

H. KIHN, Patrologie. Paderborn, 1904–1908 (2 vols.).

O. BARDENHEWER, Patrologie. 3rd edit. Freiburg im Breisgau, 1910. English translation from the 2nd edit. by J.J. SHAHAN, Patrology, The Lives and Works of the Fathers of the Church. Freiburg and St. Louis, 1908.

H. JORDAN, Geschichte der altchristlichen Literatur. Leipzig, 1911.

O. BARDENHEWER, Geschichte der altkirchlichen Literatur. Freiburg im Breisgau, 1913–1932 (5 vols., vol. 1 and 2 in 2nd edit., reprint of vol. 3 with additions).

P. G. FRANCESCHINI, Manuale di Patrologia. Rome, 1919.

E. LEIGH–BENNET, Handbook of the Early Christian Fathers. London, 1920.

J. TIXERONT, Mélanges de patrologie et d'histoire des dogmes. Paris, 1921. English transl. based upon the 4th French edition by S. A. RAEMERS, A Handbook of Patrology. St. Louis, 1934.

A. F. FINDLAY, By-Ways in Early Christian Literature. London, 1923.

H. LIETZMANN, Christliche Literatur, in: Einleitung in die Altertumswissenschaft, herausgegeben von A. Gercke und E. Norden, vol. I, Heft 5 and 6. Third edit., Leipzig, 1923.

M. DIBELIUS, Geschichte der urchristlichen Literatur. Berlin, 1926.

F. CAYRÉ, Précis de Patrologie. Paris, 1927–1930 (2 vols.). English transl. by H. HOWITT, Manual of Patrology and History of Theology. Paris, 1936–1940.

M. DIBELIUS, A Fresh Approach to the New Testament and Early Christian Literature. New York, 1936.

B. STEIDLE, Patrologia. Freiburg im Breisgau, 1937.

B. ALTANER, Patrologie. Second edit., Freiburg im Breisgau, 1950. Ital. translation by S. Mattei. Second edit., Rome, 1944 (with additions). French translation by M. Grandclaudon. Mulhouse, 1941.

A. CASAMASSA, Patrologia. Rome, 1939 ff.

B. STEIDLE, Die Kirchenväter. Eine Einführung in ihr Leben und ihr Werk. Ratisbon, 1939.

K. KASTNER, Patrologie. Im Umriss dargestellt. Paderborn, 1940.

U. MANUCCI, Istituzioni di Patrologia. Fifth edit. by P. A. Casamassa. Rome, 1940.

E. J. GOODSPEED, A History of Early Christian Literature. Chicago, 1942.

J. DE GHELLINCK, Patristique et moyen âge. Vol. I, Brussels and Paris, 1946, vol. II, 1947.

Special Works on Greek Literature

P. BATIFFOL, La littérature grecque (Bibliothèque de l'enseignement de l'histoire ecclésiastique. Anciennes littératures chrétiennes). Paris, 1897. 3rd edit., 1901.

K. KRUMBACHER–A. EHRHARD, Geschichte der byzantinischen Literatur.

2nd. edit. Munich, 1897, pp. 37–218: The Greek theologians of the Byzantine period.

O. STÄHLIN, Die altchristliche griechische Literatur, in: W. v. Christ, Geschichte der griechischen Literatur. 2. Teil, 2. Hälfte. 6th edit. Munich, 1924, pp. 1105–1500.

Q. CATAUDELLA, Critica ed estetica nella letteratura greca cristiana. Turin, 1928.

A. PUECH, Histoire de la littérature grecque chrétienne jusqu'à la fin du IVe siècle. Paris, 1928–1930 (3 vols.).

G. BARDY, Littérature grecque chrétienne. Paris, 1928.

J. M. CAMPBELL, The Greek Fathers. London and New York, 1929.

F. A. WRIGHT, A History of Later Greek Literature (to A. D. 565). London, 1932.

A. EHRHARD, Ueberlieferung und Bestand der hagiographischen und homiletischen Literatur der griechischen Kirche. Von den Anfängen bis zum Ende des XVI. Jahrhunderts. Leipzig, 1936 ff.

Special Works on Latin Literature

P. MONCEAUX, Histoire littéraire de l'Afrique chrétienne depuis les origines jusqu'à l'invasion arabe. Paris, 1901–1923 (7 vols.).

R. PICHON, Etudes sur l'histoire de la littérature latine dans les Gaules. Paris, 1906.

W. S. TEUFFEL, Geschichte der römischen Literatur, Vol. III. 6th edit. by W. Kroll and F. Skutsch, the Christian authors by E. Klostermann. Leipzig, 1913.

M. SCHANZ, Geschichte der römischen Literatur, 3rd Part: Die Zeit von Hadrian bis auf Konstantin. 3rd edit. Munich, 1922; 4th Part: Die Literatur des vierten Jahrhunderts. Munich, 1914; Die Literatur des fünften bis sechsten Jahrhunderts. Munich, 1920.

U. MORICCA, Storia della letteratura latina cristiana, vol. I–II, 1–2, III, 1–2. Turin, 1925–1934.

P. MONCEAUX, Histoire de la littérature latine chrétienne. Paris, 1924.

P. DE LABRIOLLE, Histoire de la littérature latine chrétienne. Paris, 1924. English transl. by H. WILSON, History and Literature of Christianity from Tertullian to Boethius. London, 1924. 3rd French edit., by G. BARDY, Paris, 1947.

A. GUDEMANN, Geschichte der altchristlichen lateinischen Literatur. Leipzig, 1925.

C. WEYMAN, Beiträge zur Geschichte der christlich-lateinischen Poesie. Munich, 1926.

G. BARDY, Littérature latine chrétienne. Paris, 1929.

E. S. DUCKETT, Latin Writers of the Fifth Century. New York, 1930.

L. W. LAISTNER, Thought and Letters in Western Europe A.D. 500–900. London, 1931.

N. TERZAGHI, Storia della letteratura latina da Tiberio a Giustiniano. Milan, 1934.

A. KAPPELMACHER and M. SCHUSTER, Die Literatur der Römer bis zur Karolingerzeit. Berlin, 1935.

H. J. Rose, A Handbook of Latin Literature from the Earliest Times to 430. London, 1936.
L. Salvatorelli, Storia della letteratura latina cristiana, dalle origini alla metà del VI sec. Milan, 1936.
E. Bickel, Lehrbuch der Geschichte der römischen Literatur. Bibliothek der klassischen Altertumswissenschaft No. 8. Heidelberg, 1938. Cf. J. Quasten, RQ (1938) 63–66.
E. K. Rand, The Latin Literature of the West from the Antonines to Constantine, in: The Cambridge Ancient History 12. Cambridge, 1939, 571—610.
J. de Ghellinck, Littérature latine au moyen âge. Paris, 1939 (2 vols.).

Special Works on Oriental Literature

K. Brockelmann, F. N. Finck, J. Leipoldt, E. Littmann, Geschichte der christlichen Literaturen des Orients. Leipzig, 1907.
A. Baumstark, Die christlichen Literaturen des Orients. Leipzig, 1911 (2 vols.).

Syriac:

G. Bickel, Conspectus rei Syrorum literariae. Münster, 1871.
W. Wright, A Short History of Syriac Literature. London, 1894.
R. Duval, La littérature syriaque, in: Anciennes littératures chrétiennes, vol. II, 3rd edit., Paris, 1907.
A. Baumstark, Geschichte der syrischen Literatur. Bonn, 1922.
J. B. Chabot, Littérature syriaque. Paris, 1935.
W. Kutsch, Zur Geschichte der syrisch-arabischen Uebersetzungsliteratur: Orientalia 6 (1937) 68–82.

Ethiopic:

J. M. Harden, An Introduction to Ethiopic Christian Literature. London, 1926.
J. Guidi, Storia della letteratura etiopica. Rome, 1932.

Georgian:

J. Karst, Littérature géorgienne chrétienne. Paris, 1934.
G. Peradze, Die altchristliche Literatur in der georgischen Ueberlieferung: OC 3-4 (1928–29) 109-116, 282–288; 5 (1930) 80–98, 232–236; 6 (1932) 240–244; 8 (1933) 86–92, 180–198.

Armenian:

J. Karst, Geschichte der armenischen Literatur. Leipzig, 1930.
H. Leclercq, Littérature Arménienne: DAL 9, 1576—1599.

Coptic:

O'Leary, Littérature Copte: DAL 9, 1599-1635.

Arabic:

G. GRAF, Exegetische Schriften zum Neuen Testament in arabischer Sprache:
  BZ (1933) 22–40, 161–169.
G. GRAF, Geschichte der christlichen arabischen Literatur. Rome 1944 and
  1947. 2 vols.

3. THE 'FATHERS' OF THE CHURCH

We are accustomed to call the authors of early Christian writings 'Fathers of the Church'. In ancient times the word 'Father' was applied to a teacher; for in biblical and early Christian usage, teachers are the fathers of their students. Thus, for instance, St. Paul, in his first *Letter to the Corinthians* (4, 15), says: 'For although you have ten thousand instructors in Christ, yet you have not many fathers. For in Christ Jesus, through the Gospel, I have begotten you.' Irenaeus declares (*Adv. Haer.* 4, 41, 2): 'For when any person has been taught from the mouth of another he is termed the son of him who instructs him, and the latter is called his father.' Clement of Alexandria remarks (*Strom.* 1, 1, 2–2,1): 'Words are the progeny of the soul. Hence we call those that instructed us fathers . . . and every one who is instructed is in respect of subjection the son of his instructor.'

In Christian antiquity, the teaching office was the bishop's. Thus the title 'Father' was first applied to him. Doctrinal controversies of the fourth century brought about further development. The use of the term 'Father' became more comprehensive; it was now extended to ecclesiastical writers in so far as they were accepted as representatives of the tradition of the Church. Thus St. Augustine numbers St. Jerome among the witnesses to the traditional doctrine of original sin, although he was not a bishop (*Cont. Jul.* 1, 7, 34).

Vincent of Lerins, in his *Commonitory* of 434 applies the term 'Father' to all ecclesiastical writers without distinction of hierarchical grade:

> If some new question should arise on which no such decision has been given, they should then have recourse to the opinions of the holy Fathers, of those, at least, who, each in his own time and place, remaining in the unity of communion and the faith, were accepted as approved masters; and whatsoever

these may be found to have held, with one mind and one consent, this ought to be accounted the true and catholic doctrine of the Church, without any doubt or scruple (Chapter 41). — Nothing ought to be believed by posterity save what the sacred antiquity of the holy Fathers consentient in Christ has held (Chapter 43).

This principle of Vincent of Lerins shows the importance already attached to the 'proof from the Fathers'.

The first list of ecclesiastical writers who had been approved or rejected as Fathers is contained in the *Decretum Gelasianum de recipiendis et non recipiendis libris*, which belongs to the sixth century. After mentioning a number of the most important Fathers, the text continues:

Item opuscula atque tractatus omnium patrum orthodoxorum, qui in nullo a sanctae Romanae ecclesiae consortio deviarunt nec ab eius fide vel praedicatione seiuncti sunt, sed ipsius communicationis per gratiam Dei usque in ultimum diem vitae suae fuere participes, legendos decernit (Romana ecclesia).

Today only those are to be regarded as 'Fathers of the Church' who combine these four necessary qualifications: orthodoxy of doctrine, holiness of life, ecclesiastical approval, and antiquity. All other theological writers are known as *ecclesiae scriptores* or *scriptores ecclesiastici*, a term which St. Jerome coined (*De viris ill., Prol.; Ep.* 112, 3). The title 'Doctor of the Church' is not identical with 'Father of the Church', because some of those known as Doctors of the Church lack the distinction of 'antiquity', but they have in addition to the three distinctions of *doctrina orthodoxa, sanctitas vitae,* and *approbatio ecclesiae,* the two qualifications of *eminens eruditio* and *expressa ecclesiae declaratio*. In the West, Boniface VIII declared (1298) that he wished Ambrose, Jerome, Augustine and Gregory the Great known as *egregii doctores ecclesiae*. These four Fathers are also called 'the great Fathers of the Church'. The Greek Church venerates only three 'great ecumenical teachers', Basil the Great, Gregory of Nazianzus, and Chrysostom, while the Roman Church adds St. Athanasius to these three, and thus counts four great Fathers of the East, and four of the West.

Although the Fathers of the Church hold an important position in the history of Hellenistic and Roman literature, their authority in the Catholic Church is based on entirely different grounds. It is the ecclesiastical doctrine of Tradition as a source of faith which makes the writings and opinions of the Fathers so important. The Church regards the *unanimis consensus patrum* as infallible, if it concerns the interpretation of Scripture (Vatic. sess. 3, c. 2). J. H. Cardinal Newman describes well the importance of this *consensus*, and its difference from private opinions of the Fathers, when he says:

'I follow the ancient Fathers, not as thinking that on such a subject they have the weight they possess in the instance of doctrines or ordinances. When they speak of doctrines, they speak of them as being universally held. They are witnesses to the fact of these doctrines having been received, not here or there, but everywhere. We receive those doctrines which they thus teach, not merely because they teach them, but because they bear witness that all Christians everywhere then held them. We take them as honest informants, but not as a sufficient authority in themselves, though they are an authority too. If they were to state these very same doctrines, but say, 'These are our opinions: we deduced them from Scripture, and they are true,' we might well doubt about receiving them at their hands. We might fairly say, that we had as much right to deduce from Scripture as they had; that deductions of Scripture were mere opinions; that if our deductions agreed with theirs, that would be a happy coincidence in them; but if they did not, it could not be helped — we must follow our own light. Doubtless, no man has any right to impose his own deductions upon another, in matters of faith. There is an obvious obligation, indeed, upon the ignorant to submit to those who are better informed; and there is a fitness in the young submitting implicitly for a time to the teaching of their elders; but, beyond this, one man's opinion is not better than another's. But this is not the state of the case as regards the primitive Fathers. They do not speak of their *own private* opinion; they do not say, 'This is true, *because* we see it in Scripture' — about which there might be differences of judgment — but, 'this is true, because in matter of fact it is held, and has ever been held, by all the Churches, down to our times, without interruption, ever since the Apostles':

where the question is merely one of testimony, viz., whether they had the means of knowing that it had been and was so held; for if it was the belief of so many and independent Churches at once, and that, on the ground of its being from the Apostles, doubtless it cannot be but true and Apostolic' (*Discussions and Arguments* II, 1).

J. Madoz, El concepto de la tradición en S. Vincento de Lerins. Madrid, 1923. — A. Deneffe, Der Traditionsbegriff. Münster, 1931. — J. Ranft, Der Ursprung des katholischen Traditionsprinzips. Würzburg, 1931. — J. Madoz, El concilio de Efeso ejemplo de argumentación patrística: EE 10 (1931) 305-338. — B. Steidle, Heilige Vaterschaft: BM 14 (1932) 215ff., 387ff., 454ff. — B. Reynders, Paradosis. Le progrès de l'idée de tradition jusqu'à S. Irénée: RTAM 5 (1933) 155-191. — D. van den Eynde, Les normes de l'enseignement chrétien dans la littérature patristique des trois premiers siècles. Paris, 1933. — I. Backes, Der Väterbeweis in der Dogmatik: ThQ 114 (1933) 208-221. — J. Ranft, Die Traditionsmethode als älteste theologische Methode des Christentums. Würzburg, 1934. — H. du Manoir, L'argumentation patristique dans la controverse nestorienne: RSR 25 (1935) 441-461. — L. Dürr, Heilige Vaterschaft im antiken Orient: Heilige Ueberlieferung, ed. by O. Casel. Münster i. W., 1938, 1-20. — R. Forni, Problemi della tradizione. Ireneo di Lione. Milan, 1939. — J. Quasten, Tertullian and "Traditio": Traditio 2 (1944) 481-484. — A. C. Cotter, Abbé Migne and Catholic Tradition: TS 7 (1946) 46-71.

4. GENERAL WORKS ON THE DOCTRINE OF THE FATHERS

Since the teaching of the Fathers has contributed so much to the development of the doctrine of the Church and since many of them took a leading part in the controversies preceding the definition of Christian dogmas, a history of ancient Christian literature is intimately connected with the history of dogma. For this reason the principal works dealing with this young branch of theology should be mentioned:

Catholic authors:

Dionysius Petavius, S. J. (1652), De theologicis dogmatibus. Paris, 1644-1650, 4 vols.

H. Klee, Lehrbuch der Dogmengeschichte. Erlangen, 1837.

J. H. Newman, Essay on the Development of Christian Doctrine. London, 1845; 2nd edit. 1878.

A. Ginoulhiac, Histoire du dogme catholique. Paris, 1852. This work is unfinished and deals with the first three centuries.

J. A. Schwane, Dogmengeschichte. 2nd edit. Freiburg im Breisgau, 1892, 4 vols.

J. N. Zob, Dogmengeschichte der katholischen Kirche. Innsbruck, 1865.

J. Tixeront, Histoire des dogmes. 11th edit. Paris, 1930, 3 vols. English transl. from the fifth French edition. Vol. I The Ante-Nicene Theology, 3rd edit. St. Louis and London, 1930. Vol. II From St. Athanasius to St. Augustine, 2nd edit., 1923. Vol. III The End of the Patristic Age, 2nd edit., 1926.

B. J. Otten, A Manual of the History of Dogmas. London, 1917, 2 vols.

R. M. Schultes, Introductio in historiam dogmatum. Paris, 1924.

F. Marin-Sola, L'évolution homogène du dogme catholique. Paris, 1924, 2 vols.

J. Creusen et F. van Eyen, Tabulae fontium traditionis christianae ad annum 1926. Louvain, 1926.

J. F. de Groot, Conspectus historiae dogmatum ab aetate PP. apostolicorum usque ad saec. XIII. Rome, 1931, 2 vols.

Non-Catholic authors:

W. Münscher, Handbuch der christlichen Dogmengeschichte. 1797 ff. 4 vols. The fourth vol. reaches to the 6th century.

A. Harnack, Lehrbuch der Dogmengeschichte. 5th edit. Tübingen, 1931/32, 3 vols. English transl. from the third German edit. by N. Buchanan, History of Dogma. London 1894 ff. 7 vols.

J. F. Bethune-Baker, Introduction to the Early History of Christian Doctrine, 5th. edit. London, 1933.

R. Seeberg, Lehrbuch der Dogmengeschichte. Vol. 1-2, 3rd edit. Leipzig, 1922/23, vol. 3-4, 4th edit., 1930-33.

R. Seeberg, Grundriss der Dogmengeschichte, 7th edit. Leipzig, 1936.

F. Loofs, Leitfaden zum Studium der Dogmengeschichte, 4th edit. Halle, 1906.

N. Bonwetsch, Grundriss der Dogmengeschichte, 2nd edit., 1919.

F. Wiegand, Dogmengeschichte der alten Kirche, 1912; Dogmengeschichte des Mittelalters und der Neuzeit, 1919.

F. Wiegand, Dogmengeschichte, vol. I (Sammlung Göschen 993), vol. II (Sammlung Göschen 994). Berlin and Leipzig, 1928.

D. Balanos, Εἰσαγωγὴ εἰς τὴν ἱστορίαν τῶν δογμάτων. Athens, 1919.

J. Turmel, Histoire des dogmes. Paris, 1931-1936, 6 vols.

A. Cuchman McGiffert, History of Christian Thought, 1931 ff. 2 vols.

M. Werner, Die Entstehung des christlichen Dogmas problemgeschichtlich dargestellt. Bern and Leipzig, 1941.

5. EDITIONS OF EARLY CHRISTIAN LITERATURE

I. The first printed editions of the writings of the early ecclesiastical writers cannot be regarded as critical editions, since scientific rules for the selection of the manuscripts were not in existence. Nevertheless, many of these first editions are now very valuable, because the manuscript on which their text is based has been lost.

II. Of all the older printed editions of early Christian literature which have appeared since the sixteenth century, there is one collection which still has its critical value: the editions which the French Benedictines of St. Maur published in the seventeenth and eighteenth centuries. The congregation was founded in 1618 in Paris. Learned scholars like Luc d'Achéry, Mabillon, Thierry, Ruinart, Maran, Montfaucon and Marmiet were attracted to its ranks. Some of their editions of the Fathers have not been surpassed. The Greek texts are here furnished with a Latin translation and excellent indices are added to each volume.

III. The most complete collection of patristic texts is *Patrologiae cursus completus*, edited by Abbé J. P. Migne (d. 1875). It reprints all texts which had been published until then in order to make them available for theologians and to give as many as possible access to them. Unfortunately, the Migne edition has many misprints. For this reason it is always better to use the older editions which Migne reprinted if no modern critical edition of the text has appeared. However, Migne's Patrologia remains for many patristic writings the only available text.

For an appreciation of the services which Migne rendered for the promotion of patristic research see W. JACOB, Bemerkungen zu Ausgaben theologischer Texte vom XVI bis zum XIX Jahrh.: ZNW 28 (1939) 193-195.

IV. To the Academies of Vienna and Berlin falls the honor of having started two series of patristic writings that endeavour to combine philological accuracy and completeness. Both series, the Greek as well as the Latin, are still in progress of publication.

Editions of Patristic Texts

J. P. MIGNE, Patrologiae cursus completus, series latina. Paris, 1844-1855. 221 vols. including four vols. of indexes. This Latin series comes down to Innocent III (d. 1216).

J. P. MIGNE, Patrologiae cursus completus, series graeca. Paris, 1857-1866. 161 vols. All texts are furnished with a Latin translation. This series reaches to the Council of Florence (1438-1439). It was published without indexes. However, D. Scholarios published a catalogue of the Greek writings in the Migne edition and F. Cavallera and Th. Hopfner supplied general indexes. Cf. D. SCHOLARIOS, Κλεὶς πατρολογίας καὶ

3 υζαντινῶν συγγραφέων ἤτοι εὑρετήριον πάντων τῶν συγγραφέων τῶν περιεχομένων ἐν τῇ Πατρολογίᾳ ὑπὸ Μιγνίου. Athens, 1879.

F. CAVALLERA, Migne, Patrologiae cursus completus, Series graeca. Indices digessit. Paris, 1912. Th. HOPFNER, Migne, Patrologiae cursus completus, Series graeca. Index locupletissimus. Paris, 1928 ff.

Die griechischen christlichen Schriftsteller der ersten drei Jahrhunderte, edited by the Academy of Berlin since 1897 with introductions and indexes in German. In spite of its official title this series goes beyond the third century. It comprises so far 41 vols.

Corpus scriptorum ecclesiasticorum latinorum, edited by the Academy of Vienna since 1866. 70 vols. have been published so far.

Monumenta Germaniae historica, Auctores antiquissimi. Berlin, 1877–1898, 13 vols. This series comprises the later Latin writers of the period from Christian Antiquity to the Middle Ages.

Bibliotheca Teubneriana, Leipzig, includes many patristic writings.

The Loeb Classical Library, edited by T. E. PAGE, E. CAPPS and W. H. D. ROUSE, London and New York, includes a great number of Greek and Latin Christian authors.

Corpus scriptorum christianorum orientalium, edited by J. B. CHABOT, J. GUIDI, H. HYVERNAT, B. CARRA DE VAUX, J. FORGET. This Corpus published at Paris since 1903 comprises four séries: scriptores syriaci, coptici, arabici, aethiopici. 100 vols. so far.

Patrologia orientalis, edited by R. GRAFFIN and F. NAU. Paris, 1907 ff. 25 vols. so far.

Patrologia syriaca, edited by R. GRAFFIN. Paris, 1894–1926. 3 vols.

Sources chrétiennes, edited by H. DE LUBAC and J. DANIÉLOU. Paris, 1941 ff.

Stromata patristica et mediaevalia, edited by CHR. MOHRMANN and J, QUASTEN. Utrecht and Brussels, 1950 ff.

Collections of Texts and Studies

Texte und Untersuchungen zur Geschichte der altchristlichen Literatur, edited by O. v. GEBHARDT and A. HARNACK. Leipzig, 1882–1897. 15 vols. Neue Folge, Leipzig, 1897–1906, 15 vols. Dritte Reihe, edited by A. HARNACK and C. SCHMIDT, Leipzig, 1907 ff.

Texts and Studies. Contributions to Biblical and Patristic Literature, edited by J. ARMITAGE ROBINSON. Cambridge, 1891 ff.

Studi e Testi. Pubblicazioni della Bibliotheca Vaticana. Rome, 1900 ff.

Studies and Documents, edited by K. LAKE and S. LAKE. London and Philadelphia, 1934 ff.

Collections of Patristic Texts for Students

SS. patrum opuscula selecta, edited by H. HURTER. The Greek authors are given in a Latin translation only. First series, Innsbruck, 1868–1885, 48 vols.; second series Innsbruck, 1884–1892, 6 vols. Most of the volumes went through several editions.

Florilegium Patristicum, tam veteris quam medii aevi auctores complectens,

2

ediderunt B. GEYER et J. ZELLINGER. Bonn, 1904 ff. 44 vols. so far. The Greek texts with Latin translation.

Cambridge Patristic Texts, edit. by A. J. MASON. Cambridge, 1899 ff.

Sammlung ausgewählter kirchen- und dogmengeschichtlicher Quellenschriften, edited by G. KRÜGER. Tübingen, 1891 ff. First series, 12 fascicules; 2nd series, 9 fasc.; new series, 6 fascicules.

Kleine Texte, edited by H. LIETZMANN. Bonn, 1902 ff.

Bibliotheca sanctorum patrum, edited by J. VIZZINI. Rome, 1902 ff.

Textes et documents pour l'étude historique du christianisme, edited by H. HEMMER and P. LEJAY. Paris, 1904-1912. 20 vols.

Scrittori cristiani antichi. Rome, 1921.

Testi cristiani, edited by G. MANACORDA. Florence, 1930 ff.

Corona Patrum Salesiana, edited by P. RICALDONE. Turin, 1937 ff.

Textus et documenta in usum exercitationum et praelectionum academicarum. Series theologica, edited by the Gregorian University. Rome, 1932 ff.

Translations

English:

Library of the Fathers, edited by PUSEY, KEBLE and NEWMAN. Oxford, 1838—1888. 45 vols.

The Ante-Nicene Christian Library. Translations of the writings of the Fathers down to A.D. 325, edited by A. ROBERTS and J. DONALDSON. Edinburgh, 1866-1872. 24 vols. with a supplementary volume, edited by A. MENZIES, Edinburgh, 1897.

The Ante-Nicene Fathers. American reprint of the Edinburgh edition revised by A. CLEVELAND COXE. Buffalo, 1884-1886, 8 vols., with a supplement by A. MENZIES (vol. 9) and A. CLEVELAND COXE (vol. 10). The 10th vol. contains a bibliographical synopsis and a general index.

A Select Library of Nicene and Post-Nicene Fathers of the Christian Church, edited by PH. SCHAFF and H. WACE. Buffalo and New York, 1886-1900, 28 vols.

Translations of Christian Literature, edited by W. J. SPARROW-SIMPSON and W. K. LOWTHER CLARKE. This collection, published by the Society for Promoting Christian Knowledge in London, comprises a series of I. Greek Texts, II. Latin Texts, III. Liturgical Texts, IV. Oriental Texts. London, 1917 ff.

Ancient Christian Writers, edited by J. QUASTEN and J. C. PLUMPE. Westminster, Md., 1946 ff.

The Fathers of the Church, edited by L. SCHOPP. New York, 1947 ff.

German:

Sämtliche Werke der Kirchenväter. Aus dem Urtext ins Teutsche übersetzt. Kempten, 1830-1854. 39 vols.

Bibliothek der Kirchenväter. Auswahl der vorzüglichsten patristischen Werke in deutscher Uebersetzung, edited by F. X. REITHMAYR, continued by V. THALHOFER. Kempten, 1869-1888, 80 vols.

Bibliothek der Kirchenväter. Eine Auswahl patristischer Werke in deutscher

Uebersetzung, edited by O. BARDENHEWER, TH. SCHERMANN, C. WEY-
MAN. Kempten, 1911—1930, 61 vols. and two vols. of indexes. A second
series of this collection was edited by O. BARDENHEWER, J. ZELLINGER
and J. MARTIN. Kempten, 1932-1939, 20 vols.

French:

Les Pères de l'Eglise, edited by A. DE GENOUDE. Paris, 1835-1849. 10 vols.
Bibliothèque choisie des Pères de l'Eglise, edited by N. S. GUILLON. Paris,
1828, 36 vols. Reprinted at Brussels and Louvain, 1828-1834, 27 vols.
Chefs-d'oeuvre des Pères de l'Eglise. Paris, 1837. 15 vols.
Textes et documents pour l'étude historique du christianisme, edited by
H. HEMMER and P. LEJAY. Paris, 1904-1912. 20 vols. Text and trans-
lation.
Bibliothèque patristique de spiritualité. Paris, 1932 ff.
Moralistes chrétiens. Textes et commentaires. Paris, 1924-1932. 12 vols.
Sources chrétiennes, edited by H. DE LUBAC et J. DANIÉLOU. Paris, 1941 ff.
Text and translation.
Les grands écrivains chrétiens. Lyon-Paris, 1942 ff.

Italian:

I classici cristiani, edited by P. MISCIATELLI. Siena, 1928 ff.
Scrittori cristiani antichi. Rome, 1921 ff.
Testi cristiani, edited by G. MANACORDA. Florence, 1930 ff.
Corona Patrum Salesiana. Sanctorum Patrum Graecorum et Latinorum
opera selecta, addita interpretatione vulgari, edit. by P. RICALDONE.
Turin, 1936 ff.

Spanish:

Biblioteca clásica del Catolicismo. Madrid, 1889 ff.
Biblioteca de autores griegos y latinos, edited by L. SEGALA and C. PARPAL.
Barcelona, 1916 ff.
Los grandes Maestros de la doctrina cristiana, edited by F. RESTREPO.
Madrid, 1925 ff.
Collección Excelsa. Madrid, 1940.

Catalan:

Biblioteca Sant Jordi. Barcelona, 1925.
Biblioteca Sant Pacia. Barcelona, 1931.
Biblioteca de La Paraula cristiana. Barcelona, 1933.

Dutch:

Oudchristelijke geschriften in Nederlandsche vertaling, edited by H. U.
MEYBOOM. Leiden, 1906 ff. More than 50 vols. so far.
Monumenta Christiana. Utrecht-Brussels, 1948 ff.

Polish:

Pisma Ojcow Kocsiola, edited by J. SAJDAK. Poznan. 20 vols. so far.

Norwegian:

Vidnesbyrd af Kirkefaedrene. Kristiania, 1880-1887. 15 vols.

6. WORKS OF REFERENCE, ANTHOLOGIES AND BIBLIOGRAPHIES

Works of Reference

Du Cange, Glossarium ad scriptores mediae et infimae graecitatis. Lyons, 1688 and 1890 ff.

H. Stephanus, Thesaurus linguae graecae. Paris, 1831/65.

E. Forcellini, Lexicon totius latinitatis. Prato, 1858/79.

W. Smith and H. Wace, Dictionary of Christian Biography, Literature, Sects and Doctrines. London, 1877/87.

Du Cange-Henschel-Favre, Glossarium mediae et infimae latinitatis. Niort, 1882/87.

E. A. Sophocles, Greek Lexicon of the Roman and Byzantine Periods. (146 B.C. to 1100 A.D.). New York, 3rd edition, 1888.

Pauly-Wissowa-Kroll, Realenzyklopädie der klassischen Altertumswissenschaft. Stuttgart, 1893 ff.

A. Hauck, Realenzyklopädie für protestantische Theologie und Kirche; 3rd edition. Leipzig 1896-1913 (24 volumes).

Thesaurus linguae latinae, editus auctoritate et consilio Academiarum quinque Germanicarum: Berolinensis, Gottingensis, Lipsiensis, Monacensis, Vindobonensis. Leipzig, 1900 ff.

A. Vacant—E. Mangenot—E. Amann, Dictionnaire de théologie catholique (DTC). Paris, 1903 ff.

F. Cabrol—H. Leclercq, Dictionnaire d'archéologie chrétienne et de liturgie (DAL). Paris, 1907 ff.

The Catholic Encyclopedia. An International Work of Reference on the Constitution, Doctrine, Discipline, and History of the Catholic Church. New York, 1907-1914 (15 vols. and Index).

J. Brun, Dictionarium Syriacum Latinum, second edition. Beyrouth, 1911.

A. Baudrillart—A. de Meyer—E. van Gauwenbergh, Dictionnaire d'histoire et de géographie ecclésiastiques. Paris, 1912 ff.

A. d'Alès, Dictionnaire apologétique de la foi catholique, 4th edition. Paris, 1914-1922 (4 vols.).

J. Hastings, Dictionary of the Apostolic Church. Edinburgh, 1915-18.

C. Brockelmann, Lexicon Syriacum, 2nd edition. Berlin, 1923 ff.

V. Villien—E. Magnin—R. Naz, Dictionnaire de droit canonique. Paris, 1924 ff.

F. Preisigke—E. Kiessling, Wörterbuch der griechischen Papyrusurkunden. Leipzig, 1925-31.

H. Gunkel—L. Zscharnack, Die Religion in Geschichte und Gegenwart, 2nd edition. Tübingen, 1927-1931 (5 vols. and Index).

M. Buchberger, Lexikon für Theologie und Kirche. Freiburg im Breisgau, 1930-1938 (10 vols.).

M. Viller, Dictionnaire de spiritualité ascétique et mystique. Paris, 1932 ff.

W. Bauer, Griechisch-deutsches Wörterbuch zu den Schriften des Neuen Testaments und der übrigen urchristlichen Literatur. 4th edition. Giessen, 1949 ff.

H. G. LIDDELL—R. SCOTT, A Greek-English Lexicon. A new edition rev.
and augmented by H. St. Jones. Oxford, 1925–1940 (2 vols.).
G. KITTEL, Theologisches Wörterbuch zum Neuen Testament. Leipzig,
1932 ff.
TH. KLAUSER, Reallexikon für Antike und Christentum. Leipzig, 1941 ff.

Enchiridia and Anthologies

M. J. ROUËT DE JOURNEL, Enchiridion Patristicum. 14th edit. Barcelona, 1946.
C. KIRCH, Enchiridion fontium historiae ecclesiasticae antiquae. 6th edit.
Barcelona, 1947.
M. J. ROUËT DE JOURNEL—J. DUTILLEUL, Enchiridion Asceticum. 4th edit.
Barcelona 1947.
H. DENZINGER, Enchiridion Symbolorum. 25th edit. edited by J. B. UMBERG.
Barcelona, 1948.
J. QUASTEN, Monumenta eucharistica et liturgica vetustissima (FP 7). Bonn,
1935—1937. 7 vols.
B. J. KIDD, Documents Illustrative to the History of the Church. Vol. I
to A.D. 313, vol. II 313–461 A.D. London and New York, 1938.
J. T. SHOTWELL and L. R. LOOMIS, The See of Peter. New York,
1927.
C. MIRBT, Quellen zur Geschichte des Papsttums und des römischen Katho-
lizismus. 5th edit. Tübingen, 1934.
L. V. RUDLOFF, Das Zeugnis der Väter. Ein Lesebuch zur Dogmatik.
Ratisbon, 1937.
H. KOCH, Quellen zur Geschichte der Askese und des Mönchtums in der
alten Kirche. Tübingen, 1933.
A. HEILMANN, Gottesträger. Das Schönste aus den Kirchenvätern. Freiburg
im Breisgau, 1921.
E. AMANN, Le dogme catholique dans les Pères de l'Eglise. Paris, 1922.
G. BARDY, En lisant les Pères. 2nd edit. Paris, 1933.
F. CAVALLERA, Thesaurus doctrinae catholicae ex documentis magisterii
ecclesiastici ordine methodico dispositus. 2nd edit. Paris, 1937.
J. DE GUIBERT, Documenta ecclesiastica christianae perfectionis studium
spectantia. Rome, 1931.
F. P. BERRO, Anthologia patristica Graeca. Turin, 1931. 2 vols.
J. MADOZ, La Iglesia de Jesucristo. Fuentes y documentos para el estudio
de su constitución e historia. Madrid, 1935.
J. MADOZ, El Primado romano. Fuentes y documentos para el estudio de
su constitución e historia. Madrid, 1936.
W. VÖLKER, Quellen zur Geschichte der christlichen Gnosis. Tübingen, 1932.
H. BETTENSON, Documents of the Christian Church. New York—London,
1947.

Bibliographies

A. EHRHARD, Die altchristliche Literatur und ihre Erforschung seit 1880.
Freiburg im Breisgau, 1894.

A. EHRHARD, Die altchristliche Literatur und ihre Erforschung von 1884—
1900. Erste Abteilung: Die vornicänische Literatur. Freiburg im Breisgau,
1900.

H. HURTER—FR. PANGERL, Nomenclator literarius theologiae catholicae
vol. I, 4th edit. Innsbruck, 1926.

F. DREXL, Zehn Jahre griechischer Patristik (1916–1925), I. Teil: Die
Jahrhunderte 2 und 3 n. Chr.: Bursians Jahresbericht über die Fort-
schritte der klassischen Altertumswissenschaft 220 (1929), 131—263; II.
Teil: Die Jahrhunderte 4 und 5 n. Chr.: ibidem 230 (1931) 163–273. —
J. MARTIN, Christlich-lateinische Dichter: ibidem 221 (1929) 65–140. —
W. WILBRAND, Die altchristlich-lateinische Literatur (1921/24): ibidem
226 (1930) 157–206.

G. KRÜGER, A Decade of Research in Early Christian Literature (1921–
1930): HThR 26 (1933) 173–321.

J. MADOZ, Un decennio de estudios patrísticos en España (1931–1940):
RES 1 (1941) 919–962.

B. ALTANER, Der Stand der patrologischen Wissenschaft und das Problem
einer neuen altchristlichen Literaturgeschichte: Miscellanea Mercati
(Rome, 1946) 483–520.

J. MAROUZEAU, L'année philologique. Bibliographie critique et analytique
de l'antiquité gréco-latine. Paris, 1926 ff. gives an annual report which
includes all publications regarding the Greek and Latin writers of Christian antiquity.

Bulletin de théologie ancienne et médiévale. Supplement of RTAM.

Bibliographie de la Revue d'histoire ecclésiastique. Louvain.

Bibliographisches Beiblatt der Theologischen Literaturzeitung. Leipzig.

7. THE LANGUAGE OF THE FATHERS

As far as language is concerned, Christianity was a Greek
movement until almost the end of the second century. During
the first centuries of the Empire, Greek had spread throughout
the Mediterranean. Hellenistic civilization and literature had
made such a thorough conquest of the Roman world, that there
was hardly any town in the West in which the Greek language
was not in everyday use. Even in Rome, North Africa, and
Gaul, the use of Greek was prevalent up to the third century.
For this reason, Greek must be regarded as the original language
of patristic literature. It was partly superseded in the East by
Syriac, Coptic, and Armenian, and entirely displaced in the
West, by Latin.

Both the authors of the New Testament writings, as well as
the Greek Fathers, do not write in classical Greek, but in the

Koine, which could be best described as a compromise between literary Attic and the popular language, and which became the language of the entire Hellenic world from the third century B.C. to the end of Christian antiquity, that is, to the beginning of the sixth century A.D.

Regarding the Koine see: C. P. CASPARI, Ungedruckte, unbeachtete und wenig beachtete Quellen zur Geschichte des Taufsymbols und der Glaubensregel, vol. 3. Christiania, 1875 (Universitätsprogramm) 267–466: Griechen und Griechisch in der römischen Gemeinde in den drei ersten Jahrhunderten ihres Bestehens. — A. THUMB, Die griechische Sprache im Zeitalter des Hellenismus. Beiträge zur Geschichte und Beurteilung der Koine. Strasbourg, 1901. — W. SCHMID, Ueber den kulturgeschichtlichen Zusammenhang und die Bedeutung der griechischen Renaissance in der Römerzeit. Leipzig, 1908. — A. DEISSMANN, Die Urgeschichte des Christentums im Lichte der Sprachforschung. Tübingen, 1911. — A. DEISSMANN, Licht vom Osten. Das Neue Testament und die neuentdeckten Texte der hellenistisch-römischen Welt. 4th edit. Tübingen, 1923. English transl. by L. Strachan, Light from the Ancient East, 2nd edit. New York, 1927. — J. H. MOULTON, A Grammar of New Testament Greek, vol. I. Prolegomena, 3rd edit. London, 1908; vol. II by J. H. Moulton and Howard. Edinburgh, 1919/1929. — H. REINHOLD, De graecitate patrum apostolicorum librorumque apocryphorum Novi Testamenti quaestiones grammaticae. Diss. phil. Halle, 1901. — L. RADEMACHER, Neutestamentliche Grammatik. Das Griechisch des Neuen Testaments in Zusammenhang mit der Volkssprache dargestellt, 2nd edit. Tübingen, 1925. — F. BLASS, Grammatik des neutestamentlichen Griechisch, 6th edit. by A. Debrunner. Göttingen, 1931. — P. S. COSTAS, An Outline of the History of the Greek Language with Particular Emphasis on the Koine and the Subsequent Periods. Chicago, 1936. — E. SCHWYZER, Griechische Grammatik (Handbuch der Altertumswissenschaft. Zweite Abteilung. Erster Teil. Erster Band). Munich, 1939, pp. 116–130; Das Griechische als Weltsprache des Hellenismus: Die Koine. — M. J. HIGGINS, Renaissance of the First Century and the Origin of Standard Late Greek: Traditio 3 (1945) 51–108.

Latin Christian literature had its beginnings in translations of the Bible, which must have been made during the second century. Until recently it was the predominant view that North Africa was the cradle of ecclesiastical Latin, that the Acts of the Martyrs of Scilli (ca. 180) represented the oldest Christian document in Latin, and that it was especially Tertullian who created the ecclesiastical terminology of the West. It is now maintained, however, with considerable probability that here the influence of Rome has been underestimated. More than fifty years before Tertullian composed his writings and thirty years

before the Acts of the Martyrs of Scilli were written, the process
of transition from Greek to Latin had begun in the Christian
community of Rome, as the Shepherd of Hermas indicates.
Furthermore, Clement of Rome's Epistle to the Corinthians was
translated into Latin at Rome in the first half of the second
century. The text of this version, published by G. Morin in 1894,
suggests that the translator used a Latin version of the Old Testament already in existence. For this reason it seems that ecclesiastical Latin had its beginnings at Rome, not in North Africa.

G. KOFFMANE, Geschichte des Kirchenlateins. Vol. I Entstehung und
Entwicklung des Kirchenlateins bis auf Augustinus-Hieronymus. Heft 1,
Breslau, 1879; Heft 2, 1881. — J. FELDER, Die lateinische Kirchensprache
nach ihrer geschichtlichen Entwicklung. (Progr.). Feldkirch, 1905. — J.
STIGLMAYR, Kirchenväter und Klassizismus, 1913. - E. NORDEN, Die antike
Kunstprosa, 3rd edit. Leipzig—Berlin, 1915-1918, 2 vols. — R. J. DEFER-
RARI, Early Ecclesiastical Literature and its Relation to the Literature of
Classical and Medieval Times: Philological Quarterly 6 (1927) 102-110. —
T. BIRT, Marginalien zu lateinischen Prosaikern: Phil 83 (1928) 164-182.
— G. THORNELL, Ad diversos scriptores conjectanea et interpretatoria:
Strena philologica Upsalensia. Upsala, 1922, 383-392. — E. LÖFSTEDT,
Syntactica. Studien und Beiträge zur historischen Syntax des Lateins,
I-II. Lund, 1928 and 1933. — H. P. V. NUNN, An Introduction to Ec-
clesiastical Latin. New York, 1928. — M. B. O'BRIEN, Titles of Address in
Christian Latin Epistolography. Washington, 1930. — J. SCHRIJNEN, Cha-
rakteristik des altchristlichen Latein. Nijmegen, 1932. — W. MATZKOW,
De vocabulis quibusdam Italae et Vulgatae christianis quaestiones lexico-
graphae. Berlin, 1933. — E. LÖFSTEDT, Vermischte Studien zur lateinischen
Sprachkunde und Syntax. Lund, 1936. — G. B. PIGHI, Latinità Cristiana
negli scrittor ipagani del IV secolo. Parte prima. Milan, 1936. — G. BARDY,
La latinisation de l'Eglise d'Occident: Irenikon 14 (1937) 113-130. —
H. JANSSEN, Semantische opmerkingen over het oudchristelijk latijn. Nij-
megen, 1938. — H. JANSSEN, Kultur und Sprache. Zur Geschichte der alten
Kirche im Spiegel der Sprachentwicklung. Nijmegen, 1938. — A. SIZOO,
Eloquentia divina. Het stijlprobleem der oude christenen. Delft, 1939. —
M. A. SAINIO, Untersuchungen der christlichen Latinität (Annales Academi-
cae Scientiarum Fennicae, vol. 47, 1). Helsinki, 1940. — M. MÜLLER, Der
Uebergang von der griech. zur latein. Sprache in der Abendländ. Kirche von
Hermas zu Novatian. Diss. Rome, 1943. — C. MOHRMANN, Quelques traits
caractéristiques du latin des chrétiens: Miscellanea Mercati (Rome, 1946)
437-466; C. MOHRMANN, Le latin commun et le latin des chrétiens: VC 1
(1947) 1-12; C. MOHRMANN, Laatlatijn en Middeleeuwsch Latijn. Utrecht—
Brussels, 1947. — G. BARDY, La question des langues dans l'Eglise ancienne,
vol. I. Paris, 1948. — C. MOHRMANN, Les éléments vulgaires du latin des
chrétiens: VC 2(1948) 163-184; C. MOHRMANN, Les origines de la latinité
chrétienne à Rome: VC 3(1949) 67-106; 163-183.

CHAPTER I

THE BEGINNINGS OF LITURGICAL FORMULAS AND CANONICAL LEGISLATION

I. THE APOSTLES' CREED

The Apostles' Creed (*Symbolum Apostolicum*) is a brief summary of the principal doctrines of Christianity; hence it may be called a compendium of the theology of the Church. Its present form, consisting of twelve articles, does not antedate the sixth century. From that time on it was used in Gaul, Spain, Ireland and Germany in courses of instruction intended for catechumens. The name *Symbolum Apostolicum*, however, is older. Rufinus, at the end of the fourth century, had composed a commentary 'on the symbol of the Apostles' in which he explains its origin. According to him there was a tradition which stated that the Apostles, after having received the Holy Ghost and before departing upon their mission to the various nations and countries, agreed upon a brief summary of the Christian doctrine as a basis of their teaching and as a rule of faith for the believers (ML 21, 337). Ambrose seems to share Rufinus' opinion, for in his 'Explanation of the symbol' he deliberately points to the number twelve of the articles as corresponding to the twelve Apostles: *Ecce secundum duodecim apostolos et duodecim sententiae comprehensae sunt.* In the sixth century we meet for the first time with the assertion that each of the Apostles composed one of the twelve articles of the apostolic symbol. A pseudo-Augustinian sermon of that century thus explains its origin: 'Peter said: I believe in God the Father Almighty, Creator of heaven and earth. . . Andrew said: And in Jesus Christ his only Son, our Lord. . . .' (ML 39, 2189–2190), each of the Apostles contributing one of the twelve articles. This sixth century explanation of the origin of the Apostles' Creed remained the prevailing belief throughout the Middle Ages. It created great surprise therefore when Marcus Eugenicus, the Greek Archbishop of Ephesus, declared at the Council of Ferrara (1438) that the Eastern Churches knew nothing either of the form of Creed used in the Western Church nor of its derivation from the Apostles. A few years later the Italian humanist Lorenzo Valla denied emphatically the apostolic authorship of the *Symbolum Apostolicum.*

Recent investigations on this subject are proof sufficient that its essential content is of apostolic age; the present form, however, developed gradually. Its long history is closely linked with the constant growth of the liturgy of baptism and the preparation of catechumens for this sacrament. Nothing contributed more to the composition of a 'Creed' than the need of just such a formula of profession of faith for candidates to the sacrament of initiation. From the time of the Apostles onward it was the Christian practice to require before baptism an explicit profession of faith in the essential doctrines of Jesus Christ. The candidates had to learn a set wording by heart and they had to pronounce it clearly before the assembled congregation. From this custom originated the solemn rite of the *traditio* and *redditio symboli.* The confession of faith was an integral part of the liturgy and only when we take full cognizance of this fact shall we be able to grasp its history.

A study of the earliest history of the Creed reveals two distinct orms: the christological and the trinitarian formula.

I.   THE CHRISTOLOGICAL FORMULA

The most primitive form of the Creed is preserved in the *Acts of the Apostles,* 8, 37. Philip baptized the eunuch of Ethiopia after the latter had professed his faith thus: 'I believe that Jesus Christ is the Son of God.' This passage proves that the starting point of the Creed was the confession of faith in Jesus Christ as the Son of God. There was no need to require more from the candidates for baptism. The confession of Jesus as Messias proved sufficient, especially for converts from Judaism. As time went on more and more titles were added. Soon afterwards the word 'Saviour' was included in the formula, and thus the acrostic *IXΘYΣ* appeared, a favorite Creed in the Hellenistic world, because *IXΘYΣ* 'fish' contains the initials of the five Greek words for 'Jesus Christ, Son of God, Saviour'. Tertullian and the inscription of Abercius testify to the popularity of this formula in the second half of the second century. Far earlier, however, are to be found in ancient Christian literature expressions of faith in Christ, at once more formal in character and more extensive in scope. Already St. Paul's *Epistle to the Romans* (1,3) formulates the Gospel of God as the message of 'His Son, who was made to him of the seed of David, according to the flesh, who was predestinated the Son of God in power, according to the spirit of sanctification by the resurrection of our Lord Jesus Christ from the dead'. Similar formulas can be found in *I Cor.* 15, 3, and in *I Petr.* 3, 18–22. It is possible that these formulas had been in liturgical use. This conclusion suggests itself especially with respect to the summary of the work of redemption which St. Paul gives in *Phil.* 2, 5–11. About the year 100, Ignatius of Antioch (*Trall.* 9) declares his faith in Jesus Christ in words that remind us very much of the second article in the Apostle's Creed: 'Jesus Christ, who was of the race of David and of Mary, who was truly born, both ate and drank, was truly persecuted under Pontius Pilate, was truly crucified and died while beings heavenly and earthly and under the earth beheld it, who was also truly raised from the dead, his Father having raised him up, as likewise his Father will raise us up in Christ Jesus as we believe in Him, without whom we do not have true life.'

2. THE TRINITARIAN FORMULA

Besides the christological formula there existed from the time of the Apostles a trinitarian confession of faith for the baptismal rite which finally became the dominant form. The Lord's command to baptize all nations 'in the name of the Father, of the Son and of the Holy Ghost' suggested this rule of faith. About the year 150 Justin, the Martyr, mentions (*Apol.* 1, 61) that the candidates for baptism 'receive the washing with water in the name of God the Father and Lord of the universe, and of our Saviour Jesus Christ, and of the Holy Spirit'. Moreover, the so-called *Epistola Apostolorum*, composed about the same time, already expands this profession of faith from three sections to five. Its Creed contains not only the faith 'in the Father, the ruler of the entire world, and in Jesus Christ, our Saviour, and in the Holy Ghost, the Paraclete', but adds 'and in the Holy Church and in the forgiveness of sins'.

Whereas in the *Epistula Apostolorum* the basic triple formula was expanded by addition of two new items, there remained another method of development, namely, to give greater detail to the separate articles of the Creed. The latter device is represented by a type that we may call the combination formula, combining, as it does, both the christological and the trinitarian. The insertion of the originally distinct confession of Christ (which still kept its independent existence in the *praefatio* of the eucharistic liturgy) disturbed the symmetry of the primitive trinitarian symbol. The result was a formula of eight or nine clauses with an extensive christological rule of faith similar to that current at Rome about the year 200. So the Roman rite of baptism described in Hippolytus' *Apostolic Tradition* had this Creed:

> Credo in Deum patrem omnipotentem
> Et in Christum Jesum, filium Dei
>> Qui natus de Spiritu Sancto ex Maria Virgine
>>> Et crucifixus sub Pontio Pilato et mortuus est et sepultus,
>>> Et resurrexit die tertia vivus a mortuis,
>>> Et ascendit in caelis,
>>> Et sedit ad dexteram patris
>>> Venturus judicare vivos et mortuos
>> Et in Spiritum Sanctum et sanctam ecclesiam,
>>> et carnis resurrectionem.

Tertullian at the end of the second century was already familiar with this early Roman Creed and there are many reasons for believing that it had been drawn up long before we first hear of it. Profound and extensive research has demonstrated that this Roman form of the Creed must be regarded as the mother of all the Western Creeds and of our Apostolic Symbol as well. During the third century it passed from one Church to another and finally prevailed universally. But it cannot be proved (as Kattenbusch attempted to do) that this Roman Creed was also the archtype of the oriental forms of the Creed. It seems more probable that the Eastern forms and the Roman symbol are two independent offshoots of a common stock that had its roots in the Orient.

However, a process of development similar to that which we followed in the West can be seen in the East. To a simple trinitarian confession were added christological pronouncements. But whereas the birth from the Virgin Mary was stressed in the West, the Orient introduced new phrases regarding the birth from eternity before the creation of the world. These additions have been called 'anti-heretical'. But only in a few isolated cases can we be certain that the extensions were due to any opposition to heresy. Most of them were introduced because the necessity arose within the Church to bring the principal dogmas of Christianity in abbreviated form more and more into the Creed for the instruction of the catechumens. In much the same way as the liturgy of baptism evolved from a simple rite to a solemn ceremonial, so the baptismal Creed developed from a simple trinitarian confession to a brief summary of the doctrines of Christianity. And as there existed various liturgies so there were various Creed formulas. The best known in the Orient is that of Jerusalem which is preserved in Cyril's *Catechetical Instructions*, and that of Caesarea, as given by Eusebius, the historian. Whether the Nicene Creed is an altered form of the Caesarean or of the Jerusalem type is still a matter of dispute among scholars.

Hence it is evident that the present text of the Apostles' Creed does not appear before the beginning of the sixth century. It is found first in Caesarius of Arles. The Roman Creed of the fifth century still differs considerably from ours in that it does not include the words *creatorem caeli et terrae – conceptus – passus, mortuus, descendit ad inferos – catholicam – sanctorum communionem – vitam aeternam*. However, all the doctrinal elements to be found in the Apostles' Creed appear already about the end of the first century in the numerous and varied formulas of faith which are contained in early Christian literature.

Editions: ES 1–14. — A. HAHN, Bibliothek der Symbole. 3rd ed. Breslau 1897. — E. HENNECKE, Neutestamentliche Apokryphen. 2nd ed. Tübingen 1924, 587f. — H. LIETZMANN, Symbole der alten Kirche. 2nd edit. (KT 17 and 18). Berlin, 1931. *Studies:* F. KATTENBUSCH, Das Apostolische Symbol. 2 vols. Leipzig, 1894 and 1900. — B. DÖRHOLT, Das Taufsymbol der alten Kirche. Paderborn, 1898. — H. WHEELER, The Apostles' Creed, its History and its Contents. New York, 1912. — HOLL-HARNACK-LIETZMANN: SAB (1919) 2–11; 112–116: 269–274. — H. LIETZMANN, Die Anfänge des Glaubensbekenntnisses: Festgabe für A. v. Harnack. Tübingen, 1921, 226–242; *idem*, Symbolstudien: ZNW 21 (1922) 1–34; 22 (1923) 257–279; 24 (1925) 193–203; 26 (1927)

75–95; *idem*, The Founding of the Church Universal (translated by L. Woolf). New York, 1938, 136–160. — J. Brinktrine, Die trinitarischen Bekenntnisformeln und Taufsymbole: ThQ 102 (1921) 156–190. — A. Nussbaumer, Das Ursymbolum nach der Epideixis des hl. Irenaeus und dem Dialog Justins des Märtyrers. Paderborn, 1921. — R. Seeberg, Zur Geschichte der Entstehung des apostolischen Symbols: ZKG 40 (1922) 1–41. — F. J. Badcock, The old Roman Creed: JThSt 23 (1922) 362–389; *idem*, Le credo primitif d'Afrique: RBd 45 (1933) 3–9; *idem*, The Apostles' Creed: ChQ 118 (1934) 40–56; *idem*, The History of the Creeds. 2nd ed. London 1938. — F. Loofs, Das Nicaenum: Festgabe für K. Müller. Tübingen, 1922, 68–82. — M. Wanach, Die Rhythmik im altrömischen Symbol: ThStKr 95 (1923) 125–133. — E. Norden, Agnostos Theos. Leipzig 1923, 263–276. — A. J. Coan, The Rule of Faith in the Ecclesiastical Writings of the First Two Centuries. Diss. Washington, 1924. — A. Westphal, Le symbole des apôtres: ses origines, sa formation, la valeur religieux de son enseignement. Neuilly, 1924. — K. Lake, The Apostles' Creed: HThR 17 (1924) 173–183. — R. H. Connolly, On the Text of the Baptismal Creed of Hippolytus: JThSt 25 (1924) 131–139. — P. Feine, Die Gestalt des apostolischen Glaubensbekenntnisses in der Zeit des Neuen Testamentes. Leipzig, 1925. — A. MacDonald, The Apostles' Creed. 2nd ed. New York, 1925. — E. Schwartz, Das Nicaenum und das Constantinopolitanum auf der Synode von Chalkedon: ZNW 25 (1926) 38–88. — O. Smital, Symbolum apostolicum. New York, 1929. — B. Capelle, Le symbole romain au deuxième siècle: RBd 39 (1927) 37–45; *idem*, Les origines du symbole romain: RTAM (1930) 5–20; *idem*, Alcuin et l'histoire du symbole de la messe: RTAM 6 (1934) 249–60. — J. de Ghellinck, L'histoire du symbole des apôtres. A propos d'un texte d'Eusèbe: RSR 18 (1928) 118–125. — J. Lebreton, Histoire du dogme de la Trinité II. 1928 141 ff.; *idem*, Les origines du symbole baptismal: RSR 20 (1930) 97–124. — L. Froldevaux, Le symbole de saint Grégoire le Thaumaturge: RSR 18 (1929) 193–247. — H. Koch, Lo stilo delle antiche formule di fede: RR 5 (1929) 50–59. — A. Jeremias, Die Bedeutung des Mythos für das Apostolische Glaubensbekenntnis. Leipzig, 1930. — R. Abramowski, Das Symbol des Amphilochius: ZNW 29 (1930) 129–135. — J. Burr, Studies on the Apostles' Creed. London, 1931. — H. du Manoir, Le symbole de Nicée au concile d'Ephèse: Greg 12 (1931) 104–137. — N. Akinian et R. P. Casey. Two Armenian Creeds: HThR 24 (1931) 143–151. — A. Müller, Werdestufen des Glaubensbekenntnisses. Stuttgart, 1932. — J. Kroll, Gott und Hölle. Der Mythos vom Descensuskampfe. Leipzig, 1932. — E. v. Dobschütz, Das Apostolicum in biblisch-theologischer Beleuchtung. Giessen, 1932. — G. Morin, L'origine du symbole d'Athanase: témoignage inédit de S. Césaire d'Arles: RBd 44 (1932) 207–219. — G. Morin, Le symbole de S. Césaire d'Arles: RBd 46 (1934) 178–189. — F. J. Dölger, Die Eingliederung des Taufsymbols in den Taufvollzug nach den Schriften Tertullians: AC 4 (1933) 138–46. — C. H. Moehlman, The Origin of the Apostles' Creed: JR 13 (1933) 301–319. — A. M. Hunter, The Apostles' Creed: ExpT 45 (1933) 123–128. — J. Ruiz Goyo, Los orígenes del Símbolo apostólico: EE 13 (1934) 316–337. — J. A. de Aldama, El símbolo Toledano T .I.: Su texto, su origen, su posición en la historia de los símbolos (Analecta Gregor. T. VII). Rome, 1934. — K. Prümm, Der christliche Glaube und die altheidnische Welt. 2 vols. Leipzig, 1935. — A. d'Alès, Nicée-Constantinople. Les premiers symboles de foi: RSR 26 (1936) 85–92. — J. Lebon, Nicée-Constantinople. Les premiers symboles de foi: RHE 32 (1936) 537–547. — J. Lebon, Les anciens symboles dans la définition de Chalcédoine: RHE (1936) 809–876. — I. Ortiz de Urbina, Textus symboli Nicaeni: OCP 2 (1936) 330–350. — J. Madoz, Le symbole du XIe concile de Tolède. Ses sources, sa date, sa valeur. (Spicilegium sacrum Lovaniense. Fasc. 19). Louvain 1938. — J. Madoz, Le symbole du IVe concile de Tolède: RHE 34 (1938) 5–20. — F. Cavallera, Le De Fide de Bachiarius, Egeria, le symbole du Toletanum I: BLE (1938) 88–97. — P. J. de Perez, La Cristología en los Símbolos Toletanos IV, VI, y XI. Rome, 1939. — A. C. Outler, Origen and the regulae fidei: CH 8 (1939) 212–21. — F. R. M. Hitchcock, Holy Communion and Creed in Clement of Alexandria: ChQ 129 (1939) No. 257. — W. M. Peitz, Das vorephesinische Symbol der Papstkanzlei (Miscellanea historiae pontificiae 1, 1). Rome, 1939. — H. J. Carpenter, The Birth from Holy Spirit and the Virgin in the Old Roman Creed: JThSt 40 (1939) 31–36. — G. Hoffmann, De praeparatione definitionis Concilii Florentini de Symbolo: Acta Acad. Velehradensis XIV (1940) 161ff. — J. Creyghton, Credo. Het geheim van de Apost. Geloofsbelijdenis. 's Hertogenbosch, 1941. — W. Robinson, Historical Survey of the Church's Treatment of New Converts with Reference to Pre- and Post-baptismal Instruction: JThSt 42 (1941) 42–53. — O. Cullmann, Les origines des premières confessions de foi: RHPR 21 (1941) 77–110. — H. J. Carpenter, Symbolum as a Title of the Creed: JThSt 43 (1942) 1–11. — O. Cullmann, L'essence de la foi chrétienne d'après les premières Confessions: RHPR 22(1942) 30–42. — I. Ortiz de Urbina, L' 'homousios' preniceno: OCP 8(1942) 194–209. — H. J. Carpenter, Creeds and Baptismal Rites in the First Four Centuries: JThSt 44 (1943) 1–11. — M. Villain, Rufin d'Aquilée commentateur du symbole des apôtres: RSR (1944) 129–156. — S. Liberty, The Importance of Pontius Pilate in Creed and Gospel: JThSt 45 (1944) 38–56. — J. Madoz, El Símbolo del Concilio XVI de Toledo. Madrid, 1946. — J. de Ghellinck, Patristique et moyen âge. Tome I: Les recherches sur les origines du symbole des apôtres. Brussels-Paris, 1946. — P. Nautin, Je crois à l'Esprit Saint dans la Sainte Eglise pour la résurrection de la chair. Etude sur l'histoire et la théologie du symbole. Paris, 1947. — I. Ortiz de Urbina, El Símbolo Niceno. Madrid, 1948. — L. Bieler, The 'Creeds' of St. Victorinus and St. Patrick: TS 9(1948) 121–124.

2. THE DIDACHE

The index of the codex in which the *Didache* was found lists it in the abbreviated form: Διδαχὴ τῶν δώδεκα ἀποστόλων. The complete title of this work is however: Διδαχὴ τοῦ κυρίου διὰ τῶν δώδεκα ἀποστόλων τοῖς ἔθνεσιν, i.e. 'The Lord's Instruction to the Gentiles through the Twelve Apostles'. The latter seems to have been the title by which it was originally known. The author does not reveal his name. Nevertheless, it would be rash to presume, as Duchesne suggested, that the title points to apostolic autorship. The text in no wise justifies this. This author's intention, evidently, was to give a brief summary of the doctrine of Christ as taught to the nations by the Apostles. This then would explain its title.

The Didache is the most important document of the subapostolic period, and the oldest source of ecclesiastical law which we possess. Until the year 1883 it was quite unknown. The Greek Metropolitan of Nicomedia, Philotheos Bryennios, then published it from a Greek parchment codex (1057) of the patriarchate of Jerusalem. It has since enriched and deepened, in an amazing way, our knowledge of the beginnings of the Church. Scholars, constantly drawn to its precious contents, have gained repeated inspiration and enlightenment from this little book.

Judging by the title only, one might expect the Didache to reveal the evangelical preaching of Christ, but we find it to be more on the order of a compendium of precepts of morality, of instructions on the organization of communities, and of regulations pertaining to liturgical functions; we possess here a summary of directions which offer us an excellent picture of Christian life in the second century. In fact we have here the oldest Church-Order and the venerable prototype of all the later collections of Constitutions or Apostolic Canons with which ecclesiastical law in the East and the West began.

CONTENT

The entire treatise is divided into sixteen chapters in which two main divisions are clearly discernible. The first part (chapters 1–10) presents liturgical instructions; the second part (chapters 11–15) comprises disciplinary regulations. The chapter on the *parousia* of the Lord and the Christian duties arising therefrom constitutes the conclusion.

The first section (ch. 1–6) of the liturgical part contains directions for imparting instructions to catechumens. The form in which these instructions are couched is most interesting. The rules of morality are set forth by means of a description of two ways, that of good and that of evil. The text begins thus:

> Two Ways there are, one of Life and one of Death, and there is a great difference between the Two Ways. Now the

100 – 150 AD in Syria

Way of Life is this: first, love the God who made you; secondly, your neighbor as yourself; do not do to another what you do not wish done to yourself (1,1–2).
The description of the Way of Death ushers in the fifth chapter:

But the Way of Death is this: first of all it is wicked and altogether accursed: murders, adulteries, lustful desires, fornications, thefts, idolatries, magical arts, sorceries, robberies, false testimonies, hypocrisy, duplicity, fraud, pride, malice, surliness, covetousness, foul talk, jealousy, rashness, haughtiness, false pretension, the lack of the fear of God.

This two-way device, which here becomes a basic method of training catechumens, bears the stamp of a time-honored Greek concept. It was used in the Hellenistic synagogues to instruct proselytes. – Most important for the historian of liturgy are chapters 7–10. Directions for administering baptism are given first:

Baptize as follows: after first explaining all these poinst, baptize in the name of the Father and of the Son and of the Holy Spirit, in running water. But if you have no running water, baptize in other water; and if you cannot in cold, then in warm. But if you have neither, pour water on the head three times in the name of the Father and of the Son and of the Holy Spirit (7,1–3).

According to this quotation, baptism by immersion in running water, namely in rivers and springs, was the customary manner of administering this sacrament; baptism by infusion was sanctioned in cases of neccessity. This is the sole reference from the first and second centuries regarding baptism by infusion.

The Didache contains, moreover, an express precept enjoining fasting. Both the candidate and the minister of baptism are required to fast before the administration of the sacrament (7,4). Wednesdays and Fridays are prescribed as fixed fast days, a custom which was directed against the Jewish practice, for the latter kept Mondays and Thursdays as traditional fast days (8,1).

Prayer and the liturgy

The recital of the Lord's prayer three times daily is for the faithful a matter of obligation. Ch. 9 and 10 are of importance for the history of liturgy for they contain the oldest eucharistic prayers yet recorded:

Regarding the Eucharist. Give thanks as follows:
First, concerning the cup:
'We give Thee thanks, Our Father,
for the Holy Vine of David Thy servant,
which Thou hast made known to us through
Thy Servant Jesus. To Thee be the glory for evermore.'
Next, concerning the broken bread:
'We give Thee thanks, Our Father, for
the life and knowledge Thou hast made known
to us through Jesus Thy Servant.
To Thee be the glory for evermore.
As this broken bread was scattered
over the hills and then, when gathered, became
one mass, so may Thy Church be gathered
from the ends of the earth into Thy kingdom. For Thine is
the glory and the power
through Jesus Christ for evermore.'
Let no one eat and drink of your Eucharist but those
baptized in the name of the Lord; for concerning this also
did the Lord say: Do not give to dogs what is sacred (9).

The opinion advanced more than once, that we have here no
specific Eucharistic prayers but simply table prayers, is untenable. The discussion of the Eucharist is closely connected with
that of baptism and the two are evidently associated in the
author's mind. Unbaptized persons are moreover expressly excluded from the reception of the Eucharist. The tenth chapter
cites a prayer to be said after receiving:

After you have taken your fill of food, give thanks as follows:
'We give Thee thanks, O Holy Father, for Thy holy
name, which Thou hast enshrined in our hearts,
and for the knowledge and faith and immortality
which Thou hast made known to us through Jesus
Thy Servant.
To Thee be the glory for evermore.
Thou, Lord Almighty, hast created
all things for the sake of Thy name,
and hast given food and drink for men
to enjoy, that they may give thanks to Thee;
but to us Thou hast vouchsafed spiritual

food and drink and eternal life through
(Jesus) Thy Servant. Above all, we give
Thee thanks because Thou art mighty.
To Thee be the glory for evermore' (10,1-4).
The Eucharist is here clearly called a spiritual food and drink
(πνευματικὴ τροφὴ καὶ ποτόν) and the author adds: 'If anyone is
holy, let him advance; if anyone is not, let him be converted'
(10,6).

Not only numerous other indications but especially the context warrants the assumption that these prescriptions were
intended to regulate the First Communion of the newly baptized
on Easter eve. The ordinary Eucharistic service held on Sundays
is described in chapter 14:

On the Lord's own day, assemble in common to break
bread and offer thanks; but first confess your sins, so that
your sacrifice may be pure. However, no one quarreling
with his brother may join your meeting until they are
reconciled; your sacrifice must not be defiled. For here we
have the saying of the Lord: In every place and time offer
me a pure sacrifice; for I am a mighty King, says the Lord;
and my name spreads terror among the nations (ACW).

The definite reference to the Eucharist as a sacrifice (θυσία)
and the allusion to *Malach.* 1,10 are significant.

Confession

No less interesting is the insistence on confession prior to the
partaking of the Eucharist. The confession of sins in question is
most likely a liturgical confession much after the manner of
our *Confiteor*. In a similar way chapter 4,14 demands a confession
of sins preceding the prayer in church: 'In church confess your
sins, and do not come to your prayer with a guilty conscience.'

Hierarchy

There are no indications whatever in the Didache which
would warrant the assumption of a monarchial episcopate. The
heads of the communities are called *episcopoi* and *diakonoi*; but
whether these *episcopoi* were simple priests or bishops is not clear.
Nowhere is mention made of presbyters:

Accordingly, elect for yourselves bishops and deacons,

men who are an honor to the Lord, of gentle disposition, not attached to money, honest and well-tried; for they, too, render you the sacred service of the prophets and teachers. Do not, then, despise them; for they are your dignitaries together with the prophets and teachers (15,1-2).

This reference prompts us to conclude that beside the local hierarchy the so-called prophets played an important role. In ch. 13,3 we read regarding them: 'They are your high priests.' They are entitled to celebrate the Eucharist: 'Permit the prophets to give thanks (εὐχαριστεῖν) as much as they desire' (10,7). They are entitled to tithes of all earnings: 'Therefore, take all first fruits of vintage and harvest, of cattle and sheep, and give these first fruits to the prophets . . . Likewise, when you open a fresh jar of wine or oil, take the first draught and give it to the prophets. Of money and cloth and any other possession, first set aside a portion according to your discretion and give it according to the commandment' (13,3-7). The position they occupied was evidently held in high esteem for it was said of them that they could not be judged: 'He (the prophet) is not liable to your judgment, for his judgment rests with God' (11,11). To criticize them is in effect a sin against the Holy Spirit: 'If any prophet speaks in ecstasy, do not test him or entertain any doubts; for any sin may be forgiven, but this sin cannot be forgiven' (11,7).

Charity and Social Work

Very interesting are the principles of charity and social work as expressed in the Didache. Although almsgiving is highly recommended, the duty of earning a livelihood by work is likewise stressed. The obligation of providing for others was conditioned upon their incapacity for work:

If the arrival is a transient visitor, assist him as much as you can but he may not stay with you more than two days, or, if necessary, three. But if he intends to settle among you, then, in case he is a craftsman, let him work for his living; if he has no trade or craft, use your judgment in providing for him, so that a follower of Christ will not live idle in your midst. But if he is not satisfied with this arrangement, then he is a Christmonger. Be on your guard against such people (12,2-5 ACW).

Ecclesiology

The concept 'Church' has in the Didache the connotation of universality. In the foreground of Christian consciousness is the idea of an all-embracing world church. The word ἐκκλησία means not only the congregation of believers assembled for prayer, but also the new people or the new race of Christians that shall one day be firmly established in God's kingdom. The attributes *one* and *holy* are particularly stressed. The symbol of this unity of all unities is the Eucharistic bread which from a multitude of grains became one bread. As one of the prayers puts it:

As this broken bread was scattered over the hills and then, when gathered, became one mass, so may Thy Church be gathered from the ends of the earth into Thy kingdom (9,4).

And in another passage we find the following petition:

Remember, O Lord, Thy Church: deliver her from all evil, perfect her in Thy love, and from the four winds assemble her, the sanctified, in Thy kingdom, which Thou hast prepared for her (10,5).

Eschatology

The eschatological attitude is prominent in the Didache. It shows now and again in the eucharistic prayers, 'May Grace come, and this world pass away', prompts their final conclusion, the Aramaic *Maran atha*, 'My Lord, come!', and entirely pervades the final chapter of the work. The uncertainty of the hour is known to all the Christians but also the imminence of the *parousia*, the second coming of the Lord. Therefore, the faithful should frequently be gathered together to seek the things which are profitable for their souls. The Didache points to the signs that are to herald the *parousia* and the resurrection of the dead: false prophets and perverters will multiply, sheep will turn into wolves, love will change to hate; then the deceiver of the world will appear as the Son of God and he will do sign and wonder and the earth will be given into his hands. 'Then humankind will undergo the fiery test.' Although many will be offended and lost, they who persevere in their faith shall be saved. Then shall the world see the Lord coming on the clouds of heaven and all his saints with him. Therefore the Christians are admonished: 'Watch over your life; your lamps must not go out, nor your loins be ungirded; on the contrary, be ready. You do not know the hour in which Our Lord is coming' (16,1).

TIME OF COMPOSITION

The all-important question concerning the Didache is when it was written. Recent critical examinations of the text have disclosed that chapters 1–6 of the Didache parallel closely chapters 18–20 of Barnabas' Epistle. But whether this similarity is tantamount to actual dependence of the Didache upon Barnabas' Epistle is a matter of serious doubt. In any event, such a relationship cannot be incontestably established. Another explanation is quite plausible; since in the passages under discussion each work is treating the Two Ways, it is possible that both are indebted to still another source. The attempts to link the Didache with the *Shepherd of Hermas* or with the *Diatessaron* of Tatian have so far led to no definite result. One thing is certain, namely, that section 1, 3 c to 2, 1 is a later insertion in the text of the Didache. Perhaps this is also the case in regard to chapters 6 and 14. The Didache, as a whole, is not a coherent product, but rather an artless compilation of existing texts. It is little more than a collection of ecclesiastical regulations, which had been in use for some time and had thereby acquired the force of law. This would also explain many a contradiction in the Didache. The compiler failed in the attempt to achieve a consistent unit from the material before him.

Internal evidence is much more helpful in determining the date at which the Didache was compiled. The contents clearly reveal that the document does not go back to apostolic times, because opposition to the Jews is already discernible. The process of abandoning the customs of the synagogue is in progress. Furthermore, such a collection of ecclesiastical ordinances presupposes a period of stabilization of some duration. Scattered details indicate that the apostolic age is no longer contemporary, but has passed into history. Baptism by infusion has found sanction; the regard for the prophets of the New Dispensation is waning and has to be stressed anew. On the other hand, many features point to an origin proximate to apostolic times: the liturgy as described in chapters 7–10 is of the utmost simplicity; baptism in living water, that is in rivers, is still the rule; baptism by infusion is permitted by way of exception only; there are, moreover, no traces to be found of a universal creed formula or a New Testament canon; the prophets still celebrate the eucharist, and it is necessary to stress that the actual liturgical ministers, the bishops and deacons, are entitled to no less honor and respect on the part of the faithful. All these facts aid in attesting that the Didache must have originated between 100 A.D. and 150 A.D. It was, in all likelihood, written in Syria.

Such regard and reverence were accorded to the Didache in Christian antiquity that many considered it equal in importance to the books of the New Testament. Hence Eusebius (*Hist. eccl.* 3, 25, 4), Athanasius (*Ep. fest.* 39) and Rufinus (*Comm. in symb.* 38) find it necessary to stress that the Didache does not possess canonical character and must therefore be numbered among the apocryphal books. It served subsequent liturgical works and ecclesiastico-juridical writings as model, e.g., the *Syriac Didascália*, the *Apostolic Tradition* of Hippolytus of Rome, and the *Constitutions of the Apostles*; and it was used, as Athanasius tells us, for the instruction of catechumens.

TEXT TRADITION

The following are the authorities for the text of the Didache:

Greek: 1) The Codex Hierosolymitanus of the Greek Patriarchate at Jerusalem, formerly in the library of the Hospice of the Holy Sepulchre Church in Constantinople. It was written in 1056 by a certain Notary, Leo. Here the text is inserted after the epistles of Barnabas and of Clement and before those of St. Ignatius. 2) The Greek text of chapters 1, 3–4 and 2, 7 – 3, 2 is preserved in a fourth-century Oxyrhynchos parchment. 3) Chapters 1–6 are embodied in chapters 18–20 of the Epistle of Barnabas. 4) The Canons of the Apostles compiled in Egypt in the fourth century contains chapters 1, 1 – 3 and 2, 2–4, 8. The seventh book of the Apostolic Constitutions, written in Syria in the fourth century, includes almost all of the Greek text of the Didache.

Latin: Two fragments of an old Latin translation which must have been made in the third century are preserved. The shorter of the two, from a codex of Melk of the ninth or tenth century, consists of chapters 1, 1 – 3 and 2, 2 – 6 of the Didache. The second has been found in a Munich manuscript (Cod. Monac. lat. 6264) of the eleventh century and comprises chapters 1, 1–2 and 2,2–6, 1. Recently a considerable portion (chapters 10, 3b–12, 2a) of a Coptic translation of the fifth century has been found in a papyrus (927) of the British Museum. According to this fragment, a prayer to be said over the oil of unction (μύρον) followed the eucharistic prayers. The oil in question is probably the chrism used in the administration of the sacraments of baptism and confirmation. In addition to the aforementioned manuscripts we possess fragments of Syriac, Arabic, Ethiopic and Georgic translations.

Editions: J. RENDEL HARRIS, The Teaching of the Twelve Apostles (with Facsimile of the Manuscript). Baltimore and London, 1887. — J. B. LIGHTFOOT and J. R. HARMER, The Apostolic Fathers. London and New York, 1893. — A. HARNACK. Die Lehre der 12 Apostel (TU 2). Leipzig, 2nd ed. 1893. — F. X. FUNK, Patres Apostolici I 2. Tübingen, 1901, 2–37. — K. BIHLMEYER, Die apostolischen Väter. Tübingen, 1924, 1–9. — G. RAUSCHEN, Monumenta aevi apostolici (FP 1). Bonn, 1904, 2nd ed. 1914, 9–29. — K. LAKE, The Apostolic Fathers (LCL). London and New York, 1930, 303–33. — H. LIETZMANN, Die Didache, mit kritischem Apparat (KT 6). Berlin. 1936. — TH. KLAUSER, Doctrina duodecim Apostolorum (FP 1). Bonn, 1940.

Translations. English: J. B. LIGHTFOOT and J. R. HARMER, l. c. — C. BIGG, The Doctrine of the Twelve Apostles. London, 1898. Revised edition by A. J. MACLEAN. London and New York, 1922. — K. LAKE, l. c. — F. X. GLIMM, FC 1, 165–184 — J. A. KLEIST, ACW 6 (1948) 3–25. *German:* HARNACK, l. c. — R. KNOPF, Handbuch zum Neuen Testament, Ergänzungsband. Tübingen, 1920, 1–40. — F. ZELLER, Die Apostolischen Väter (BKV²35). Kempten and Munich, 1918, 6–16. — E. HENNECKE, Neutestamentliche Apokryphen. Tübingen, 2nd ed. 1924, 560–65. — H. LILJE, Die Lehre der 12 Apostel. Berlin, 1938. — *French:* H. HEMMER, Les Pères Apostoliques. Paris, 1907 — *Italian:* M. DAL PRADA, La Didache. Vicenza, 1938. — G. BOSIO, I Padri Apostolici. Turin, 1940, 1–59.

Studies: J. A. ROBINSON, Barnabas, Hermas and the Didache. London, 1920. J. V. BARTLET, The Didache Reconsidered: JThSt 22 (1921) 239–249. — A. LOISY, La Didache et les lettres des Pères Apostoliques: RHL 7 (1921) 433–81. — R. H. CONNOLLY, The Use of the Didache in the Didascalia: JThSt 24 (1923) 147–57. — F. R. M. HITCHCOCK, Did Clement of Alexandria know the Didache?: JThSt 24 (1923) 297–401. — R. H. CONNOLLY, New Fragments of the Didache: JThSt 25 (1924) 151–53. — G. HORNER, A New Papyrus Fragment of the Didache in Coptic: JThSt 25 (1924) 225–31. —

C. Schmidt, Das koptische Didache-Fragment des British Museum: ZNW 24 (1925) 81–99. — J. Muilenburg, The Literary Relations of the Epistle of Barnabas and the Teaching of the Twelve Apostles. Marburg, 1929. — U. Hüntemann, Ad cap. I Doctrinae XII apostolorum: Ant 6 (1931) 195–96. — F. C. Burkitt, Barnabas and the Didache: JThSt 33 (1932) 25–27. — R. H. Connolly, The Didache in Relation to the Epistle of Barnabas: JThSt 33 (1932) 237–53. — G. Peradze, Die Lehre der zwölf Apostel in den georgischen Ueberlieferungen: ZNW 31 (1932) 111–16. — G. Dix, Didache and Diatessaron: JThSt 34 (1933) 242–50. — Athenagoras, Νεώτεραι ἀπόψεις ἐπὶ τῆς Διδασκαλίας, Διδαχῆς καὶ τῶν ἀποστολικῶν Διαταγῶν: EPh 32 (1933) 481–510. — J. A. Robinson,The Didache, with Additional Notes by R.H. Connolly: JThSt 35 (1934) 113–46; 225–247. — A. Broekutne, Eine schwierige Stelle in einer alten Gemeindeordnung (Did. 11, 11): ZKG 54 (1935) 576–582. — H. J. Cadbury, The Epistle of Barnabas and the Didache: JQR 26 (1936) 403–6. — H. Streeter, The Much-belaboured Didache: JThSt 37 (1936) 369–74. — R. H. Connolly, Canon Streeter on the Didache: JThSt 38 (1937) 364–78. — H. Lietzmann, The Beginnings of the Christian Church. New York, 1937, 270–73. — R. H. Connolly, Barnabas and the Didache: JThSt 38 (1937) 165–67; idem, The Didache and Montanism: Downside Review 55 (1937) 339–47. — J. M. Creed, The Didache: JThSt 39 (1938) 370–87. — F. E. Vokes, The Riddle of the Didache: Fact or Fiction, Heresy or Catholicism? (SPCK) London, 1938. — Th. Klauser, Taufet in lebendigem Wasser (Zum religions - und kulturgeschichtl. Verständnis von Didache 7, 1–3): Pisciculi, Münster, 1939, 157–64. — W. L. Knox, Περικαθαίρων (Didache 3,4): JThSt 40 (1939) 146–49. — W. Telfer, The Didache and the Apostolic Synod of Antioch: JThSt 40 (1939) 133–46; 258–71. — J. E. L. Oulton, Clement of Alexandria and the Didache: JThSt 41 (1940) 177–79. — E. J. Goodspeed, The Didache, Barnabas and the Doctrina: AThR 27 (1945) 228–247. — For the Eucharistic prayers see: J. Quasten, Monumenta eucharistica et liturgica vetustissima (FP 7). Bonn, 1935–37, 8–13. — H. Lietzmann, Messe und Herrenmahl (Arbeiten zur Kirchengeschichte 8). Bonn, 1926, 230–38. — A. Greiff, Das älteste Pascharitual der Kirche, Didache 1–10 und das Johannesevangelium (Johanneische Studien 1). Paderborn, 1929. — R. D. Middleton, The Eucharistic Prayers of the Didache: JThSt 37 (1935) 259–67. — H. J. Gibbins, The Problem of the Liturgical Section of the Didache: JThSt 36 (1935) 373–87. — R. H. Connolly, Agape and Eucharist in the Didache: Downside Review 55 (1937) 477–89. — A. Arnold, Der Ursprung des christlichen Abendmahles. Freiburg i. B., 1937. — M. Dibelius, Die Mahlgebete in der Didache: ZNW 37 (1938) 32–41. — G. Dix, Primitive Consecration Prayers: TJHC 37 (1938) 261–83. — E. Peterson, Didache cap. 9 e 10: EL 58 (1944) 3–13. — J. A. Jungmann, Missarum Solemnia. Vienna, 1948, I, 17–19. For the passages dealing with penance cf. J. Hoh, Die kirchliche Busse im zweiten Jahrhundert. Breslau, 1932, 103–111. — B. Poschmann, Paenitentia secunda. Bonn, 1940, 88–97. For the social question, see A. T. Geoghegan, The Attitude Towards Labor in Early Christianity and Ancient Culture (SCA 6). Washington, 1945, 122–133.

CHAPTER II

THE APOSTOLIC FATHERS

The Apostolic Fathers were the Christian writers of the first and early second centuries whose teaching may be considered a fairly immediate echo of the preaching of the Apostles: they had either been in personal contact with the Apostles, or had received instructions from their disciples. The term 'Apostolic Fathers' was entirely unknown in the early Church. It was introduced by scholars of the seventeenth century. J. B. Cotelier brought together under this name (*Patres aevi apostolici*, 2 vols. 1672) the following five ecclesiastical writers: Barnabas, Clement of Rome, Ignatius of Antioch, Polycarp of Smyrna, and Hermas. In later times it became the custom to extend the number of Apostolic Fathers to seven, and to include Papias of Hieropolis, and the unknown author of the *Epistle to Diognetus*. In modern times the Didache has been added. It is, of course, self evident that this classification does not indicate a homogeneous group of writings. The *Shepherd of Hermas* and the *Letter of Barnabas* belong, as far as form and content are concerned, to the Apocrypha, while, because of its purpose, the *Letter to Diognetus* should be put with the works of the Greek Apologists.

The writings of the Apostolic Fathers are of a pastoral character. With regard to content and style, they are closely related to the writings of the New Testament, especially to the Epistles of the Apostles. Consequently, they may be regarded as connecting links between the time of revelation and the time of tradition, and as very important witnesses to the Christian faith. The authors belong to very different regions of the Roman Empire, for instance, Asia Minor, Syria, and Rome. They wrote for special occasions. Nevertheless, they present a unified world of ideas that gives us a picture of the Christian doctrine at the turn of the century.

Typical of all these writings is their eschatological character. The second coming of Christ is regarded as imminent. On the other hand, the person of Christ is still vividly remembered on account of the direct relation of the authors to the Apostles. Thus the writings of the Apostolic Fathers reveal a deep longing for Christ, the departed and expected Saviour, a longing which very often takes a mystical form, as for instance in Ignatius of Antioch. The Apostolic Fathers do not aim at a scientific exposition of the Christian faith: their writings contain occasional utterances rather than doctrinal definitions. In general, however, they do present a uniform christological doctrine. Christ is, to them, the Son of God, who is pre-existent, and who collaborated in the creation of the world.

Editions: O. GEBHARDT, A. HARNACK and TH. ZAHN, Patrum Apostolicorum Opera 1-3. Leipzig, 1875-77; Vol. I in 2nd ed. 1876-78. Ed. minor 2nd ed. 1920. — J. B. LIGHTFOOT, The Apostolic Fathers. Pt. I, vols. 1 and 2, S. Clement of Rome. London, 1890; Pt. II, vols. 1-3, St. Ignatius and Polycarp. 2nd ed. London, 1889. — J. B. LIGHTFOOT and J. R. HARMER, The Apostolic Fathers. London and New York, 1893. — F. X. FUNK, Patres Apostolici 1-2. Tübingen, 1901. 3d ed. of vol. 2 ed. F. DIEKAMP. Tübingen, 1913. Ed. minor 2nd ed. 1906.—K. BIHLMEYER, Die apostolischen Väter. Tübingen, 1924.—K. LAKE, The Apostolic Fathers (LCL). London and New York, 1930. — H. HEMMER, G. OGER, A. LAURENT, A. LELONG, Les Pères apostoliques, 4 vols. Paris, 1907-12; 2nd ed. of vols. 1 and 2, 1926. — S. COLOMBO, Patrum apostolicorum opera. Turin, 1934. — E. J. GOODSPEED, Index Patristicus sive clavis Patrum apost. Leipzig, 1907.

Translations: English: A. ROBERTS, J. DONALDSON and F. CROMBIE, The Writings of the Apostolic Fathers (Ante-Nicene Christian Library, Vol. 1). Edinburgh, 1870. — A. C. COXE, The Apostolic Fathers with Justin Martyr and Irenaeus (ANF 1). New York, 1903. — J. B. LIGHTFOOT, l.c. — J. B. LIGHTFOOT and J. R. HARMER, l.c. — K. LAKE, l.c. — F. X. GLIMM, G. G. WALSH, J. M. F. MARIQUE, The Apostolic Fathers. New York, 1947. — J. A. KLEIST, ACW 1 (1946), ACW 6 (1948). — E. J. GOODSPEED, The Apostolic Fathers. New York, 1950. — *German:* F. ZELLER, Die Apostolischen Väter (BKV² 35). Kempten and Munich, 1918. — H. LIETZMANN, Handbuch zum Neuen Testament. Ergänzungsband. Tübingen, 1920-23. — E. HENNECKE, Neutestamentliche Apokryphen. Tübingen, 2nd ed., 1924, 480-540; 588-595. — *French:* H. HEMMER, G. OGER, A. LAURENT, A. LELONG, l.c. — *Italian:* G. BOSIO, I Padri apostolici. Vol. I. Turin, 1940; Vol. II, 1942.— *Spanish:* C. RICCI, Los padres apostólicos I. Buenos-Aires, 1929. — *Dutch:* H. U. MEYBOOM, Apost. Vaders. Leiden, 1907. — D. FRANSES, De Apostolische Vaders. Hilversum, 1941.

Studies: A. STRUCKER, Die Gottebenbildlichkeit des Menschen in der christlichen Literatur der ersten zwei Jahrhunderte. Münster, 1913. — E. UNDERHILL, The Mystic Way, a Psychological Study in Christian Origins. London, 1914. — J. BAUER, Untersuchungen über die Vergöttlichungslehre in der Theologie der griechischen Väter: ThQ 98 (1916) 467-91; 99 (1918) 225-52. — A. HARNACK, Die Terminologie der Wiedergeburt und verwandter Erlebnisse in der ältesten Kirche (TU 42,3). Leipzig, 1918. — F. CAVALLERA, Les plus anciens textes ascétiques chrétiens: RAM 1 (1920) 155-60; 351-60. —

G. André, La vertu de simplicité chez les Pères apostoliques: RSR 11 (1921) 306–27. — J. Deblavy, Les idées eschatologiques de S. Paul et des Pères apostoliques. Alençon, 1924. — L. Choppin, La Trinité chez les Pères apostoliques. Paris, 1925. — H. Korn, Die Nachwirkungen der Christusmystik des Paulus in den apostolischen Vätern. Borna-Leipzig, 1928. — J. Marty, Etude des textes cultuels de prière conservés par les Pères apostoliques: RHPR 10 (1930) 90–98. — W. v. Loewenich, Das Johannesverständnis des 2. Jahrhunderts. 1932, 4–38. — E. Mersch, Le corps mystique du Christ. Louvain, 1933, 230–34. — W. Roslan, Les caractères essentiels de la grâce d'après les Pères apostoliques. Warsaw, 1934. — H. Schumacher, Kraft der Urkirche. Das 'neue Leben' nach den Dokumenten der ersten zwei Jahrhunderte. Freiburg i. B., 1934. — G. Bardy, La spiritualité des Pères apostoliques: VS 42 (1935) 140–61; 251–60; 43 (1935) 40–60; idem, La vie spirituelle d'après les Pères des trois premiers siècles. Paris, 1935. — J. Brosch, Das Wesen der Heresie. Bonn, 1936. — K. Rahner, Sünde als Gnadenverlust in der frühchristlichen Literatur: ZkTh 60 (1936) 471–91. — H. D. Simonin, Le 'doute' (δυψυχία) d'après les Pères apostoliques: VS 51 (1937) 165–78. — G. Bardy, Le sacerdoce chrétien d'après les pères apostoliques: VS 53 (1937) 1–28. — A. Casamassa, I padri apostolici. Studio introduttivo. Rome, 1938. — I. Giordani, Il messagio sociale dei primi padri della chiesa. Turin, 1939. English transl. by A. I. Zizzamia, The Social Message of the Early Church Fathers. Paterson, N.J., 1944. — G. del Ton, L'azione cattolica negli scritti dei Padri apostolici: SC (1940) 358–372; 465–480. — G. Bardy, La Théologie de l'Eglise de saint Clément de Rome à saint Irénée. Paris, 1945.

CLEMENT OF ROME

According to the oldest list of Roman bishops bequeathed to posterity by Irenaeus (*Adv. Haer.* 3, 3, 3), Clement was the third successor of St. Peter in Rome. Irenaeus does not tell us when Clement entered upon his reign, nor does he say how long he ruled the Church. Eusebius, the historian (*Hist. eccl.* 3, 15, 34), who likewise mentions Clement as the third successor of St. Peter, sets the twelfth year of Domitian's reign as the beginning, and the third year of Trajan's reign as the end, of his office. Clement, in other words, was Pope from 92 A.D. to 101 A.D. Tertullian states that Clement received consecration from St. Peter himself. Epiphanius confirms this but adds that Clement for the sake of harmony relinquished the pontificate to Linus, and resumed it again after the death of Anacletus. We know next to nothing of the early life of Clement of Rome. Irenaeus points out that Clement was personally acquainted with both St. Peter and St. Paul. Origen (*Comm. in Joan.* 6, 36) and Eusebius

(*Hist. eccl.* 6, 3, 15) identify him with the Clement whom St. Paul praises as his collaborator in the Epistle to the Philippians (IV, 3). But this opinion lacks corroboration. The *Pseudo-Clementines*, which make Clement a member of the imperial family of the Flavii, are anything but trustworthy. Still less reliable is the opinion of Dio Cassius (*Hist. Rom.* 67, 14) who tells us that Clement was none other than the consul Titus Flavius Clemens, a member of the imperial family, executed in 95 A.D., or 96 A.D., for professing Christ. We can put no faith in the story that this fourth Bishop of Rome was martyred. The Greek *Martyrium S. Clementis* is of the fourth century and moreover of purely legendary character. The Roman liturgy commemorates him on the 23rd of November, and his name is enshrined in the Canon of the Mass.

THE EPISTLE TO THE CORINTHIANS

The high esteem in which Clement was held is evident from the one and only writing that we have from him, namely his *Epistle to the Corinthians.*

It is among the most important documents of subapostolic times, the earliest piece of Christian literature outside the New Testament for which the name, position and date of the author are historically attested. The outbreak of disputes within the Church of Corinth during the reign of Domitian impelled the author to intervene. Factions, so severely reprimanded on occasion by St. Paul, raged anew. Some arrogant and impudent individuals had rebelled against ecclesiastical authority and driven the incumbents from office. Only a very small minority of the community remained loyal to the deposed presbyters. Clement's intention was to settle the differences and to repair the scandal given to the pagans. We do not know how word of the disputes reached Rome. There is no foundation for the opinion formerly frequently subscribed to that the Corinthians had appealed to the Bishop of Rome to proceed against the rebellious element. Far more plausible is the theory that Rome was apprized of existing conditions by Roman Christians who had sojourned in Corinth and been witnesses to the dissensions or discords.

The Epistle consists of an introduction (1–3), two main parts (4–36 and 37–61) and a recapitulation (62–65).

The introduction calls attention to the flourishing state of the Christian community of Corinth before the quarrel, the harmony that had then existed among its members and their zeal for good. The third chapter, by way of contrast, points to the entirely changed condition of the community. The first main part is of a rather general character. It deprecates discord and envy, and cites numerous instances of these vices from both Old Testament and Christian times (4–6). This part, furthermore, exhorts to penance, hospitality, piety and humility, and substantiates its argument with a host of quotations and examples. The author then expatiates upon the goodness of God, the harmony existing in his creation, his omnipotence, the resurrection and the judgment; humility, temperance, faith and good works lead to reward, to Christ. The second main part deals more immediately with the quarrel among the Christians in Corinth. God, the Creator of order in nature, requires order and obedience from his creatures. This necessity for discipline and subjection is proved by pointing to the rigorous training of the Roman army and to the existence of a hierarchy in the Old Testament. So, too, Christ called the Apostles and they in turn appointed bishops and deacons. Love should take the place of discord and charity should prompt forgiveness. The instigators of contention are exhorted to do penance and to be submissive. The conclusion summarizes the exhortation and expresses the fervent hope that those commissioned to deliver the Epistle may return in haste to Rome with the glad tidings of peace reborn in Corinth.

The letter is of great consequence for the study of ecclesiastical antiquities as also for the study of the history of dogma and of liturgy.

Church History

1) Very important is the first chapter. It bears reliable testimony to St. Peter's sojourn in Rome, St. Paul's journey to Spain and the martyrdom of the two Princes of the Apostles:

Let us take the noble examples of our own generation.

It was due to jealousy and envy that the greatest and most holy pillars were persecuted and fought to the death. Let us pass in review the good Apostles: a Peter who through unmerited jealousy underwent not one or two, but many hardships and after thus giving testimony, departed to the place of glory that was his due. Through jealousy and strife Paul demonstrated how to win the prize of patient endurance. Seven times he was imprisoned, he was forced to leave and stoned, he preached in the East and in the West; and, finally, won the splendid renown which his faith had earned. He taught the right manner of life to the whole world, travelled as far as the Western boundary, and, when he had given testimony before the authorities, ended his earthly career and was taken up into the holy place as the greatest model of patient endurance (ACW).

2) Again, the sixth chapter gives us information about Nero's persecution of the Christians, speaks of a multitude of martyrs and mentions that many of them were women:

These men who had led holy lives were joined by a great multitude of the elect that suffered numerous indignities and tortures through jealousy and thus became illustrious examples among us. Owing to jealousy, Danaids and Dircae suffered frightful and abominable outrages and, securely reaching the goal in the racecourse of the faith, obtained a noble prize, in spite of the weakness of their sex (ACW).

History of Dogma

1) The document is precious from the dogmatic viewpoint. It may well be called the manifesto of ecclesiastical jurisdiction. Here for the first time we find a clear and explicit declaration of the doctrine of apostolic succession. The fact is stressed that the presbyters cannot be deposed by the members of the community because authority is not bestowed by them. The right to rule derives from the Apostles, who exercised their power in obedience to Christ, who in turn was sent by God:

The Apostles preached to us the Gospel received from Jesus Christ, and Jesus Christ was God's Ambassador. Christ, in other words, comes with a message from God and the Apostles with a message from Christ. Both of these orderly arrangements, therefore, originate from the will of God. And so, after receiving their instructions and being fully assured through the Resurrection of our Lord Jesus Christ, as well as confirmed in faith by the word of God, they went forth, equipped with the fullness of the Holy Spirit, to preach the good news that the Kingdom of God was close at hand. From land to land, accordingly, and from city to city they preached, and from their earliest converts appointed men whom they had tested by the Spirit to act as bishops and deacons for the future believers. And this was no innovation, for, a long time before the Scripture had spoken about bishops and deacons; for somewhere it says: 'I will establish their overseers in observance of the law and their ministers in fidelity' (42). — Our Apostles, too, were given to understand by our Lord Jesus Christ that the office of the bishop would give rise to intrigues. For this reason, equipped as they were with perfect foreknowledge, they appointed the men mentioned before, and afterwards laid down a rule once for all to this effect: when these men die, other approved men shall succeed to their sacred ministry. Consequently, we deem it an injustice to eject from the sacred ministry the persons who were appointed either by them, or later, with the consent of the whole Church, by other men in high repute (44, 1–3 ACW).

2) The Epistle of St. Clement is also of supreme importance for another point of dogma, the primacy of the Roman Church, of which it furnishes unequivocal proof. That it contains no categorical assertion of the primacy of the Roman See is undeniable. The writer nowhere states expressly that his intervention binds and obligates by law the Christian community of Corinth. Nevertheless the very existence of the Epistle is in itself a testimony of great moment to the authority of the Roman Bishop. The Church of Rome speaks to the Church of Corinth as a superior speaks to a subject. In the first chapter the author apologizes forthwith because he had been unable to devote his attention earlier to the irregularities existing in far-off Corinth. This clearly proves that primitive Christian vigilance and solicitude of community for community did not alone inspire the composition of the letter. Had this been the case an apology for

meddling in the controversy would have been in order. But the Bishop of Rome regards it as a duty to take the matter in hand and he considers it sinful on their part if they do not render obedience to him: 'But if some be disobedient to the words which have been spoken by him through us, let them understand that they will entangle themselves in transgression and no little danger but we shall be guiltless of this sin' (59, 1–2). Such an authoritative tone cannot be adequately accounted for on the ground of the close cultural relations existing between Corinth and Rome. The writer is convinced that his actions are prompted by the Holy Spirit: 'For you will give us joy and gladness, if you render obedience to the things written by us through the Holy Spirit' (63, 2).

3) Chapters 24 and 25 treat of the resurrection of the dead and the symbolic Phoenix legend. It is the oldest Christian allusion to this ancient story. The legend plays a great role in early Christian literature and art.

4) The treatise, in the twentieth chapter, on the harmony existing in the world order reveals the influence of Stoic philosophy:

Let us consider how unimpassioned He is in dealing with all His creation.

The heavens revolve by His arrangement and are subject to Him in peace.

Day and night complete the revolution ordained by Him, and neither interferes in the least with the other.

Sun and moon and the starry choirs, obedient to His arrangement, roll on in harmony, without any deviation, through their appointed orbits.

The earth bears fruit according to His will in its proper seasons, and yields the full amount of food required for men and beasts and all the living things on it, neither wavering nor altering any of His decrees.

The unsearchable decisions that govern the deeps are maintained by the same decrees.

The basin of the boundless sea, firmly built by His creative act for the collecting of the waters, does not burst the barriers set up all around it, and does precisely what has been assigned to it. For He said: Thus far shalt thou come, and thy billows shall be turned to spray within thee.

The ocean, impassable for men, and the worlds beyond it are governed by the same decrees of the Master.

The seasons — spring, summer, autumn, and winter — make room for one another in peaceful succession.

The stations of the winds at the proper time render their service without disturbance.

Ever-flowing springs, created for enjoyment and for health, without fail offer to men their life-sustaining breasts.

The smallest of the animals meet in peaceful harmony.

All these creatures the mighty Creator and Master of the universe ordained to act in peace and concord, thus bene-fitting the universe, but most abundantly ourselves who have taken refuge under His mercies through our Lord Jesus Christ.

To whom be the glory and majesty forever and evermore. Amen (ACW).

Liturgy

1) The Epistle points to a clear distinction between hierarchy and laity. After explaining the various divisions of the Old Testament hierarchy the author adds: 'The layman is bound by the rules laid down for the laity' (40, 5). And then he draws the following conclusion: 'Each of us, brethren, must in his own place endeavor to please God with a good conscience, reverently taking care not to deviate from the established rule of service (Λειτουργία)' (41, 1).

2) The members of the Christian hierarchy are called ἐπίσκοποι καὶ διάκονοι. In other passages they are called cumulatively πρεσβύτεροι (cf. 44,5 and 57,1). Their most important function is the celebration of the liturgy: to offer the gifts or to present the offerings (44, 4).

3) The section of the letter preceding the conclusion (chapter 59, 4–61, 3) contains a beautiful prayer. It is quoted here to show that the Roman Church has the welfare of all Christendom at heart. We shall not be mistaken if we assume that it is nothing less than a liturgical prayer of the Church of Rome. It would be meaningless in this context if it did not reproduce with almost entire fidelity a prayer customary in public worship. Its form and language are throughout liturgical and poetical. It bears

witness to Christ's divinity, who is called 'the beloved child' of God (ἠγαπημένος παῖς) 'through whom God has taught us, made us holy, and brought us to honor'. Christ is the 'High Priest' and 'Guardian of our souls' (61, 3). In addition Clement sings the praises of God's providence and mercy. The conclusion is a petition in behalf of the secular rule; it is of great interest in the study of the primitive Christian concept of the state:

Thou, O Master, through Thy transcendent and indescribable sovereignty hast given them the power of royalty, so that we, acknowledging the honor and glory conferred upon them by Thee, may bow to them, without in the least opposing Thy will. Grant to them, O Lord, health, peace, concord, and firmness, so that they may without hindrance exercise the supreme leadership Thou hast conferred on them. For it is Thou, O Master, O heavenly King of all ages, that conferrest upon the sons of men glory and honor and authority over the things which are upon the earth. Do Thou, O Lord, direct their counsels in accord with what is good and pleasing in Thy sight, so that they may piously exercise in peace and gentleness the authority Thou hast granted them, and thus experience Thy graciousness (61, 1-2 ACW).

To turn from consideration of detail to the Epistle as a whole, we can determine some facts as to time of composition, personality of the author and the purpose which prompted him to write.

TIME OF COMPOSITION

In addition to being told of the persecution of Nero (5,4) we learn of another then in progress, to which reference is made in these words: 'Owing to the suddenly bursting and rapidly succeeding calamities and untoward experiences that have befallen us' (1,1). After describing Nero's persecution Clement says: 'We are in the same arena and face the same conflict' (7,1). In these unmistakable allusions to another persecution he must have in mind that of Domitian in the years 95 A.D. and 96 A.D. Furthermore, the context suggests that the Apostles had been dead for some time, and even the presbyters appointed by them had relinquished their offices to others and now too reposed in the Lord (42–44,2). These data gained from a study of the Letter itself agree with the testimony of tradition, particularly that of Hegesippus (ca. 180) in Eusebius, that the quarrels which induced Clement to write occured during Domitian's reign. In addition, Polycarp resorted to Clement's Epistle when he wrote to the Philippians.

AUTHOR'S PERSONALITY

In his letter Clement does not mention himself by name. The sender is: 'The Church of God sojourning in Rome.' When referring to himself the author uses the plural pronoun 'we'. Nevertheless the work was undoubtedly composed by a single person. A certain unity of style and thought lends proof to this assertion. Clement, it seems, took into consideration that his communication would be regarded as destined for public, rather than private use; he envisioned its being read to the Christian community assembled for divine worship. Hence the Epistle is highly elaborated and embellished with many rhetorical conceits. The first part takes the form of a sermon addressed to the entire congregation and has little bearing upon the particular conditions existing in Corinth. Bishop Dionysius of Corinth actually mentions that the Epistle of St. Clement was still read to his congregation during divine worship (ca. 170 A.D.). He says in a letter to Pope Soter (Eusebius, *Hist. eccles.* 4, 23, 11): 'Today we observed the holy day of the Lord and read out your letter, which we shall continue to read from time to time for our admonition, as we do with that formerly sent to us through Clement.' Eusebius states in another passage (*Hist. eccles.* 3, 16) that this custom was not confined to Corinth: 'There is one recognized epistle of Clement, long and wonderful, which he drew up for the Church of the Corinthians in the name of the Church of the Romans when there had been dissension in Corinth. We have learned that this letter was publicly read in the common assembly in many churches both in the days of old and in our time.' Clement's evident intention, to invest the document with an importance transcending its immediate occasion, attained its purpose and assured it, furthermore, a lasting place in ecclesiastical literature. The author, as far as we are able to ascertain, seems to have been of Jewish descent. The frequent references to the Old Testament and the comparatively few citations from the New Testament lend weight to this conjecture.

TEXT TRADITION

The text of the Epistle is preserved in the following manuscripts:

1. The Codex Alexandrinus of the fifth century in the British Museum, though it lacks chapters 57, 6–64, 1.

2. The Codex Hierosolymitanus written by Leo the Notary in 1056. This manuscript contains the entire text of the Letter.

An old Syriac translation is preserved in a twelfth-century (1170) manuscript of the New Testament which is housed in the Cambridge University Library. G. Morin discovered a Latin version in an eleventh-century manuscript in the *Grand Séminaire* of Namur. The translation is almost verbatim and most likely from the first half of the second century (cf. p. 21). Then there are two Coptic translations in the Akhmimic dialect. One of the two was edited from a papyrus (MS. orient., fol. 3065), which is in possession of the Berlin *Staatsbibliothek*. Chapters 34, 5–42 are missing because five pages of this manuscript have been lost. The papyrus dates back to the fourth century and was the property of the famous *White Monastery* of Shenute. The other Coptic version was discovered at Strasbourg in a seventh-century papyrus; it is fragmentary and does not go beyond Chapter 26, 2.

Editions: See the editions and translations of the Apostolic Fathers on p. 41. — *Separate edition:* TH. SCHAEFER, S. Clementis Epistula ad Corinthios (FP 44). Bonn, 1941. — *Separate translation:* W. K. L. CLARKE, First Epistle of Clement to the Corinthians (SPCK). London 1937. — J. A. KLEIST, The Epistles of Clement of Rome and Ignatius of Antioch (ACW 1). Westminster, 1946.

Studies: W. SCHERER, Der erste Klemensbrief an die Korinther nach seiner Bedeutung für die Glaubenslehre der katholischen Kirche untersucht. Regensburg, 1902. — H. BRUDERS, Die Verfassung der Kirche bis zum Jahre 175 n. Chr. Mainz, 1904. — E. METZNER, Die Verfassung der Kirche in den ersten zwei Jahrhunderten (mit besonderer Berücksichtigung der Schriften Harnacks). Danzig, 1920. — G. BARDY, Expressions stoiciennes dans la Prima Clementis: RSR 12 (1922) 73–85. — C. SCHMIDT, Der erste Clemensbrief in altkoptischer Uebersetzung (TU 32,1). Leipzig, 1908. — A. HARNACK, Der erste Klemensbrief, eine Studie zur Bestimmung des Charakters des ältesten Christentums (SAB 1909) 38–63. — W. L. LORIMER, Clement of Rome, Epistle 1,44: JThSt 25 (1924) 404. — J. LEBRETON, La Trinité chez Saint Clément de Rome: Greg 6 (1925) 369–404. — I. GIOR-

DANI, S. Clemente Romano e la sua lettera ai Corinti. Turin, 1925. — H.
LIETZMANN, Petrus und Paulus in Rom. 2nd ed. Berlin, 1927, 226–36. —
P. BATIFFOL, L'Eglise naissante et le catholicisme. 12th ed. Paris, 1927, 146–
56. — J. SHOTWELL and L. ROPES LOOMIS, The See of Peter. New York,
1927, 66–69. — H. DELAFOSSE (J. TURMEL), La Lettre de Clément Romain
aux Corinthiens: RHR 97 (1928) 53–89. — A. HARNACK, Einführung in die
alte Kirchengeschichte. Das Schreiben der römischen Gemeinde an die
korinthische aus der Zeit Domitians (Erster Clemensbrief). Leipzig, 1921. —
O. COLMANN, Les causes de la mort de Pierre et de Paul d'après le témoignage
de Clément Romain: RHPR 10 (1930) 294–300. — ST. LÖSCH, Epistula
Claudiana. Rottenburg, 1930, 33–44. — F. GERKE, Die Stellung des ersten
Clemensbriefes innerhalb der Entwicklung der altchristlichen Gemeinde-
verfassung und des Kirchenrechts (TU 47, 1). Leipzig, 1931. — H. DANNEN-
BAUER, Die römische Papstlegende: HZ 146 (1932) 239–62. — A. S. BARNES,
The Martyrdom of St. Peter and St. Paul. New York, 1933. — W. BAUER,
Rechtgläubigkeit und Ketzerei im ältesten Christentum. Tübingen, 1934,
99–109. — E. BARNIKOL, Spanienreise und Römerbrief. Halle, 1934. — O.
MARRUCCHI, Pietro e Paolo a Roma. 2nd ed. Turin, 1934. — F. R. VAN
CAUWELAERT, L'intervention de l'église de Rome à Corinthe vers l'an 96:
RHE 31 (1935) 267–306, 765f. — K. HEUSSI, War Petrus in Rom? Gotha,
1936; idem, War Petrus wirklich römischer Martyrer?: Die Christl. Welt 51
(1937); idem, Neues zur Petrusfrage. 1939. — H. LIETZMANN, Petrus römischer
Martyrer. (SAB 29) Berlin, 1936. — L. HERRMANN, La mort de S.
Paul et de S. Pierre 811 U.C. = 58 ap. J. C.: Revue de l'Université de
Bruxelles 41 (1936) 189–99. — E. BARNIKOL, Die präexistenziöse Christologie
des I. Clemensbriefes: Theologische Jahrbücher 4 (1936) 61–76. — J. MADOZ,
El primado romano. Madrid, 1936. — E. BARNIKOL, Die vorsynoptische
Auffassung von Taufe und Abendmahl im I. Clemensbriefe: Theologische
Jahrbücher 4 (1936) 77–80. — E. METZNER, Die Petrustradition und ihre
neuesten Gegner. Schwerin (Warthe), 1937. — ST. LÖSCH, Der Brief des
Clemens Romanus. Die Probleme und ihre Beurteilung in der Gegenwart:
Studi dedicati alla memoria di Paolo Ubaldi. Milan, 1937, 177–88. — J. A.
DE ALDAMA, Ia Clementis: Greg. 18 (1937) 107–110. — E. BARNIKOL, Die
Marcionitische Deutung und Datierung des 1. Clemensbriefes durch Turmel
(Delafosse): Theologische Jahrbücher 6 (1938) 10–14; idem, Die Nicht-
kenntnis des Markusevangeliums in der römischen Clemensgemeinde um
100: Theologische Jahrbücher 4 (1938) 142–43. — A. HÖDUM, De brief van
den H. Clemens van Rome: Collationes Brugen. 38 (1938) 454–60. — L.
LEMARCHAND, La composition de l'épître de saint Clément aux Corinthiens:
RSR 18 (1938) 448–57. — H. KATZENMAYER, Zur Frage ob Petrus in Rom
war. I. Klemensbrief, Kap. 5 bis 6: IKZ 28 (1938) 129–40. — H. DANNEN-
BAUER, Nochmals die römische Petruslegende: HZ 159 (1938) 81–88. —
E. FASCHER, PWK 19 (1938) 1345–61. — L. HERTLING, 1 Kor. 15,15 und
1 Clem. 42: Bibl 20 (1939) 276–83. — P. MEINHOLD, Geschehen und Deutung
im I. Clemensbrief: ZKG 58 (1939) 82–129. — B. POSCHMANN, Paenitentia
secunda. Bonn, 1939, 112ff. — H. KATZENMAYER, Das Todesjahr des Petrus:
IKZ 29 (1939) 85–93. — W. L. LORIMER, Clement of Rome, Ep. 1, 6, 2:
Δαναΐδες καὶ Δίρκαι: JThSt 42 (1941) 70. — M. SCHULER, Klemens von Rom

und Petrus in Rom: Trierer Theologische Studien 1 (1941) 94–116. — M. DIBELIUS, Rom und die Christen im ersten Jahrhundert: SAH (1942) 18–29. — E. STAUFER, Zur Vor- und Frühgeschichte des Primatus Petri: ZKG 62 (1943/44) 3–34. — L. SANDERS, L'Hellénisme de saint Clément de Rome et le Paulinisme. Louvain, 1943. — H. RAHNER, Abendländische Kirchenfreiheit. Dokumente über Kirche und Staat im frühen Christentum. Einsiedeln-Cologne, 1943. — G. BARDY, La théologie de l'Eglise de saint Clément de Rome à saint Irénée. Paris, 1945, 108–109; 110–113; 128–129. — ST. SCHMUTZ, Petrus war dennoch in Rom: BM 22 (1946), 128–141. —B. ALTANER, Neues zum Verständnis von I Klemens 5,1-6,2: HJG 62 (1950) 25–30. — For the liturgical passage cf. J. QUASTEN, Monumenta eucharistica et liturgica vetustissima. Bonn, 1937, 327–334. — TH. SCHERMANN, Griechische Zauberpapyri und das Gemeinde- und Dankgebet im I. Klemensbrief (TU 34, 2b). Leipzig, 1909. — J. BRINKTRINE, Der Messopferbegriff in den ersten zwei Jahrhunderten (FThSt 21). Freiburg i. Br., 1918, 68–76. — A. BAUMSTARK, Trishagion und Qeduscha: JL 3 (1923) 18–32. — J. MARTY, Etude des textes cultuels de prière conservés par les 'Pères apostoliques': RHPR 10 (1930) 99 ff. — U. WILCKEN, Mitteilungen aus der Würzburger Papyrussammlung. Nr. 3 : Ein liturgisches Fragment (3. Jahrh.) : AAB, phil.-hist. Klasse Nr. 6. Berlin, 1934, 31–36.

NON-AUTHENTIC WRITINGS

The universal esteem in which Clement was held in antiquity is responsible for the attribution to him of several other writings.

I.   THE SO-CALLED SECOND EPISTLE OF CLEMENT

In the two manuscripts that contain the Greek text of the authentic Clementine Epistle and also in the Syriac version we find added a second Letter likewise addressed to the Corinthians. But this document is neither a letter nor is it from Clement's hand. Its literary form and style give ample proof of this. The work is nevertheless of value to us. It is the oldest Christian sermon extant. The homiletic character and tone are unmistakable. Two passages in particular strengthen this opinion: 'And let us not seem to believe and pay attention now only, while we are being admonished by the presbyters, but also, when we have gone back to our homes, let us remember the commandments of the Lord' (17,3). The second passage says: 'Hence, brothers and sisters, now that the God of truth has spoken, I read to you an exhortation to take to heart that which is written, that you may save yourselves and him who reads this in the midst of you' (19,1). The preacher alludes here to the reading of the Scriptures, which most likely preceded his sermon. The style is unliterary, hence completely different from that of the genuine Clementine Epistle. Moreover, the preacher does not refer to himself in the first person plural but employs the singular form. He quotes not only from the Sacred Scriptures but also from the apocryphal gospels, e.g., the *Gospel of the Egyptians*. Opinions still differ, to a great extent, regarding the place of origin of this sermon. Repeated attempts to approximate the time of origin more closely or to determine the author have failed because of the lack of chronological data in the sermon. Harnack's hypothesis that this document is the letter addressed by Pope Soter (165–173) to the Christian community of Corinth, meets with the insuperable objection that it has none of the characteristics of a letter. Harris and Streeter hold that the composition is in fact an Alexandrian homily because the theology of the author betrays Alexandrian influence and the *Gospel of the Egyptians* is used as a source. But how then could the work ever have been attributed to Clement? The most attractive suggestion is that made by Lightfoot, Funk and Krüger that the homily originated in Corinth. The Isthmian athletic contests held nearby might explain the imagery which the author uses in the seventh chapter. One could then understand also why the work was attributed to Clement and attached to the first Clementine Letter. The homily, more than likely, was preserved together with Clement's Epistle in the archives of Corinth and both were discovered simultaneously. We possess only one clue as to time of composition, the development of Christian doctrine as evidenced in the homily. Hence it is impossible to assign an exact date. The opinion regarding penance, as put forward in the sermon, indicates that it was written not long after the *Shepherd of Hermas*, that is, about 150 A.D. Even though the document was included in the Scriptures in the Syrian Church, Jerome and Eusebius, nevertheless, declared it unauthentic. Eusebius, for instance, says: 'It must be known that there is also a second letter ascribed to Clement, but we have not the same assurance of its acceptance as we have of the former (I Clem.), for we do not even know if the primitive writers used it' (*Hist. eccles.* 3, 38,4). Jerome repudiates the document absolutely: 'There is a second letter circulating under Clement's name but it has not been acknowledged as such by the men of antiquity' (*De viris illustr.* 15).

CONTENT

The content of the homily is rather general in character. The Christian's conception of Christ, the Judge of the living and the dead, must correspond to God's majesty. We must glorify him through the observance of his commandments and the contempt of worldly pleasures and thereby gain for ourselves eternal life.

1. *Christology*

The divinity of Christ and his humanity are clearly expressed:
> Brethren, we ought so to think of Jesus Christ as of God, as of the Judge of the living and the dead (1,1). — If Christ, the Lord who saved us, though he was originally spirit, was made flesh and so called us, so also we shall in this flesh receive our reward (9, 5).

Christ endured great sufferings for our sake (1,2):
> For he had pity on us and saved us in his mercy, and he beheld the great error and destruction which was in us and he saw that we had no hope of salvation save only through him (1,7).

Christ is called 'the prince of incorruptibility (ἀρχηγὸς τῆς ἀφθαρσίας) through whom God made manifest to us truth and heavenly life' (20,5).

2. *Notion of the Church*

Interesting is the concept of the Church which we find in this Letter. According to the author the Church existed before the creation of the sun and the moon. But she was invisible, spiritual and barren. Now she has become flesh. She is the body of Christ; she is his spouse and we have been given to her as children:
> Thus brethren, if we do the will of God our Father we shall be of the first Church, the spiritual, which was created before the sun and moon; . . . Therefore let us choose to belong to the Church of life, that we may be saved. But I do not think that you are ignorant that the living Church is the body of Christ. For the Scriptures say: 'God made them male and female.' The male is Christ, the female is the Church. And moreover the Books and the Apostles say that the Church is not of the present but has been from

the beginning. For she was spiritual, as was also our Jesus but he was manifested in the last days that he might save us. Now the Church, being spiritual, was manifested in the flesh of Christ, thereby showing us that if any one of us shall guard her in the flesh and defile her not, he shall receive her back again in the Holy Spirit. For this flesh itself is an anti-type of the spirit; no man, therefore, who has defiled the anti-type shall receive the real. This, therefore, is what he means, brethren: Guard the flesh that you may partake of the Spirit. Now if we say that the flesh is the Church and the Spirit is Christ then verily he who has dishonored the flesh has dishonored the Church. Such a one, therefore, shall not partake of the Spirit, which is Christ (14, 1–4).

The author shows here that he was greatly influenced by St. Paul's line of thought, particularly by the latter's Epistle to the Ephesians (1, 4, 22; 5, 23, 32), for he calls the Church the mystical body of Christ and represents her as his bride. We find this sermon interesting and valuable also from another viewpoint; we meet here the first reference to the Church as *Mother* even though the author does not employ the word itself: 'In saying, 'Rejoice thou barren that bearest not', he speaks of us, for our Church was barren before children were given her' (2, 1).

3. *Baptism*

Baptism is called the seal (σφραγίς); and this seal must be kept inviolate; 'For of those who have not kept the seal he says: Their worm shall not die, and their fire shall not be quenched, and he shall be a spectacle for all flesh' (7, 6). 'This therefore is what he says: Keep the flesh pure and the seal without spot that we may receive eternal life' (8, 6). Pauline theology is here again in evidence. Cf. Ephes. 4 and 2 Cor. 1, 21–22.

4. *Penance*

The last part of the sermon contains a direct testimony to the *paenitentia secunda*, i.e. penance for sins committed after baptism. Christians are exhorted to penance much as in the *Shepherd of Hermas*:

Therefore, brethren, let us repent forthwith. Let us be sober for our good, for we are full of much madness and evil. Let us wipe off from ourselves our former sins and let us be saved by repenting with all our hearts. Let us not be pleasers of men nor desirous only to please ourselves by our righteousness but also those who are without, that the name be not blasphemed through us (13, 1-2). So then, brethren, having received no small opportunity for repentance let us, now that we have time, turn to God who calls us while we yet have one who awaits us (16, 1). Let us, so long as we are in this world, repent with all our heart of whatsoever evil we have done in the flesh, that we may be saved by the Lord, while we have yet time for repentance. For after we have departed from this world, we shall no longer be able to confess our sins or repent them (8, 2-3).

5. *Efficacy of good works for salvation*

The sermon is very clear on the necessity of good works. Almsgiving is the principal means by which sins are remitted. It is better than fasting and prayer:

Almsgiving is therefore good even as penance for sin. Fasting is better than prayer but almsgiving is better than both. Love covers a multitude of sins, but prayer from a good conscience delivers from death. Blessed is every man that is found full of these things, for almsgiving removes the burden of sin (16, 4).

Translations: English: A. ROBERTS, J. DONALDSON and F. CROMBIE, The Writings of the Apostolic Fathers (Ante-Nicene Christian Library 1). Edinburgh, 1870, 55-63. — J. B. LIGHTFOOT, The Apostolic Fathers I, 2. London and New York, 1890, 306-316. — T. W. CRAFER, Second Epistle of Clement to the Corinthians (SPCK). London, 1921. — K. LAKE, The Apostolic Fathers. London and New York, 1930, 129-163. — *German:* R. KNOPF, Die Apostolischen Väter, Handbuch zum Neuen Testament, ed. by H. LIETZMANN, Ergänzungsband I. Tübingen, 1920, 151-84. — H. V. SCHUBERT, in E. HENNECKE, Neutestamentliche Apokryphen. 2nd ed. Tübingen, 1924, 588-95.

Studies: H. WINDISCH, Das Christentum im zweiten Clemensbrief: Harnack-Ehrung. Tübingen, 1921, 119-134. — J. RENDEL HARRIS, The Authorship of the So-called Second Epistle of Clement: ZNW (1924) 193-200. — H. WINDISCH, Julius Cassianus und die Clemenshomilie: ZNW 25 (1926) 258-62. — J.T. SHOTWELL and L. ROPES LOOMIS, The See of Peter. New York,

1927. 251-55. — G. Krüger, Bemerkungen zum zweiten Klemensbrief: Studies in Early Christianity, ed. by S. J. Case. New York and London, 1928, 417-439. — K. Müller, Die Forderung der Ehelosigkeit für alle Getauften in der alten Kirche. Tübingen, 1927, 14-16. — H. Streeter, The Primitive Church Studied with Special Reference to the Origins of the Christian Ministry. London, 1929, 243ff. — J. Hoh, Die kirchliche Busse im 2. Jahrhundert. Breslau, 1932, 35-40. — G. Krüger, Zu II Klem., 14, 2: ZNW 31 (1932) 204-5. — I. Rucker, Florilegium Edessenum anonymum (SAM). Munich, 1933, 4f. — B. Poschmann, Paenitentia secunda. Bonn, 1939, 124ff. — C. Chavasse, The Bride of Christ. London, 1940, 115-116. — J. C. Plumpe, Mater Ecclesia (SCA 5). Washington, 1943, 22-23.

II. THE TWO LETTERS ADDRESSED TO VIRGINS

Two letters, dealing with virginity and addressed to the unmarried of both sexes, have been handed down to us under Clement's name. They belong actually to the first half of the third century and are referred to in literature for the first time in the writings of Epiphanius (*Haer.* 30, 15))and of Jerome (*Adv. Jovin.* 1,12). The original Greek text has been lost except for a few fragments found in the Πανδέκτης τῆς ἁγίας γραφῆς of the Monk Antiochos of St. Saba (ca. 620). The two epistles have been preserved to us entire, however, in a Syriac translation, discovered in 1470 in a manuscript of the Peshitta version of the New Testament. Moreover, for Chapters 1-8 of the first letter we have a Coptic version, which mentions Athanasius as the author. In reality, the two letters constitute a single work, which in course of time came to be divided.

The first letter begins with instructions on the nature and meaning of virginity. The author looks upon continency as something divine: to him it is a supernatural life, the life of angels. The celibate and the virgin have, in truth, put on Christ. They are imitators of Christ and the Apostles; they are only seemingly of this earth. They have the right to a higher place in heaven than other Christians. The author, however, stresses strongly that virginity in itself without corresponding works of charity, e.g., care of the sick, will not guarantee eternal life. He is acquainted with the abuses prevalent among his addressees and feels compelled to point out that a life of virginity imposes particularly serious responsibilities upon those who embrace it. He exhorts and cautions and does not hesitate sharply to rebuke.

The document ends (chapters 10–13) with directions against the communal life of men and women ascetics and with deploring the evils of idleness. It has, however, no formal conclusion. The second letter begins abruptly without any introduction whatever and goes on in the tenor of the first. The admonitions continue, and no break in thought is discernible. The writer passes next to a description of the customs and laws prevailing among the ascetics of his own country, cites a number of examples from the Bible, and in conclusion points to that of Christ.

As is clear from the above summary, the author vigorously opposes the abuses of the *syneisaktoi* or the so-called *virgines subintroductae*, in other words, he inveighs against the communal life of ascetics of both sexes living together under one roof. Since objections against this curious custom are voiced for the first time in ecclesiastical literature towards the middle of the third century, we may conclude that these two letters likewise originated about this time. The birthplace of the writer seems to have been Palestine: his name is not disclosed. But the work leads one to believe that the composer must have been a prominent and highly revered ascetic. The letters are valuable as one of the oldest sources for the history of early Christian asceticism.

Editions: F. Diekamp, Patres Apostolici, II, 2. Tübingen, 1913, 1–49 gives the Latin translation from the Syriac by J. Th. Beelen and the Greek passages. *Translations: English:* B. P. Pratten, ANF, 8, 51–66. — A German translation by P. Zingerle, Briefe der Päpste I. Wien, 1827.

Studies: A. Harnack, Die pseudo-klementinischen Briefe de virginitate und die Entstehung des Mönchtums (SAB). Berlin, 1891, 361–85. — H. Koch, Virgines Christi. Die Gelübde der gottgeweihten Jungfrauen in den ersten drei Jahrhunderten (TU 31, 2). Leipzig, 1907, 99f. — F. Martinez, L'ascétisme chrétien pendant les trois premiers siècles. Paris, 1913, 171–186. — R. Reitzenstein, Historia monachorum und Historia Lausiaca. Göttingen, 1916, 53–55. — L. Th. Léfort, Le 'de virginitate' de S. Clément ou de S. Athanase?: Le Muséon 40 (1927) 249–264; *idem*, S. Athanase, Sur la virginité: Le Muséon 42 (1929) 197–274; *idem*, Une citation copte de la Ia pseudo-clémentine 'de virginitate': Bulletin de l'institut français d'archéologie orientale 30 (1931) 509–511. — H. Koch, Quellen zur Geschichte der Askese und des Mönchtums in der alten Kirche (SQ 6). Tübingen, 1933, 42–48.

III.   THE PSEUDO-CLEMENTINES

Pseudo-Clementines is the title of a comprehensive novel with a didactic purpose whose protagonist is Clement of Rome. The unidentified author of this edifying narrative represents Clement as a scion of the Roman imperial family, who, searching for truth, tries in vain the various schools of philosophers for a solution of his doubts concerning the immortality of the soul, the origin of the world and problems of a similar nature. Finally news of the appearance of the Son of God in faraway Judea prompts him to take a trip to the Orient. In Caesarea he meets St. Peter, who instructs him in the doctrine of the true prophet, dispels his doubts and invites him to accompany him on his missionary journeys. By far the greatest part of the work is devoted to Clement's experiences as St. Peter's companion on the latter's apostolic journeys and to the encounter between St. Peter and Simon Magus. The narrative is in the last analysis merely an introduction to the missionary sermons of St. Peter and belongs properly to the class of apocryphal acts of the Apostles. It differs from other legends of the Apostles in that its purpose is less to entertain than to furnish theological instructions and weapons for defending Christianity effectively.

The following fragments of the Pseudo-Clementines are extant:

1) *The Twenty Homilies*, containing the missionary sermons of St. Peter, reputedly excerpted by Clement and forwarded by him to the brother of our Lord, Bishop James of Jerusalem (Κλήμεντος τοῦ Πέτρου ἐπιδημίων κηρυγμάτων ἐπιτομή). Two letters, one by Peter, the other by Clement, addressed to James and intended as a guide to the proper use of the collection, precede the homilies. In the letters the Church of Jerusalem is accorded great distinction and the Apostle James is called bishop of bishops. The characteristic feature of the discourses is that they espouse the tenets of the Judaist Ebionites and Elkasaites, according to whom Christianity is nothing more than a purged Judaism. God reveals himself to man through the instrumentality of the true prophet who comes in various guises. He appeared first in the person of Adam, then as Moses and finally as Jesus Christ. The title 'Son of God' is, however, restricted to Christ; but even he is only a prophet and teacher and not a redeemer. It was Moses' task to restore religion dimmed by sin to its pristine brightness, and when in the course of time the truths that he had proclaimed had become obscured and corrupted, a new manifestation in the person of Jesus Christ became necessary. Christ's

teaching is essentially an exaggerated monotheism which excludes any distinction of divine persons.

A precise concept of God is lacking. He is conceived on the one hand as a personal being and portrayed as the creator and judge (17,7). On the other hand, he is called, pantheistically, the heart of the world (17,9), and the development of the world is set forth as an evolution of God himself.

2) *The Ten Books of Recognitions.* They are available in their entirety only in the Latin translation of Rufinus. The narrative material, basically the same as in the *Homilies,* is likewise an autobiography of Clement, but it is worked out in greater detail. Curious circumstances caused the separation of the members of his family; father, mother and three sons were dispersed. Each seeks in vain for information of the whereabouts of the others. Through Peter's intervention they are, after many and varied adventures, finally reunited. The document takes its name *Recognitions* from the various recognition scenes in which the long separated members of the family meet again. Greater differences exist between the *Recognitions* and the *Homilies* as to didactic content. The Judaistic element is toned down and subordinated. Christ is called *solus fidelis ac verus propheta.* Judaism is merely regarded as a preparation for Christianity. The doctrine of the trinity is clearly stated: *filium Dei unigenitum dicimus, non ex alio initio, sed ex ipso ineffabiliter natum; similiter etiam de paracleto dicimus* (1,69). Such statements may, of course, have been inserted by the translator, Rufinus. It is difficult to determine whether or not he added them to the original.

3) Besides the *Homilies* and *Recognitions* two Greek excerpts (ἐπιτομαί) from the *Homilies* are preserved; these excerpts are expanded by additions from Clement's letter to James, from the *Martyrium Clementis* by Symeon Metaphrastes and by Bishop Ephraim of Cherson's account of a miracle performed by Clement over a child.

4) In addition to these Greek texts there are extant also two Arabic excerpts from the *Homilies* and *Recognitions.* These selections confine themselves to the narrative element and omit the lengthy discourses.

It would be greatly to our advantage if we could determine the time when the *Homilies* and *Recognitions* were written. But this question involves extremely intricate literary problems that have thus far defied every attempt at solution, and opinions vary widely. It seems to be a general conviction that the *Homilies* and the *Recognitions* rest on a common basic document. But there is no agreement about the sources of this basic document, which was probably of considerable bulk. Its nucleus must have been the biography of Clement, to whom the work was attributed. That explains why the narrative element of both, *Homilies* and *Recognitions*, is identical if we ignore minor deviations, whereas the accompanying discourses vary considerably. The author was most likely of heretical Jewish-Christian association. The basic document was probably written in Syria in the early decades of the third century.

Recognitions

Editions: PG 2. — P. DE LAGARDE, Clementis Romani Recognitiones syriace. Leipzig, 1861. — A new edition by B. REHM will be published soon in GCS. — The Arabic extracts with an English translation in M. D. GIBSON, Apocrypha Sinaitica. London, 1896.

Translations: English: TH. SMITH, ANF 8, 73–212; *German:* G. ARNOLD, Berlin, 1702. — E. HENNECKE, Neutestamentliche Apokryphen. 2nd ed. Tübingen, 1924, 151–63; 212–26. *Dutch:* H. U. MEYBOOM, De Clemensroman, I. Groningen, 1902.

Homilies:

Editions: PG 1. — P. DE LAGARDE, Clementina. Leipzig, 1865.
Translations: English: TH. SMITH, P. PETERSON, J. DONALDSON, ANF 8, 223–346; *French:* A. SIOUVILLE, Les homilies clémentines (Les textes du christianisme II). Paris, 1934. *Dutch:* MEYBOOM, l. c.

The two Greek Epitomes. Editions: A. R. M. DRESSEL, Clementinorum Epitomae duae. 2nd ed. Leipzig, 1873. — W. FRANKENBERG, Die syrischen Clementinen mit dem griechischen Paralleltext (TU 48, 3). Leipzig, 1937.

Studies: A. HILGENFELD, Die clementinischen Recognitionen und Homilien. Jena and Leipzig, 1848. — G. UHLHORN, Die Homilien und Recognitionen des Clemens Romanus. Göttingen, 1854. — J. LEHMANN, Die clementinischen Schriften. Gotha, 1889. — C. BIGG, The Clementine Homilies (Studia biblica et ecclesiastica II). Oxford, 1890. — W. CHAWNER, Index of Noteworthy Words and Phrases Found in the Clementine Homilies. London, 1893. — H. U. MEYBOOM, De Clemens-Roman, II. Groningen, 1904. — H. WAITZ, Die Pseudoklementinen (TU 25,4). Leipzig, 1904. — F. NAU, Notes sur les Clémentines: Actes du XIVe Congrès international des Orientalistes, 6e section. Paris, 1906. — F. NAU, Clémentines (apocryphes): DTC 3 (1908) 201–216. — J. CHAPMAN, On the Date of the Clementines: ZNW 9 (1908)

21ff., 147ff. — W. Heintze, Der Clemensroman und seine griechischen Quellen (TU 40,2). Leipzig, 1914. — L. Cerfaux, La gnose simonienne: RSR 15 (1925) 459ff., 16 (1926), 265ff.; 481ff.; *idem*, Le vrai prophète des Clémentines: RSR 18 (1928) 143–163. — A. Siouville, Introduction aux homélies clémentines: RHR 100 (1929) 142–204. — C. Schmidt, Studien zu den Pseudo-Clementinen (TU 46,1). Leipzig, 1929. — H. Waitz, Die Pseudo-klementinen und ihre Quellenschriften: ZNW 28 (1929) 241–272. — R. Cadiou, Origène et les reconnaissances clémentines: RSR 20 (1930) 506–528. — O. Cullmann, Le problème littéraire et historique du roman pseudo-clémentin. Paris, 1930. — A. Puech, Quelques observations sur les écrits pseudo-clémentins: RSRUS 10 (1930) 40–46. — H. Waitz, Pseudoklementinische Probleme: ZKG 50 (1931) 186–94. — E. Schwarz, Unzeitgemässe Beobachtungen zu den Clementinen: ZNW 31 (1932) 151–199. — J. Lowe, The First Christian Novel. A Review of the Pseudo-Clementines: Can. J. of Rel. Thought 7 (1931) 292–301. — H. J. Rose, Pseudo-Clement and Ovid: JThSt 33 (1932) 382–84. — M. R. James, A Manual of Mythology in the Clementines: JThSt 33 (1932) 262–65. — H. Waitz, Neues zur Text- und Literarkritik der Pseudoklementinen: ZKG 52 (1933) 305–18. — J. Thomas, Les ébionites baptistes: RHE 30 (1934) 257–96; *idem*, Le mouvement baptiste en Palestine et Syrie. Louvain, 1935. — E. Donckel, Sale sumpto. Randbemerkungen zu den verschiedenen Mahlberichten der Pseudoklementinen: EL 7 (1933) 101–112. — J. Svennung, Handschriften zu den ps.-klementinischen Recognitiones: Phil 88 (1933) 473–6. — K. Pieper, Offene Antwort an Herrn Prof. Hugo Koch in München (Mt. 16, 18): ThGl 28 (1936) 164–68. — H. Hoppe, Rufin als Uebersetzer (Studi dedicati alla memoria di Paolo Ubaldi). Milan, 1937, 133–150. — W. Frankenberg, Zum syrischen Text der Clementinen: ZDMG 91 (1937) 577–604. — B. Rehm, Zur Entstehung der pseudoklementinischen Schriften: ZNW 37 (1936) 77–184; *idem*, Bardesanes in den Pseudoklementinen: Phil 93 (1938) 218–247. — R. Abramowski, Pseudoclemens. Zu W. Frankenbergs Clemensausgabe: ThBl 18 (1939) 147–51. — B. Rehm, Zur Entstehung der pseudoklementinischen Schriften. Munich, 1939. — H. Waitz, Die Lösung des pseudoclementinischen Problems?: ZKG 59 (1940) 304–341. — F. X. Murphy, Rufinus of Aquileia. His Life and Works. Washington, 1945, 112–116; 195–200.

IGNATIUS OF ANTIOCH

Ignatius, second bishop of Antioch, an inimitable personality, was sentenced during Trajan's reign (98–117) to be devoured by wild beasts. He was ordered from Syria to Rome to suffer his martyrdom. On the way to the Eternal City he composed seven Epistles — the only memorial bequeathed to us of his extensive labors. Of these, five were addressed to the Christian communities of Ephesus, Magnesia, Tralles, Philadelphia and Smyrna — cities that had sent representatives to greet him as he passed through. Another letter was directed to Bishop Polycarp of Smyrna. The most important of all was written to the Christian community of his destination, Rome. The missives intended for Ephesus, Magnesia and Tralles were penned at Smyrna. In these he thanks the communities for their many proofs of sympathy with him in his fate, exhorts them to obedience to their ecclesiastical superiors and warns them against heretical doctrines. It was from the same city that he dispatched his affectionate greetings to the members of the Church at Rome, begging them to take no steps whatever which might defraud him of his most ardent desire — to die for Christ; for death to him was but the beginning of true life: 'How glorious to be a setting sun — away from the world, on to God. May I rise in his presence' (*Rom.* 2,2). 'I fear that your love will cause me damage for I shall not have such another occasion to enter into the possession of God. I am the wheat of God, and I must be ground by the teeth of wild beasts, that I may become the pure bread of Christ' (*Rom.* 1, 2; 2,1; 4, 1). The messages to his coreligionists at Philadelphia and Smyrna, as well as that to Polycarp, were forwarded from Troas. Ignatius had received word while there that persecution had ceased in Antioch. Hence he urges the Christians of Philadelphia and of Smyrna as well as the bishop of the last-mentioned city to send delegates to congratulate the brethren of Antioch. In subject matter, these communications resemble strongly those sent from Smyrna. They contain earnest pleas for unity of faith and of sacrifice and urge the readers to intimate contact with the bishop appointed to guide them. The Epistle to Polycarp has in addition specific directions for the administration of the episcopal office. He offers the counsel: 'Stand firm like an anvil under the hammer. It is like a great athlete to take blows and yet win the fight' (*Pol.* 3,1). These letters are a welcome enlightenment as to internal conditions of early Christian communities. They give us a glimpse, too, into the very heart of the great bishop-martyr and breathe forth a profound religious enthusiasm that catches us up and fires us. His language, spirited and intensely original, scorns the tricks and niceties of style. His soul in its inimitable zeal and ardor soars above and beyond the ordinary modes of expression. Finally, the letters are of inestimable importance for the history of dogma.

I. THE THEOLOGY OF ST. IGNATIUS

1. The idea of divine 'economy' in the universe is the core of Ignatius' theology. God wishes to deliver world and humanity from the despotism of the prince of this world. He prepared mankind for salvation in Judaism through the instrumentality of the prophets; their expectation found its fulfillment in Christ:

> Jesus Christ is our only teacher, of whom even the prophets were disciples in the Spirit and to whom they looked forward as their teacher (*Magn.* 9,1–2).

2. The Christology of Ignatius is exceedingly clear as to both, ✓ the divinity and the humanity of Christ:

> There is only one physician both carnal and spiritual, born and unborn (γέννητος καὶ ἀγέννητος), God become man, true life in death, sprung both from Mary and from God (καὶ ἐκ Μαρίας καὶ ἐκ θεοῦ), first subject to suffering, and then incapable of it — Jesus Christ Our Lord (*Eph.* 7,2). — He is really of the line of David according to the flesh, and the Son of God by the will and power of God; was really born of a Virgin, and baptized by John in order to comply with every ordinance (*Smyrn.* 1,1).

Christ is timeless (ἄχρονος) and invisible (ἀόρατος):

> Look for Him who is above time — the Timeless, the Invisible, who for our sake became visible, the Impassible, who became subject to suffering on our account and for our sake endured everything (*Pol.* 3,2).

At the same time he attacks the form of heresy called Docetism, ✓ which denied a human nature and especially suffering to Christ:

> But if, as some atheists, that is, unbelievers, say, His suffering was but a make-believe — when in reality they themselves are make-believes — then why am I in chains? Why do I even pray that I may fight with the beast? In vain, then, do I die! My testimony is, after all, but a lie about the Lord! Shun these wildlings, then, which bear but deadly fruit, and when one tastes it, he is outright doomed to die (*Trall.* 10–11,1). From Eucharist and prayer they hold aloof, ✓ because they do not confess that the Eucharist is the Flesh of our Savior Jesus Christ, which suffered for our sins, and which the Father in His loving-kindness raised from the

dead. And so, those who question the gift of God perish in their contentiousness. It would be better for them to have love, so as to share in the resurrection. It is proper, therefore, to avoid associating with such people and not to speak about them either in private or in public, but to study the prophets attentively and especially the Gospel, in which the Passion is revealed to us and the Resurrection shown in its fulfillment (*Smyrn.* 7, ACW).

All in all, the foundation of Ignatius' Christology is St. Paul, but influenced and enriched by the theology of St. John.

3. The Church is called 'the place of sacrifice' θυσιαστήριον (*Eph.* 5,2; *Trall.* 7,2; *Phil.* 4). It seems that the conception of the Eucharist as the sacrifice of the Church suggested this designation, for in the Didache, the Eucharist is called θυσία. Ignatius calls the Eucharist, 'the medicine of immortality, the antidote against death, and everlasting life in Jesus Christ' (*Eph.* 20,2). He admonishes:

> Take care, then, to partake of one Eucharist; for one is the Flesh of our Lord Jesus Christ, and one the cup to unite us with His Blood, and one altar, just as there is one bishop assisted by the presbytery and the deacons, my fellow servants (*Phil.* 4). — (Clear and unmistakable is the following quotation): The Eucharist is the Flesh of our Saviour Jesus Christ, which suffered for our sins, and which the Father in His loving-kindness raised from the dead (*Smyrn.* 7,1).

4. Ignatius is the first to use the term 'Catholic Church', to mean the faithful collectively:

> Where the bishop appears, there let the people be, just as where Jesus Christ is, there is the Catholic Church (*Smyrn.* 8,2).

5. We obtain from Ignatius' letters a vivid picture of the hierarchical dignity and prestige accorded a bishop in the midst of his flock. St. Ignatius mentions nothing of the prophets, who prompted by the Spirit were still going from one Church to another, as described in the Didache. A monarchical episcopate reigns over the communities. We all but see the bishop surrounded by his priests and deacons. The bishop presides as God's representative, the priests form the apostolic senate and the deacons perform the services of Christ:

I exhort you to strive to do all things in harmony with God: the bishop is to preside in the place of God, while the presbyters are to function as the council of the Apostles, and the deacons, who are most dear to me, are entrusted with the ministry of Jesus Christ (*Magn.* 6,1).

The idea that the bishop represents Christ invests his office with such dignity and supernatural eminence that even the authority of a young bishop is never to be questioned:

But for you, too, it is fitting not to take advantage of the bishop's youth, but rather, because he embodies the authority of God the Father, to show him every mark of respect; and your presbyters, so I learn, are doing just that: they do not seek to profit by his youthfulness, which strikes the bodily eye; no, they are wise in God and therefore defer to him, or, rather, not to him, but to the Father of Jesus Christ, the bishop of all men (*Magn.* 3,1).

6. The bishop is above all the responsible teacher of the faithful, and to be in communion with him is to be safeguarded against error and heresy (*Trall.* 6; *Phil.* 3). Hence the bishop constantly admonishes his flock to peace and unity, which can only be attained through solidarity with the hierarchy:

Hence it is proper for you to act in agreement with the mind of the bishop; and this you do. Certain it is that your presbytery, which is a credit to its name, is a credit to God; for it harmonizes with the bishop as completely as the strings with a harp. This is why in the symphony of your concord and love the praises of Jesus Christ are sung. But you, the rank and file, should also form a choir, so that, joining the symphony by your concord, and by your unity taking your keynote from God, you may with one voice through Jesus Christ sing a song to the Father. Thus He will both listen to you and by reason of your good life recognize in you the melodies of His Son. It profits you, therefore, to continue in your flawless unity, that you may at all times have a share in God (*Eph.* 4, ACW).

7. The bishop is according to Ignatius also the high priest of the liturgy and the dispenser of the mysteries of God. Neither baptism, nor agape, nor Eucharist may be celebrated without him:

It is not permitted without authorization from the bishop either to baptize or to hold an agape; but whatever he approves is also pleasing to God. Thus everything you do will be proof against danger and valid (*Smyrn.* 8,2). — Let no one do anything touching the Church apart from the bishop. Let that celebration of the Eucharist be considered valid which is held under the bishop or anyone to whom he has committed it (*Smyrn.* 8,1).

Hence marriages likewise must be contracted before him:

For those of both sexes who contemplate marriage it is proper to enter the union with the sanction of the bishop; thus their marriage will be acceptable to the Lord and not just gratify lust (*Pol.* 5,2).

8. St. Ignatius' interpretation of matrimony and virginity shows the stamp of St. Paul's influence. Matrimony symbolizes the eternal bond between Christ and His bride, the Church:

Tell my sisters to love the Lord and to be content with their husband in body and soul. In like manner, exhort my brethren in the name of Jesus Christ to love their wives as the Lord loves the Church (*Pol.* 5,1).

But he also counsels virginity:

If anyone is able to remain continent, to the honor of the Flesh of the Lord, let him persistently avoid boasting (*Pol.* 5,2).

9. When one compares the opening words of the various epistles to the communities of Asia Minor with the salutation of that addressed to the Church of Rome, there is no doubt that Ignatius holds the Church of Rome in far higher regard. The significance of this salutation cannot be overestimated; it is the earliest avowal ✓ of the Primacy of Rome that we possess from the pen of a non-Roman ecclesiastic:

Ignatius, also called Theophorus, to the Church that has found mercy in the transcendent Majesty of the Most High Father and of Jesus Christ, His only Son; the Church by the will of Him who willed all things that exist, beloved and illuminated through the faith and love of Jesus Christ our God; which also presides in the chief place of the Roman territory; a church worthy of God, worthy of honor, worthy of felicitation, worthy of praise, worthy of success, worthy of sanctification, and presiding in love, maintaining the law of

Christ, and bearer of the Father's name: her do I therefore salute in the name of Jesus Christ, the Son of the Father. Heartiest good wishes for unimpaired joy in Jesus Christ our God, to those who are united in flesh and spirit by every commandment of His; who imperturbably enjoy the full measure of God's grace and have every foreign stain filtered out of them (ACW).

Among these titles of encomium lavished upon the Church of Rome by Ignatius, one in particular, namely, 'presiding in love' προκαθημένη τῆς ἀγάπης, has attracted the attention of scholars. But they are very much divided as to the meaning of this phrase. A. Harnack saw in the phrase merely a grateful acknowledgment of the pre-eminent charity displayed by the Roman Christians. According to him, the Roman Church is called 'presiding in love' because she is the most charitable, generous and helpful of all the Churches and therefore the protectress and patroness of charity. The fact cannot be ignored, however, that the expression appears twice in the salutation and with no apparent change in meaning. At its first occurence it runs thus: 'Which also presides in the chief place of the Roman territory' (ἥτις καὶ προκάθηται ἐν τόπῳ χωρίου Ρωμαίων). Here the suggestion of ecclesiastical authority is inescapable and Harnack's interpretation is inapplicable. Proof of this is that the same Greek idiom, in the only other place in Ignatius' works in which it is met with (*Magn.* 6, 1, 2), unmistakably refers to the exercise of supervision by bishop, presbyters, and deacons. A more difficult problem is the sense of τῆς ἀγάπης. The reader of the Epistles will soon realize that the word ἀγάπη, as used in them, has various meanings. F. X. Funk, basing his solution upon the fact that in several instances (*Phil.* 11,2; *Smyrn.* 12,1; *Trall.* 13,1 and *Rom.* 9,3) Ignatius makes the term ἀγάπη a synonym for the respective Churches, turned the passage in the letter to the Romans by, 'presiding over the bond of love' — 'bond of love' being merely another way of saying 'the Church universal'. But more recent investigations by J. Thiele and A. Ehrhard have proved that this translation is scarcely correct, given the context and the trend of Ignatius' thought. Moreover, the old Latin, Syriac, and Armenian versions of Ignatius' Epistles do not favor such a rendition. Rather convincing is the suggestion of J. Thiele, namely, to give the word in this passage a wider and profounder meaning, and to understand by 'agape' the totality of that supernatural life which Christ enkindled in us by his love. Then Ignatius would by the phrase 'presiding in love' assign to the Roman Church authority to guide and lead in that which constitutes the essence of Christianity and of the new order brought into the world by Christ's divine love for men. But, aside from the problem presented by so difficult an expression, the Epistle to the Romans, taken in its entirety, shows beyond cavil that the position of honor accorded the Roman Church is acknowledged by Ignatius as her due, and is founded not on the extent of her charitable influence but on her inherent right to universal ecclesiastical supremacy. This is borne out by the passage in the salutation, 'which also presides in the chief place of the Roman territory'; again by the remark, 'you taught others' (3,1); and still again by the plea to espouse the Church in Syria as Christ would and as a bishop should: 'Remember in your prayers the Church in Syria which has God for its shepherd instead of me. Its bishop shall be Jesus Christ alone and your love' (9,1). Significant also is the fact that although Ignatius admonishes to unity and harmony in all his Epistles he does not do so in the one addressed to the Romans. He does not presume to issue commands to the Roman community, for it has its authority from the Princes of the Apostles: 'I do not issue any orders to you as did Peter and Paul; they were Apostles, I am a convict' (*Rom.* 4,3). This testimony also makes Ignatius an important witness to Peter and Paul's sojourn in Rome.

II. MYSTICISM OF ST. IGNATIUS

Just as the Christology of Ignatius combines the theological doctrine of St. Paul and St. John, so too his mysticism is influenced by both: St. Paul's idea of union with Christ is joined to St. John's idea of life in Christ and there emerges the ideal favored by Ignatius — the imitation of Christ.

1. *Imitation of Christ*

Perhaps no author of early Christian times is as eloquent on the 'imitation of Christ' as Ignatius. If we wish to live the life of Christ and of God, then we must adopt the principles and virtues of God and of Christ:

The carnal cannot live a spiritual life, nor can the spiritual live a carnal life, any more than faith can act the part of infidelity, or infidelity the part of faith. But even the things you do in the flesh are spiritual, for you do all things in union with Jesus Christ (*Eph.* 8,2).

As Christ imitated his Father so must we imitate Christ: 'Do as Jesus Christ did, for He, too, did as the Father did' (*Phil.* 7,2). But this imitation of Christ consists not only in the observance of the moral law, not only in a life not at variance with Christ's teaching, but in conforming oneself particularly to his passion and death. Hence he entreats the Romans: 'Permit me to be an imitator of my suffering God' (*Rom.* 6,3).

2. *Martyrdom*

From his conception of resemblance to his Lord spring his ardor and enthusiasm for martyrdom. He conceives martyrdom as the perfect imitation of Christ; hence only he is the true disciple of Christ who is ready to sacrifice his life for him:

I am not yet perfected in Jesus Christ; indeed, I am now but being initiated into discipleship, and I address you as my fellow disciples (*Eph.* 3,1). — Pardon me — I know very well where my advantage lies. At last I am well on the way to being a disciple. May nothing seen or unseen fascinate me, so that I may happily make my way to Jesus Christ! Fire, cross, struggles with wild beasts, wrenching of bones, mangling of limbs, crunching of the whole body, cruel tortures inflicted by the devil — let them come upon me, provided only I make my way to Jesus Christ. Of no use to me will be the farthest reaches of the universe or the kingdoms of this world. I would rather die and come to Jesus Christ than be king over the entire earth. Him I seek who died for us; Him I love who rose again because of us. The birth pangs are upon me. Forgive me, brethren; do not obstruct my coming to life — do not wish me to die; do not make a gift to the world of one who wants to be God's. Beware of seducing me with matter; suffer me to receive pure light. Once arrived there, I shall be a man (*Rom.* 5, 3–6). — Why, moreover, did I surrender myself to death, to fire, to the sword, to wild beasts? Well, to be near the

sword is to be near God; to be in the claws of wild beasts
is to be in the hands of God. Only let it be done in the name
of Jesus Christ! To suffer with Him I endure all things, if
He, who became perfect man, gives me the strength (*Smyrn.*
4,2).

3. *Inhabitation of Christ*

The Pauline idea of God's immanence in the human soul is a
favorite theme of St. Ignatius. The divinity of Christ dwells in
the souls of Christians as in a temple:

> Let us therefore do all things in the conviction that He
> dwells in us. Thus we shall be His temples and He will be
> our God within us. And this is the truth, and it will be made
> manifest before our eyes. Let us, then, love Him as He
> deserves (*Eph.* 15,3).

Ignatius is so thoroughly permeated and inspired by the consciousness of this immanence that he coins new words in the
cultural vein of his time. He calls Christians θεοφόροι, χριστοφόροι,
ναοφόροι. 'And thus you all are fellow travellers, God-bearers and
temple-bearers, Christ-bearers' (*Eph.* 9,2). He styles himself
θεοφόρος; all his letters begin with the words: 'Ignatius, also
called Theophorus'.

4. *Being in Christ*

But Christ is not only in us, we are also one with Christ, hence
all Christians are linked by a divine union. Ignatius again and
again repeats the Pauline expression, 'being in Christ'. He desires,
'to be found in Jesus Christ'. 'Union with Christ is the bond
which encircles all Christians.' And therefore he beseeches the
Ephesians to be imitators of the Lord, 'that you may remain in
all purity and sobriety in Jesus Christ, both in the flesh and in
the spirit' (10,3). In his Epistle to the Magnesians he writes that
he prays for the Churches:

> I pray that in them there may be a union based on the
> flesh and spirit of Jesus Christ, who is our everlasting life, a
> union of faith and love, to which nothing is to be preferred,
> but especially a union with Jesus and the Father (1,2).

It is characteristic of Ignatius to stress repeatedly that Christians
are united with Christ only when they are one with their bishop

through faith, obedience and particularly through participation in divine worship. He does not recognize individual independence in the spiritual life or in the mystical union with Christ but acknowledges only one divine union with the Savior, namely that accomplished through liturgical worship. His mysticism springs from the divine cult, which means that it does not center around the individual soul but around the community of the faithful functioning as a liturgical body. This also explains why his mystical terminology and the spirituality which permeates his style are partial to symbols and phrases from cult and liturgy.

AUTHENTICITY OF THE EPISTLES

The authenticity of the Epistles was for a long time questioned by Protestants. On their view, it would be unlikely to find at the time of Trajan the monarchical episcopate and so clear cut an organization of the hierarchy into bishop, presbyter and deacon. They suspected the Letters of Ignatius of being a forgery, made with the very purpose of creating the hierarchical organization. But such a falsification is incredible. After the brilliant defense of their authenticity by J. B. Lightfoot, A. v. Harnack, Th. Zahn and F. X. Funk they are generally accepted as genuine today. Both the external and the internal evidence are in their favor. Testimony is extant which reaches back to the time of their composition. Polycarp, Bishop of Smyrna, and one of the addressees, writes in his *Epistle to the Philippians*, which was penned soon after Ignatius' death: 'The Epistles of Ignatius which were sent to us by him, and others which we had by us, we send you as requested. They are enclosed herewith. You will be able to benefit greatly from them. For they are conducive to faith and patience and to every kind of edification pertaining to our Lord' (13,2). This description fits the letters exactly. Both Origen and Irenaeus refer to the Epistles, and Eusebius specifically names all seven in their traditional order, recording them as integral parts of a compact collection (Euseb., *Hist. eccles.* 3, 36, 4ff).

TEXT TRADITION OF THE EPISTLES

The letters are preserved in three recensions:

1. *The short recension*

This is the original recension which exists in Greek only and is preserved in the *Codex Mediceus Laurentianus* 57,7; the recension dates back to the second century. The Epistle to the Romans, however, is missing; but its text was found in the tenth-century *Codex Paris Graec.* No. 1457.

2. *The long recension*

In the fourth century the original collection was tampered with and interpolated. This recension was executed by a contemporary of the compiler of the *Apostolic Constitutions*, a person closely associated with the Apollinarists. He added six spurious letters to the seven authentic Epistles. This longer recension is extant in numerous Greek and Latin manuscripts.

The longer recension became known first. It was printed in Latin in 1489 and in Greek in 1557. The original short recension of the Epistles to the Ephesians, to the Christian communities of Magnesia, Tralles, Philadelphia and Smyrna and to Bishop Polycarp was published in 1646 and that of the Letter to the Romans in 1689. Since then the conviction has prevailed that the long recension is spurious.

3. *The Syriac Abridgment*

In 1845, W. Cureton published a Syriac text of a collection of the Epistles to the Ephesians, to the Romans and to Polycarp. The editor considered these abbreviated recensions as genuine. Lightfoot and others, however, proved them to be only an abridgment of a Syriac version of the short recension.

Editions and translations: See the editions and translations of the Apostolic Fathers, p. 41. *Separate editions:* P. G. Crone, Ignatius von Antiochien, Briefe. Münster, 1936. — Th. Camelot, Ignace d'Antioche, Lettres (SCH 10). Paris, 1946. *Separate translations: English:* J. H. Srawley, The Epistles of St. Ignatius, Bishop of Antioch (SPCK). 3d ed. London, 1935. —J. A. Kleist, The Epistles of Clement of Rome and Ignatius of Antioch (ACW 1). Westminster, Md., 1946. — *French:* A. Lelong, Paris, 1927. — H. Delafosse (J. Turmel), Lettres d'Ignace d'Antioche. Paris, 1929. Cf. G. Bardy, RAp 46 (1928) 476ff. — Th. Camelot, SCH 10, Paris, 1946. — *German:* L. A. Winterswyl, Die Briefe des hl. Ignatius von Antiochien. Freiburg i. B., 1938. — *Italian:* M. Monachesi, L'Epistolario Ignaziano. Rome, 1925. — U. Moricca,

Ignazio di Antiochia e Policarpo, vescovo di Smirna. Le lettere, il martirio
di Policarpo. Rome, 1923.

Studies: TH. ZAHN, Ignatius von Antiochien. Gotha, 1873. — J. H. NEWMAN,
On the Text of the Seven Epistles of St. Ignatius: Tracts, Theological and
Ecclesiastical. London, 1874, 95-123. — A. HARNACK, Die Zeit des Ignatius
und die Chronologie der antiochenischen Bischofe bis Tyrannus. Leipzig,
1878. — J. NIRSCHL, Die Theologie des hl. Ignatius. Mainz, 1880. — F. X.
FUNK, Die Echtheit der Ignatianischen Briefe aufs neue verteidigt. Tübingen,
1883. — E. V. D. GOLTZ, Ignatius von Antiochien als Christ und Theologe
(TU 12, 3). Leipzig, 1894. — F. X. FUNK, Der Primat der römischen Kirche
nach Ignatius und Irenaeus: Kirchengeschichtliche Abhandlungen und Unter-
suchungen I. Paderborn, 1897, 1-23. — H. DE GENOUILLAC, L'Eglise chrétienne
au temps de Saint Ignace d'Antioche. Paris, 1907. — W. M. RAMSAY, The
Church in the Roman Empire. 7th ed. London, 1913, 311-19. — M. RACKL,
Die Christologie des heiligen Ignatius von Antiochien. Freiburg i. B., 1914.
— P. BATIFFOL, Ignatius of Antioch, in: J. HASTINGS, Dictionary of the
Apostolic Church I (1916) 594ff. — L. BAUR, Untersuchungen über die
Vergöttlichungslehre in der Theologie der griechischen Väter: ThQ 99
(1918) 234-52. — H. DELAFOSSE (J. TURMEL), Nouvel examen des lettres
d'Ignace d'Antioche: RHL 8 (1922) 303-337; 477-533. — S. REINACH,
Ignatius, Bishop of Antioch and Archeia: Anatolian Studies Presented to
W. M. Ramsay. Manchester, 1923, 339f. — J. LEBRETON, La théologie de
la Trinité d'après Saint Ignace d'Antioche: RSR 25 (1925) 97-126; 393-419.
— J. RENDEL HARRIS, Genuine and Apocryphal Works of Ignatius of Antioch: Bulletin John Rylands Library II (1927) 204-31. — J. THIELE, 'Vor-
rang in der Liebe': Theologie und Glaube 19 (1927) 701-709. — P. BATIFFOL,
L'Eglise naissante et le catholicisme. 12th ed. Paris, 1927, 157-70. — H.
SCHLIER, Religionsgeschichtliche Untersuchungen zu den Ignatius-Briefen.
Giessen, 1929. Cf. A. D. NOCK, JThSt 31 (1930) 308-13. — GOOSSENS, RHE 26
(1930) 439 ff. — H. KOCH, ThLZ 56 (1931) 539ff. — O. CASEL, JL 10 (1930)
295-98. — C. P. S. CLARKE, St. Ignatius and St. Polycarp. London, 1930.
— F. LOOFS, Theophilus von Antiochien Adv. Marcionem und die andern
theologischen Quellen bei Irenaeus (TU, 46,2). Leipzig, 1930, 194-205. —
J. MOFFAT, Two Notes on Ignatius, Magnesians I and Justin Martyr, Apologia 1, 62ff.: HThR 23 (1930) 153-159; *idem,* Ignatius of Antioch.
A Study in Personal Religion: JR 10 (1930) 169-186. — J. RIVIÈRE, Le
dogme de la rédemption. Louvain, 1931, 61-73. — G. A. MITCHELL, Canon
Streeter and S. Ignatius: ChQ 102 (1931) 219-32. — F. A. SCHILLING, The
Mysticism of Ignatius of Antioch. Philadelphia, 1932. — J. HOH, Die kirchliche Busse im 2. Jahrhundert. Breslau, 1932, 72-77. — E. MERSCH, Le corps
mystique du Christ. Louvain, 1933, 234-44. — F. J. DÖLGER, Christophorus
als Ehrentitel für Märtyrer und Heilige im christlichen Altertum: AC 4 (1933)
73-80. — R. ROCA-PUIG, La redemcio segons sant Ignasi martir: PC 28
(1933) 36-45. — W. BAUER, Rechtgläubigkeit und Ketzerei im ältesten
Christentum. Tübingen, 1934, 65-73, — J. F. MONTANA, S. Ignacio martyr
y sus cartas. Madrid, 1934. — A. D'ALÈS, Ἐὰν γνωσθῇ πλέον τοῦ ἐπισκόπου
ἔφθαρται (Ignat., Pol., V, 2): RSR 25 (1935) 489-91. — C. CH. RICHARDSON,

The Christianity of Ignatius of Antioch. New York, 1935. — P. N. Harrison, Polycarp's Two Epistles to the Philippians. Cambridge, 1936, 121–140. — J. Moffatt, An Approach to Ignatius: HThR 29 (1936) 1–38. — F. J. Dölger, θεοῦ φωνή. 'Die Gottesstimme' bei Ignatius von Antiochien, Kelsos und Origenes: AC 5 (1936) 218–223. — C. C. Richardson, The Church in Ignatius of Antioch: JR 17 (1937) 428–43. — H. Lietzmann, The Beginnings of the Christian Church. New York, 1937, 315–32. — M. Villain, Une vive conscience de l'unité du corps mystique: S. Ignace d' Antioche et S. Irénée: RAp 66 (1938) 257–71. — Th. Preiss, La mystique de l'imitation du Christ et de l'unité chez Ignace d'Antioche: RHPR 18 (1938) 197–241.—G. Cloin, De verhouding van den bisschop tot het πνεῦμα in de Ignatiaanse brieven: StC 14 (1938) 19–42; idem, De verhouding van den bisschop tot de ἀγάπη in de Ignatiaansche brieven: StC 14 (1938) 231–54; idem, De Spiritualiteit van de Ignatiaansche bisschops-idee. Nijmegen, 1938. — A. Hödum, De H. Ignatius van Antiochië, leeraar der eenheid: Coll. Brugenses 39 (1939) 137–145. — H. B. Bartsch, Gnostisches Gut und Gemeindetradition bei Ignatius von Antiochien. Gütersloh, 1940. Cf. B. Nisters, ThR 39 (1940) 253–54. — M. H. Shepherd, Smyrna in the Ignatian Letters. A Study in Church Order: JR 20 (1940) 141–159. — K. Prümm, Christentum als Neuheitserlebnis. Freiburg i. B., 1939, 281–284. — M. Viller and K. Rahner, Aszese und Mystik in der Väterzeit. Freiburg i. B., 1939, 22–27. — W. J. Burghardt, Did Saint Ignatius of Antioch Know the Fourth Gospel?: ThSt 1 (1940) 1–26. — A. Heitmann, Imitatio Dei. Die ethische Nachahmung Gottes nach der Väterlehre der zwei ersten Jahrhunderte. Rome, 1940, 71–74. — R. Spörri, Vom Geiste des Urchristentums. Basel, 1941, 31–53. — H. v. Torre, Het vocabularium van Ignatius van Antiochië. Diss. Louvain, 1942. — O. Perler, Ignatius von Antiochien und die römische Christengemeinde: DT 22 (1944) 413–451. — G. Bardy, La Théologie de l'Eglise de saint Clément de Rome à saint Irénée. Paris, 1945, 31–33; 44–49; 83–84; 102–104; 113–117.

For the Eucharistic passages see: A. Scheiwiler, Die Elemente der Eucharistie in den ersten drei Jahrhunderten (FLDG 3, 4). Mainz, 1903, 17–26. — Th. Schermann, Zur Erklärung der Stelle Epistula ad Ephes. 20,2 des Ignatius von Antiocheia φάρμακον ἀθανασίας: ThQ 92 (1910) 6–19. — J. Brinktrine, Der Messopferbegriff in den ersten zwei Jahrhunderten (FThSt 21). Freiburg i. B., 1918, 76–84. — W. Scherer, Zur Eucharistielehre des hl. Ignatius: TPQ 76 (1923) 627ff. — P. Batiffol, L'Eucharistie. La présence réelle et la transsubstantiation (Etudes d'histoire et de théologie positive. 2. series). 9th ed. Paris, 1930, 39–50. — J. Quasten, Monumenta eucharistica et liturgica vetustissima. Bonn, 1935-37, 334–336.

POLYCARP OF SMYRNA

Polycarp was Bishop of Smyrna. The high regard in which he was held is explained by the fact that he had been a disciple of the Apostles. Irenaeus (Eusebius, *Hist. eccles.* 5, 20, 5) records that Polycarp sat at the feet of St. John, furthermore that he was appointed to the see of Smyrna by the Apostles (*Adv. Haer.* 3, 3, 4). It was to him as Bishop of Smyrna that St. Ignatius addressed one of his letters. The discussions which Polycarp and Pope Anicetus carried on in Rome in the year 155, relative to various ecclesiastical matters of moment, particularly the settlement of a date for the celebration of Easter, give added proof of the esteem in which Polycarp was held. No mutually satisfactory solution was arrived at, however, in this burning controversy, for Polycarp appealed to St. John and the Apostles as his authority for the quartodeciman usage while Anicetus declared himself in favor of the custom adhered to by his predecessors, namely the dominical usage. Although pope and bishop differed, nevertheless they parted on the best of terms. Irenaeus relates (*Adv. Haer.* 3, 3, 4) that Marcion when meeting Polycarp asked him if he recognized him: 'Of course', replied the latter, 'I recognize the first-born of Satan'.

I.   POLYCARP'S MARTYRDOM

Through a letter (A.D. 156) from the Church of Smyrna to the Christian community of Philomelium in Greater Phrygia, we possess a detailed account of Polycarp's heroic martyrdom which occurred shortly after his return from Rome (probably February 22, 156). This document is the oldest detailed account extant of the martyrdom of a single individual and is therefore often regarded as the first 'Acts of the Martyrs'. Judged by its literary form it does not, however, belong to this category but to early Christian epistolography. The letter bears the signature of a certain Marcion and was written shortly after the death of Polycarp. To this document some notes with additional information were later appended. From it we gain an excellent impression of the noble personality of the Bishop of Smyrna. When the Proconsul Statius Quadratus ordered Polycarp: 'Swear and I shall release thee; revile Christ!' he replied: 'For six and eighty years I have been serving Him, and he has done no wrong to me; how, then, dare I blaspheme my King who has saved me!' (9,3). When his torturers were on the point of fastening him with nails, he said: 'Leave me just as I am. He who enables me to endure the fire will also enable me to remain on the pyre unbudging, without the security afforded by your nails' (13,3). This, the oldest narrative of a martyrdom known to modern research, is very important to a proper understanding of that term. Already we find stressed the notion that martyrdom is an imitation of Christ, the imitation consisting in the similarity in suffering and death. This document is, furthermore, the earliest evidence for the cult of the martyrs: 'We afterwards took up his remains, more precious than costly stones, and more excellent than gold, and interred them in a decent place. There the Lord will permit us, as far as possible, to assemble in rapturous joy and celebrate his martyrdom — the day of his birth!' (18,2). It is striking how positively this document asserts and justifies the honor paid to martyrs: 'Him we worship as being the Son of God, the martyrs we love as being disciples and imitators of the Lord; and deservedly, because of their unsurpassable affection for their King and Teacher' (17,3). The intrinsic purpose and the dogmatic character of the veneration of martyrs, as distinguished from the adoration paid to Christ, is herewith indicated with unmistakable clearness. The prayer which the author of the acts puts into the mouth of the dying martyr is important for the history of early Christian prayer. Not only in the precise trinitarian doxology, but throughout, this prayer reminds one of liturgical formulas:

O Lord, Almighty God,
Father of your beloved and blessed Son
Jesus Christ,
through whom we have received the perfect knowledge of
you,
God of angels and hosts and of all creation
and of the whole race of saints
who live under your eyes!
I bless you,
because you have seen fit to bestow on me
this day and this hour,
that I may share, among the number of the martyrs,
the cup of your Anointed
and rise to eternal life
both in soul and in body,
in virtue of the immortality of the Holy Spirit.

May I be accepted among them in your sight today
as a rich and pleasing sacrifice,
such as you, the true God that cannot utter a falsehood
have prearranged, revealed in advance, and consummated.
And therefore I praise you for everything;
I bless you,
I glorify you
through the eternal and heavenly High Priest
Jesus Christ,
your beloved Son,
through whom be glory to you
together with him and the Holy Spirit,
both now and for the ages to come.
Amen (14 ACW).

Spurious, on the other hand, is the so-called *Vita Polycarpi* by Pionius. As far as authorship is concerned, the presbyter Pionius of Smyrna, who suffered martyrdom under Decius, is out of the question. The work is purely legendary in character and may have been composed about 400 A.D. to supplement the older authentic account of Polycarp's death.

2. EPISTLE TO THE PHILIPPIANS

Irenaeus tells us (Euseb., *Hist.* 5, 20, 8) that Polycarp addressed several letters to neighboring Christian communities and to some of his fellow-bishops. But one of these letters is extant, that to the Philippians. Its complete text has come down to us only in a Latin translation. The Greek manuscripts contain nothing beyond chapters 1–9,2. Eusebius (*Hist.* 3, 36, 13–15) refers also to a Greek text of chapters 9 and 13.

The Christian community of Philippi had asked Polycarp for a copy of the letters of St. Ignatius. Polycarp sent these together with a communication in his own hand. In this he requested reliable information regarding St. Ignatius: hence it must have been written shortly after the death of St. Ignatius. It is a moral exhortation comparable to St. Clement's *First Epistle to the Corinthians*. Polycarp actually used Clement's Epistle as a source. We get a faithful portrayal of the doctrine, organization, and the Christian charity of the Church at that time.

P. N. Harrison advanced the theory that the document we

call the Epistle of Polycarp really consists of two letters which Polycarp wrote to the Philippians at different times and which were copied out at an early date on to the same papyrus roll, and so fused into one. The first, consisting of chapter 13, possibly also 14, was a short covering note sent by Polycarp along with a batch of Ignatian Epistles directly after the visits paid by Ignatius as a prisoner to Smyrna and Philippi on his way to Rome. The date of this note is in all probability early in September of the year in which Ignatius was martyred (ca. 110). The second Epistle, consisting of the first twelve chapters, was written by Polycarp twenty years later. At that time the name of Ignatius had become a blessed memory, and the story of his martyrdom had passed into history. The arch-heretic denounced in the main body of this Epistle is Marcion. In view of this and other internal evidence, it cannot be dated earlier than the thirties of the second century. Harrison's theory is very convincing and removes the one serious objection to an early dating of the Epistles of Ignatius.

a. *Doctrine*

The Epistle defends the christological doctrine of the Incarnation and of Christ's death upon the Cross against 'false teaching' with the following words:

> For every one who shall not confess that Jesus Christ is come in the flesh is antichrist: and whoso shall not confess the testimony of the Cross is of the devil: and whoso shall distort the words of the Lord to his own desires, and say that there is neither resurrection nor judgment, this is the first-born of Satan (7,1).

b. *Organization*

Polycarp makes no mention of a bishop of Philippi but he does speak of the obedience due to presbyters and deacons. One might be justified in concluding that the Christian community of Philippi was governed by a committee of presbyters. The letter portrays the ideal priest in the following terms:

> The presbyters must be tenderhearted, merciful toward all, turning back (the sheep) that have gone astray, visiting all the sick, not neglecting widow or orphan or poor man,

but always taking thought for that which is honorable in the sight of God and of man, abstaining from all anger, respect of persons, unrighteous judgment, being far from all love of money, not hastily believing (anything) against any one, not stern in judgment, knowing that we are all debtors because of sin (6,1).

c. *Charity*

Almsgiving is earnestly recommended:
When it is in your power to do good, withhold not, because alms deliver from death. All of you be subject to one another, having your behavior blameless among the Gentiles, that by your good works both you may receive praise, and the Lord may not be blasphemed in you (10,3).

d. *Church and State*

Worthy of notice is the attitude of the Church toward the State. Prayer for the civil authorities is expressly enjoined:
Pray also for kings and powers and rulers, and for them that persecute and hate you, and for the enemies of the Cross, that your fruit may be manifest unto all, that you may be perfect in Him (12,3).

For *editions* and *translations* of the Epistle see those of the Apostolic Fathers on p. 41 f.

Studies: H. J. BARDSLEY, The Testimony of Ignatius and Polycarp to the Apostleship of St. John: JThSt 14 (1913) 489ff.; *idem*, The Testimony of Ignatius and Polycarp to the Writings of St. John: JThSt 14 (1913)207ff. — P. BATIFFOL, Polycarp, in: HASTING's Dictionary of the Apostolic Church, vol. II. Edinburgh, 1918. — C. P. S. CLARKE, St. Ignatius and St. Polycarp. London, 1930. — W. v. LOEWENICH, Das Johannes-Verständnis im zweiten Jahrhundert. Giessen, 1932, 22-25. — W. BAUER, Rechtgläubigkeit und Ketzerei im ältesten Christentum.Tübingen, 1934, 73-78. — J. M. BOVER, Un fragmento attribuido a san Policarpo sobre los principios de los Evangelios: EE 14 (1935) 5-19. — P. N. HARRISON, Polycarp's Two Epistles to the Philippians. Cambridge, 1936. — A. C. GLOUCESTER, The Epistle of Polycarp to the Philippians: ChQ 141 (1945) 1-25.

Editions: For the *Martyrium Polycarpi* see LIGHTFOOT's and FUNK's editions of the Apostolic Fathers, p. 41. — O. v. GEBHARDT, Ausgewählte Märtyreracten. Berlin, 1902, 1-12. — G. RAUSCHEN, Monumenta aevi apostolici (FP 1). Bonn, 1914, 40-60. — R. KNOPF, Ausgewählte Märtyrerakten, 3rd ed. rev. by G. KRÜGER (SQ 3). Tübingen, 1929, 1-7.

Translations: See the translations of the Apostolic Fathers p. 41f. *English:* B. JACKSON, St. Polycarp (SPCK). London, 1898, 49–74. — E. C. E. OWEN, Some Authentic Acts of the Early Martyrs. Oxford, 1927, 19–39. — J. A. KLEIST, ACW 6 (1948) 85–102. *German:* G. RAUSCHEN, in: Frühchristliche Apologeten II (BKV²14). Kempten and Munich, 1913, 9–20. — H. RAHNER, Die Märtyrerakten des zweiten Jahrhunderts. Freiburg i. B., 1941, 23–37. *Studies:* H. BADEN, Der Nachahmungsgedanke im Polykarpmartyrium: ThGl 3 (1911) 115–122. — B. SEPP, Das Martyrium Polycarpi. Regensburg, 1911. — W. REUNING, Zur Erklärung des Polykarpmartyriums. Giessen, 1917. Cf. H. DELEHAYE, AB (1920) 200–202. — J. A. ROBINSON, The 'Apostolic Anaphora' and the Prayer of St. Polycarp: JThSt 21 (1920) 97–108; *idem,* Liturgical Echoes in Polycarp's Prayer: JThSt 21 (1920) 97–105; 24 (1923) 141–144. — J. W. TYRER, The Prayer of St. Polycarp and its Concluding Doxology: JThSt 23 (1922) 390ff. — R. H. CONNOLLY, The Doxology in the Prayer of St. Polycarp: JThSt 24 (1923) 144ff. — W. M. RAMSAY, The Date of St. Polycarp's Martyrdom: Jahreshefte des Oesterreichischen Archaeologischen Institutes 27 (1932) 245–248. — H. W. SURKAU, Martyrien in jüdischer und frühchristlicher Zeit. Göttingen, 1938, 126–134.

PAPIAS OF HIERAPOLIS

Papias was Bishop of Hierapolis in Asia Minor. Irenaeus says of him (*Adv. Haer.* 5, 33, 4) that he had heard St. John preach, also that he was a friend of Polycarp, Bishop of Smyrna. Eusebius (*Hist. eccles.* 3, 39, 3) informs us that, 'he was a man of very little intelligence, as is clear from his books'. The books thus referred to by Eusebius can only be the treatise written by Papias about 130 A.D., in five books, 'Explanation of the Sayings of the Lord' (*Λογίων κυριακῶν ἐξηγήσεις*). The harsh criticism which Eusebius meted out to Papias is justified on several counts: first, Papias defended the belief in the millenium, and secondly, he showed very little critical judgment in the selection and interpretation of his sources. But the work, as much as we possess of it, is important in spite of these defects, since it contains what is of great value to us, the oral teaching of disciples of the Apostles. Papias in his preface sums up his work thus:

And I shall not hesitate to append for you to the interpretations all that I ever learnt and remember well, for of their truth I am confident. For unlike the many I did not take pleasure in those who have so very much to say, but in those who teach the truth, nor in those who recount the commandments of others, but in those who recorded such as were given by the Lord to faith and derived from truth itself. And again if ever anyone came who had been a follower of the presbyters I inquired into the words of the presbyters, what Andrew or Peter or Philip or Thomas or James or John or Matthew or any other of the Lord's disciples and what Aristion and the presbyter John, the disciples of the Lord, were saying. For I did not think that information from books would help me so much as the utterances of a living and surviving voice (Euseb. *Hist. eccles.* 3, 39, 3–4).

From this quotation it is clear that the utterances of the Lord which Papias undertook to explain were drawn not only from the written gospels before him but also from oral tradition. His work therefore was not merely a commentary on the gospels, even though he took the majority of the passages from the gospel narratives.

Among the few remaining fragments of the work which Eusebius has preserved for us the remarks on the first two gospels have become famous. The first fragment reads:

And the presbyter said this: Mark became the interpreter of Peter and wrote down accurately all that he remembered without, however, recording in order the things said or done by the Lord. For he had not heard the Lord, nor had he followed him, but afterwards, as I said, followed Peter, who used to give instructions as necessity demanded but had no design of giving an arrangement of the Lord's oracles, so that Mark made no mistake in thus writing down single points as he remembered them. For he made it his one care to leave out nothing of what he had heard and to make no false statement in them (Euseb. *Hist. eccl.* 3, 39, 15–16).

We have here the best attestation of the canonicity of the gospel of St. Mark. No satisfactory explanation, however, has thus far been found why John should be mentioned twice by Papias (3, 39, 4). Of the origin of St. Matthew's gospel he has the following to say: 'Matthew composed the sayings in the Hebrew language, and each one interpreted them as best as he could' (Euseb. *Hist. eccl.* 3, 39, 16). This statement proves that in Papias' days the original work of Matthew had already been superseded by a Greek translation. The translations which Papias had in mind were not written translations of the gospel but oral rendi-

84 THE APOSTOLIC FATHERS

tions of our Lord's sayings contained in the gospel. They were, in all probability, a translation of the pericopes used in liturgical assemblies among Greek or bilingual communities.

Eusebius says, furthermore, of Papias: 'The same writer adduces other accounts which came to him from unwritten tradition and some strange parables and teachings of the Saviour as well as other more fabulous accounts. Among them he says there will be a thousand years after the resurrection of the dead when the kingdom of Christ will be set up in a material form in this earth. I suppose that he got these notions by a misunderstanding of the apostolic accounts, not realizing that they had spoken mystically and figuratively' (*Hist. eccl.* 3, 39, 11–12). Eusebius intimates that Papias' prestige lured many Christian writers to chiliastic beliefs: 'He is responsible for the fact that so many ecclesiastical writers after him held the same opinion relying on his antiquity, as, for instance, Irenaeus and whoever else seems to have held the same ideas' (3, 39, 13).

To the 'more fabulous accounts' which Eusebius relates, belong, no doubt, the legend of the ghastly end of the traitor Judas, the murder of John, brother of James, perpetrated by the Jews, and also what he had heard from the daughters of Philip (*Acts of the Apostles* 21,8) who resided in Hierapolis; they told him of the miracles which happened in their day, namely, of the raising to life of the mother of Manaimus, and of Justus Barsabbas, who swallowed a draught of poison with no ill effects to himself.

Editions and translations: See the editions and translations of the Apostolic Fathers, p. 41f. — M. Bucellato, Papias di Hierapoli. Frammenti e testi monianze nel testo greco (Studi Biblici III). Milan, 1936.

Studies: J. Chapman, John the Presbyter and the Fourth Gospel. Oxford, 1911. — H. J. Lawlor, Eusebius on Papias: Hermathena 43 (1922) 167-222. — W. Larfeld, Ein verhängnisvoller Schreibfehler bei Eusebius: BNJ 3 (1922) 282-285; *idem,* Das Zeugnis des Papias über die beiden Johannes von Ephesus: NKZ 33 (1922) 410-512; *idem,* Bischof Papias ein urchristlicher Stenograph?: BNJ 5 (1927) 36-41. — J. Donovan, The Logia in Ancient and Recent Literature. Cambridge, 1924. — J. Sykutris, Ein neues Papiaszitat: ZNW 26 (1927) 210-212. — G. Goetz, Papias von Hierapolis oder der Glottograph?: ZNW 27 (1928) 348. — B. W. Bacon, Adhuc in corpore constituto: HThR 23 (1930) 305ff. — C. Lambot, Les presbytres et l'exegesis de Papias: RB 43 (1931) 116-123. — J. Donovan, The Papias Presbyteri Puzzle: IER (1928) 124-37; *idem,* IER (1931) 483-500. — P. de Ambroggi, Appunti sulla questione di Giovanni presbitero presso Papia:

SC 16 (1930) 374–376; *idem*, Giovanni Apostolo e Giovanni presbitero, una persona o due: SC 5 (1931) 389–396. — P. VANUTELLI, De presbytero Joanne apud Papiam: SC 16 (1930) 366–74. — F. LOOFS, Theophilus von Antiochien adv. Marcionem und die andern theologischen Quellen bei Irenaeus (TU 46,2). Leipzig, 1930, 328–338. — A. FRÖVIG, Das Matthaeus-evangelium und die aramäische Matthäusschrift des Papias: NKZ 42 (1931) 67–97. — P. VANUTELLI, Iterum de presbytero Joanne apud Papiam: SC 59 (1931) 219–232; *idem*, De presbytero Joanne apud Papiam. Rome, 1933. — D. G. DIX, The Use and Abuse of Papias on the Fourth Gospel: Th 24 (1932) 8–20. — J. V. BARTLET, Papias' 'Exposition': its Date and Contents: Amicitiae Corollae edited by H. G. WOOD. London, 1933, 15–44. — P. VANUTELLI, De argumentis externis de Matthaeo et Marco apud Papiam: Synoptica 1 (1935) XII–XXX. — N. J. HOMMES, Het Testimonialboek. 1935, 230–255. — P. GAECHTER, Die Dolmetscher des Apostel: ZkTh 60 (1936) 161–187. — A. VACCARI, Un preteso scritto perduto di Papia: Bibl 20 (1939) 413–414. — G. PERRELLA, DTP (1940) 47–56. — R. M. GRANT, Papias and the Gospels: HThR 25 (1943) 218–222. — J. A. KLEIST, Rereading the Papias Fragment on St. Mark: St. Louis University Studies. Series A. Vol. I, No. 1 (1945) 1–17.

THE EPISTLE OF BARNABAS

The Epistle of Barnabas is a theological tract and a letter only in appearance. Actually it contains nothing personal and lacks the ordinary introduction and conclusion. The content is general and gives no indication of being directed at particular individuals. Hence its form is merely a literary convention. Early Christian writers looked upon the epistle as the only proper genre for instruction in piety and resorted to it even when they were not addressing a limited circle of readers. The author, whose name is not mentioned, purposes to teach 'perfect knowledge' (γνῶσις) and faith.

CONTENTS

The letter is divided into two parts: one section is theoretical, the other, practical.

I. The first section, the theoretical, comprises chapters 1–17 and is of a dogmatic character. In chapter 1,5 the author states the purposes of his work in these words: 'that your knowledge may be perfected along with your faith'. This knowledge, however, is unique. The author, first of all, wishes to expound and prove to his readers the value and meaning of the revelation of the Old Testament; he seeks to show that the Jews completely misunderstood the Law because they interpreted it literally. After repudiating this interpretation he presents what is in his opinion the genuinely spiritual meaning, i.e., the τελεία γνῶσις. It consists of an allegorical explanation of Old Testament doctrines and commandments. God does not desire material gifts of bloody sacrifices but the offering of one's heart in the form of repentance. He does not want the circumcision of the flesh but the circumcision of our hearing that our mind may incline to truth. He does not insist that man abstain from the flesh of unclean animals but he insists upon his renunciation of the various sins symbolized by the unclean animals (chapters 9 and 10). Swine, for example, are numbered among forbidden animals, because there are men who resemble swine, which forget the hand that feeds them when they are surfeited with food. Eagle, hawk, kite and raven are prohibited because they are symbolical of such men as seize upon their daily bread by rapine and all manner of iniquity rather than earn it by honest toil and sweat (chapter 10,4). Proof of the daring allegories of the author is offered in the ninth chapter. He tells of the circumcision, ordered by Abraham, of 318 of his servants. The mystery of redemption through Christ's crucifixion and death was, according to the author's interpretation, to be revealed thereby to Abraham. The digits 10 and 8 are written in Greek: ιη = ιη (σούς), the number 300 = τ. This letter τ signifies the cross. Hence the number 318 signifies the redemption through Jesus Christ's death upon the cross. The Old Law was not intended for Jews. 'Moses received it, but they were not worthy.' It was intended for the Christians from the very beginning: 'But learn how we received it. Moses received it when he was a servant, but the Lord himself gave it to us, as the people of the inheritance, by suffering for our sake' (14,4). The Jewish interpretation of the Old Law was not that sponsored by God; the Jews were deceived through the machinations of a wicked angel: 'They erred because an evil angel was misleading them' (9,4). The author even dares to say that the Jewish form of worship resembles pagan idolatry (16,2).

II. The second section (chapters 18–21) takes up morals and manifests no special bias. It describes, exactly like the *Didache*, the two ways of man, that of life and that of death, but it calls the one that of light and the other that of darkness. To sketch the way of light it offers a large number of moral precepts which reflect the decalog. The passage dealing with the way of darkness consists of a catalog of various kinds of vices and sins.

DOCTRINE

Even though the doctrinal element is sparse in this book, nevertheless some details are worth notice.

1) Barnabas proclaims the preexistence of Christ. He was with God the Father when the latter created the world, and the words, 'Let us make man after our image and likeness' were spoken by the Father to his divine Son (5,5). Barnabas, moreover, employs the parable of the sun, so popular in Alexandrian theology, in order to explain the incarnation:

> For if he had not come in the flesh how could men have been able to look upon him that they might be saved, seeing that they have not the power when they look at the sun to gaze straight at its rays? (5, 10).

Two motives prompted the incarnation:

> First: 'the Son of God came in the flesh for this reason that he might fill up the measure of the iniquity of those who had persecuted his prophets to death. For this cause he endured'. Secondly: 'he was willing to suffer for us' (5, 11-13).

2) Chapters 6 and 11 describe beautifully how baptism confers upon man adoption to sonship and stamps upon his soul God's image and likeness:

> He has renewed us by the remission of our sins and has made us another type that we should have the soul of children as though he were creating us afresh. For thus the scripture says concerning us where it introduces the Father speaking to the Son, 'Let us make man after our likeness and image' (6, 11-12).

3) Baptism makes God's creatures temples of the Holy Ghost:

> It remains yet that I speak to you concerning the temple; how those miserable men (the Jews) erred by putting their trust in the house, and not in God himself who made them; as if it were the habitation of God. For much after the same manner as the Gentiles, they consecrated him in the temple. But learn how the Lord speaks, rendering the temple vain: 'Who has measured the heaven with a span, and the earth

with his hand? Is it not I?' Thus saith the Lord: 'Heaven is my throne, and the earth is my footstool. What is the house that ye will build me?' Know therefore that all their hope is vain. And again he says: 'Behold, they who destroyed his temple, they shall again build it up.' And so it came to pass; for through their wars it was destroyed by the enemies; and the servants of their enemies build it up at present. . .

Let us inquire, therefore, whether there can be any temple of God. Yes, there is; and that, there where he himself declares that he would both make and perfect it. For it is written: 'And it shall be, that as soon as the week shall be completed, the temple of the Lord shall be gloriously built in the name of the Lord.' I find then that there is a temple. But how shall it be built in the name of the Lord? I will show you. Before we believed in God, the habitation of our heart was corruptible and weak, as a temple really built with hands. For it was a house full of idolatry, a house of devils, inasmuch as there was done in it whatsoever was contrary unto God. But it shall be built in the name of the Lord. Consider that the temple of the Lord may be gloriously built; and by what means that shall be, learn. Having received remission of our sins, and trusting in the name of the Lord, we become renewed, being again created from the beginning. Wherefore God truly dwells in our house, that is, in us (16, 1–8,9).

4) The celebration of the eighth day of the week, i.e., Sunday, because it is the day of the resurrection, instead of the Sabbath of the Jews is particularly stressed in chapter 15, 8:

He (God) says to them (the Jews): 'Your new moons and your sabbaths, I cannot bear them'. Consider what he means by it: Not the sabbaths of the present era are acceptable to me, but that which I have appointed to mark the end of the world and to usher in the eighth day, that is the beginning of the other world. Wherefore we joyfully celebrate the eighth day on which Jesus rose from the dead, and having manifested himself to his disciples he ascended into heaven.

5) The life of the infant, unborn or born, is protected by law: 'Thou shalt not procure abortion nor kill the child after it has been born' (19,5).

6) The author is a follower of chiliasm. The six days of creation mean a period of six thousand years because a thousand years are like one day in the eyes of God. In six days, that is in six thousand years, everything will be completed, after which the present evil time will be destroyed and the Son of God will come again and judge the godless and change the sun and the moon and the stars and he will truly rest on the seventh day. Then will dawn the sabbath of the millenial kingdom (15, 1–9).

AUTHOR

The letter nowhere asserts that Barnabas is its author, nor does it lay any claim even to an Apostolic origin; yet from earliest times it has been attributed by tradition to the Apostle Barnabas, the companion and co-worker of St. Paul. The fourth-century Codex Sinaiticus ranks the Epistle among the canonical books of the New Testament and lists it immediately after the Apocalypse of St. John. Clement of Alexandria culls from it many quotations which he credits to the Apostle Barnabas. Origen calls it καθολικὴ ἐπιστολή and numbers it among the books of Sacred Scripture. Eusebius relegates it to the controverted writings and Jerome counts it among the apocryphal works. Modern research has definitely established that the Apostle Barnabas was not the author of this Letter, because of the decidedly harsh and absolute repudiation of the Old Testament. Because of this pronounced antipathy to everything Jewish, Barnabas cannot possibly come into consideration as the author of the Epistle. A wide chasm, furthermore, yawns between the teachings of St. Paul, to whom Barnabas was a missionary companion, and the views voiced in the Epistle of Barnabas. Paul recognized the Old Law as a divinely ordained institution, but the Epistle of Barnabas speaks of it as a diabolical deception (9,4). The authorship of Barnabas must be rejected also on historical grounds, since it is absolutely certain that the Epistle was penned after the destruction of Jerusalem; chapter 16 proves this clearly.

The use of the allegorical method of interpretation in the Epistle points to Alexandria as the home of the author. The influence of Philo is unmistakable. That in part would also explain why the Epistle was regarded so highly among the theologians of Alexandria.

TIME OF COMPOSITION

Although the *terminus post quem* is quite definite because the destruction of the Temple of Jerusalem is mentioned, opinions are widely divergent regarding the *terminus ante quem*. The wording of chapter 16, 3–4, is as follows: 'Furthermore he says again, Lo, they who destroyed this temple shall themselves build it. That is happening now. For owing to the war it was destroyed by the enemy; at present even the servants of the enemy build it up again.' The sentence beginning with 'at present' leads us to conclude that some time had elapsed since the Temple's destruction. In the reference to the contemplated rebuilding of the Temple Harnack sees an allusion to the construction of the temple of Jupiter in Jerusalem during Hadrian's reign (117–138). Relying on this he dates the composition of the Epistle to 130 or 131. Funk's assertion that the passage has to do with the erection of the *supernatural* temple of God's Church is far from convincing. Even less satisfactory is the conclusion he draws concerning the date from chapter 4,4–5. At this point the Epistle cites Daniel 7,24 and 7,7–8. The citation reads: 'And the prophet also says thus: 'Ten kingdoms shall reign upon the earth and there shall rise up after them a little king, who shall subdue three of the kings under one.' Daniel says likewise concerning the same: 'And I beheld the fourth Beast, wicked and powerful and fiercer than all the beasts of the sea, and ten horns sprang from it, and out of them a little excrescent horn, and that subdued under one three of the great horns.' As the eleventh little king of this prophecy Funk identifies the Roman Emperor Nerva (96–98). According to Funk, he 'subdued three kings under one' in the sense that he gained the throne upon the assassination of Domitian in whom was extinguished the dynasty of the Flavians consisting of three members, the Emperors Vespasian, Titus and Domitian. But it is only through so arbitrary an interpretation that the words of Daniel can be made to apply to Nerva. On the other hand, Harnack's method of fixing the date has also its difficulties. It hinges upon which destruction and which reconstruction of the Temple are alluded to in the Epistle. Lietzmann thinks that the author refers to the second destruction of the Temple in the War of Barcochba. This would lead us to believe that the work originated after the beginning of this insurrection, the end of which coincides with the last year of Hadrian's reign (138). A later date than this can not possibly be defended. Formerly, the homogeneity of Barnabas' Epistle was questioned and attemps made to detect interpolations. Muilenburg has, however, successfully established that the document is from beginning to end by one and the same author and that no subsequent additions are discernible. Its frequent lapses into incoherence may be ascribed to clumsy language and unskilful composition. The writer strays now and then suddenly from one theme to another, and often he disrupts the thread of his discourse to interject a moral exhortation that has no connection with what he is saying. The exposition of the Two Ways, that of good and that of evil, was drawn from the same source as the Didache. Nevertheless we can be certain that the author did not use the Didache. The analysis of Barnabas' Epistle leads to the conclusion that he had at his disposal not only this common source and the Sacred Scriptures but also others that cannot now be identified.

TEXT TRADITION

We have the following authorities for the Greek text:

1) The *Codex Sinaiticus* of the fourth century, formerly at St. Petersburg, now in London. Here it is included among the books of the New Testament immediately after the Apocalypse.

2) The *Codex Hierosolymitanus* of the year 1056, formerly at Constantinople, now at Jerusalem. This codex was discovered by Bryennios in 1875 and contains the Epistle of Barnabas, the Didache and the First Letter of Clement.

3) The *Codex Vaticanus graec.* 859 of the eleventh century contains among others the Epistles of St. Ignatius, St. Polycarp, and the Epistle of Barnabas. Chapters 1, 1–5, 7, however, are missing. This lacuna also appears in later manuscripts which derive from the same archtype.

The work is also extant in a Latin translation dating back to the third century. This was copied in the tenth century in the Monastery of Corby and is now preserved in St. Petersburg. In this manuscript, however, chapters 18, 1–29, 9 are missing.

Editions and Translations: See the editions and translations of the Apostolic Fathers, p. 41f. *Separate Edition:* TH. KLAUSER, (FP 1). Bonn, 1940. — A new

German translation in: K. THIEME, Kirche und Synagoge. Olten, 1945, 27–65.
— English: J. A. KLEIST, ACW 6, Westminster, Md., 1948.

Studies: PH. HÄUSER, Der Barnabasbrief neu untersucht und erklärt (FLDG 11,2). Paderborn, 1912. — J. MUILENBURG, The Literary Relations of the Epistle of Barnabas and the Teaching of the Twelve Apostles. Marburg, 1929. — F. C. BURKITT, Barnabas and the Didache: JThSt 33 (1932) 25–27. — A. L. WILLIAMS, The Date of the Epistle of Barnabas: JThSt 34 (1933) 337–346. — R. H. CONNOLLY, Barnabas and the Didache: JThSt 38 (1937) 165–167. — H. J. CADBURY, The Epistle of Barnabas and the Didache: JQR 26 (1936) 403–406. — H. LIETZMANN, The Beginnings of the Christian Church. New York, 1937, 289–294. — P. MEINHOLD, Geschichte und Exegese im Barnabasbrief: ZKG (1940) 255–303. — G. BARDY, La Théologie de l'Eglise de S. Clément de Rome à S. Irénée. Paris, 1945, 157–162.

THE SHEPHERD OF HERMAS

Although numbered among the Apostolic Fathers, the *Shepherd* of Hermas belongs in reality to the apocryphal apocalypses. It is a book of revelations which were granted to Hermas in Rome by the agency of two heavenly figures, the first an old woman and the second an angel in the form of a shepherd. It is to the latter that the entire book owes its title. It contains only one statement from which to determine the time of composition. According to a passage in the second vision (4,3) Hermas receives the command from the Church to make two copies of the revelation, one of which he is to turn over to Clement, who will send it to distant cities. The Clement indicated is undoubtedly Pope Clement of Rome, who wrote his Epistle to the Corinthians about 96 A.D. But this seems to contradict the *Muratorian Fragment,* which has this to say about the author: 'And very recently in our own times, in the city of Rome, Hermas wrote the Shepherd, when his brother Pius, the bishop, sat upon the chair of the city of Rome.' The testimony of the *Muratorian Fragment,* which dates from the close of the second century, creates an impression of trustworthiness. But the reign of Pius I falls within 140 A.D.–150 A.D., hence Hermas' reference to Pope Clement in the second vision was looked upon as a fiction. There is no valid reason why it should be so labelled. The two dates are accounted for by the way in which the book was compiled. The older portions would most likely go back to Clement's day while the present redaction would be of Pius' time. Critical examina-

tion of the contents leads to the same conclusion. This shows
that parts of the work belong to different periods. Origen's opinion, on the other hand, that the author of the Shepherd of
Hermas and the Hermas mentioned by St. Paul in the Epistle
to the Romans are one and the same person, is unacceptable.
The author says of himself that he was sold into slavery in early
youth and sent to Rome, and that he was there purchased by
his mistress, a certain Rhode. His frequent Hebraisms indicate
that he was either of Jewish descent or that he was educated by
Jewish teachers. With good-natured sincerity he relates all manner of intimate matters concerning himself and his relatives. He
speaks of his business transactions, of the loss of the property
which he had accumulated as a freedman and of farming his
acres located on the highway leading from Rome to Cumae.
This last fact explains why so much rural imagery flows uncon-
sciously from his pen. He tells us that his children apostatized
during the persecution, that they betrayed their own parents,
and that they led a disorderly life. He has nothing good to say
of his wife, who talks too much and cannot bridle her tongue.
This information prompts us to conclude that we are dealing
here with an earnest, pious and conscientious man, one who had
proven himself steadfast in time of persecution.

His work consists of a sermon on penance, apocalyptic in character, and, all in all, curious in form and subject. Externally it
exhibits a division into three sections containing five visions,
twelve precepts or mandates and ten parables. Although this is
the author's own arrangement, yet, internally, the work itself
discloses no logical ground for either the triple partitioning or
the various subheadings, since even the precepts and parables
are apocalyptic. Logically, it has only two main sections and a
conclusion.

CONTENT

I. In the first main section, vision 1-4, Hermas receives his
revelations from the Church, which appears to him first as an old
and venerable matron, who gradually casts off the signs of age
and emerges in the fourth vision as a bride, symbol of God's elect.

First Vision. The first vision is prefaced by an account of a sin
of thought which disturbs Hermas' conscience. The apparition

manifests itself as the Church in the guise of an old lady and exhorts him to penance for his sins and those of his family.

Second Vision. In the second vision the old matron gives him a booklet to copy and to circulate; the contents thereof again exhort to penance, and quite clearly prophesy that a persecution is impending.

Third Vision. In this vision the aged lady employs the symbol of a tower under construction and points out to him the destiny of Christianity, which in a short time shall grow into the ideal Church. As every stone not suitable for the masonry of the tower is rejected, so every sinner who does not do penance shall be excluded from the Church. Prompt penance is necessary, for the time is limited.

Fourth Vision. This vision shows the seer grievous and imminent calamities and persecution under the aspect of a hideous dragon. As terrible as the monster is, it will do no harm to the seer and to those who are armed with a steadfast faith. Behind the beast he sees the Church in the attire of a beautiful bride, a symbol of bliss to those loyal, and a guarantee of their reception into the eternal Church of the future.

Fifth Vision. In this vision, which forms the transition from the first to the second main section, the angel of penance appears in the guise of a shepherd, who will sponsor and direct the whole penitential mission, who is to revitalize Christianity, and who now proclaims his commands and his parables.

II. The second main section comprises the twelve commands and parables one to nine.

1) *The Twelve Commands* represent an abridgment of Christian morality: they proclaim the precepts to which the new life of penitents should conform, and treat in detail: (1) faith, fear of the Lord and sobriety, (2) single-heartedness and innocence, (3) truthfulness, (4) purity and proper deportment in wedlock and widowhood, (5) patience and restraint of temper, (6) whom one must believe and whom one should disregard respectively, the Angel of Justice and the Angel of Iniquity, (7) whom one should fear and whom one should not fear: God and the devil, (8) what one must avoid and what one must do: evil and good, (9) concerning doubts (δυψυχία), (10) of sadness and pessimism, (11) of false prophets, (12) that one ought to extirpate all evil

desire from one's heart and fill it with goodness and joy. The entire section ends like each mandate with an exhortation and a promise. The faint-hearted soul who doubts his ability to comply with the commandments is assured that one who strives with trust in God to keep them will find it easy to persevere in the observance of them; and that all who adhere to the commandments will attain to eternal life.

2) *The Ten Similitudes.* The first five of these parables likewise consist of moral precepts. The *first* styles the Christians strangers upon earth: 'You know that you who are the servants of God dwell in a strange land, for your city is far away from this one. If then you know your city in which you are to dwell, why do you here provide lands and make expensive preparations and accumulate dwellings and useless buildings? He who makes such preparations for this city cannot return to his own... Instead of lands therefore buy afflicted souls, according as each one is able, and visit widows and orphans, and do not overlook them and spend your wealth and all your establishments which you received from God upon such lands and houses... This is a noble and sacred expenditure.' The *second* parable enjoins upon the rich, under the allegory of vine and elm which depend upon each other, the duty to help the needy. In return for the assistance rendered, the poor shall pray for their well-to-do brethren. To the question so perplexing to Christianity, why the sinner and the just man are in no wise distinguishable upon earth, the *third* parable replies by comparing them to the trees of a forest in winter. When trees have shed their leaves and snow is upon the boughs they too are indistinguishable. The *fourth* parable adds by way of parenthesis that the world to come is like to a forest in summertime, for then the dead as well as the healthy trees are readily distinguishable. The *fifth* similitude refers to the practice of public fasts observed by the whole community — the stations, as they were called — and it criticizes not the institution itself nor fasting in general, but the vain trust which some men had in this practice. A fast demands, first and foremost, moral reform, strict observance of the law of God, and then the practice of charity. On fast days he allows bread and water alone. The saving thus made in the usual daily expenditure goes to the poor. The last four parables treat of submission to penance. So the *sixth* simil-

itude presents the angel of gluttony and deceit and the angel of punishment in the shape of two shepherds and treats of the duration of the punishment which follows. In the *seventh* parable Hermas pleads with the angel of punishment, who torments him, for delivery, but is exhorted to patience and told, for his consolation, that he is suffering for the sins of his family. The *eighth* similitude compares the Church to a large willow tree whose branches are quite hardy; for though torn from the parent trunk and apparently dried up they blossom into vitality if they are planted in the ground and kept moist. Thus also those who have been deprived of the life-giving union with the Church through mortal sin, may by penance and the use of the means of grace offered by the Church be again roused to life. The *ninth* similitude was most likely inserted later; it is, to some extent, a correction. The parable of the tower is taken up again and the different stones used in its construction represent the various types of sinners. But what is entirely new is that the construction of the tower is delayed for a time, in order to afford opportunity for many sinners to repent and thus be received into the tower. But unless they hasten to repent, they will be excluded. In other words the time of penance at first restricted is extended more than was originally announced. It is quite possible that Hermas himself undertook to make these changes because the expected parousia had not taken place. The *tenth* parable forms the conclusion of the work. Hermas is admonished once again by the angel of penance to cleanse his own family of all evil and he is charged once more with the mission to summon everyone to penance.

There is extant hardly a work of ancient Christian times in which the life of the community passes before us with such vividness as in the Shepherd of Hermas. We meet here all classes of Christians — good as well as evil. We read of bishops, priests and deacons who have administered their office worthily before God, but also of priests who were given to judgment, proud, negligent and ambitious, and of deacons who had appropriated for themselves money intended for widows and orphans. We read of martyrs whose hearts never faltered a moment, but also of apostates, traitors and informers; of those who apostatized merely for the sake of worldly interests and of such as were not ashamed publicly to curse God and their fellow Christians. We are told of converts who are without stain of sin as well as of all kinds of sinners; of wealthy persons who disdain poorer brethren and also of charitable and good Christians; of heretics as well as of doubters who struggle to find the way of righteousness; of good Christians with minor faults and of simulators and hypocrites. So the book of Hermas is a great self-examination on the part of the Church of Rome. The cowardly conduct of a large number of Christians was evidently due to the period of comparative peace in which these members had established themselves in comfort, amassed wealth and even gained prestige among their pagan neighbours only to find themselves taken completely by surprise by the horrors of a terrible persecution. These happenings mark the reign of Trajan and hence point strongly to the first half of the second century; they correspond to the date mentioned above. But in spite of this, it is clear that in the eyes of Hermas, the exemplary Christians, not the sinners, were in the majority.

The author's intention is not only to smite the wicked with his exhortations to penance but also to comfort the timid souls. Hence, there is discernible in the entire discourse a certain optimistic view of life.

THE DOGMATIC ASPECT OF THE SHEPHERD

1) *Penance*

The doctrine of penance as stated in Hermas has been the core of violent controversy. This controversy centers about mandate 4, 3, 1–6 which presents a colloquy between Hermas and the angel of penance:

> I have heard, sir, said I, from certain teachers that there is no other repentance than that one when we went down into the water and received remission of our former sins. He said to me, you have heard correctly for so it is. He who has received remission of sin ought never to sin again, but to live in purity. But since you ask diligently about all things, I will explain this also to you, not as giving excuse to those who in the future shall believe or to those who have already believed in the Lord. For those who have already believed or are about to believe have no repentance of sins, but have

remission of their former sins. For them that were called before these days, the Lord appointed repentance, for the
Lord knows the heart and foreknowing all things he knew
the weakness of man and the cunning craftiness of the devil,
that he will do some evil to the servants of God and will
deal wickedly with them. The Lord therefore being full of
compassion had mercy on his creation and established this
repentance and to me was given the power over this repentance. But I tell you, said he, after that great and solemn
calling, if a man should be tempted by the devil and sin, he
has one repentance. But if he sin repeatedly and repent,
it is unprofitable for such a man, for hardly shall he live. I
said to him, I attained life when I heard these things thus
accurately from you, for I know that if I do not again add
to my sins I shall be saved. You shall be saved, said he,
and all who do these things.

According to this passage the doctrine of penance as presented
by Hermas may be reduced to the following points:

a) There is a saving repentance after baptism. This is not a
new doctrine or one first announced by Hermas, as has frequently and mistakenly been assumed, but an old institution in the
Church. Hermas was prompted to write his work for the very
reason that some teachers insisted that there was no penance
except baptism and that any person who committed a mortal sin
ceased to be a member of the Church. It is not Hermas' intention
to give the impression that he is the first to announce to the
Christian sinner pardon for his sins or that this is only an exceptional concession. In reality the author wishes to make it clear to
Christians, that his message offers not the first but the last opportunity to obtain pardon for sins committed. This is what constitutes the new element of his message.

b) Penance has a universal character: no sinner is excluded
therefrom, neither the impure nor the apostate. Only the culprit
who will not repent is excluded.

c) Penance must be prompt and must produce amendment;
the opportunity it provides must not be abused by falling back
into sin. He argues for necessity of amendment by stressing the
psychological aspect, the difficulty the recidivist has in attaining
eternal life. He has in mind here the point of view of pastoral

rather than of dogmatic theology. Promptness in penance is urged on eschatological grounds. It must be effected before the construction of the tower, the Church, has become an accomplished fact, for building operations were suspended to grant the sinner time for repentance.

d) The intrinsic purpose of penance is μετάνοια, a complete reform of the sinner, and a willingness to make atonement by voluntary chastisement and fasting, by praying for the pardon of the sins committed.

e) The justification attained by penance is to be not only a purification but a positive sanctification such as produced in baptism by the infusion of the Holy Spirit (*Sim.* 5,7, 1-2).

f) The doctrine of penance in Hermas is already thoroughly permeated with the idea that the Church is an institution necessary for our salvation. Hence Hermas speaks of prayer offered for sinners by the elders of the Church. Reconciliation as such is not mentioned but must, for weighty reasons, be accepted as certain.

2) *Christology*

The Christology of Hermas has aroused serious doubts. He never uses the term Logos, or the name Jesus Christ. He invariably calls the Saviour, Son of God or Lord. But in the parable 9, 1,1 we read of the angel of penance who says to Hermas: 'I wish to show you what the Holy Spirit (τὸ πνεῦμα τὸ ἅγιον), who spoke with you in the form of the Church, showed you, for that Spirit is the Son of God.' Here the Holy Spirit is identified with the Son of God, in other words, we have only two divine persons, God and the Holy Spirit, whose relations are represented as those of Father and Son. Still more significant is *Parable* 5,6,5-7:

The pre-existent Holy Spirit which created all things did God make to dwell in a body of flesh chosen by himself. This flesh, in which dwelt the Holy Spirit, served the Spirit well in all purity and all sanctity without ever inflicting the least stain upon it. After the flesh had thus conducted itself so well and chastely, after it had assisted the Spirit and worked in all things with it, always showing itself to be strong and courageous, God admitted it to share with the Holy Spirit; for the conduct of this flesh pleased him, because it was not defiled while it was bearing the Holy Spirit on earth. He therefore consulted His Son and His glorious angels, in order that this flesh, which had served the Spirit without any cause for reproach, might obtain a place of habitation, and might not lose the reward of its services. There is a reward for all flesh which through the indwelling of the Holy Spirit shall be found without stain.

According to this passage the Trinity of Hermas seems to consist of God the Father, of a second divine person, the Holy Spirit, whom he identifies with the Son of God and finally the Saviour, who was elevated to be their companion as the reward of his merits. In other words Hermas regards the Saviour as the adopted son of God as far as his human nature is concerned.

3) *The Church*

In Hermas' opinion the Church is the first created of all creatures, hence she comes to him in the guise of a venerable old lady. The whole world was created just for her sake:

> And a revelation was made to me, brethren, while I slept, by a very beautiful young man who said to me, Who do you think that the old lady was from whom you received the book? I said, The Sibyl. You are wrong, he said, she is not. Who is she then? I said. The Church, he said. And I said to him, Why then is she an old lady? Because, he said, she was created the first of all things. For this reason is she old; and for her sake was the world established (*Vis.* 2,4,1).

But the most prominent figure under which the Church appears to Hermas is that of the mystical tower (*Vis.* 3,3,31; *Simil.* 8,13,1). This symbol, however, designates the Church of the predestined and elect, the Church triumphant, not the Church militant in which saints and sinners live side by side. This Church is founded upon a rock, the Son of God.

4) *Baptism*

No one is received into this Church except by the reception of baptism:

> Hear then why the tower has been built upon the water; because your life was and shall be saved by the water, and the tower has been founded by the word of the almighty

and glorious name and is maintained by the unseen power of the Master (*Vis.* 3, 3, 5).

Similitude 9, 16 calls baptism the seal and mentions its effect: Why Sir, said I, did the stones come up from the deep and were placed into the building of the tower, after they had borne these spirits? It was necessary for them, said he, to ascend through the water that they might be made alive, for they could not otherwise enter into the kingdom of God unless they put away the mortality of their former life. Accordingly these also who had fallen asleep received the seal of the son of God (τὴν σφραγῖδα τοῦ υἱοῦ τοῦ θεοῦ) and entered into the kingdom of God. For before, said he, a man bears the name of the Son of God, he is dead. But when he receives the seal he puts away mortality and receives life. The seal, then, is the water. They descend then into the water dead, and ascend alive. Therefore to these also was this seal preached and they made use of it to enter into the kingdom of God. And I said, Why then, Sir, did the forty stones also ascend with them out of the deep, although they had received the seal already? Because, he said, those Apostles and teachers who preached the name of the Son of God, and died in the power and faith of the Son of God, preached also to those who had died before them and they gave to them the seal of the preaching. They descended, therefore, with them into the water and ascended again; but the latter descended alive and ascended alive while the former, who had fallen asleep before, went down dead but came up alive. Through them, therefore, they were made alive, and received the knowledge of the name of the Son of God. For this cause they also came up with them and were put into the building of the tower, and without being hewn they were used together with them for the building. For they died in righteousness and in great purity; this seal alone they did not have. Here you have the explanation of these things.

Thus Hermas is so thoroughly convinced that baptism is absolutely necessary for salvation that he teaches that the Apostles and teachers descended into limbo after death (*descensus ad inferos*) to baptize the righteous departed of pre-Christian times.

THE ETHICS OF THE SHEPHERD

More important than the dogmatic is the ethical teaching contained in Hermas.

1. Noteworthy and important is the fact that here already we find a differentiation between commandment and counsel, between obligatory and supererogatory works, the *opera supererogatoria*:

> I will show you his commandments and if you do anything good beyond the commandments of God you will gain for yourself greater glory and be more in favor with God than you were destined to be (*Sim.* 5, 3, 3).

As such works of supererogation Hermas mentions fasting, celibacy and martyrdom.

2. Worthy of note also is the clear-sighted observation regarding the spirits that sway the heart of man:

> There are two angels in man, one of righteousness and one of wickedness. . . The angel of righteousness is mild and modest and meek and gentle. When, therefore, he comes into your heart he immediately speaks with you of righteousness, of purity, of holiness, of self-control, of every righteous deed and of all glorious virtue. When all these things come into your heart, know that the angel of righteousness is with you. Therefore, believe him and his works. Now see also the works of the angel of wickedness. He is, first of all, bitter and angry and foolish and his deeds are evil and cast down the servants of God. Whenever therefore he comes into your heart know him from his works (*Mand.* 6, 2, 1–4).

In another passage he takes pains to explain that it is impossible for a good and a bad angel to occupy man's heart simultaneously:

> For when these spirits dwell in one vessel, where also the Holy Spirit dwells, there is no room in that vessel, but it is overcrowded. Therefore the tender Spirit, which is not accustomed to dwell with an evil spirit or with hardness, departs from such a man and seeks to dwell with gentleness and quietness. When, therefore, it is departed from the man in whom it dwelt, that man becomes destitute of the righteous Spirit and afterwards is filled with the evil spirits, and is disorderly in all his actions, being dragged here and

there by the evil spirits, and is wholly blinded from goodness of thought (*Mand.* 5, 2, 5–7).

3. Of adultery he says that a husband must put away his wife
should she be guilty of this sin and refuse to do penance. He
himself, however, may not enter upon another union during her
lifetime. If the adulterous wife repents and reforms, the husband
is obliged to receive her back:

> If the husband do not receive her he sins and brings great
> sin upon himself. It is necessary to receive the sinner who
> repents, yet not often; for the servants of God there is but
> one repentance (*Mand.* 4, 1, 8).

4. Hermas, contrary to a number of early Christian authors,
permits remarriage:

> If, Sir, said I, a wife, or on the other hand a husband die,
> and the survivor marry does he sin so doing? He does not
> sin, said he, but if he shall remain single, he shall thereby
> gain for himself more exceeding honor and great glory be-
> fore the Lord; but even if he marry he does not sin (*Mand.*
> 4,4,1–2).

5. In *Vision* 3, 8, 1–7 we meet with a catalog of seven virtues:
Faith, Continence, Simplicity, Knowledge, Innocence, Reverence
and Love. They are symbolized by seven women, a conception
that played a great role in the development of Christian art.

The high regard in which the Shepherd of Hermas was held
in Christian antiquity is attested by the fact that several ecclesiastical writers, among them Irenaeus, Tertullian in his pre-Montan-
istic period and Origen considered him an inspired prophet, and
numbered his work among the books of Holy Scripture. He
seems to have enjoyed greater popularity in the East than in
the West, since St. Jerome remarks that in his day the book was
almost unknown among the Latin-speaking people (*De vir. ill.* 10).
From the *Muratorian Fragment* we learn that the book could be
read privately but that it was not to be read publicly in Church.
Yet Origen bears witness to the fact that it was read publicly in
some Churches but that this practice was not general.

TEXT TRADITION

The authorities for the Greek text of the Shepherd are as
follows:

1) *Codex Sinaiticus,* written in the fourth century, contains only the first quarter of the entire work, i.e. to *Mand.* 4, 3, 6.

2) An Athos manuscript of the fifteenth century contains the whole work except the very end, namely, *Simil.* 9, 30, 3–10, 4, 5.

3) The University of Michigan collection of papyri possesses two fragments, which have been published by Campbell Bonner and form a welcome addition to our knowledge of the text. The larger is of considerable importance because it has preserved most of the sentences missing from the Athos manuscript. It contains *Similitudes* 2, 8–9, 5, 1, and is older than most of the manuscripts of the Shepherd hitherto published. It was written at the end of the third century. The smaller fragment dates from the same time and it comprises the end of *Mand.* 2 and the opening words of *Mand.* 3.

4) A small fragment of vellum manuscript in Hamburg contains *Sim.* 4, 6–7 and 5, 1–5 (SBA 1909 pp. 1077ff.).

5) Fragments of the text have also been found in Amherst Papyrus CXC, Oxyrh. Pap. 404 and 1172, Berlin Pap. 5513 and 6789.

The text is preserved furthermore in two Latin and in an Ethiopic translation; extant also are fragments of a Sahidic Coptic version in Papyri now in the Bibl. Nat. at Paris and in the library of the Louvre, and a fragment of a middle-Persian translation.

Editions and Translations: See the editions and translations of the Apostolic Fathers, p. 41. C. BONNER, A Papyrus Codex of the Shepherd of Hermas (Similitudes 2-9) with a Fragment of the Mandates (Univ. of Michigan Studies, Humanistic Series 22). Ann Arbor, 1934. — *English translation:* C. TAYLOR, The Shepherd of Hermas (SPCK). London, 1903-06, 2 vols.

Studies: V. SCHWEITZER, Der Pastor Hermae und die opera supererogatoria: ThQ 86 (1904) 539–556. — A. BAUMEISTER, Die Ethik des Pastor Hermae. Freiburg i. B., 1912. — A. D'ALÈS, L'Edit de Calliste. Etude sur les origines de la pénitence chrétienne. Paris, 1914, 52-113. — G. RAUSCHEN, Eucharist and Penance. St. Louis, 1913, 155-159. — K. LAKE, Landmarks in the History of Early Christianity. London, 1920, 137-140. The Interpretation of the Shepherd of Hermas by F. S. MACKENZIE.—G. BAREILLE, Hermas: DTC 5, 2268-2288. — K. LAKE, The Shepherd of Hermas: HThR 18 (1925) 279ff. — W. J. WILSON, The Career of the Prophet Hermas: HThR 20(1927) 21-62. — C. BONNER, A Codex of the Shepherd of Hermas in the Papyri of the University of Michigan: HThR 18 (1925), 115-127; *idem,* A New Fragment of the Shepherd of Hermas, Michigan Papyrus 44: HThR 20

(1927) 105–116. — G. SCHLAEGER, Der Hirt des Hermas eine ursprünglich jüdische Schrift: NTT 16 (1927) 327–342. — P. BATIFFOL, L'Eglise naissante et le catholicisme. 12th ed. Paris, 1927, 222–224. — D. W. RIDDLE, The Messages of the Shepherd of Hermas: JR 7 (1927) 561–577. — J. RENDEL HARRIS, The Shepherd of Hermas in the West: ExpT 39 (1928) 259–261. — R. VAN DEEMTER, Der Hirt des Hermas Apokalypse oder Allegorie? Amsterdam Dissertation. Delft, 1929. — J. TIXERONT, History of Dogmas. 3rd ed. St. Louis and London, 1930, 111–119. — J. HOH, Die kirchliche Busse im zweiten Jahrhundert. Breslau, 1932, 10–34.— J. SCHÜMMER, Die altchristliche Fastenpraxis (LQF 27). Münster, 1933, 124f., 135f., 138f. — J. SVENNUNG, Statio = 'Fasten': ZNW 32 (1933) 294–308. — G. GHEDINI, Nuovi codici del Pastore di Erma: SC 62 (1934) 576–580. — A. PUECH, La langue d'Hermas: Mélanges Navarre (1935) 361–363. — A. V. STRÖM, Allegorie und Wirklichkeit im Hirten des Hermas (Arbeiten und Mitteilungen aus dem neutestamentl. Seminar zu Upsala, F. 3). Leipzig, 1936. — M. DIBELIUS, A Fresh Approach to the New Testament and Early Christian Literature. New York, 1936, 130–134; 224–226. — J. LEBRETON, Le texte grec du Pasteur d'Hermas d'après les papyrus de l'Université de Michigan: RSR 26 (1936) 464–67. — A. PUECH, Observations sur le Pasteur d'Hermas: Studi ded. alla memoria di Paolo Ubaldi. Milan, 1937, 83–85. — L. TH. LEFORT, Le Pasteur d'Hermas, en copte sahidique: Le Muséon 51 (1938) 239–276; idem, Le Pasteur d'Hermas. Un nouveau codex sahidique: Le Muséon 52 (1939) 223–228. — B. POSCHMANN, Paenitentia secunda. Bonn, 1939, 134–205. — R. C. MORTIMER, The Origins of Private Penance in the Western Church. Oxford, 1939. — G. MERCATI, Nuove note di letteratura biblica e cristiana antica (ST 95). Vatican City, 1941, 81ff. — J. BARBEL, Christos Angelos (Theophaneia 3). Bonn, 1941, 47–50. — J. RUWET, Les Antilegomena dans les oeuvres d'Origène: Bib (1942) 18–42. — J. C. PLUMPE, Mater Ecclesia (SCA 5). Washington, 1943, 19–25. — M. M. MUELLER, Der Uebergang von der griechischen zur lateinischen Sprache in der abendländischen Kirche von Hermas bis Novatian. Diss. Rome, 1943. — J. M. RIFE, Hermas and the Shepherd: Classical Weekly 37 (1943/44) 81. — O. J. F. SEITZ, Relationship of the Shepherd to the Epistle of James: JBL 63 (1944) 131–140. — G. D. KILPATRICK, A New Papyrus of the Shepherd of Hermas.: JThSt 48 (1947) 204–205. — O. J. SEITZ, Antecedents and Signification of the term δίψυχος: JBL 66 (1947) 211–219. — C. MOHRMANN, Les origines de la latinite chrétienne à Rome: VC 3 (1949) 74–78.

CHAPTER III

THE BEGINNINGS OF CHRISTIAN ROMANCE, FOLK STORIES, AND LEGENDS

THE APOCRYPHAL LITERATURE OF THE NEW TESTAMENT

It is a fact that the New Testament offers little information concerning the youth of Our Lord, the life and death of his Mother, and the missionary travels of his Apostles. No wonder that pious imaginations were moved to supply the details. For the purpose of edification the legend-making processes were given free scope. On the other hand, heretics felt the need of Gospel narratives to support their doctrines, particularly the Gnostics. Thus there grew up around the canonical Scriptures the collection of legends which comprise the so-called Apocrypha of the New Testament. Non-canonical Gospels, Apocalypses, Letters and Acts of the Apostles appeared as counterparts of the canonical writings.

Originally the words *apocryphal* and *apocrypha* did not mean that which is spurious or untrue, at least not in the minds of those who first employed them. Some of these works were regarded as canonical, according to the testimony of St. Jerome (*Epist.* 107, 12 and *Prol. gal. in Samuel et Mal.*) and St. Augustine (*De civitate Dei*, 15, 23, 4). An apocryphal book was in the beginning one too sacred and too secret to be known by everybody. It must be hidden (*apocryphos*) from the public at large and restricted to the initiates of the sect. In order to gain acceptance, such books usually made their appearance under the names of Apostles and pious disciples of Jesus. With the recognition of the falsity of these attributions the meaning of the word apocryphal changed; henceforth, apocryphal meant spurious, false, to be rejected.

Even the most superficial reader of these writings perceives their inferiority to the canonical. They abound in accounts of alleged miracles which at times descend to absurdity. Nevertheless, the Apocrypha are of the utmost importance for the Church historian in as much as they supply valuable information about tendencies and customs which characterize the early Church. Moreover, they represent the beginnings of Christian legends, folk stories and romantic literature. They are indispensable to the understanding of Christian art. The mosaics of Santa Maria Maggiore in Rome and the reliefs of ancient Christian sarcophagi owe their inspiration to them. The miniatures of the liturgical books and the stained-glass windows of the cathedrals of the Middle Ages would be indecipherable without reference to the stories of these Apocrypha. Their influence on the later miracle or mystery plays was considerable. Even Dante used them as a source for the eschatological scenes of his *Divine Comedy*. Accordingly, we possess in them a picturesque and first hand source on Christian thought.

M. R. James has given an excellent appreciation of their place in the history of Christian literature:

People may still be heard to say, 'After all, these Apocryphal Gospels and Acts, as you call them, are just as interesting as the old ones. It was only by accident or caprice that they were not put into the New Testament'. The best answer to such loose talk has always been, and is now, to produce the writings and let them tell their own story. It will very quickly be seen that there is no question of anyone's having excluded them from the New Testament: they have done that for themselves.

'But, it may be said, if these writings are good neither as books of history, nor of religion, nor even as literature, why spend time and labour on giving them a vogue which on your own showing they do not deserve?' Partly of course, in order to enable others to form a judgment on them; but that is not the whole case. The truth is that they must not be regarded only from the point of view which they claim for themselves. In almost every other aspect they have a great and enduring interest...

If they are not good sources of history in one sense, they are in another. They record the imaginations, hopes, and fears of the men who wrote them; they show what was acceptable to the unlearned Christians of the first ages, what interested them, what they admired, what ideals of conduct they cherished for this life, what they thought they would find in the text. As folklore and romance, again, they are precious; and to the lover and student of mediaeval literature and art they reveal the source of no inconsiderable part of his material and the solution of many a puzzle. They have, indeed, exercised an influence (wholly disproportionate to their intrinsic merits) so great and so widespread, that no one who cares about the history of Christian thought and Christian art can possibly afford to neglect them [1].

Editions: J. A. FABRICIUS, Codex apocryphus Novi Testamenti. 2 vols. Hamburg, 1703-19. Vol I reprinted .1719, vol. II repr. 1743. — A. BIRCH, Auctuarium codicis apocryphi Novi Testamenti Fabriciani, I. Hauniae, 1804. — J. C. THILO, Codex apocryphus Novi Testamenti. Leipzig, 1832. — A. HILGENFELD, Novum Testamentum extra canonem receptum. 2nd ed. Leipzig, 1884. — M. R. JAMES, Apocrypha anecdota. Cambridge, 1893-1897. — E. KLOSTERMANN und A. HARNACK, Apocrypha I (KT 3) 3rd ed. Bonn, 1921; II (KT 8) 2nd ed. Bonn, 1910; III (KT 11) 2nd ed. Bonn, 1911; IV (KT 12) 2nd ed. Bonn, 1912.

Translations: M. R. JAMES, The Apocryphal New Testament. Oxford, 1924. — E. HENNECKE, Neutestamentliche Apokryphen. 2nd ed. Tübingen, 1924; *idem,* Handbuch zu den neutestamentlichen Apokryphen. Tübingen, 1914. — J. BOUSQUET et E. AMANN, Les apocryphes du Nouveau Testament. Paris, 1910, 1913, 1922. — H. BAKELS, Nieuw Testamentische apocriefen. Vert. met inl. en aant. voorzien. Amsterdam, 1922, 2 vols. — C. RUTS, De apocriefen uit het Nieuw-Testament I. Evangeliën en Kerkstemmen. Brussels, 1927.

Studies: B. J. SNELL, The Value of the Apocrypha. London, 1905. -- S. N. SEDGWICK, Story of the Apocrypha. A Series of Lectures on the Books and Times of the Apocrypha. London, 1906. — J. GEFFCKEN, Christliche Apokryphen. Tübingen, 1908. — W. C. PROCTOR, The Value of the Apocrypha. 1926. — E. HENNECKE, Zur christlichen Apokryphenliteratur: ZKG 45 (1926) 309-315. — J. A. ROBINSON, Excluded Books of the New Testament. 1927. — E. AMANN, Apocryphes du Nouveau Testament: DB (Supplement) I (1928) 460-533. — SH. E. JOHNSON, Stray Pieces of Early Christian Writing: Journal of Near Eastern Studies 5 (1946) 40-54.

Syriac Versions: W. WRIGHT, Contributions to the Apocryphal Literature of the New Testament, Collected and Edited from Syriac Manuscripts in the British Museum with an English Translation and Notes. London, 1865.

Coptic Versions: E. REVILLOUT, Apocryphes coptes du Nouveau Testament. Paris, 1876; *idem,* PO 2, 2 (1907); 9,2 (1913). — E. A. W. BUDGE, Coptic Apocrypha in the Dialect of Upper Egypt. London, 1913. — F. H. HALLOCK, Coptic Apocrypha: JBL 52 (1933) 163-174. — W. GROSSOUW, De Apocriefen van het O. en N.T. in de Koptische letterkunde: StC 10 (1934) 434-446; 11 (1935) 19-36. — O. H. E. BURMESTER, Egyptian Mythology in the Coptic Apocrypha: Orientalia 7 (1938) 355-367. — L. TH. LEFORT, Fragments d'apocryphes en copte-akhminique: Muséon 52 (1939) 1-10.

[1]) M. R. James, The Apocryphal New Testament, Oxford, 1924, XI, XIII.

Ethiopic Versions: R. BASSET, Les Apocryphes éthiopiens traduits en français. Paris, 1893. — GUERRIER and GRÉBAUT, PO 9,3 (1913); 12,4 (1919); CSCO 1,7-8. — A. Z. AESCOLY, Les noms magiques dans les apocryphes chrétiens des Éthiopiens. Paris, 1932.

Armenian Versions: Editions of the Mechitarists of S. Lazzaro, 2 vols., 1898–1904.

Old Slavonic Versions: N. BONWETSCH, in: A. HARNACK, Geschichte der altchristlichen Literatur 1, 902–917. — J. FRANKO, Beiträge aus dem Kirchenslavischen zu den Apokryphen des Neuen Testamentes: ZNW 3 (1902) 146-155; 315-335; *idem*, Beiträge aus dem Kirchenslavischen zu den neutestamentlichen Apokryphen: ZNW 7 (1906) 151-171. — J. FRANKO, Codex apocryph. 1-5. Lemberg, 1896-1910.

I. EARLY CHRISTIAN INTERPOLATIONS IN OLD TESTAMENT APOCRYPHA

The custom of imitating Biblical books can be traced back to pre-Christian times. The authors of these apocryphal writings ascribed their work to some notable figure and dated it back into a much earlier period. Thus originated in the second century before Christ the *Third Book of Esdras*, which gives a reconstruction of the story of the decline and fall of the kingdom of Juda from the time of Josias. This work was continued in the Christian era by the so-called *Fourth Book of Esdras*. Composed about the time of the destruction of Jerusalem, this latter book was considerably affected by Christian hopes, and had no mean influence on the formation of Christian eschatology. It is not surprising, therefore, that it was regarded as canonical.

In a similar way the Enoch literature arose. This consists of a collection of Apocalypses, the kernel of which, chapters 1–36 and 72–104, originated in the second century before Christ. It contains probably the oldest piece of Jewish literature dealing with the general resurrection of Israel. Interpolations of Christian authors extended this *Book of Enoch* more and more during the first century A.D. It is particularly interesting that in chapters 32,2–33,3 of the (Slavonic) *Secrets of Enoch* we find the first reference to the millenium. Similar interpolations may be found in the *Testaments of the Twelve Patriarchs*, a composite work purporting to preserve the last words of the twelve sons of Jacob, and in the *Apocalypse of Baruch*.

Translation: R. H. CHARLES, The Testament of the Twelve Patriarchs (SPCK). London, 1917.

The most important example of Christian adaptation of Jewish writings is the *Ascension of Isaias*. The basis of this valuable document from the end of the first or the beginning of the second century is a group of Jewish legends dealing with Beliar and the martyrdom of the prophet Isaias. The second part (chs. 6 to 11) contains a rhapsodical description of the seven heavens, and of the incarnation, passion, resurrection and ascension of Christ as seen by Isaias after he was taken up into heaven. This section is undoubtedly of Christian origin. It gives besides prophecies regarding Christ and his Church an unmistakable description of the emperor Nero and is of special importance as the most ancient of surviving testimonies as to the manner of Peter's death. We possess the complete text of this Apocalypse in Ethiopic only. But large fragments are preserved in Greek, Latin, and Slavonic recensions.

Editions and translations: The *Greek* fragments in B. C. GRENFELL and A. S. HUNT, The Amherst Papyri, vol I. London, 1900. *Ethiopic Version:* E. TISSERANT, Ascension d'Isaie de la version éthiopienne. Paris, 1909, with a French translation. *English translations:* R. H. CHARLES, The Apocrypha and Pseudepigrapha of the Old Testament in English, vol II. Oxford, 1913, 155ff; *idem*, The Ascension of Isaiah (SPCK). London, 1919. *German:* E. HENNECKE, Neutestamentliche Apokryphen, 2nd ed. Tübingen, 1924, 303–314.

Studies: E. SCHÜRER, Geschichte des jüdischen Volkes im Zeitalter Christi, vol. III. 4th ed., Leipzig, 1919. — A. L. DAVIES, Ascension of Isaiah, in: J. HASTINGS, Dictionary of the Apostolic Church, vol. I. New York, 1916. — V. BURCH, Ascensio Isaiae: JThSt 21 (1920) 249ff. — J. T. SHOTWELL and L. ROPES LOOMIS, The See of Peter. New York, 1927, 69–71.

II. APOCRYPHAL GOSPELS

Editions and translations: C. TISCHENDORF, Evangelia apocrypha. Leipzig, 1853, 2nd ed. by Fr. WILBRANDT, Leipzig, 1876. — E. PREUSCHEN, Antilegomena. Die Reste der ausserkanonischen Evangelien und urchristlichen Ueberlieferungen (with a German translation). 2nd ed. Giessen, 1905. — R. ROBINSON, Coptic Apocryphal Gospels with an English Transl. (Texts and Studies, 4,2). Cambridge, 1896. — CH. MICHEL et P. PEETERS, Evangiles apocryphes I–II (Textes et documents pour l'étude historique du christianisme). Paris, 1911–1914. — E. KLOSTERMANN, (KT 3,8). Bonn, 1910. — B. PICK, Paralipomena. Remains of Gospels and Sayings of Christ. Chicago, 1908. — L. SCARABELLI. I Vangeli apocrifi. Bologna, 1867. — C. RUTS, De apocriefen uit het Nieuw-Testament I. Evangeliën en Kerkstemmen. Brussels, 1927.

Studies: C. TISCHENDORF, De evangeliorum apocryphorum origine et usu. Haag, 1851. — R. HOFMANN, Das Leben Jesu nach den Apokryphen. Leipzig, 1851. — W. BAUER, Das Leben Jesu im Zeitalter der neutestamentlichen Apokryphen. Tübingen, 1909. — L. COUARD, Altchristliche Sagen über das Leben Jesu und der Apostel. Gütersloh, 1909. — F. HAASE, Literarkritische Untersuchungen zur orientalisch-apokryphen Evangelienliteratur. Leipzig, 1913. — A. F. FINDLAY, Byways in Early Christian Literature. Studies in the Uncanonical Gospels and Acts. Edinburgh, 1923. — PLUMMER, The Apocryphal Gospels: ExpT (1923) 473f.— C. RUTS, De Apocryphen uit het N.T. 1 : Evangeliën en kerkstemmen. Brussels, 1927. — P. SAINTYVES, De la nature des évangiles apocryphes et de leur valeur hagiographique: RHR 106 (1932) 435-457. — H. J. BARDSLEY, Reconstructions of Early Christian Documents (SPCK) vol. I. London, 1935. — L. CERFAUX, Un nouvel évangile apocryphe: ETL 12 (1935) 579-80; *idem*, Parallèles canoniques de l'évangile inconnu: Muséon 49 (1936) 55-78. — G. GHEDINI, La lingua dei Vangeli apocrifi greci: Studi dedicati alla memoria di Paolo Ubaldi. Milan, 1937, 443-480. — H. WAITZ, Neue Untersuchungen über die sogenannten judenchristlichen Evangelien: ZNW 36 (1937) 60-80. — M. BLACK, The Palestinian Syriac Gospel and the Diatessaron: OC 35 (1939) 101-111. — M. DIBELIUS, A Fresh Approach to the New Testament and Early Christian Literature. New York, 1936, 72-95; *idem*, Auf der Spur eines unbekannten apokryphen Evangeliums: Die christliche Welt 54 (1940) 221-2. — H. IDRIS BELL and T. C. SKEAT, Fragments of an Unknown Gospel and Other Early Christian Papyri. Oxford, 1935.

1. *The Gospel according to the Hebrews*

In his work, *De Viris Illustribus* (ch. 2), St. Jerome, speaking of James, the Lord's brother, says the following:

Also the Gospel called According to the Hebrews, lately translated by me into Greek and Latin speech, which Origen often uses, tells, after the Resurrection of the Saviour: *Now the Lord, when He had given the linen cloth unto the servant of the priest, went unto James and appeared to him (for James had sworn that he would not eat bread from that hour wherein he had drunk the Lord's cup until he should see him risen again from among them that sleep)* and again after a little, *Bring ye, saith the Lord, a table and bread,* and immediately is added, *He took bread and blessed and brake and gave it unto James the Just and said unto him: My brother, eat thy bread, for the Son of Man is risen from among them that sleep.*

The *Gospel According to the Hebrews*, from which St. Jerome quotes this interesting passage, was originally written in the Aramaic language, but in Hebrew letters. The original text was, in

Jerome's time, in a library at Caesarea, in Palestine. Both the Ebionites and the Nazarenes used this Gospel, and it was from them that Jerome obtained a copy for his Greek and Latin translations. The fact that it was in use by Palestinian Christians who spoke Hebrew (Aramaic) explains the name 'According to the Hebrews'. It explains also why James 'the brother of the Lord', the representative of strict Jewish Christianity, comes here into the center of the Easter narrative, contrary to the canonical records. At Jerome's time, most people regarded this apocryphal gospel as the Hebrew original of the canonical Gospel of Matthew which Papias mentioned (Eusebius, *Historia ecclesiastica* 3, 39, 16; 6, 25, 4; Irenaeus 1, 1). In fact, the few fragments which are preserved indicate a close relationship to Matthew. The safest conclusion is, probably, that this Gospel According to the Hebrews was some sort of reworking and extension of the Hebrew original of the canonical Gospel of Matthew. The passage quoted above shows that it included sayings of Jesus which   nonical Gospels do not contain. This characteristic is vouch   for also by others than St. Jerome, e.g. Eusebius, *Theophany*, 22.

The gospel which has come down to us in Hebrew characters gave the threat as made not against him who hid (his talent) but against him who lived riotously; for (the parable) told of three servants, one who devoured his lord's substance with harlots and flute-girls, one who gained profit manyfold, and one who hid his talent, and how in the issue one was accepted, one merely blamed, and one shut up in prison.

The time of composition of this apocryphal gospel must be in the second century, because Clement of Alexandria used it in his *Stromata* (2,9,45) in the last quarter of this century.

M. R. James, The Apocryphal New Testament. Oxford, 1924, 1–8. — R. Handmann, Das Hebräerevangelium (TU 5,3). Leipzig, 1888. — A. Rouvanet, Etude exégétique et critique de l'Evangile des Hébreux. Thèse, Cahors, 1904. — A. S. Barnes, The Gospel according to the Hebrews: JThSt 6 (1905) 356ff. — V. Burch, The Gospel according to the Hebrews (Coptic sources): JThSt 21 (1920) 310ff. — M. J. Lagrange, L'Evangile selon les Hébreux: RBibl 31 (1922) 161–181; 321–349. — J. T. Dodd, The Gospel according to the Hebrews. London, 1933. — W. Bauer, Rechtgläubigkeit und Ketzerei im ältesten Christentum. Tübingen, 1934, 55–57. — A. Schmidtke, Zum Hebräerevangelium: ZNW 35 (1936) 24–43.

2. *The Gospel of the Egyptians*

Clement of Alexandria is also our chief source of knowledge for the so-called *Gospel of the Egyptians*. Its name seems to indicate that it was in circulation among the Christians of Egypt. This would explain why Clement of Alexandria and Origen were acquainted with it. The *Gospel of the Egyptians* belongs to that class of apocrypha which were written for the support of certain heresies. It is most probably of Gnostic origin. Its distinctive doctrinal elements evince a sectarian and heretical bias. Clement of Alexandria has preserved from it a few sayings of Jesus from the Lord's conversation with Salome, which are the best proof of its tendencies:

When Salome inquired how long death should have power, the Lord (not meaning that life is evil, and the Creation bad) said: *As long as you women bear* (*Stromata*, 3,6,45). — And those who opposed the creation of God through shameful abstinence allege also those words spoken to Salome whereof we made mention above. And they are contained, I think, in the Gospel according to the Egyptians. For they said that the Saviour Himself said: *I came to destroy the works of the female,* — the female being lust and the works birth and corruption (*Stromata*, 3,9,63). — And why do not they who walk any way rather than by the Gospel rule of truth adduce the rest also of the words spoken to Salome? For when she said, *Therefore have I done well in that I have not brought forth,* as if it were not fitting to accept motherhood, the Lord replies, saying, *Eat every herb, but that which has bitterness eat not* (*Stromata*, 3, 9, 66). — Therefore Cassian says: When Salome inquired when those things should be concerning which she asked, the Lord said: *When ye trample on the garment of shame, and when the two shall be one, and the male with the female, neither male nor female* (*Stromata*, 3,13,92).

3. *The Ebionite Gospel*

The Ebionite Gospel is most probably identical with the *Gospel of the Twelve Apostles* which Origen mentions (*Hom. in Luc.* 1). If that is the case, it most likely dates from the beginning of the third century. Jerome, however, is evidently mistaken in identifying it with the *Gospel According to the Hebrews*, although A Schmidtke supports this opinion.

All our knowledge regarding the Gospel of the Ebionites is derived from Epiphanius (*Adv. Haer.* 30, 13–16, 22), who gives fragments of it. To judge from these fragments it was written in the interests of some sect of Christians opposed to sacrifice. Thus, Jesus is represented as saying: 'I come to put an end to sacrifice, and unless you cease from sacrificing, anger will not cease from you' (30,16).

4. The Gospel According to Peter

A large fragment of this gospel was discovered in 1886–87 by Bouriant in the tomb of a monk at Akhmim, in Upper Egypt. He published it with a translation in 1892. It relates the passion, death and burial of Jesus, and embellishes the narrative of his resurrection with interesting details regarding the miracles which followed. There are slight traces of the Docetic heresy in it. Perhaps this is the reason why the words of Jesus on the cross, 'My God, My God, why hast Thou forsaken me', have been changed to read, 'My power, my power, thou hast forsaken me'. It is also interesting that Herod, not Pilate, gives the order for execution; the responsibility for the death of Jesus is thus put exclusively on the Jews. But it remains doubtful whether this gospel is really of heretical origin. The trifling indications of sectarianism in it are scarcely enough to be convincing. The author seems to have worked over the narratives of the canonical gospels, adapting them freely.

There are references to the *Gospel According to Peter* in the ecclesiastical writers. The first who mentions it is Origen, in his *Commentary on Matthew* (10,17). He reports that some, relying on a 'tradition of the gospel entitled According to Peter', thought the so-called 'brothers of Jesus' were sons of Joseph by a former wife, who had lived with him before Mary. Eusebius states that Bishop Serapion of Antioch rejected this gospel about the year 190 A.D. as of Docetic character. Accordingly, it must have been written, at the latest, in the second half of the second century.

Editions and translations: Cf. above, p. 110. — U. BOURIANT, Fragments du texte grec du livre d'Enoch et de quelques écrits attribués à saint Pierre:

Mémoires publiés par les membres de la mission archéologique française au Caire 9,1. Paris, 1892, 93-147. — E. KLOSTERMANN, Apocrypha I: Reste des Petrusevangeliums, der Petrusapokalypse und des Kerygma Petri (KT 3). 2nd ed. Bonn, 1933, 3-8. — G. RAUSCHEN, Monumenta minora saeculi secundi (FP 3). 2nd. ed. Bonn, 1914, 47-58. — L. VAGANAY, L'évangile de Pierre (Etudes bibliques). Paris, 1930.

Studies: H. B. SWETE, Gospel of Peter. New York, 1893. — TH. ZAHN, Das Evangelium des Petrus. Erlangen, 1893. — A. HARNACK, Bruchstücke des Evangeliums und der Apokalypse des Petrus (TU 9,2). 2nd ed. Leipzig, 1893. — O. V. GEBHARDT, Das Evangelium und die Apokalypse des Petrus. Leipzig, 1893. — H. V. SCHUBERT, Die Composition des pseudopetrinischen Evangelienfragments. Berlin, 1893. — D. VÖLTER, Petrusevangelium oder Aegypterevangelium? Tübingen, 1893. — V. H. STANTON, The Gospel of Peter: JThSt 2 (1900) 1-25. — F. H. CHASE, The Gospel of Peter, in: HASTINGS, Dictionary of the Bible 3 (1900) 776. — C. H. TURNER, The Gospel of Peter: JThSt 14 (1913) 161ff. — P. GARDNER-SMITH, The Gospel of Peter: JThSt 27 (1926) 255ff.; *idem*, The Date of the Gospel of Peter: JThSt 27 (1926) 401ff. — E. FASCHER, Petrusapokryphen: PWK 19 (1938) 1373-1381.

5. *The Gospel of Nicodemus*

The tendency to minimize the guilt of Pilate which is found in the *Gospel According to Peter* shows the keen interest with which ancient Christianity regarded his person. The prominent position occupied by Pontius Pilate in early Christian thought is further evidenced by the *Gospel of Nicodemus*. Into this narrative have been incorporated the so-called *Acts of Pilate*, a supposed official report of the procurator concerning Jesus. Some Acts of Pilate, it seems, were known as early as the second century. Justin Martyr remarks in his first *Apology* (35) after he has mentioned the passion and crucifixion of Jesus: 'And that these things happened you can ascertain from the Acts of Pontius Pilate.' A similar statement occurs in chapter 48. Tertullian refers twice to a report made by Pilate to Tiberius. According to him, Pontius Pilate informed the Emperor of the unjust sentence of death which he had pronounced against an innocent and divine person; the Emperor was so moved by his report of the miracles of Christ and his resurrection, that he proposed the reception of Christ among the gods of Rome. But the Senate refused (*Apologeticum* 5). In another place Tertullian says that the 'whole story of Christ was reported to Caesar — at that time it was Tiberius — by Pilate, himself in his secret heart already a

Christian' (*Apol.* 21,24). We see here the tendency at work to use the Roman procurator as a witness for the history of the death and resurrection of Christ and the truth of Christianity. The same tendency must have given rise to the so-called *Acts of Pilate* which form the *Gospel of Nicodemus*. As it now stands, this gospel gives in the first part, chapters 1 to 11, an elaborate account of the trial, crucifixion, and burial of Jesus. This part has the special title, *Acta Pilati*. The second part (chapters 12 to 16) describes the debates held in the Sanhedrin about the Resurrection of Christ, and constitutes an addition to the *Acta Pilati*. The third part (chapters 17 to 27) is designated 'Descensus Christi ad Inferos'. It purports to be the account of Christ's descent to hell by two witnesses, the 'sons of Simeon', who have arisen from the dead after having seen Christ in Hades.

The whole work, which in a later Latin manuscript is called the *Evangelium Nicodemi*, must have been composed at the beginning of the fifth century, but it seems to be more or less a compilation of older material. Eusebius tells us that during the persecution of Maximin Daia in 311 or 312 the Roman government spread pagan forgeries of these *Acts of Pilate* to stir up hate against the Christians:

> Having forged, to be sure, Memoirs of Pilate and Our Saviour, full of every kind of blasphemy against Christ, with the approval of their chief they sent them round to every part of his dominions, with edicts that they should be exhibited openly for everyone to see in every place, both town and country, and that the primary teachers should give them to the children, instead of lessons, for study and committal to memory (*Hist. eccl.* 9,5,1; cf. 1,9,1; 1,11,9; 9,7,1).

It is possible that the *Acts of Pilate* which formed the *Evangelium Nicodemi* were originally written to counteract the bad effects of these pagan acts.

The oldest piece of Christian Pilate literature seems to be 'The Report of Pilate to the Emperor Claudius', which is inserted in Greek into the late *Acts of Peter and Paul* and is given in Latin translation as an appendix of the *Evangelium Nicodemi*. It is probable that this report is identical with that mentioned by Tertullian. If that is true, it must have been composed before the year 197 A.D., the time of Tertullian's *Apologeticum*. Based on the Greek text, the English translation of M. R. James runs as follows:

Pontius Pilate unto Claudius, greeting.

There befell of late a matter which I myself brought to light (*or*, made trial of): for the Jews through envy have punished themselves and their posterity with fearful judgements of their own fault; for whereas their fathers had promises (*al.* had announced unto them) that their God would send them out of heaven his holy one who should of right be called their king, and did promise that he would send him upon earth by a virgin; he then (*or* this God of the Hebrews, then) came when I was governor of Judea, and they beheld him enlightening the blind, cleansing lepers, healing the palsied, driving devils out of men, raising the dead, rebuking the winds, walking upon the waves of the sea dry-shod, and doing many other wonders, and all the people of the Jews calling him the Son of God: the chief priests therefore, moved with envy against him, took him and delivered him unto me and brought against him one false accusation after another, saying that he was a sorcerer and did things contrary to their law.

But I, believing that these things were so, having scourged him, delivered him unto their will: and they crucified him, and when he was buried they set guards upon him. But while my soldiers watched him he rose again on the third day: yet so much was the malice of the Jews kindled that they gave money to the soldiers, saying: Say ye that his disciples stole away his body. But they, though they took the money, were not able to keep silence concerning that which had come to pass, for they also have testified that they saw him arisen and that they received money from the Jews. And these things have I reported (unto thy mightiness) for this cause, lest some other should lie *unto thee* (*Lat.* lest any lie otherwise) and thou shouldest deem right to believe the false tales of the Jews.

The other apocryphal *Reports of Pilate*, as for instance, the *Anaphora Pilati*, the *Letter of Pilate to Tiberius*, *The Paradosis Pilati*, i.e., the sentence of Pilate by the Emperor, and the correspondence between Pilate and Herod, belong to the Middle Ages.

The *Acts of Pilate* in the *Gospel of Nicodemus*, which have been preserved in the Greek text as well as in Syriac, Armenian,

Coptic, Arabic and Latin translations, have had interesting results. The Christians of Syria and Egypt venerated Pilate as a
saint and martyr, and even today he is in the liturgical calendar
of the Coptic church. During the Middle Ages, the influence of
the Acts in the field of literature and art was tremendous.

Editions: In Greek: C. TISCHENDORF, Evangelia apocrypha. 2nd ed. Leipzig,
1876, 210–486. — G. F. ABBOT, The Report and Death of Pilate: JThSt 4
(1903) 83–86. — M. R. JAMES, Apocrypha anecdota, Ser. 2. Cambridge,
1897, 65–70; 77–81. — *Syriac version with Latin translation:* J. E. RAHMANI,
Apocrypha hypomnemata Domini nostri seu Acta Pilati, antiqua versio
syriaca (Studia Syriaca II). Scharfa, Libanon, 1908. — *Coptic version with
French translation:* E. REVILLOUT, PO, 9. Paris, 1913, 61ff. — P. VANUTELLI,
Actorum Pilati textus synoptici. Rome, 1938.

Other translations: English: A. WALKER, ANF 8, 416–467. — A. WESTCOTT,
The Gospel of Nicodemus and Kindred Documents. London, 1915. — M. R.
JAMES, The Apocryphal New Testament. Oxford, 94–147. — W. P. CROZIER,
Letters of Pontius Pilate, Written during his Governorship of Judea to his
Friend Seneca in Rome. New York, 1928. — *German:* J. SEDLACEK, Neue
Pilatusakten (Sitzungsberichte der böhmischen Gesellschaft der Wissen-
schaften). Prag, 1908.

Studies: R. A. LIPSIUS, Die Pilatusakten kritisch untersucht. Kiel, 1871, 2nd
ed., 1886. — E. v. DOBSCHÜTZ, Christusbilder (TU 18). Leipzig, 1899,
205ff.; *idem,* Der Prozess Jesu nach den Acta Pilati: ZNW 3 (1902) 89ff.;
idem, Gospel of Nicodemus in: J. HASTINGS' Dictionary of the Bible. —
K. LAKE, Texts from Mount Athos (Studia Biblica et ecclesiastica 5,2).
Oxford, 1902, 152–163. — TH. MOMMSEN, Die Pilatusakten: ZNW 3 (1902)
198–205. —VITTI, Verbum Domini (1927) 138–144; 171–181.— A. MINGANA,
The Lament of the Virgin and the Martyrdom of Pilate. Manchester, 1928.
— J. KROLL, Gott und Hölle. Leipzig, 1932, 83–95.

6. *The Protoevangelium of James*

The *Protoevangelium of James* belongs to the group of *Infancy
Gospels*, which narrate at some length the youth of the Virgin
Mary and the birth and childhood of Jesus. The term *Protoevangelium* is modern: it was first applied to the *Gospel of James* in 1552
in a Latin translation of Guillaume Postel. Origen is the first who
refers to the *Book of James*, mentioning that this book states that
the 'brethren of the Lord' were sons of Joseph by a former wife.
But even before Origen, his teacher, Clement of Alexandria, and
Justin Martyr report incidents connected with the birth of Jesus
which are also related in the *Protoevangelium.*

The book, most probably, was a product of the middle of the second century, and certainly was in existence at the end of this century. It contains the oldest extant account of the miraculous birth, and of the infancy and youth of the Virgin Mary. In it the names of Mary's parents, Joachim and Anna, appear for the first time. Most interesting is the account of the dedication of the child and her presentation in the temple, whither she was brought by her parents when she was three years of age (Ch. 6–8):

And day by day the child waxed strong, and when she was six months old her mother stood her upon the ground to try if she would stand; and she walked seven steps and returned unto her bosom. And she caught her up, saying: As the Lord my God liveth, thou shalt walk no more upon this ground until I bring thee into the temple of the Lord. And she made a sanctuary in her bedchamber and suffered nothing common or unclean to pass through it. And she called for the daughters of the Hebrews that were undefiled, and they carried her hither and thither.

And the first year of the child was fulfilled, and Joachim made a great feast and invited the priests and the scribes and the assembly of the elders and the whole people of Israel. And Joachim brought the child to the priests, and they blessed her saying: O God of our fathers, bless this child and give her a name renowned for ever among all generations. And all the people said: So be it, so be it. Amen. And he brought her to the high priests, and they blessed her, saying: O God of the high places, look upon this child, and bless her with the last blessing which hath no successor.

And her mother caught her up into the sanctuary of her bedchamber and gave her suck.

And Anna made a song unto the Lord God saying: I will sing a hymn unto the Lord my God, because he hath visited me and taken away from me the reproach of mine enemies, and the Lord hath given me a fruit of his righteousness, single and manifold before him. Who shall declare unto the sons of Reuben that Anna giveth suck? Hearken, hearken, ye twelve tribes of Israel, that Anna giveth suck. And she laid the child to rest in the bedchamber of her sanctuary, and went forth and ministered unto them. And when the feast was ended, they departed rejoicing and glorifying the God of Israel.

And unto the child her months were added: and the child became two years old. And Joachim said: Let us bring her up to the temple of the Lord that we may pay the promise which we promised; lest the Lord require it of us, and our gift become unacceptable. And Anna said: Let us wait until the third year, that the child may not long after her father or mother. And Joachim said: Let us wait.

And the child became three years old, and Joachim said: Call for the daughters of the Hebrews that are undefiled, and let them take every one a lamp and let them be burning, that the child turn not backward and her heart be taken captive away from the temple of the Lord. And they did so until they had gone up into the temple of the Lord.

And the priest received her and kissed her and blessed her, and said: The Lord hath magnified thy name among all generations: in thee in the last days shall the Lord make manifest his redemption unto the children of Israel. And he made her to sit upon the third step of the altar. And the Lord laid his grace upon her and she danced with her feet and all the house of Israel loved her.

And her parents returned down marvelling, and praising the Lord God because the child had not turned back.

And Mary was in the temple of the Lord as a dove that is nurtured; and she received food from the hand of an angel.

And when she was twelve years old, there was a council of priests, saying: Behold Mary is become twelve years old in the temple of the Lord. What then shall we do with her lest she pollute the sanctuary of the Lord? And they said unto the high priest: Thou standest over the altar of the Lord. Enter in and pray concerning her: and whatsoever the Lord shall reveal to thee that let us do.

The gospel goes on to narrate Mary's espousal to Joseph, then an old man with children. The birth of Jesus in a cave and accompanying miracles of the most extravagant sort are given in detail.

The principal aim of the whole writing is to prove the perpetual and inviolate virginity of Mary before, in, and after the birth of Christ. Thus, she drinks of 'the water of the conviction of the Lord' in order to remove all suspicion (ch. 16). Her *virginitas in partu* is attested by a mid-wife who was present at the Nativity (ch. 20). In this connection, it seems that Clement of Alexandria knew this gospel, or its legendary source, because he says in *Stromata* (7, 93, 7): 'For after she had brought forth, some say that she was attended by a midwife and was found to be a virgin.'

With the account of the martyrdom of Zacharias, father of St. John the Baptist, and the death of Herod, the gospel comes to a close. At the very end, there comes a statement regarding the authorship of the gospel: 'Now I, James, who wrote this history in Jerusalem, when there arose a tumult when Herod died, withdrew myself into the wilderness until the tumult ceased in Jerusalem, glorifying the Lord God which gave me the gift and the wisdom to write this history.'

There is no doubt that the author seeks to give the impression that he is none other than James the Less, the Bishop of Jerusalem. Who he really was cannot be ascertained. He shows an astonishing ignorance of the geography of Palestine; on the other hand, he seems to be strongly influenced by the Old Testament in his narratives. This suggests that he was a Christian of Jewish descent residing somewhere outside of Palestine, perhaps Egypt.

In its present form, the gospel cannot be regarded as the work of one author. The incidents of the death of Zacharias and of the escape of John the Baptist appear to be later additions to the work. The sequence of the narrative is broken several times. Thus, in chapter 18, Joseph breaks in suddenly and starts to speak without having been introduced.

The present form of the Greek text dates from the fourth century, in the latter part of which it was used by Epiphanius. The wide diffusion of the *Protoevangelium* can be seen from the fact that the Greek text has been preserved in no less than thirty manuscripts. Moreover, we possess early translations of it into Syriac, Armenian, Coptic, and Slavic. But no Latin manuscript of the gospel has yet been discovered.

The *Decretum Gelasianum de libris recipiendis et non recipiendis* of the sixth century condemns the writing as heretical. Nevertheless, the influence of this Nativity Gospel cannot be overestimated. Liturgy, literature, and art — all have been alike affected by it. The cult of St. Anne and the ecclesiastical feast of the Presentation of the Virgin in the temple have their source in the traditions of this book. Many of the charming legends of Our Lady are based upon the stories of the *Protoevangelium*, and artists have been inspired by it again and again.

Editions and translations: C. TISCHENDORF, Evangelia apocrypha 2nd ed. Leipzig, 1876, 1–50. — G. RAUSCHEN, Monumenta minora saeculi secundi (FP 3). 2nd ed. Bonn, 1914, 59–68 gives the text of chapters 1–11. — E. AMANN, Le protévangile de Jacques et ses remaniements latins. Introduction, textes, traduction et commentaire. Paris, 1910. — CH. MICHEL, Evangiles apocryphes I. Paris, 1911. — An *Ethiopic* version was published by M. CHAINE, CSCO, Scriptores aethiopici, Series I, tom. VII. Leipzig, 1909.— F. C. CONYBEARE, Protoevangelium Jacobi (from an Armenian Manuscript in the Library of the Mechitarists in Venice): The American Journal of Theology 1 (1897) 424–442. — A fragment of a *Syriac* version with an English translation is found in W. WRIGHT, Contributions to the Apocryphal Literature of the New Testament. London, 1865, 3ff., and a complete Syriac text in: A. SMITH LEWIS, Studia Sinaitica 9. London, 1902. — For papyrus fragments of the Protoevangelium see A. EHRHARD, Ueberlieferung und Bestand der hagiographischen und homiletischen Literatur der griechischen Kirche von den Anfängen bis zum Ende des 16. Jahrhunderts I (TU 50,1). Leipzig, 1937, 57–69. *English translations:* A. WALKER, ANF 8, 361–367. — M. R. JAMES, The Apocryphal New Testament. Oxford, 1924, 38–49.; *idem*, Latin Infancy Gospels, a New Text with a Parallel Version from Irish. Cambridge, 1927. — *German:* L. LEMME, Das Jakobus-Evangelium. Berlin, 1920. — E. HENNECKE, Neutestamentliche Apokryphen, 2nd ed. Tübingen, 1924, 84ff. — *Italian:* E. PISTELLI, Il Protevangelo di Jacopo. Lanciano, 1919.

Studies: F. HAASE, Literarkritische Untersuchungen zur orientalisch-apokryphen Evangelienliteratur. Leipzig, 1913, 49ff. — G. DURIEZ, Les apocryphes dans le drame religieux en Allemagne au moyen âge. Lille, 1914. — M. J. LAGRANGE, Un nouvel Evangile de l'Enfance édité par M. R. James: RBibl 37 (1928) 544–557. — A. JANSSENS, De H. Maagd en Moeder Gods Maria: het Dogma en de Apocriefen, 2nd ed. Amsterdam, 1930. — B. KLEINSCHMIDT, Die hl. Anna. Ihre Verehrung in Geschichte, Kunst und Volkstum. Düsseldorf, 1930. — A. E. W. BUDGE, Legends of Our Lady the Perpetual Virgin and her Mother Anna. Oxford, 1933. — A. KLAWEK, Motivum immobilitatis naturae in Protevangelio Jacobi (Polish): CT 17 (1936) 327–338. — P. VANUTELLI, Protevangelium Jacobi synoptice: Synoptica 5 (1940) 65–96. — M. J. KISHPAUGH, The Feast of the Presentation of the Virgin Mary in the Temple. An Historical and Literary Study. Washington, 1941, 1–5.

7. The Gospel of Thomas

In his *First Homily on Luke*, Origen remarks, 'There is also current the Gospel According to Thomas'. This apocryphal gospel originated in heretical, probably Gnostic, circles. Hippolytus of Rome attributes it to the Naassenes (*Philos.* 5,7), while Cyril of Jerusalem speaks of it as a Manichean product. In his *Catecheses* (4,36) Cyril says: 'And of the New Testament read the four Gospels only. The others are apocryphal and harmful. The Manicheans also wrote a Gospel According to Thomas, which though colored with the fragrance of a gospel in name, corrupts the souls of the simpler.' In *Catechesis* 6,31, he makes a similar statement: 'Let no one read the Gospel According to Thomas, for it is not by one of the twelve Apostles, but by one of the three wicked disciples of Manes.' It seems that Hippolytus has this same Gospel in mind. Hippolytus speaks of the author as one of the Naassenes, while Cyril ascribes the writing to the Manicheans. But this difficulty may be gotten over by presuming that the Manichean *Gospel of Thomas* was merely a redaction, a working over of the Gnostic *Evangelium Thomae*. At any rate, both the Manichean and the Gnostic gospel have been lost. The Infancy *Gospel According to Thomas*, which we possess in Greek, Syriac, Armenian, Slavonic, and Latin recensions, is most probably an expurgated and abbreviated edition of the original. It gives an account of the childhood of Jesus; stories of His miraculous knowledge and power are knitted together to show that Jesus was possessed of divine power before His Baptism. The daily life in a little village forms the background for these narratives, as for instance in the following story:

> This little child Jesus when he was five years old was playing at the ford of a brook: and he gathered together the waters that flowed there into pools, and made them straightway clean, and commanded them by his word alone. And having made soft clay, he fashioned thereof twelve sparrows. And it was the sabbath when he did these things (*or* made them). And there were also many other little children playing with him.

> And a certain Jew when he saw what Jesus did, playing upon the sabbath day, departed straightway and told his

father Joseph: Lo, thy child is at the brook, and he hath taken clay and fashioned twelve little birds, and hath polluted the sabbath day. And Joseph came to the place and saw: and cried out to him saying: Wherefore doest thou these things on the sabbath, which it is not lawful to do? But Jesus clapped his hands together and cried out to the sparrows and said to them: Go! and the sparrows took their flight and went away chirping. And when the Jews saw it they were amazed, and departed and told their chief men that which they had seen Jesus do (Ch. 2).

Some of the miracles do not show much taste. The author seems to have had a queer concept of divinity, because he pictures the boy Jesus as using his power to take revenge:

After that again he went through the village, and a child ran and dashed against his shoulder. And Jesus was provoked and said unto him: Thou shalt not finish thy course (*lit.* go all thy way). And immediately he fell down and died. But certain when they saw what was done said: Whence was this young child born, for that every word of his is an accomplished work? And the parents of him that was dead came unto Joseph, and blamed him, saying: Thou that hast such a child canst not dwell with us in the village: or do thou teach him to bless and not to curse: for he slayeth our children.

And Joseph called the young child apart and admonished him, saying: Wherefore doest thou such things, that these suffer and hate us and persecute us? But Jesus said: I know that these thy words are not thine: nevertheless for thy sake I will hold my peace: but they shall bear their punishment. And straightway they that accused him were smitten with blindness (49f. James).

The present expurgated form of this Infancy Gospel is probably later than the sixth century.

Editions and translations: C. TISCHENDORF, Evangelia apocrypha. 2nd ed. Leipzig, 1876, 140ff., 158ff., 164ff. — P. PEETERS, Evangiles apocryphes II. L'évangile de l'Enfance, rédactions syriaques, arabes et armén. trad. et annotées. Paris, 1914. — *English:* A. WALKER, ANF 8, 395–404. — W. HAYES, London, 1921. — M. R. JAMES, The Apocryphal New Testament. Oxford, 1924, 49–67. — *German:* E. HENNECKE, Neutestamentliche Apokryphen, 2nd ed. Tübingen, 1924, 93ff. — E. BOCK, Die Kindheit Jesu. 1924.

Studies: F. HAASE, Literarkritische Untersuchungen zur orientalisch-apokryphen Evangelienliteratur. Leipzig, 1913, 38ff. — M. R. JAMES, The Gospel of St. Thomas: JThSt 30 (1928) 51ff. — W. LÜDTKE, Die slavischen Texte des Thomas-Evangeliums: BNJ 6 (1929) 490–508.

8. *The Arabic Gospel of the Childhood of Jesus*

The *Protoevangelium of James* and the *Gospel of Thomas* have led to many other Infancy Gospels, which enlarge on the narratives of these two sources and add more stories. A striking example is offered by the so-called *Arabic Gospel of the Childhood of Jesus*. This late compilation derives the material for its first part from the *Protoevangelium*, for the final section from the *Gospel of Thomas*. But many new and strange incidents are added. Thus, this apocryphal gospel reports that Jesus, as He was lying in the cradle, said to His mother: 'I am Jesus, the Son of God, the Logos whom thou hast brought forth.'

9. *The Arabic History of Joseph, the Carpenter*

A similar work is the so-called *Arabic History of Joseph the Carpenter*. It narrates the life and death of Joseph, and the eulogy spoken over him by Jesus. The author embodies material of the *Protoevangelium*, of the *Gospel of Thomas*, which he develops and to which he makes various additions. The object of the book is the glorification of Joseph and the fostering of his cult, which was very popular in Egypt. We possess the complete text in Arabic and Bohairic, and fragments of it in Sahidic; a Latin translation was made in the fourteenth century. As for the time of composition, the gospel must have been written not before the fourth, and not later than the fifth, century.

10. *The Gospel of Philip*

Apocryphal gospels were attributed not only to Peter, James and Thomas but to the rest of the Apostles as well. Speaking of the Egyptian Gnostics of his time, Epiphanius (*Haer.* 26,13) says: "They produce a Gospel forged in the name of Philip the holy disciple, which says: The Lord revealed unto me what the soul must say as it goeth up into heaven, and how it must answer each of the Powers above. 'I have taken knowledge (it saith) of myself, and have gathered myself together out of every quarter and have not begotten children unto the Ruler, but I have rooted out his roots and gathered together the members that were scattered abroad. And I know thee who thou art, for I (it saith) am of them that are from above.' " The fragment of the *Gospel of Philip* which is here given by Epiphanius reveals a strong tendency to Gnostic asceticism, which maintained that the sparks of the divine dispersed through the material world must be reunited and delivered from the influence of matter. It seems that the Coptic book, *Pistis Sophia*, refers to this *Gospel of Philip* when it mentions that Philip the Apostle wrote down secret doctrines which the Lord taught in His conversations with His disciples after His Resurrection. From this reference the conclusion may be drawn that the gospel was in existence in the third century.

11. *The Gospel of Matthias*

Origen (*Hom. I on Luke*) states that a Gospel according to Matthias was known at his time. M. R. James and O. Bardenhewer think that the *Traditions of Matthias* which Clement of Alexandria mentions may be identical with this gospel. Others, like O. Stählin and J. Tixeront doubt this. The passages of Clement are the following: 'The beginning (of truth) is to wonder at things, as Plato says in the *Theaetetus*, and Matthias in the *Traditions*, advising us: Wonder thou at the things that are before thee, making this the first step to further knowledge' (*Strom.* 2,9,45). 'They (the Gnostics around Basilides) say that Matthias also taught thus: that we should fight with the flesh and abuse it, not yielding to it at all for licentious pleasure, but should make the soul grow by faith and knowledge' (*Strom.* 3,4,26). 'They say that in the *Traditions*, Matthias the Apostle said that on every occasion, if the neighbor of a chosen one sin, the chosen one hath sinned: for had he behaved himself as the word enjoins, the neighbor also would have been ashamed of his way of life, so as not to sin' (*Strom.* 7,13,82).

Whether or not these passages of the *Traditions of Matthias* once formed part of the *Gospel of Matthias*, the latter must have been written before the time of Origen.

12. The Gospel According to Barnabas

Nothing of this Gospel has been preserved. We know of it from the *Gelasian Decree* of the sixth century, which lists it among the apocrypha; it also occurs in the Greek *List of the Sixty Books* of the seventh or eighth century. An entirely different work, however, is the Italian *Gospel of Barnabas*, which Lonsdale and Laura Ragg published in 1907. This latter work was written by a Christian of the fourteenth century who apostatized to Islam, and its principal aim is to prove that Mohammed was the Messias and that Islam is the only true religion.

13. The Gospel of Bartholomew

This gospel is mentioned by Jerome in the Prologue to his *Commentary on Matthew*, and by the *Gelasian Decree*. It is most probably identical with the *Questions of Bartholomew*, which we know was originally composed in Greek. Besides two Greek manuscripts, one at Vienna, one at Jerusalem, we possess fragments of the *Questions of Bartholomew* in Slavonic, Coptic and Latin versions. It contains in the form of answers to questions of Bartholomew revelations by the Lord after his resurrection and an account of the annunciation by Mary. Even Satan appears and replies to Bartholomew's investigations regarding the sin and downfall of the angels, and the *Descensus ad Inferos* is described in detail.

Editions and translations: A. VASILIEV, Anecdota Graeco-byzantina I. Moscow, 1893. — N. BONWETSCH, Die apokryphen Fragen des Bartholomäus: NGWG Phil.-Hist. Kl. (1897) 1–42 gives the Greek and Slavonic texts. — E. REVIL-LOUT, Evangile de St. Barthélémy: PO 2 (Paris, 1907) 185–198. — A. WILMART et E. TISSERANT, Fragments grecs et latins de l'Evangile de Barthélémy: RBibl 19 (1913) 161–190; 321ff. — U. MORICCA, Un nuovo testo dell'Evangelo di Bartolommeo: RBibl 30 (1921) 489f.; 31 (1922) 20ff. gives the complete Latin version. — The *Coptic* text with an *English translation* in: E. A. BUDGE, Coptic apocrypha. London, 1913, 1ff., 179ff., 216ff. — *English translation:* M. R. JAMES, The Apocryphal New Testament. Oxford, 1924, 166–186. — A *Syriac* fragment was published by F. S. MARSH, JThSt 23 (1922) 400 ff.

Studies: F. HAASE, Zur Rekonstruktion des Bartholomäusevangeliums: ZNW 16 (1915) 93ff. — J. KROLL, Gott und Hölle. Der Mythos vom Descensus-kampfe. Leipzig-Berlin, 1932, 71–82.

14. *Other Apocryphal Gospels*

Since it was the practice of the heretical sects, especially the Gnostics, to write gospels in support of their peculiar doctrines, there existed a large number of such apocrypha. Most of them we know only by name, as for instance:

1. *The Gospel of Andrew.* It was probably of Gnostic origin, and St. Augustine seems to refer to it (*Contra Adversarios Legis et Prophetarum*, 1,20).

2. *The Gospel of Judas Iscariot*, which was used by the Gnostic sect of the Cainites.

3. *The Gospel of Thaddeus*, which is listed in the *Gelasian Decree*.

4. *The Gospel of Eve*: Epiphanius tells us that this circulated among the Borborites, an Ophite sect of the Gnostics.

Some of these gospels have the names of famous heretics, for instance:

5. *The Gospel according to Basilides*: Origen says that this heretic 'had the audacity' to write a gospel, and this work is mentioned by Ambrose and Jerome. It is possible that Basilides reworked the canonical Gospels to make them favorable to Gnostic doctrine.

6. *The Gospel of Cerinthus*, which is mentioned by Epiphanius.

7. *The Gospel of Valentinus*: Tertullian is the source for our knowledge of this work.

8. *The Gospel of Apelles*, to which Jerome and Epiphanius refer.

A common feature of all these Gnostic gospels is their arbitrary treatment of the canonical material. The narratives of the canonical Gospels are used as a framework for Gnostic revelations, which are given by the Lord or by Mary in conversations with the disciples of Jesus after His Resurrection. On account of the cosmological speculations they contain, these gospels assume a certain apocalyptic character. For this reason they have been called *Gospel-Apocalypses*.

III.   THE APOCRYPHAL ACTS OF THE APOSTLES

The apocryphal Acts of the Apostles have this in common with the apocryphal gospels that they too try to furnish information lacking in the New Testament. Just as the gospels invent material to fill out the life of Jesus and His parents, so the Acts of the Apostles recount the life and death of the Apostles in a manner reminiscent of pagan romances. Apparently, the design of creating a popular literature to displace the erotic pagan narratives had an important role in the formation of these apocryphal acts. They revel in adventure and descriptions of foreign countries and strange peoples; their heroes pass through all kinds of dangers. Even more than on the apocryphal gospels the influence of current fairy tales, of folklore, and legends can be seen. But sometimes an historical tradition appears at the bottom of all these miraculous and fantastic stories. Such is the case, for instance, when the *Acts of Peter and Paul* report the martyrdom of both Apostles at Rome, or when the *Acts of John* mention John's residence at Ephesus.

Although most of these Acts reveal heretical tendencies, they are of great importance for the history of the Church and the history of culture. They throw considerable light on the history of Christian worship in the second and third centuries; they describe the earliest forms of religious services in private homes; they contain hymns and prayers which constitute the beginnings of Christian poetry. They reflect as well the ascetic ideals of the common heretical sects, and show the syncretism in Gnostic circles of Christian beliefs with pagan ideas and superstitions. M. R. James says, 'Among the prayers and discourses of the apostles in the spurious Acts, some utterances may be found which are remarkable and even beautiful; not a few of the stories are notable and imaginative and have been consecrated and made familiar to us by the genius of mediæval artists. But the authors do not speak with the voices of Paul or of John, or with the quiet simplicity of the three first Gospels. It is not unfair to say that when they attempt the former tone, they are theatrical, and when they essay the latter, they are jejune. In short, the result of anything like an attentive study of the literature, in bulk and in detail, is an added respect for the sense of the Catholic Church, and for the wisdom of the scholars of Alexandria, Antioch, and Rome: assuredly in this case, they were tried money-changers, who proved all things and held fast that which was good.'

The real authors of these Acts are unknown. Since the fifth century a certain Leukios is mentioned as the author of heretical Acts of the Apostles. Photios (*Bibl. cod.* 114) names a Leukios

Charinos as author of a collection of Acts of Peter, Paul, Andrew, Thomas, and John. It seems, however, that Leukios was first regarded as author of the *Acts of John* only; later on, all heretical Acts were attributed to him. To avoid the spread of heretical doctrines by these Acts, some of them were rewritten by Catholic authors. Thus the lack of canonical reports regarding the missionary travels of the Apostles was made up for. Many lections of the Roman Breviary for the feasts of the Apostles are based on these Acts.

Editions: Greek Texts: R. A. LIPSIUS and M. BONNET, Acta Apostolorum Apocrypha. Leipzig, vol. I, 1891; vol. II, 1, 1898; vol. II, 2, 1903. — *Syriac version:* W. WRIGHT, Apocryphal Acts of the Apostles. Text and translation. 2 vols. London, 1871. — *Ethiopic version:* E. A. W. BUDGE, The Contendings of the Apostles. Text and translation. 2 vols. London, 1901. — *Arabic version:* A. SMITH LEWIS, The Mythological Acts of the Apostles (Horae Semiticae IV). Cambridge, 1904. — *Armenian version:* P. VETTER, OC 1901, 217ff; 1903, 16ff, 324ff; ThQ 1906, 161ff. *Coptic version:* I. GUIDI, Frammenti copti. Rome, 1888; *idem,* Gli atti apocrifi degli apostoli nei testi copti, arabi ed etiopici: Giornale della società Asiatica Italiana 3 (1888) 1–66 gives an Italian translation. — O. v. LEMM, Koptische apokryphe Apostelakten: Bulletin de l'académie des sciences de St. Pétersbourg, Nouvelle série 1,33 (1890) 509–581; 3,35 (1892) 233–326.

Studies: R. A. LIPSIUS, Die apokryphen Apostelgeschichten und Apostellegenden. 2 vols. and Suppl. Braunschweig, 1883–90. — J. E. WEIS-LIEBERSDORF, Christus- und Apostelbilder. Einfluss der Apokryphen auf die ältesten Kunsttypen. Freiburg i. B., 1902. — F. PIONTEK, Die katholische Kirche und die haeretischen Apostelgeschichten bis zum Ausgang des sechsten Jahrh. (Kirchengesch. Abhandlungen, hersg. von M. Sdralek VI, 1–71). Breslau, 1908. — B. PICK, The Apocryphal Acts of Paul, Peter, John, Andrew and Thomas. Chicago, 1909. — F. HAASE, Apostel und Evangelisten in den orientalischen Ueberlieferungen. Leipzig, 1922. — H. LJUNGVIK, Studien zur Sprache der apokryphen Apostelgeschichten. Diss. Uppsala. Lundequist, 1926. — R. SÖDER, Die apokryphen Apostelgeschichten und die Literatur der Antike (Würzburger Studien zur Altertumswissenschaft 3). Stuttgart, 1932. — M. BLUMENTHAL, Formen und Motive in den apokryphen Apostelgeschichten (TU 48,1). Leipzig, 1933.

1.   *The Acts of Paul* (Πράξεις Παύλου)

In his treatise *On Baptism* (ch. 17) Tertullian remarks, 'But, if the writings which wrongly go under Paul's name claim Thecla's example as a license for women's teaching and baptizing, let them know that in Asia the presbyter who composed them as if he were augmenting Paul's fame from his own store, after being convicted and confessing that he had done it from love of Paul, was removed from his office.' From these words it seems clear that certain *Acts of Paul* circulated before Tertullian's time, and that their author was a priest of Asia Minor whose suspension must have taken place before the year 190 A.D. Not until C. Schmidt in the year 1904 published the fragment of a Coptic translation of these Acts in a papyrus of the University of Heidelberg was it possible to determine the whole content and extent of these Acts.

This Coptic version proved especially that three writings which we knew long before as independent treatises were originally simply parts of the Acts of Paul. These are 1) the *Acts of Paul and Thecla*, 2) the *Correspondence of St. Paul with the Corinthians*, and 3) the *Martyrdom of St. Paul*.

1. The so-called Greek *Acta Pauli et Theclae* (Πράξεις Παύλου καὶ Θέκλης). St. Jerome (*De vir. ill.* 7) calls them *Periodi Pauli et Theclae*. They contain the story of Thecla, a Greek girl from Iconium who had been converted by Paul's preaching. She breaks off her engagement and follows the Apostle, assisting him in his missionary work. She escapes persecutions and death in a miraculous way, and retires finally to Seleucia. The narrative has all the appearances of fiction and seems to be without any historical foundation. Nevertheless the cult of St. Thecla became very popular and spread over the East and West. In fact, her name occurs in the prayer for the departing soul (*Proficiscere*) in the Roman Ritual. It cannot be stated with certainty whether the Acts account for her veneration, or whether the story contains a historical nucleus. The Greek text of these Acts has been preserved in a number of manuscripts. There are five Latin and a great many Oriental translations extant.

The content of this novel has had and still has a great influence on Christian literature and art. The description of Paul given in ch. 3 set the type for this Apostle's portraits from an early time: 'And he saw Paul coming, a man little of stature, with bald head and bent legs, strong, with eyebrows joining and nose somewhat hooked, full of charm; sometimes he appeared like a man, and at others he had the face of an angel.'

2. *The Correspondence of St. Paul with the Corinthians*, which forms

another part of the *Acta Pauli*, contains the answer of the Corinthians to his second letter, and the third letter of the Apostle addressed to them. Cf. Apocryphal Letters, p. 155.

3. In addition, the *Acts of Paul* include the *Martyrium* or *Passio Pauli*. The text is preserved in two Greek manuscripts, in an incomplete Latin translation, and in Syriac, Coptic, Ethiopic and Slavonic versions. The contents are legendary. The work deals with Paul's preaching and missionary work in Rome, the persecution of Nero, and the execution of the Apostle. The description of his death which is given here has strongly influenced Christian art and liturgy: 'Then Paul stood with his face to the east and lifted up his hands unto heaven, and prayed a long time, and in his prayers he conversed in the Hebrew tongue with the Fathers, and then stretched forth his neck without speaking. And when the executioner struck off his head, milk spurted upon the cloak of the soldier.' After his death Paul appears to the Emperor and prophesies the judgment to come upon him. The idea of Christ the King and the *militia Christi* is very pronounced throughout this work. He is called the 'Eternal King' and the 'King of the Ages', and the Christians are 'soldiers of the great King'. The clash of the worship of Christ with the cult of the Roman Emperor is clearly depicted.

The recent discovery of a major portion of the Acts in the original Greek text proved that C. Schmidt's conclusion as to the original form of the Acts was correct. Eleven pages of a papyrus written about A.D. 300, which is now at Hamburg, have given us a large part of the text which was lacking.

Editions: The Greek text is found in C. TISCHENDORF, Acta apostolorum apocrypha, 40ff. and R. A. LIPSIUS-M. BONNET, Acta apostolorum apocrypha I. Leipzig, 1891, 235–272. — Greek papyrus fragments with translations were published by W. SCHUBART and C. SCHMIDT, Πράξεις Παύλου Acta Pauli. Nach dem Papyrus der Hamburger Staats- und Universitätsbibliothek, Hamburg, 1936. Cf C. SCHMIDT, Neue Funde zu den alten Πράξεις Παύλου: SAB 94 (1929) 176–83; *idem*, Ein Berliner Fragment der alten Πράξεις Παύλου: SAB 96 (1931) 37–41. — *Latin versions:* O. v. GEBHARDT, Passio S. Theclae virginis (TU 22,2). Leipzig, 1902. — *Coptic versions:* E. J. GOODSPEED, The Book of Thekla: The American Journal of Semitic Languages and Literature 17 (1901) 65–95 with English translation. — C. SCHMIDT, Acta Pauli, 2nd ed. Leipzig, 1905; *idem*, Ein neues Fragment der Heidelberger Acta Pauli: SAB (1909) 216ff. — *Syriac version* (with English translation): W. WRIGHT, Apocryphal Acts of the Apostles. London, 1871, vol. I, 128–169; vol. II, 116–145.

Translations: English: A.WALKER, ANF 8, 487–492. — B. PICK, The Apocryphal Acts of Paul, Peter, John, Andrew and Thomas. Chicago, 1909. — M. R. JAMES, The Apocryphal New Testament. Oxford, 1924, 270–299. — *French:* L. VOUAUX, Les Actes de Paul et ses lettres apocryphes. Introduction, textes, traduction et commentaire (Les apocryphes du Nouveau Testament). Paris, 1913. — *Italian:* M. ZAPPALÀ, Il romanzo di Paolo e Tecla. Milan, 1924. — *German:* E. HENNECKE, Neutestamentliche Apokryphen. 2nd ed. Tübingen, 1924.

Studies: J. GWYN, Thecla, in Dictionary of Christian Biography, vol. 4, London, 1887, 882–896. — W. M. RAMSAY, The Church in the Roman Empire before A.D. 170. 2nd ed. London, 1893, 375–428. — F. C. CONYBEARE, The Armenian Apology and Acts of Apollonius and Other Monuments of Early Christianity. 2nd ed. London, 1896, 49–88. — A. HARNACK, Drei wenig beachtete Cyprianische Schriften und die Acta Pauli (TU 19,3). Leipzig, 1899. — C. HOLZHEY, Die Thekla-Akten. Ihre Verbreitung und Beurteilung in der Kirche (Veröffentlichungen aus dem kirchengeschichtlichen Seminar München 2,7). Munich, 1905. — M. R. JAMES, A Note on the Acta Pauli: JThSt 6 (1905) 244. — C. F. M. DEELEMAN, Acta Pauli et Theclae: ThStKr (1908) 273–301. — F. ROSTALSKI, Die Sprache der griechischen Paulusakten mit Berücksichtigung ihrer lateinischen Uebersetzungen. Progr. Myslowitz, 1913. — A. SOUTER, The Acta Pauli in Tertullian: JThSt 25 (1924) 292f. — F. J. DÖLGER, Der heidnische Glaube an die Wirkungskraft des Fürbittgebetens für die vorzeitig Gestorbenen nach den Theklaakten: AC 2 (1930) 13–16. — F. LOOFS, Theophilus von Antiochien Adv. Marcionem und die andern theol. Quellen bei Irenäus. Leipzig, 1930, 148–157. — H. A. SANDERS, A Fragment of the *Acta Pauli* in the Michigan Collection: HThR 31 (1938) 73–90. — J. DE ZWAAN, Een papyrus van de Acta Pauli: Nederlandsch Archief voor Kerkgeschiedenis (1938) 48–57. — A. KURFESS, Zu dem Hamburger Papyrus der Πράξεις Παύλου: ZNW 38 (1939) 164–170. — E. PETERSON, Einige Bemerkungen zum Hamburger Papyrus-Fragment der Acta Pauli: VC 3 (1949) 142–162.

2. The Acts of Peter

The Acts of Peter were composed about the year 190. The author seems to have lived in Syria or Palestine rather than in Rome. We do not possess the complete text, but about two-thirds of it have been recovered from various sources.

1. The main part of the Acts is extant in a Latin translation, which was found in a manuscript at Vercelli (*Actus Vercellenses*). This version, entitled *Actus Petri cum Simone*, reports 1) how Paul takes leave of the Roman Christians and sets out for Spain, 2) how Simon Magus comes to Rome and embarrasses the Christians with his apparent miracles, 3) how Peter travels to Rome and triumphs over the magician, who dies in an attempt to fly from

the Roman forum to heaven. The document concludes with an account of the martyrdom of Peter.

In determining the intellectual milieu of the author, it is important that in Chapter 2 the Acts mention St. Paul celebrating the Eucharist with bread and water: 'Now they brought unto Paul bread and water for the sacrifice, that he might make prayer and distribute it to every one.' This fact points to an author who shares the Docetic views. The same sectarian influence can be seen in Peter's preaching against matrimony, and his prevailing upon wives to leave their husbands.

2. The *Martyrdom of St. Peter*, which forms the third part of the *Actus Vercellenses*, is extant also in the original Greek (Μαρτύριον τοῦ ἁγίου ἀποστόλου Πέτρου). It contains the story of the 'Domine, quo vadis?' As Peter feels compelled to leave Rome, he meets Jesus. 'And when he saw him, he said: Lord, whither goest thou? And the Lord said unto him: I go into Rome to be crucified. And Peter said unto him: Lord, art thou being crucified again? He said unto him: Yes, Peter, I am being crucified again. And Peter came to himself, and having beheld the Lord ascending up into Heaven, he returned to Rome, rejoicing and glorifying the Lord, for that he said: I am being crucified, which was about to befall Peter' (ch. 35, p. 333 James). The story continues with Peter's condemnation to death by the prefect Agrippa. He is crucified head downward, at his own request. Before his death, he delivers a long sermon on the cross and its symbolic meaning, which again shows Gnostic influence.

3. The *Martyrium beati Petri Apostoli a Lino conscriptum* does not belong to the same author. It was written in Latin, probably in the sixth century. The author, consequently, cannot have been the first successor of St. Peter, Linus, to whom it is attributed. The story is purely legendary. It follows the original martyrdom as given in the *Actus Vercellenses*, but adds some details, for instance, the names of Processus and Martinian, Peter's jailers.

Editions: R. A. Lipsius-M. Bonnet, Acta apostolorum apocrypha I. Leipzig, 1891, 1–22; 45–103. — A. H. Salonius, Martyrium beati Petri apostoli a Lino episcopo conscriptum. Helsingfors, 1926. — L. Vouaux, Les actes de Pierre. Paris, 1922, gives an edition of all texts with a French translation. — *English translations:* B. Pick, The Apocryphal Acts of Paul, Peter, John, Andrew and Thomas. Chicago, 1909. — M. R. James, The Apocryphal New

Testament. Oxford, 1924, 300–336. — *German:* E. HENNECKE, Neutestamentliche Apokryphen. 2nd ed. Tübingen, 1924, 226–249.
Studies: G. FICKER, Die Petrusakten. Leipzig, 1903. — C. SCHMIDT, Die alten
Petrusakten im Zusammenhang mit der apokryphen Apostelliteratur untersucht (TU 9,1). Leipzig, 1903. — A. STRUCKMANN, Die Gegenwart Christi
in der hl. Eucharistie nach den schriftlichen Quellen der vornicänischen Zeit.
Wien, 1905, 105–109. — C. F. M. DEELEMAN, Acta Petri: Geloof en Vrijheid
44 (1910) 193–244. — C. ERBES, Ursprung und Umfang der Petrusakten:
ZKG 32 (1911) 161–185; 353–377; 497–530. — J. N. REAGAN, The Preaching
of Peter. Chicago, 1923. — G. STUHLFAUT, Die apokryphen Petrusgeschichten
in der altchristlichen Kunst. Berlin, 1925. — C. SCHMIDT, Studien zu den
alten Petrusakten: ZKG 47 (1926) 481–513; *idem,* Studien zu den Pseudo-
Clementinen (TU 46,1). Leipzig, 1929; *idem,* Zur Datierung der alten
Petrusakten: ZNW 29 (1930) 150–155. — J. T. SHOTWELL and L. ROPES
LOOMIS, The See of Peter. New York, 1927, 133–153. — C. H. TURNER, The
Latin Acts of Peter: JThSt 32 (1931) 119–133. — D. DE BRUYNE, Deux
citations apocryphes de l'Apôtre Pierre: JThSt 34 (1933) 395–396. — G.
BOTTOMLEY, The Acts of St. Peter. London, 1933. — J. QUASTEN, Monumenta
eucharistica et liturgica vetustissima. Bonn, 1935—37, 341. — H. DANNEN-
BAUER, Nochmals die römische Petruslegende: HZ 159 (1938) 81–88. —
E. FASCHER, PWK 19 (1938) 1377–1381.

3. The Acts of Peter and Paul

Quite different and distinct from the *Acts of Paul* and the *Acts
of Peter*, both of which have just been mentioned, are the *Acts of
Peter and Paul* (Πράξεις τῶν ἁγίων ἀποστόλων Πέτρου καὶ Παύλου),
which stress the close relationship and companionship between
the two Apostles. The text begins with Paul's journey from the
island of Gaudomelete to Rome, and then relates the apostolic
work and the martyrdom of both Apostles in that city. The
author evidently used the canonical Acts of the Apostles as a
basis for his description of Paul's journey. It is possible that he
intended his work to supersede heretical Acts. The writing originated perhaps in the third century. It shows scarcely any signs
of heretical influence. The Acts are extant in Greek and Latin
fragments.

4. The Acts of John

The *Acts of John* are the earliest of all the Apocryphal Acts
of the Apostles which we possess. They were composed in Asia
Minor between 150 and 180. Although there is no complete text

extant, we have a considerable part of the Greek original, sup-
plemented for several episodes by a Latin version. The work purports to give an eye-witness account of the missionary travels
of John in Asia Minor. It narrates his miracles and sermons and
his death. The sermons of the Apostle evince unmistakably Docetic tendencies, especially the description of Jesus and the im-
materiality of his body, as for instance in ch. 93: 'Sometimes
when I would lay hold on him, I met with a material and solid
body, and at other times again, when I felt him, the substance
was immaterial, and as if it existed not at all.' The hymn to the
Father which Jesus sings with his Apostles before he goes to die
is in its expression and in its structure colored by Gnosticism.
The author shows a weakness for strange stories like that of
Drusiana, and humorous incidents. The ethics which the Acts
reveal are those of popular philosophy. Nevertheless, the Acts
are very valuable for the history of Christianity. They are, for
instance, the oldest source recording the celebration of the Eucharist for the dead: 'Now on the next day, John came, accompanied by Andronicus and the brethren, to the sepulchre at dawn,
it being now the third day from Drusiana's death, that we might
break bread there' (ch. 72). In ch. 85 the Eucharistic prayer
which the Apostle uses for this funeral service is given: 'And
having thus said, John took bread and bare it into the sepulchre
to break it, and said:

We glorify thy name,
which converteth us from error and ruthless deceit:
we glorify thee who hast shown before our eyes
that which we have seen:
we bear witness to Thy loving kindness
which appeared in diverse ways:
we praise Thy merciful name, O Lord,
who hast convicted them
that are convicted of Thee:
we give thanks to Thee, O Lord Jesus Christ,
that we are persuaded of Thy grace which is unchanging:
we give thanks to Thee
who hadst need of our nature that should be saved:
we give thanks to Thee that hast given us this sure faith,
for Thou art God alone, both now and ever.

We Thy servants give Thee thanks, O Holy One,
who are assembled with good intent
and are gathered out of the world.

Editions: TH. ZAHN, Acta Joannis. Erlangen, 1880. — M. R. JAMES, Apocrypha anecdota. Ser. 3. Cambridge, 1897, 1-25. — R. A. LIPSIUS-M. BONNET, Acta apostolorum apocrypha II, 1. Leipzig, 1898, 151-216.
Translations: English: A. WALKER, ANF 8, 560-564. — B. PICK, The Apocryphal Acts of Paul, Peter, John, Andrew and Thomas. Chicago, 1909. — M. R. JAMES, The Apocryphal New Testament. Oxford, 1924, 228-269. — *German:* E. HENNECKE, Neutestamentliche Apokryphen. 2nd ed. Tübingen, 1924, 171-191.

Studies: TH. ZAHN, Die Wanderungen des Apostels Johannes: NKZ 10 (1899) 191-218. — A. SCHEIWILER, Die Elemente der Eucharistie in den ersten drei Jahrhunderten (FLDG 3,4). Mainz, 1903, 132-165. — A. STRUCKMANN, Die Gegenwart Christi in der hl. Eucharistie nach den schriftlichen Quellen der vornicänischen Zeit. Wien, 1905, 90-114. — W. BOUSSET, Hauptprobleme der Gnosis. Göttingen, 1907, 276-319. — R. H. CONNOLLY, The Original Language of the Syrian Acts of John: JThSt 8 (1907) 249-261. — R. H. CONNOLLY, The Diatessaron in the Syrian Acts of John: JThSt 8 (1907) 571f. — V. C. MACMUNN, The Menelaus Episode in the Syriac Acts of John: JThSt 12 (1911) 463-65. — F. J. DÖLGER, $IX\ThetaY\Sigma$ II. Münster, 1922, 552-560. — H. LIETZMANN, Messe und Herrenmahl. Bonn, 1926, 240-243. — E. FREISTEDT, Altchristliche Totengedächtnistage und ihre Beziehungen zum Jenseitsglauben und Totenkultus der Antike (LQF 24). Münster, 1928, 1—3. — H. STREETER, The Primitive Church Studied with Special Reference to the Origins of the Christian Ministry. London, 1929, Appendix 5. — P. BATIFFOL, L'Eucharistie. La présence réelle et la transsubstantiation. 9th ed. Paris, 1930, 189-203. — J. QUASTEN, Monumenta eucharistica et liturgica vetustissima. Bonn, 1935, 339-341. — A. C. RUSH, Death and Burial in Christian Antiquity (SCA 1). Washington, 1941, 262-264.

5. *The Acts of Andrew*

Eusebius mentions (*Hist. eccl.* 3,25,6), besides the *Acts of John*, *Acts of Andrew* as put forward by heretics. 'To none of these' he says, 'has any who belonged to the succession of the orthodox ever thought it right to refer in his writings. Moreover, the type of phraseology differs from Apostolic style, and the opinion and tendency of their contents are widely dissonant from true orthodoxy, and clearly show that they are the forgeries of heretics.'

The author of these *Acts of Andrew* is thought to be Leukios Charinos, who wrote them perhaps about the year 260. There are only a few fragments extant today which contain the following episodes:

1. The story of Andrew and Matthias among the cannibals on the Black Sea, which we possess in Latin, Syriac, Coptic, and Armenian versions, and in the Anglo-Saxon poem Andreas, ascribed to Cynewulf.

2. The story of Peter and Andrew.

3. The martyrdom of Andrew in the city of Patrai in Achaia, which was composed after 400 A.D. In form this document is an encyclical writing of the priests and deacons of Achaia about the death of Andrew. It is extant in Greek and Latin, and seems to have no connection with the Gnostic Acts of Andrew which Eusebius condemns.

4. Another fragment preserved in *Codex Vaticanus graec.* 808 reports the sufferings of Andrew in Achaia, and the discourses which he delivered in prison in Patrai.

5. An account of the martyrdom of St. Andrew, which has reached us in a number of recensions.

There is one thing which all these narrations have in common: before his death Andrew addresses the cross on which he is going to die in a long sermon which reminds us of a similar oration in the *Acts of Peter.* Just as in the *Acts of Peter,* so also in these *Acts of Andrew,* renunciation of marriage is recommended by the Apostle. This leads to similar conflicts with husbands and with the pagan authorities, and ultimately to the death of the Apostle.

R. A. Lipsius-M. Bonnet, Acta apostolorum apocrypha II, 1. Leipzig, 1898, 1–127. — M. N. Speranskij, Die apokryphen Akten des Apostels Andreas in den altrussischen Texten. Moscow, 1894 (in Russian). — J. Flamion, Les Actes apocryphes de l'apôtre André. Les Actes d'André et de Mathias, de Pierre et d'André et les textes apparentés. Louvain, 1911. — F. Blatt, Die lateinischen Bearbeitungen der Acta Andreae et Matthiae apud anthropophagos. Mit sprachl. Kommentar. Giessen, 1930. — A. Walker, ANF 8, 511–527. — B. Pick, The Apocryphal Acts of Paul, Peter, John, Andrew and Thomas. Chicago, 1909. — M. R. James, The Apocryphal New Testament. Oxford, 1924, 337–363. — E. Hennecke, Neutestamentliche Apokryphen. 2nd ed. Tübingen, 1924, 249–256. — L. Rademacher, Zu den Acta Andreae et Matthiae: WSt (1930) 108.

6. The Acts of Thomas

The *Acts of Thomas* are the only apocryphal Acts of which we possess the complete text. They were written in Syriac in the first half of the third century. The author most probably belonged to the sect of Bardaisan at Edessa. Shortly after their composition they were translated into Greek, and of this translation we possess a number of manuscripts. Also extant are an Armenian, an Ethiopic, and two different Latin versions.

The Acts picture Thomas as missionary and Apostle of India. His adventures and experiences on his journey to this country are given in detail. In India he converts King Gundafor. After many miracles he dies the death of a martyr.

The whole story consists of fourteen Acts. Although the existence of an Indian King of the name of Gundafor in the first century has been ascertained, all attempts to prove the story of Thomas' missionary work in India an historical fact have failed so far. The Acts reveal their Gnostic origin and partly Manichean tendency clearly. Their ascetic ideal is like that of the Acts of Andrew and Peter. Marriage is renounced and wives are persuaded to leave their husbands. The Acts contain several liturgical hymns of considerable beauty. Most remarkable is the hymn of the soul or of the redemption, which is most probably older than the Acts, and seems to have been forced into the narrative. The song pictures Christ as the son of the king, who was sent from his native country in the east to Egypt in the west to defeat the dragon and get the pearl. After this he returns to the light of his country in the east. The country in the east is heaven or paradise, from which Christ descends into the sinful world to redeem the soul entangled in matter.

Editions: Greek: R. A. LIPSIUS-M. BONNET, Acta apostolorum apocrypha II. Leipzig, 1903, 99–288. A later Greek recension was published by M. R. JAMES, Apocrypha anecdota, ser. 2. Cambridge, 1897, 27–45. An extract of the eleventh century from the Greek text was edited by M. BONNET, Actes de S. Thomas apôtre. Le poeme de l'âme. Version grecque remaniée par Nicétas de Thessalonique: AB 20 (1901) 159–164. — The *Syriac* original was edited and translated by W. WRIGHT, Apocryphal Acts of the Apostles. London, 1871, vol. 1: The Syriac texts, 171–333; vol. 2: The English translation, 146–298. The Syriac text is found also in: P. BEDJAN, Acta Martyrum et Sanctorum 3. Paris, 1892, 1–175. Fragments of the Syriac text in a manuscript of the fifth to the sixth century were edited and translated by F. C.

BURKITT in: Studia Sinaiticu 9. London, 1900, 23–44. Older fragments were published by A. SMITH LEWIS, The Mythological Acts of the Apostles (Horae Semiticae 4). Cambridge, 1904.

Translations: English: A. WALKER, ANF 8, 535–552. — B. PICK, The Apocryphal Acts of Paul, Peter, John, Andrew and Thomas. Chicago, 1909. — M. R. JAMES, The Apocryphal New Testament. Oxford, 1924, 364–438. — *German:* E. HENNECKE, Neutestamentliche Apokryphen. 2nd ed. Tübingen, 1924, 256–289. For other translations see above, p. 108.

Studies: K. MACKE, Syrische Lieder gnostischen Ursprungs, eine Studie über die apokryphen syrischen Thomasakten: ThQ 56 (1874) 1–70; *idem*, Hymnen aus dem Zweiströmeland. Mainz, 1882, 246–259. — A. A. BEVAN, The Hymn of the Soul, contained in the Syriac Acts of St. Thomas (Texts and Studies, 5,3). Cambridge, 1897. — G. HOFFMANN, Zwei Hymnen der Thomasakten: ZNW 4 (1903) 273–309. — A. E. MEDLYCOTT, India and the Apostle Thomas. An Inquiry with a Critical Analysis of the Acta Thomae. London, 1905. — W. BOUSSET, Hauptprobleme der Gnosis. Göttingen, 1907, 276–319. — F. HAASE, Zur bardesanischen Gnosis. Leipzig, 1910, 50–67. — F. ROSTALSKI, Sprachliches zu den apokryphen Apostelgeschichten. I. Teil: Die casus obliqui in den Thomasakten. Programm Myslowitz, 1911. — J. DAHLMANN, Die Thomaslegende und die ältesten historischen Beziehungen des Christentums zum fernen Osten. Freiburg i. B., 1912. — F. MARTINEZ, L'ascétisme chrétien pendant les trois premiers siècles. Paris, 1913, 54–72. — G. P. WETTER, Altchristliche Liturgien I. Göttingen, 1921, 89ff. — J. KROLL, Die frühchristliche Hymnodik bis zu Klemens von Alexandreia: Programm der Akademie von Braunsberg (1921–22) 52ff. — A. VÄTH, Der hl. Thomas, der Apostel Indiens. 2nd ed. Aachen, 1925. — H. LIETZMANN, Messe und Herrenmahl. Bonn, 1926, 243–247. — E. BUONAIUTI, Le origini dell' ascetismo cristiano. Pinerolo, 1928, 109–122. — J. KROLL, Gott und Hölle. Leipzig, 1932, 30–34. — T. K. JOSEPH, A Query, St. Thomas in Parthia or India?: Indian Antiquary 61 (1933) 159; *idem*, The St. Thomas Traditions of South India: Bulletin of the International Committee of Historical Research 5 (1933) 560–569. — G. BORNKAMM, Mythos und Legende in den apokryphen Thomasakten. Göttingen, 1933; *idem*, PWK II, 6 316–323. — R. H. CONNOLLY, A Negative Golden Rule in the Syriac Acts of Thomas: JThSt 36 (1935) 353–357. — D. S. MARGOLIOUTH, Some Problems in the Acta Judae Thomae: Essays in Honour of Gilbert Murray, 1936, 249–259. — J. QUASTEN, Monumenta eucharistica et liturgica vetustissima. Bonn, 1935–37, 341–345. — E. G. PANTELAKIS, Αἱ ἀρχαὶ τῆς ἐκκλησιαστικῆς ποιήσεως: Θεολογία 16 (1938) 5–31. — J. QUASTEN, The Painting of the Good Shepherd at Dura-Europos: Mediaeval Studies 9 (1947) 1–18.

7. *The Acts of Thaddaeus*

In his *Ecclesiastical History* (1,13), Eusebius indicates that he knew the *Acts of Thaddaeus*, which were composed in Syria. According to him, they narrated that King Abgar of Edessa, when he heard of Jesus and his miracles, sent a letter to him asking him to come and heal his terrible disease. Jesus did not give heed to his request, but he answered the king in a letter, in which he promised to send one of his disciples. In fact, after the resurrection, Thomas the Apostle was divinely moved to send to Edessa Thaddaeus, one of the seventy disciples of the Lord. Thaddaeus healed the king of his sickness and all Edessa was converted to Christianity. Eusebius translated the correspondence between Jesus and King Abgar from the Syriac into Greek. He tells us that he took his text from the archives at Edessa. Here is his report:

There is also documentary evidence of these things taken from the archives at Edessa which was at that time a capital city. At least, in the public documents there, which contain the things done in antiquity and at the time of Abgar, these things too are found preserved from that time to this; but there is nothing equal to hearing the letters themselves, which we have extracted from the archives, and when translated from the Syriac they are verbally as follows:

A copy of a letter written by Abgar the Toparch to Jesus and sent to him to Jerusalem by the courier Ananias:

'Abgar Uchama, the Toparch, to Jesus the Good Saviour who has appeared in the district of Jerusalem, greeting. I have heard concerning you and your cures, how they are accomplished by you without drugs and herbs. For, as the story goes, you make the blind recover their sight, the lame walk, and you cleanse lepers and cast out unclean spirits and demons, and you cure those who are tortured by long disease and you raise dead men. And when I heard all these things concerning you I decided that it is one of the two, either that you are God, and came down from heaven to do these things, or are a Son of God for doing these things. For this reason I write to beg you to hasten to me and to heal the suffering which I have. Moreover I heard that the Jews are mocking you, and wish to illtreat you. Now I have a city very small and venerable which is enough for both.'

The reply from Jesus to Abgar, the Toparch, by the courier Ananias:

'Blessed art thou who didst believe in me not having seen

me, for it is written concerning me that those who have seen me will not believe in me, and that those who have not seen me will believe and live. Now concerning what you wrote to me, to come to you, I must first complete here all for which I was sent, and after thus completing it be taken up to him who sent me, and when I have been taken up I will send to you one of my disciples to heal your suffering and give life to you and those with you' (LCL).

These letters of Jesus and King Abgar found their way all over the East and were introduced into the West by Rufinus' translation of Eusebius' *History of the Church*. King Abgar Uchama is known to have reigned from 4 B.C. until 7 A.D. and from 13 A.D. until 50 A.D. Nevertheless, the letters are not authentic. Augustine (*Cont. Faust.* 28,4; *Consens. Ev.* 1,7,11) denies the existence of any authentic letters of Jesus, and the *Decretum Gelasianum* calls the letters in question apocryphal. The *Acts of Thaddaeus* are nothing else than local legends which were written down during the third century.

There is another form of these Acts extant in Syriac, the so-called *Doctrina Addei*, which was published in 1876. The content is almost the same as given by Eusebius, but there is one new item: the messenger Ananias, who carries Abgar's letter to Jesus, paints a picture of Jesus which he brings to his king. Abgar gives it a place of honor in his palace. However the *Doctrina Addei* does not mention the letter which Jesus wrote. His answer to Abgar's letter is delivered orally by Ananias. Perhaps the author knew of Augustine's statement. The *Doctrina Addei* was probably composed about the year 400. Besides the Syriac original we possess an Armenian and a Greek version of it.

Editions and Translations: W. Cureron, Ancient Syriac Documents. London, 1864, 5–23 edited and translated extensive fragments of the Syriac Doctrina Addaei from two manuscripts of the British Museum. The complete text was found in a manuscript of St. Petersburg (saec. VI) and published by G. Phillips, The Doctrine of Addai, the Apostle, Now First Edited in a Complete Form in the Original Syriac with an English Translation and Notes. London, 1876. — The *Armenian* version of the Doctrina was first published with a *French translation* by L. Alishan, Laboubnia, Lettre d'Abgar, ou Histoire de la conversion des Edesséens par Laboubnia, écrivain contemporain des apôtres. Venice, 1868. — The *Greek* Acta Thaddaei are found in: R. A. Lipsius-M. Bonnet, Acta apostolorum apocrypha I. Leipzig, 1891,

273–278. — B. P. Pratten, ANF 8, 657–665 gives an *English translation* of the 'Teaching of Addaeus the Apostle'.

Studies: R. A. Lipsius, Die edessenische Abgarsage kritisch untersucht. Braunschweig, 1880. — K. C. A. Matthes, Die edessenische Abgarsage auf ihre Fortbildung untersucht. (Diss.). Leipzig, 1882. — G. Bonnet-Maury, La légende d'Abgar et de Thaddée et les missions chrétiennes à Edesse: RHR 16 (1887) 269–283. — L. J. Tixeront, Les origines de l'église d'Edesse et la légende d'Abgar. Etude critique suivie de deux textes orientaux inédits. Paris, 1880. — J. P. P. Martin, Les origines de l'église d'Edesse et des églises syriennes (Extrait de la Revue des sciences ecclésiastiques). Paris, 1889. — E. v. Dobschütz, Christusbilder (TU 18). Leipzig, 1889, 102–196; *idem,* Der Briefwechsel zwischen Abgar und Jesus: Zeitschrift für wissenschaftl. Theologie 43 (1900) 422–486. — F. Cumont, Nouvelles inscriptions du Pont: Revue des études grecques 15 (1902) 326. — E. Schwartz, Zur Abgarlegende: ZNW (1903) 61–66. — N. Cartojan, Legenda lui Abgar in literatura veche romaneasca. Bucarest, 1925. — St. Runciman, Some Remarks on the Image of Edessa: Cambridge Historical Journal 3 (1929–31) 238–252. — H. C. Youtie, A Gothenburg Papyrus and the Letter to Abgar: HThR 23 (1930) 299ff.; *idem,* Gothenburg Papyrus 21 and the Coptic Version of the Letter to Abgar 24 (1931) 61f. — A. M. Kropp, Ausgewählte koptische Zaubertexte. Brussels, 1930–31, II, Nr. 15ff. — J. Myslivec, Die Abgaros-Legende auf einer Ikone des 17. Jahrhunderts: Seminarium Kondakovianum 5 (1932) 185–190. — W. Bauer, Rechtgläubigkeit und Ketzerei im ältesten Christentum. Tübingen, 1934, 7–10; 15–17; 40–45.

In addition to the Acts with which we have dealt, there are others. Most of them belong to the fourth and fifth centuries. Some are of even later date. It may suffice to mention here the *Acts of Matthew,* of which only the last part is extant, and those of Philip and Bartholomew. Of the disciples and companions of the Apostles, we have the apocryphal Acts of Barnabas, Timotheus, and Marcus.

For the Acts of Philip see J. Flamion, Les trois recensions grecques du martyre de l'apôtre Philippe: Mélanges d'histoire offerts à Ch. Moeller I. Louvain, 1914. — E. Peterson, Die Haeretiker der Philippus-Akten: ZNW 31 (1932) 97–111; *idem,* Zum Messalianismus der Philippus-Akten: OC 7 (1932) 172–179; *idem,* Die Philippus-Akten im Armenischen Synaxar: ThQ 113 (1933) 289–298.

IV. APOCRYPHAL APOCALYPSES

Corresponding to the canonical Apocalypse of St. John there are also apocryphal apocalypses attributed to other Apostles. Although the literary form of the Apocalypse, or Book of

Revelation, should have been especially inviting to writers of poetic legends and edifying narratives, the number of apocryphal apocalypses is very limited.

1. *The Apocalypse of Peter*

The most important of them is the *Apocalypse of Peter*, which was written between A.D. 125 and 150. This book was held in high esteem by the ecclesiastical writers of antiquity. Clement of Alexandria (Eus. *Hist. eccl.* 6,14,1) regards it as a canonical writing. It appears in the oldest list of the Canon of the New Testament, the *Muratorian Fragment*, but with the addition: 'Some will not have it read in Church.' Eusebius declares (*Hist. eccl.* 3,3,2): 'Of the so-called Apocalypse (of St. Peter), we have no knowledge at all in Catholic tradition. For no orthodox writer of the ancient time or of our own has used its testimonies.' Jerome (*De vir. ill.* 1) also rejects it as non-canonical. But the Church historian Sozomen (7,19) in the fifth century remarks that it was still used in the Liturgy of Good Friday in some Churches of Palestine.

A large fragment of the Apocalypse in Greek was found at Akhmim in 1886–7. The complete text of it was discovered in 1910 in an Ethiopic translation. The content consists mainly of visions which picture the beauty of heaven and the ugliness of hell. The author paints in detail the hideous punishments to which sinful men and women are subjected according to their crimes. His ideas and imagination show the influence of Orphic-Pythagorean eschatology and oriental religions. It may suffice to compare the following passage:

And I saw also another place over against that one, very squalid; and it was a place of punishment, and they that were punished and the angels that punished them had their raiment dark, according to the air of the place.

And some there were there hanging by their tongues and these were they that blasphemed the way of righteousness, and under them was laid fire flaming and tormenting them.

And there was a great lake full of flaming mire, wherein were certain men that turned away from righteousness; and angels, tormentors, were set over them.

And there were also others, women, hanged by their hair

above that mire which boiled up; and these were they that adorned themselves for adultery.

And the men that were joined with them in the defilement of adultery were hanging by their feet, and had their heads hanging in the mire, and said: We believed not that we should come unto this place.

And I saw the murderers and them that were consenting to them cast into a strait place full of evil, creeping things, and smitten by those beasts, and so turning themselves about in that torment. And upon them were set worms like clouds of darkness. And the soul of them that were murdered stood and looked upon the torment of those murderers and said: O God, righteous is thy judgment.

And hard by that place I saw another strait place wherein the discharge and the stench of them that were in torment ran down, and there was as it were a lake there. And there sat women up to their necks in that liquor, and over against them many children which were born out of due time sat crying; and from them went forth rays of fire and smote the women in the eyes; and these were they that conceived out of wedlock (?) and caused abortion (508–509 James).

Editions and translations: U. BOURIANT, Mémoires publiés par les membres de la Mission archéologique française au Caire 9,1. Paris, 1892, gives a fragment in Greek. — E. KLOSTERMANN, Apocrypha I. 2nd ed. (KT 3). Bonn, 1910, 8–12. — E. PREUSCHEN, Antilegomena. 2nd ed. Tübingen, 1905, with *German* translation. — *Ethiopic* text with *French translation*: S. GRÉBAUT, Littérature éthiopienne pseudo-clémentine: ROChr 15 (1910) 198ff., 307ff, 425ff. — A later Arabic rendition was published by A. MINGANA, The Apocalypse of Peter, edited and translated (Woodbrooke Studies 3,2). Cambridge, 1931.

Other translations: A. RUTHERFORD, ANF 9, 141–147. — M. R. JAMES, The Apocryphal New Testament. Oxford, 1924, 505–524. — E. HENNECKE, Neutestamentliche Apokryphen. 2nd ed. Tübingen, 1924, 314–327.

Studies: A. DIETERICH, Nekyia. Beiträge zur Erklärung der neuentdeckten Petrusapokalypse. Leipzig, 1893. — A. HARNACK, Die Petrusapokalypse in der alten abendländischen Kirche (TU 13,1). Leipzig, 1895. — A. MARMORSTEIN, Jüdische Parallelen zur Petrusapokalypse: ZNW 10 (1909) 297–300. — F. SPITTA, Die Petrusapokalypse und der zweite Petrusbrief: ZNW 12 (1911) 237–242. — M. R. JAMES, A New Text of the Apocalypse of Peter: JThSt 12 (1911) 36–54; 362–383; 573–583. — H. DUENSING, Ein Stücke der urchristlichen Petrusapokalypse enthaltender Traktat der äthiopischen pseudo-

klementinischen Literatur: ZNW 14 (1913) 65-78. — K. Prümm, De ge-
nuino Apocalypsis Petri textu: Bibl 10 (1929) 62-80. — M. R. James, The
Rainer Fragment of the Apocalypse of Peter: JThSt 32 (1931) 270-278.—
C. M. Edsman, Le baptême de feu. Leipzig-Uppsala, 1940, 57-66.

2. *The Apocalypse of Paul*

There were several apocalypses to appear under the name of
the Apostle Paul. Epiphanius (*Haer.* 38,2) mentions a Gnostic
book, *Ascent of Paul.* Of this work nothing is extant. We have,
however, a text of an *Apocalypse of Paul* in several versions. It
was written in Greek, between 240 and 250, most probably in
Egypt. Perhaps this explains why Origen knew of it. Of the
original text nothing is preserved. We possess however a revision
of the Greek text which originated between 380 and 388. In the
Introduction to this edition, we are told that the Apocalypse was
found under the house of St. Paul at Tarsus during the consu-
late of Theodosius and Gratianus. The Church historian Sozomen in the 5th century knew of this apocryphal composition,
because in his *Ecclesiastical History* (7,19) he says, 'The work
entitled the Apocalypse of the Apostle Paul which none of the
ancients ever saw is still esteemed by most of the monks. Some
persons affirm that the book was found during this reign (of
Theodosius) by divine revelation in a marble box, buried be-
neath the soil in the house of Paul at Tarsus in Cilicia. I have
been informed that this report is false by a Cilician priest of the
Church of Tarsus. He was a man whose grey hairs showed him
to be of considerable age, and he said that no such occurrence is
known among them, and wonders if the heretics did not invent
the story.'
    In addition to the Greek text we have Syriac, Coptic, Ethio-
pic, and Latin versions. The Latin translation, which originated
about 500 A.D. and which we possess in more than a dozen
recensions, is superior to all other authorities, even to the revised
Greek text. In most of the Latin manuscripts, the Apocalypse is
entitled *Visio Pauli.* This title is the best description of the content,
because the author intends to narrate what Paul saw in the vision
which he mentions in his second Letter to the Corinthians (12,2).
The Apostle receives from Christ the task of preaching penance
to mankind. All creation, the sun, the moon, the stars, the waters,

the sea and the earth have appealed against man, saying, 'O Lord God Almighty, the children of man have defiled Thine Holy Name'. The Apostle is led by an angel to the place of the just souls: the shining land of the righteous, and to the lake Acherusa, out of which the golden city of Christ rises. After he has been shown this city in detail, he is taken by the angel to the River of Fire, where the souls of the ungodly and sinners are suffering. This part, with its description of the torments of hell, resembles the *Apocalypse of Peter*. But the *Apocalypse of Paul* goes beyond the description of the former. The different ranks of the clergy, bishops, priests, deacons, and the different kinds of heretics are included in the classes of the damned. The author is a poet of considerable skill and imaginative powers. It is not surprising then that his work had tremendous influence on the Middle Ages. Dante alludes to it when he mentions the visit of the 'chosen vessel' to hell, in Canto 2, 28 of the *Inferno*.

Interesting is the angelology of the Apocalypse. The idea of the guardian angel is very pronounced:

> When therefore the sun is set, at the first hour of the night, in the same hour goeth the angel of every people and of every man and woman, which protect and keep them, because man is the image of God: and likewise at the hour of morning, which is the twelfth hour of the night, do all the angels of men and women go to meet God and present all the work which every man has wrought, whether good or evil (528 James).

It is the office of the angels to act as protecting guides to souls (*Psychopompoi*), especially when they ascend from earth to Heaven after death. St. Michael's duties as a guide (ch. 14) remind us of the Offertory of the Requiem Mass in the *Missale Romanum*.

> And the voice of God came, saying, Like as this soul has not grieved me, neither will I grieve it . . . Let it be delivered therefore unto Michael, the angel of the Covenant, and let him lead it unto the Paradise of the Rejoicing, that it become fellow-heir with all the Saints (532 James).

The counterpart of Michael as Psychopompos is Tartarus ich. 18): And I heard a voice saying, Let that soul be delivered (nto the hands of Tartarus, and he must be taken down into hell (535 James).

Furthermore, it is interesting that we meet here (ch. 44) the idea of the *mitigatio poenarum* of the damned on Sunday:
Yet now because of Michael the Archangel of my Covenant and the angels that are with him, and because of Paul my dearly beloved, whom I would not grieve, and because of your brethren who are in the world and who offer oblations, and because of your sons, for in them are my commandments, and yet more because of my own goodness: on that day whereon I rose from the dead, I grant unto all you that are in torment refreshment for a day and a night forever (548 James).
This belief had a strong influence on the literature of the Middle Ages (Cf. Dante).

Editions: C. TISCHENDORF, Apocalypses apocryphae. Leipzig, 1866, 34–60. *Latin version:* M. R. JAMES, Apocrypha anecdota. Cambridge, 1893, 11–12. — TH. SILVERSTEIN, Visio S. Pauli, The History of the Apocalypse in Latin together with Nine Texts. London, 1935. — For the *Syriac* text cf. G. RICCIOTTI, L'apocalisse di Paolo siriaca. I: Introduzione, testo e commento, II: La cosmologia della Bibbia e la sua trasmissione fino a Dante. Brescia, 1932; *idem*, Apocalypsis Pauli syriace: Orientalia 2 (1933) 1–32.

Translations: A. RUTHERFORD, ANF 9, 149–166. — M. R. JAMES, The Apocryphal New Testament. Oxford, 1924, 525–55. — German translation of the Syriac version by P. ZINGERLE, Vierteljahrschrift für deutsch- und englisch-theologische Forschung und Kritik 4 (1871) 139ff.

Studies: H. BRANDES, Visio S. Pauli. Halle, 1885, 1–19. — E. WIEBER, De Apocalypsis S. Pauli codicibus (Diss.). Marburg, 1904. — D. SERRUYS, Une source gnostique de l'Apocalypse de Paul: RPh 35 (1911) 194–202. — ST. D. SEYMOUR, Irish Versions of the Vision of St. Paul: JThSt 24 (1923) 54ff. — R. BROTANEK, Refrigerium damnatorum (Festschrift der Philos. Fakultät der Universität Erlangen zur 55. Versammlung deutscher Philologen). Erlangen, 1925, 77–85. — R. VAN DOREN, L'oraison 'Fidelium' du Lundi: Questions Liturgiques et Paroissiales 10 (1925) 102–105. — A. MAYER, Stetit urna paullum sicca: Bayerische Blätter für das Gymnasialschulwesen 62 (1926) 331–338. — A. CABASSUT, La mitigation des peines de l'enfer d'après les livres liturgiques: RHE 23 (1927) 65–70. — L. GOUGAUD, La croyance au répit des damnés dans les légendes irlandais: Mélanges bretons et celtiques off. à M. J. Loth. Annales de Bret. 1927, 1–10. — S. MERKLE, Deutsches Dante-Jahrbuch, 1929, 24ff.; *idem*, Augustin über eine Unterbrechung der Höllenstrafen: Aurelius Augustinus. Festschrift der Görresgesellschaft zum 1500. Todestage des hl. Augustinus. Köln, 1930, 197–202. — L. G. A. GETINO, Del gran número de los que se salvan y de la mitigación de las penas eternas. Madrid, 1934. — A. LANDGRAF, ZKTh 1936, 299–370. — C. H. KRAELING, The Apocalypse of Paul and the 'Iranische Erlösungsmysterium': HThR 24

(1931) 209–244. — R. P. CASEY, The Apocalypse of Paul: JThSt 34 (1933) 1–32. — TH. SILVERSTEIN, Did Dante know the Vision of St. Paul: Harvard Studies and Notes in Philology and Literature 19 (1937), 231–247.

3. The Apocalypse of Stephen

The *Apocalypse of Paul* is condemned in the *Decretum Gelasianum*, together with two other Apocalypses, those of Stephen and of Thomas. Concerning the *Apocalypse of Stephen*, we do not have any information. It is possible that the *Decretum* means here the account of the finding and rediscovery of the relics of St. Stephen which the Greek presbyter Lucian composed about the year 415.

ML 41, 805–818. — M. J. LAGRANGE, S. Etienne et son sanctuaire à Jerusalem. Paris, 1894. — G. SEGUR VIDAL, La carta-encíclica del obispo Severo. Palma de Majorque, 1938. — M. R. JAMES, The Apocryphal New Testament. Oxford, 1924, 564–568.

4. The Apocalypse of Thomas

The *Apocalypse of Thomas* was written in Greek or Latin about 400. The author shares Gnostic Manichean views. Not until the year 1907 was it discovered in a manuscript in Munich. Here the Apocalypse is entitled, *Epistola Domini Nostri Jesu Christi ad Thomam Discipulum*. We possess an old English version of this Revelation in a sermon contained in an Anglo-Saxon manuscript at Vercelli. There are indications that the original language was perhaps Greek.

The content consists of revelations which the Lord gives to the Apostle Thomas regarding the Last Days. The signs of the approaching destruction of the world extend here over seven days. The Apocalypse was used by the Priscillianists, and was known in England in the 9th century at least.

Editions: F. WILHELM, Deutsche Legenden und Legendare. Leipzig, 1907, 40–42: Epistula domini nostri Jesu Christi ad Thomam discipulum suum. — P. BIHLMEYER, Un texte non interpolé de l'Apocalypse de Thomas: RB 28 (1911) 270–282.

Translation: M. R. JAMES, The Apocryphal New Testament. Oxford, 1924, 556–562.

Studies: E. HAULER, Zu den neuen lateinischen Bruchstücken der Thomasapokalypse und eines apostolischen Sendschreibens im Cod. Vindob. nr. 16:

WSt 30 (1908) 308–340. — M. R. James, Revelatio Thomae: JThSt 11 (1910) 288ff. — M. Förster, Der Vercelli-Codex CXVII: Studien zur englischen Philologie 50 (Festschrift f. L. Morsbach). Halle a. S., 1913, 116ff.

5. *The Apocalypses of St. John*

Even to the author of the canonical Apocalypse, the Apostle John, apocryphal apocalypses have been attributed. One of them was published by A. Birch and C. Tischendorf. It contains a series of questions and answers concerning the end of the world, and a description of Antichrist, which often follows the canonical Apocalypse. Another *Apocalypse of St. John* was edited by F. Nau from a manuscript at Paris (*Paris. graec.* 947). Here St. John addresses questions to the Lord regarding the celebration of Sunday, fasting, the liturgy and the doctrine of the Church.

6. *Apocalypses of the Virgin*

Of later origin are the Apocalypses of the Virgin, in which Mary receives revelations regarding the torments of hell and in which she intercedes for the damned. There are several texts extant in Greek and Ethiopic, which have been published by C. Tischendorf, A. Vasiliev, M. Chaine and M. R. James.

M. A. A. Jugie, La mort et l'assomption de la Sainte Vierge (ST 114). Vatican City, 1944.

V.   APOCRYPHAL EPISTLES OF THE APOSTLES

1.   *The Epistola Apostolorum*

The most important and historically the most valuable of the apocryphal epistles is the *Epistola Apostolorum*. It was first published in 1919. The letter which is addressed 'to the Churches of the East and the West, the North and the South', originated in Asia Minor or Egypt. According to C. Schmidt, it was written between 160 and 170, whereas A. Ehrhard attributes it to the period 130 to 140. Indications in the text however point to a date between 140 and 160. Of its original Greek text nothing is extant. We have a part of a Coptic version, which was discovered in 1895 at Cairo, and a complete Ethiopic translation published in 1913. There are also fragments of a Latin version. A critical edition using these three authorities was edited by C. Schmidt in 1919.

The main part of the letter consists of revelations which the Savior made to his disciples after his Resurrection. The introduction contains a confession to Christ and a summary of his miracles. The conclusion is a description of the Ascension. The epistolary form is retained for the first part only; therefore the work as a whole is rather an apocalypse than a letter. It is an example of the unofficial popular religious literature. The author bases his ideas mainly on the New Testament. His language and his concepts are influenced by the Gospel of St. John. The report about the Resurrection is a compilation from the four canonical Gospels. In addition to these sources, the author has used the apocryphal *Apocalypse of Peter*, the *Epistle of Barnabas*, and the *Shepherd of Hermas*.

The Theology of the Epistle. The Epistle is very clear on the two natures of Christ. Christ calls himself 'I who am unbegotten and yet begotten of mankind, who am without flesh and yet have borne flesh' (21). The Incarnation of the Logos is explicitly stated:

> In God the Lord the Son of God do we believe, that he is the Word become flesh: that of Mary the Virgin he took a body, begotten of the Holy Ghost, not of the will of the flesh, but by the will of God: that he was wrapped in swaddling clothes in Bethlehem and made manifest, and grew up and came to ripe age (3).

However, in another passage, Gabriel is regarded as a personification of the Logos, who is introduced saying:

> On that day whereon I took the form of the Angel Gabriel, I appeared unto Mary and spoke with her. Her heart accepted me, and she believed, and I formed myself and entered into her body. I became flesh for I alone was a minister unto myself, in that which concerned Mary, in the appearance of the shape of an angel (14).

On the other hand, the deity of the Logos is fully identified with that of the Father:

> And we said to him, Lord is it then possible that thou shouldst be both here and there? But he answered us, I am wholly in the Father and the Father in me, because of the

likeness of the form and the power and the fulness and the light and the full measure and the voice. I am the Word (17). Although there are some Gnostic ways of thought, there is a definite anti-Gnostic tendency in this writing. The beginning refers to Simon (Magus) and Cerinthus as 'the false apostles concerning whom it is written that no man shall cleave unto them, for there is in them deceit wherewith they bring man to destruction'. The same anti-Gnostic tendency can be seen in the emphasis which the author lays on the resurrection of the flesh. This resurrection is called a 'second birth', a 'vesture that shall not decay' (21). As far as the eschatology is concerned, there is not the least sign of a chiliastic view. In the description of the Last Judgment the flesh is judged together with the soul and the spirit. After that mankind will be divided, 'the one part shall rest in heaven and the other part shall be punished ever-lastingly yet living' (22).

The Epistle is also important for the history of the liturgy. It contains a short symbol in which besides the three divine Persons, the Holy Church and the remission of sins are mentioned as articles of faith (5; see above p. 1ff.). Baptism is regarded as a condition of salvation from which there can be no dispensation. Therefore Christ descends into Limbo to baptize the righteous and the Prophets:

And I poured out upon them with my right hand the water of life and forgiveness and salvation from all evil, as I have done unto you and to them that believe in me (27).

Here the author shows acquaintance with the *Shepherd of Hermas*, who has the same explanation for the *Descensus ad inferos*. On the other hand Baptism alone is not sufficient for salvation:

But if any man believe in me and do not my command-ments, although he have confessed my name he hath no profit therefrom, but runneth a vain race: for such will find themselves in perdition and destruction (27).

The celebration of the Eucharist is called *Pascha* and is re-garded as a memorial of the death of Jesus. Agape and the Eucharist are still celebrated together. Here is the text of the valuable passage (ch. 15):

But do you commemorate my death. Now when the Pascha cometh, one of you shall be cast into prison for my

Name's sake; and he will be in grief and sorrow because
you keep the Pascha while he is in prison and separated
from you . . . And I will send my power in the form of my
angel Gabriel and the doors of the prison shall be opened.
And he shall come forth and come unto you and keep the
night watch with you until the cock crow. And when you
have accomplished the memorial which is made of me, and
the Agape, he shall again be cast into prison, for a testimony,
until he shall come out of thence and preach that which I
have delivered unto you. And we said unto him: Lord, is it
then needful that we should again take the cup' and drink?
He said unto us, Yea it is needful until the day when I
come again with them that have been put to death for my
sake (489 James).

Editions and translations: L. GUERRIER, Le testament en Galilée de Notre-
Seigneur Jésus-Christ. Texte éthiopien édité et traduit avec le concours de
Sylvain GRÉBAUT (PO 9,3). Paris, 1913. — C. SCHMIDT, Gespräche Jesu mit
seinen Jüngern nach der Auferstehung. Ein katholisch-apostolisches Send-
schreiben des 2. Jahrhunderts nach einem koptischen Papyrus herausgegeben,
übersetzt und untersucht. Uebersetzung des äthiopischen Textes von I. WAJN-
BERG (TU 43). Leipzig, 1919. — H. DUENSING, Epistula Apostolorum nach
dem äthiopischen und koptischen Text herausgegeben (KT 152). Bonn, 1925.
— M. R. JAMES, The Apocryphal New Testament. Oxford, 1924, 485-503. —
E. HENNECKE, Neutestamentliche Apokryphen. 2nd ed. Tübingen, 1924,
146-150.

Studies: M. R. JAMES, The Epistula Apostolorum in a New Text: JThSt 12
(1911) 55-56. — H. J. CLADDER, Zur neuen 'Epistola Apostolorum': ThR 18
(1919) 452-453. — A. EHRHARD, Historisch-politische Blätter 165 (1920)
645-655; 717-729. — K. LAKE, The Epistola Apostolorum: HThR 14 (1921)
15ff. — H. LIETZMANN, Die Epistula Apostolorum: ZNW 20 (1921) 173-176.
— M. R. JAMES, Epistola Apostolorum: a Possible Quotation: JThSt 23
(1922) 56. — F. J. DÖLGER, *ΙΧΘΥΣ* II. Münster, 1922, 552-554. — TH.
SCHNEIDER, Das prophetische 'Agraphon' der Epistola Apostolorum: ZNW
24 (1925) 151-154. — J. DELAZER, Disquisitio in argumentum Epistolae
Apostolorum: Ant 3 (1928) 369-406; *idem,* De tempore compositionis
Epistolae Apostolorum: Ant 4 (1929) 257- 292; 387-430. — J. HOH, Die
kirchliche Busse im zweiten Jahrhundert. Breslau, 1932, 64-72. — J. DE
ZWAAN, Date and Origin of the Epistle of the Eleven Apostles: Amicitiae
Corolla dedicated to Rendel Harris, 1933, 344-355. — J. QUASTEN, Monu-
menta eucharistica et liturgica vetustissima. Bonn, 1935-37, 336-337. —
B. POSCHMANN, Paenitentia secunda. Bonn, 1939, 104ff. — L. GRY, La date de
la Parousie d'après l'Epistula Apostolorum: RBibl 49 (1940) 86-97.

2. Apocryphal Epistles of St. Paul

In the canonical Epistles of St. Paul there are several letters mentioned which are not preserved in the Canon of the New Testament. They have evidently been lost. To replace the missing letters, apocryphal Epistles of St. Paul appeared.

a. In his Epistle to the Colossians (4,16), St. Paul mentions a letter which he wrote to the Laodiceans. This reference provided the opportunity for the apocryphal *Epistle to the Laodiceans.* The content imitates and plagiarizes the authentic letters of the Apostle, especially his Epistle to the Philippians. After the author has given expression to his joy at the faith and virtue of the Laodiceans, he warns them against heretics, and exhorts them to remain loyal to the Christian doctrine and the Christian concept of life, as the Apostle instructed them. The letter purports to have been written from prison. From the content the date of its origin cannot be determined. It is true that the Muratorian Fragment does mention an *Epistle to the Laodiceans* as a forgery in the interests of Marcion's heretical doctrine, but Harnack's idea that this was the apocryphal Letter to the Laodiceans which we possess did not meet with the approval of scholars. Although there is a possibility that the letter was originally written in Greek, there is only a Latin text extant thus far. The oldest manuscript which we have is the *Codex Fuldensis* of Bishop Victor of Capua, which was written in 546. The letter was composed not later than the fourth century, because from that time onward it is mentioned by ecclesiastical writers. The translations which we have are all based on the Latin text. The letter occurs in a number of Bibles written in England.

Editions: R. ANGER, Ueber den Laodicenerbrief. Leipzig, 1843, 155–165. — J. B. LIGHTFOOT, St. Paul's Epistles to the Colossians and to Philemon. 8th ed. London, 1886, 287–289. — E. J. GOODSPEED, A Toledo MS of the Laodiceans: JBL 23 (1904) 76–78; *idem,* The Madrid MS of Laodiceans: The American Journal of Theology 8 (1904) 536–538. *Special edition:* A. HARNACK, Die apokryphen Briefe des Paulus an die Laodicener und Korinther. 2nd ed. (KT 12). Berlin, 1931. An *Arabic* version was edited by CARRA DE VAUX, L'épitre aux Laodicéens en arabe: RBibl 5 (1896) 221–226.

Translations: English: M. R. JAMES, The Apocryphal New Testament. Oxford, 1924, 478–480. *French:* L. VOUAUX, Les actes de Paul et ses lettres apocryphes. Paris, 1913. *German:* E. HENNECKE, Neutestamentliche Apokryphen. 2nd ed. Tübingen, 1924, 150f.

Studies: A. HARNACK, Marcion. 2nd ed. Berlin, 1924, 172f., 64ff. Cf. B. CAPELLE, RB (1924), Bull. I, n. 283. — W. J. MACKNIGHT, The Letter to the Laodiceans: The Biblical Review 16 (1932) 519-539.

b. The Muratorian Fragment mentions side by side with the *Letter to the Laodiceans*, a Marcionite *Epistle to the Alexandrians*, which has been lost. We have no other informations about it.

c. The so-called *Third Epistle to the Corinthians* is contained in the apocryphal *Acts of Paul* (see above, p. 132). The Letter is supposed to have been written as an answer to a letter which the Corinthians sent to Paul. In this letter the Corinthians reported about two heretics, Simon and Cleobius, who tried 'to overthrow the faith' by the following doctrines:

They say that we must not use the prophets and that God is not almighty and that there shall be no resurrection of the flesh and that man was not made by God and that Christ came not down in the flesh, neither was born of Mary, and that the world is not of God but of the angels (289 James).

The content of Paul's answer is therefore of considerable importance because it deals with such topics as the creation of the world, mankind and its Creator, the Incarnation, and the resurrection of the flesh. Both the letter from the Corinthians and Paul's letter in answer from his prison in Philippi found a place in the Syriac collection of Pauline epistles, and were for a time regarded as authentic in the Armenian and Syriac Churches. A Latin ranslation originated as early as the third century.

For *editions* and *translations* see the *Acta Pauli*, above, p. 132f. Furthermore: P. VETTER, Der apokryphe dritte Korintherbrief (Tübinger Programm). Wien, 1894. — A. HARNACK, Die apokryphen Briefe des Paulus an die Laodicener und Korinther. 2nd ed. (KT 12). Berlin, 1931. — L. VOUAUX, Les actes de Paul et ses lettres apocryphes. Paris, 1913.

Studies: D. DE BRUYNE, Un quatrième ms. latin de la correspondance apocryphe de S. Paul avec les Corinthiens: RB 45 (1933) 189-195. — W. BAUER, Rechtgläubigkeit und Ketzerei im ältesten Christentum. Tübingen, 1934, 45-48. — M. RIST, Pseudoepigraphic Refutations of Marcionism: JR 22 (1942) 39-62.

d. The *Correspondence between Paul and Seneca* is a collection of eight letters from the Roman philosopher Seneca to St. Paul and six short replies from the Apostle. They were written in Latin not later than the 3rd century. St. Jerome (*De vir. illus.*

12) testifies that they were 'read by many'. Seneca writes to the
Apostle that the content of these letters made a deep impression
on him, 'for it is the Holy Spirit which is in you and high above
you, which expresses these exalted and admirable thoughts'.
But the philosopher does not like the wretched style in which
Paul wrote these letters and so he admonishes him: 'I would
therefore have you careful of other points, that the polish of the
style may not be wanting to the majesty of the thought' (Ep. 7).
The whole correspondence was evidently invented for a definite
purpose. The author intended to have the authentic letters of
St. Paul read in Roman society circles, despite their literary
shortcomings, 'because the gods often speak by the mouth of the
simple, not of those who try deceitfully what they can do by
their learning' (*ibid.*).

Editions: C. W. BARLOW, Epistolae Senecae ad Paulum et Pauli ad Senecam
quae vocantur (Papers and Monographs of the American Academy in Rome,
vol. 10). Rome, 1938.

Translation: M. R. JAMES, The Apocryphal New Testament. Oxford, 1924,
480–484.

Studies: K. DEISSNER, Paulus und Seneca. 1917. — E. LIÉNARD, Sur la corres-
pondance apocryphe de Sénèque et de St. Paul: RBPh 11 (1932) 5–23. —
P. DE LABRIOLLE, La réaction paienne. Etude sur la polémique antichrétienne
du Ier au VIe siècle. Paris, 1934, 25–28. — A. KURFESS, Zum apokryphen
Briefwechsel zwischen Seneca und Paulus: ThGl 19 (1937) 317–322; *idem*,
Zum apokryphen Briefwechsel zwischen Seneca und Paulus: ThQ 119 (1938)
318–331; *idem*, Zur Collatio Alexandri et Dindimi: Mnem 9 (1941) 138–152.
Cf. Mnem (1938) 265–269; Mnem (1939) 239f. — E. LIÉNARD, Alcuin et les
Epistolae Senecae et Pauli: RBPh (1941) 589–598. — P. BENOIT, Sénèque
et Paul: Bibl (1946) 7–35.

3. *Apocryphal Letters of Disciples of St. Paul*

a. The Epistle of Barnabas (see above, p. 85).

b. *Epistola Titi Discipuli Pauli, de Dispositione Sanctimonii.* The
text of this Latin apocryph was first published in 1925 by
De Bruyne. It is not a letter but an address on virginity to
ascetics of both sexes which combats the abuses of the *Syneisaktoi* and the communal life of the two sexes of ascetics under one
roof. It is closely related to the Pseudo-Cyprianic writing *De
singularitate clericorum* which was used by the author. The treatise

probably originated in Priscillianist circles in Spain. Its original language seems to have been Greek.

D. DE BRUYNE, Epistula Titi, discipuli Pauli, de dispositione sanctimonii: RB 37 (1925) 47-72. Cf. A. HARNACK, SAB (1925) 180-212. — H. KOCH, Zu Ps.-TITUS, De dispositione sanctimonii: ZNW 32 (1935) 131-144. — G. MORIN, Un curieux inédit du IVe/Ve siècle. Le soidisant évêque Asterius d'Ansedunum contre la peste des agapètes: RB 47 (1935) 101-113.

CHAPTER IV

THE BEGINNINGS OF CHRISTIAN POETRY

I. THE FIRST CHRISTIAN HYMNS

Hymns were one of the essential elements of Christian worship from the very beginning. The psalms and songs of the Old Testament in the translation of the Septuagint played an important role in the earliest Christian liturgy. But at an early date the Christians created similar compositions of their own. St. Paul mentions (Col. 3,16) psalms, hymns and spiritual songs.

The New Testament contains a number of such hymns, as for instance the *Magnificat* (Luke, 1,46ff), the *Benedictus* (1,68ff), the *Gloria in Excelsis* (2,14) and the *Nunc Dimittis* (2,29ff), which are still in the liturgy of the Church. The Apocalypse of St. John (5,9ff) speaks of a 'new hymn' which the just in heaven sing in praise of the Lamb. It is probable that the author was here inspired by the liturgy of his time, representing, as he does, the heavenly worship as an echo of the liturgy here on earth. In addition to this 'new hymn' there are numerous short hymns in this book which give us an idea of the nature and content of early Christian hymns (Cf. Apoc. 1,4–7, 8–11 etc.). Of course all these songs are not what the Greeks regarded as verse since they follow no regular metrical pattern. They are written in a solemn and exalted language and in the *parallelismus membrorum*. Nevertheless they are prose. During the second century, however, the Gnostics, who were in contact with Hellenistic literature, composed a great number of metrical hymns to diffuse their special doctrines. We find many of them in the apocryphal Acts of the Apostles, for instance, the two already mentioned (above, p. 139-140) the Hymn of the Soul in the *Acts of Thomas*, and the hymn which Christ sings with his apostles in the *Acts of John*. The best example of these Gnostic hymns is the Hymn of the Naassenes which Hippolytus (*Philosophoumena* 5,10,2) has preserved. It is not merely a coincidence that Clement of Alexandria, who tried to reconcile Christianity and culture and fought for a Catholic Gnosticism, composed a metrical hymn in anapaests in honor of Christ. The Hymn to Christ the Savior is found at the end of his *Paidagogos*. Christ is praised here as:

King of Saints, Almighty Word
Of the Father, highest Lord,
Wisdom's head and chief,
Assuagement of all grief;
Lord of all time and space,
Jesus, Savior of our race (ANF 11,296).

W. CHRIST-M. PARANIKAS, Anthologia Graeca carminum christianorum. Leipzig, 1871. — J. MEARNS, The Canticles of the Christian Church, Eastern and Western. Cambridge, 1914. — A. BAUMSTARK, Hymns (Greek Christian): J. HASTINGS, Encyclopaedia of Religion and Ethics 7 (1914) 5–12. — A. J. MacLEAN, Hymns (Syriac Christian): ibidem 209–218. — H. GUNKEL, Die Lieder in der Kindheitsgeschichte Jesu bei Lukas: Festgabe Harnack. Tübingen, 1921, 43–60. — J. KROLL, Die christliche Hymnodik bis zu Klemens von Alexandreia: Programm der Akademie von Braunsberg (1921/22); idem, E. HENNECKE, Neutestamentliche Apokryphen. 2nd ed. Tübingen, 1924, 435ff.; 596–601. — J. LEBRETON, La forme primitive du Gloria in excelsis: RSR 13 (1923) 322–329. — C. DEL GRANDE, Liturgiae preces. Hymni christianorum e papyris collecti. 2nd ed. Naples, 1934. — E. T. MONETA. Caglio, La Laus angelorum. L'inno mattinale dell'antichità: Ambrosius 11 (1935) 209–223. — E. G. PANTELAKIS, Αἱ ἀρχαὶ τῆς ἐκκλησιαστικῆς ποιήσεως: Θεολογία 15 (1937) 323–339; 16 (1938) 5–31. — J. QUASTEN, The Liturgical Singing of Women in Christian Antiquity: CHR 27 (1941) 149–165.

To the second century belongs the famous Evening Hymn Φῶς ἱλαρόν which is still preserved in the evening service and the liturgy of the Presanctified of the Greek Church:
Serene light of the Holy Glory
Of the Father Everlasting
    Jesus Christ:
Having come to the setting of the sun,
And seeing the evening light
We praise the Father and the Son
And the Holy Spirit of God.
It behooveth to praise Thee
At all times with holy songs,
Son of God, who hast given life;
Therefore the world glorifieth Thee (ANF 2,298).

L. BARRAL, Le 'Phos hilaron': L'Union des églises 4 (1925) 470–472. — E. R. SMOTHERS, ΦΩΣ ΙΛΑΡΟΝ: RSR 19 (1929) 266–283. — F. J. DÖLGER, Lumen Christi: AC 5 (1936) 11–26.

In 1922 the fragment of a Christian hymn with musical notes was found at Oxyrhynchos (Oxyrh. Pap. vol. XV, no. 1786). The hymn seems to belong to the end of the third century. Only a few words have been preserved: 'All the glorious creatures of God should not remain silent and be outdone by the radiant stars. . . . The waters of the rustling stream should give praise to our Father and Son and Holy Ghost.'

Editions: B. P. GRENFELL and A. S. HUNT, The Oxyrhynchos Papyri, Part XV. London, 1922, Nr. 1786, 21–25. — C. WESSELY, Les plus anciens monuments du christianisme écrits sur papyrus II: PO 18 (1924) 506–508.

Studies: TH. REINACH, Un ancêtre de la musique de l'église: Revue musicale 3 (1922) Nr. 9. — H. ALBERT, Ein neuentdeckter frühchristlicher Hymnus mit antiken Musiknoten: Zeitschrift für Musikwissenschaft 4 (1922) 524ff.; *idem,* Das älteste Denkmal der christlichen Kirchenmusik: Antike 2 (1926) 282–290. — R. WAGNER, Der Oxyrhynchos-Notenpapyrus XV Nr. 1786: Phil 79 (1923) 201–221. — C. DEL GRANDE, Inno cristiano antico: Rivista Indo-Greco-Italica 7 (1923) 173–179. — O. URSPRUNG, Der Hymnus aus Oxyrhynchos, das älteste Denkmal christlicher (Kirchen?) Musik: Bulletin de la Société 'Union Musicologique' 3 (1923) 129: *idem,* Der Hymnus aus Oxyrhynchos im Rahmen unserer kirchenmusikalischen Frühzeit: ThGl 18 (1926) 390ff. — N. TERZAGHI, Sul P. Oxy. 1786: Raccolta di scritti in onore di Giacomo Lumbroso. Milan, 1925, 229ff. — J. QUASTEN, Musik und Gesang in den Kulten der heidnischen Antike und christlichen Frühzeit (LQF 25). Münster, 1930, 100–102. — G. B. PIGHI, Ricerche sulla notazione ritmica greca: Aegyptus (1941) 189–220.

Eusebius in his *Eccl. Hist.* (7,30,10) reports that Paul of Samosata was accused of having put a stop to hymns addressed to Jesus Christ on the ground that they were modern and the compositions of modern authors. More and more hymns were sung even at home in order to supplant the hymns to the pagan gods. Thus the hymn played an important role not only in developing the Christian liturgy but also in suffusing the surrounding culture with Christian ideas.

2.   THE ODES OF SOLOMON

The *Odes of Solomon* are the most important discovery in the field of early Christian literature since the finding of the Didache. Rendel Harris first happened upon them in 1905 in a Syriac manuscript. Though they were published as long ago as 1909 they have since baffled all attempts to determine their exact character. It is true that some of these forty-two hymns give expression to Gnostic ideas (cf. Odes 19 and 35); nevertheless, they cannot with complete assurance be dubbed a 'Hymn Book of Gnostic Churches'. The Gnostic dualism is lacking (cf. Odes 7,20f.; 16,10f.). Even more untenable is the idea that these Odes in their original form were purely Jewish, and that extensive interpolations were made by a Christian about the year 100 A.D. Two reasons have been given for the characterization of the Odes as Jewish:

1) In the extant manuscript the Odes are found in juxtaposition with the *Psalms of Solomon*, which have a definitely Jewish cast of thought.

2) The second argument is linguistic. The author of the Odes employs an idiom strongly reminiscent of the Old Testament; *parallelismus membrorum*, parables, and figures are used very frequently. But these features may be easily explained from the fact that the author evidently intends to imitate the psalms and their language.

The unity of style which the Odes exhibit is a decisive argument against any supposition of Jewish origin and Christian interpolation. They must be the work of a single author, though his identity eludes us. Bardesanes has been dismissed as a possibility. No more can they be ascribed to Aphraates or Ephraim Syrus; the numerous allusions to the doctrine and ritual of baptism scarcely prove that they are Hymns of the Baptized. There are no convincing reasons for supposing their origin to be Montanistic. It seems more likely that they actually express the beliefs and hopes of Eastern Christianity. This does not exclude the possibility that mythological material and Greek philosophy influenced the author to some degree. There are strong indications that they were written during the second century, most probably in the first half of it. Their original language was in all probability Greek — not Hebrew, nor Aramaic, nor Syriac. Burkitt discovered a second manuscript of these hymns dating from the tenth century among the Nitrian collection in the British Museum (Add. 14538). This document contains less than that published by Rendel Harris, preserving merely the Syriac text of Ode 17,7 to the end.

Up to the year 1909 all that was known of the Odes was that:

1) Lactantius (*Instit.* IV,12,3) makes a single quotation of Ode 19,6;

2) They were mentioned in the Pseudo-Athanasian *Synopsis*

Sacrae Scripturae, a sixth century catalogue of sacred books with an enumeration of the canonical books of the Old Testament. Here we read: 'There are also other books of the Old Testament, not regarded as canonical but read to the catechumens. . . . Maccabees. . . .Psalms and Odes of Solomon, Susanna.' In the *Stichometry* of Nicephorus, a list of scriptural books which, in its present form, dates from about the year 850 A.D., the Odes are listed in a similar way.

3) The complete text of five of these Odes is cited as Holy Scripture in a Gnostic treatise entitled *Pistis Sophia*. Both the Coptic translation, as found in this work, and the Syriac recension in the manuscripts of Harris and Burkitt seem to be based on the original Greek text, which has been lost.

CONTENT OF THE ODES

The content of these hymns breathes throughout the spirit of an exalted mysticism, which seems to be influenced by the Gospel of St. John. Most of them contain general praises of God with no traces of theological or speculative thought. However, some of them glorify dogmatic themes, for instance, the Incarnation, the descent into Limbo, and the privileges of divine grace. Thus, Ode 7 describes the Incarnation:

As the impulse of anger against iniquity,
So is the impulse of joy towards the beloved (object);
It brings in of its fruits without restraint:
My joy is the Lord and my impulse is towards Him:
This path of mine is excellent:
For I have a helper, the Lord.
He hath caused me to know Himself
Without grudging
By His simplicity:
His kindness hath humbled His greatness.
He became like me,
In order that I might receive Him:
He was reckoned like myself
In order that I might put Him on;
And I trembled not
When I saw Him:
Because He was gracious to me:

Like my nature He became
That I might learn Him,
And like my form
That I might not turn back from Him:
The Father of Knowledge
Is the word of Knowledge:
He who created wisdom
Is wiser than His works:
And He who created me
When yet I was not,
Knew what I should do
When I came into being:
Wherefore He pitied me
In His abundant grace:
And granted me
To ask from Him
And to receive from His sacrifice:
Because He it is
That is incorrupt,
The fulness of the ages
And the Father of them.

Ode 19 is a song exalting the conception by the Virgin; as in the *Ascension of Isaias* (XI,14) the painlessness of the birth is stressed, evidently in contrast to Eve's child-bearing:

The womb of the Virgin caught (it),
And received conception,
And brought forth:
And the Virgin became a Mother
With many mercies:
And she travailed
And brought forth a Son,
Without incurring pain.
Because it happened not emptily,
And she had not sought a midwife
(For He brought her to bear),
She brought forth,
As if she were a man,
Of her own will,

> And she brought Him forth openly,
> And acquired Him in great power,
> And loved Him in salvation,
> And guarded Him in kindness,
> And showed Him in majesty,
> Hallelujah.

Ode 12 sings of the Logos:

> He hath filled me with words of truth:
> That I may speak the same;
> And like the flow of waters flows truth from my mouth,
> And my lips shew forth His fruit.
> And He has caused His knowledge to abound in me,
> Because the mouth of the Lord is the true Word,
> And the door of His light,
> And the Most High hath given it to His worlds,
> Which are the interpreters of His own beauty,
> And the repeaters of His praise,
> And the confessors of His counsel,
> And the heralds of His thought,
> And the chasteners of His servants.
> For the swiftness of the Word cannot be expressed,
> And according to its swiftness so is its sharpness;
> And its course knows no limit.
> Never doth it fail, but it stands sure,
> And it knows not descent nor the way of it.
> For as the work is, so is its expectation:
> For it is light and the dawning of thought;
> And by it the worlds talk one to the other,
> And in the Word there were those that were silent;
> And from it came love and concord;
> And they spake one to the other
> Whatever was theirs;
> And they were penetrated by the Word;
> And they knew Him who made them,
> Because they were in concord;
> For the mouth of the Most High spake to them;
> And His explanation ran by means of it;
> For the dwelling place of the Word is man;

And its truth is love.
Blessed are they who by means thereof
Have understood everything,
And have known the Lord in His truth.
Hallelujah.

Ode 28 gives a poetical description of the Passion with occasional reminiscences of scriptural language. Christ is made to
say here:

They who saw me marvelled at me,
Because I was persecuted,
And they supposed that I was swallowed up:
For I seemed to them as one of the lost,
And my oppression was to me for salvation;
And I was their reprobation,
Because there was no zeal in me;
Because I did good to every man
I was hated,
And they came round me like mad dogs,
Who ignorantly attack their masters,
For their thought is corrupt and their understanding
                                        (perverted.
But I was carrying waters in my right hand,
And their bitterness I endured by my sweetness;
And I did not perish,
For I was not their brother
Nor was my birth like theirs,
And they sought for my death
And did not find it:
For I was older than their recollection (reached);
And vainly did they cast lots upon me;
In vain did those who were behind me
Seek to bring to nought the memory of Him
Who was before them:
For nothing is prior to the Thought of the Most High:
And His heart is superior to all wisdom. Hallelujah.

Ode 42 has as theme the Resurrection of Christ and his victory
in Limbo. The cry of the souls in the world below to the Savior

for their deliverance from death and darkness, at the end of the
hymn, is especially remarkable:

> I stretched out my hands and approached my Lord:
> For the stretching of my hands is His sign:
> My expansion is the out-spread tree
> Which was set up on the way of the Righteous One.
> And I became of no account to those
> Who did not take hold of me;
> And I shall be with those who love me.
> All my persecutors are dead;
> And they have sought me
> Who set their hope on me,
> Because I live:
> And I rose and am with them;
> And I will speak by their mouths.
> For they have despised those
> Who persecuted them;
> And I lifted up over them the yoke of my love;
> Like the arm of the Bridegroom over the Bride,
> So was my yoke over those that know me,
> And as the couch that is spread in the house of the
>   (bridegroom and bride
> So is my love over those that believe in me.
> And I was not rejected,
> Though I was reckoned to be so.
> I did not perish,
> Though they devised (it) against me.
> Sheol saw me and was made miserable;
> Death cast me up
> And many along with me.
> I was gall and bitterness to him,
> And I went down with him to the utmost of his depths:
> And the feet and the head he let go,
> For they were not able to endure my face:
> And I made a congregation of living men amongst his dead
>   men,
> And I spake with them by living lips:
> Because my word shall not be void:
> And those who had died ran towards me:

And they cried out and said,
Son of God, have pity on us
And do with us according to thy kindness,
And bring us out from the bonds of darkness:
And open to us the door by which we shall come out to thee.
Let us also be redeemed with thee:
For thou art our Redeemer.
And I heard their voice;
And my name I sealed upon their heads:
For they are free men and they are mine.
Hallelujah.

Editions and translations: J. R. HARRIS, The Odes and Psalms of Solomon.
Cambridge, 1909, 2nd ed. 1911. Re-edited by J. R. HARRIS and A. MINGANA,
The Odes and Psalms of Solomon. 2 vols., Manchester 1916/1920 with
facsimile of the Syriac text, translation and commentaries. — J. H. BERNARD,
The Odes of Solomon (Texts and Studies, 8,3). Cambridge, 1912 with an
English translation from which the passages pp. 162 to 167 are taken.
German: J. FLEMMING and A. HARNACK, Ein jüdisch-christliches Psalm-
buch aus dem 1. Jahrhundert (TU 35,4). Leipzig, 1910. — H. GRIMME,
Die Oden Salomos, syrisch-hebräisch-deutsch. Heidelberg, 1911. — A.
UNGNAD and W. STAERK, Die Oden Salomos, aus dem Syrischen über-
setzt (KT 64). Bonn, 1910. — G. DIETTRICH, Die Oden Salomos aus
dem Syrischen ins Deutsche übersetzt und mit einem Kommentar versehen
(Neue Studien zur Geschichte d. Theologie und Kirche 9). Berlin, 1911. —
E. HENNECKE, Neutestamentliche Apokryphen. 2nd ed. Tübingen, 1924,
437–472. — W. BAUER, Die Oden Salomos (KT 64). Berlin, 1933. — *French:*
J. LABOURT et P. BATIFFOL, Les Odes de Salomon. Paris, 1911. — C. BRUSTON,
Les plus anciens cantiques chrétiens. Paris, 1912. — *Italian:* L.TONDELLI, Le
Odi di Salomone. Rome, 1914. — *Dutch:* H. J. E. WESTERMAN HOLSTIJN,
Oden van Salomo. Zutphen, 1942.

Studies: W. E. BARNES, The Text of the Odes of Solomon: JThSt 11 (1910)
573ff. — R. NEWBOLD, Bardaisan and the Odes of Solomon: JBL 30 (1911)
161–204; *idem*, The Descent of Christ in the Odes of Solomon: JBL 31
(1912) 168–209. — W. STÖLTEN, Gnostische Parallelen zu den Oden Salomons: ZNW 13 (1912) 29–58. — A. J. WENSINCK, Ephrem's Hymns on
Epiphany and the Odes of Solomon: The Expositor, Ser. 8, vol. 3 (1912)
108–112. — J. R. HARRIS, Ephrem's Use of the Odes of Solomon: *ibidem*,
113–119. — W. H. WORRELL, The Odes of Solomon and the Pistis Sophia:
JThSt 13 (1912) 29ff. — R. H. CONNOLLY, The Odes of Solomon: Jewish
or Christian?: JThSt 13 (1912) 298ff. — F. C. BURKITT, A New MS of the
Odes of Solomon: JThSt 13 (1912) 372. — E. A. ABBOTT, The Original
Language of the Odes of Solomon: JThSt 14 (1913) 313ff. — R. H. CONNOLLY,
Greek the Original Language of the Odes of Solomon: JThSt 14 (1913)
530ff. — E. A. ABBOTT and R. H. CONNOLLY, The Original Language of

the Odes of Solomon: JThSt 15 (1914) 44ff. — W. K. L. CLARKE, The First Epistle of St. Peter and the Odes of Solomon: JThSt 15 (1914) 47ff. — H. M. SLEE, The Sixteenth Ode of Solomon: JThSt 15 (1914) 454ff. — G. KITTEL, Die Oden Salomons, überarbeitet oder einheitlich? Mit zwei Beilagen. I: Bibliographie der Oden Salomos, II: Syrische Konkordanz der Oden. Leipzig, 1914. — H. LEWY, Sobria Ebrietas. Giessen, 1929, 85ff. — J. R. HARRIS, The Odes of Salomon and the Apocalypse of Peter: ExpT 42 (1930) 21–23. — J. M. BOVER, La mariología en las odas de Salomón: EE 10 (1931) 349–363. — W. V. LOEWENICH, Das Johannesverständnis im zweiten Jahrhundert. Giessen, 1932, 112–115. — J. KROLL, Gott und Hölle. Leipzig, 1932, 34–44. — G. BARDY, La vie spirituelle d'après les Pères des trois premiers siècles. Paris, 1935, 94–100. — E. MERSCH, Le corps mystique du Christ, vol. 2. Brussels, 1936, 392ff.— W. C. VAN UNNIK, A Note on Ode of Solomon XXXIV, 4: JThSt 37 (1936) 172–175. — R. ABRAMOWSKI, Der Christus der Salomonoden: ZNW 35 (1936) 44–89. — J. ZIEGLER, Dulcedo Dei. Münster, 1937, 98-104. — J. DE ZWAAN, The Edessene Origin of the Odes of Solomon: Quantalacunque. Studies Presented to K. Lake. London, 1937, 285–302. — L. G. RYLANDS, The Beginnings of Gnostic Christianity. London, 1940, 23–118. — R. M. GRANT, The Odes of Salomon and the Church of Antioch: JBL (1944) 363-377.

3. THE CHRISTIAN SIBYLLINE ORACLES

Under the mythical name of the Sibyl there were fourteen books of didactic poems in hexameters, most of which were composed in the second century A.D. The compilers were Oriental Christians who made use of Jewish writings as basic material. As early as the second century B. C. Hellenistic Jews had adopted the pagan idea of the Sibyl or Seeress in order to provide propaganda for the Jewish religion in pagan circles. It is possible that they incorporated pagan oracles such as the sayings of the Sibyl of Erythraea in their writings. The same propagandistic tendency led Christian writers to compose the Sibylline oracles of the second century A.D. The work in its present form is a compilation and mixture of pagan, Jewish and Christian material of historical, political, and religious character. Of purely Christian origin are books VI, VII and large parts of Book VIII; also most probably books XIII and XIV. Books I, II, and V seem to be of Jewish origin, but they contain Christian interpolations. Books IX and X have not yet been found. Books XI to XIV were discovered by Cardinal A. Mai in 1817.

Book VI contains a hymn in honor of Christ. The miracles of the canonical Gospels are here prophesied as belonging to the future. And at the end the assumption of the Cross of the Savior into Heaven is announced. Book VII (162 verses) prophesies misfortunes and calamities against pagan nations and cities and gives a picture of the golden end of all time.

Book VIII is eschatological. The first part (1 to 216) is full of hatred and curses against Rome, and refers to Hadrian and his three successors, Pius, Lucius Verus, and Marcus. This proves that this part must have been composed shortly before 180, most probably by a Jew. The rest of the book is Christian in character, and here we find at the beginning the famous acrostic Ἰησοῦς Χριστὸς θεοῦ υἱὸς σωτὴρ σταυρός, to which Constantine (Ad coetum sanctorum, 18) and Augustine (De civ. Dei, 18,23) refer. After an eschatological description, there occur passages about the essence of God and Christ, the Nativity, and the worship of the Christians.

The prophecies of the Sibyl seem to have been used by Christians as early as the second century, because Celsus, about 177 to 178, takes pains to explain that the Christians interpolated them (Origen, Contra Celsum 7,53). Lactantius in the fourth century rejects such an idea. He quotes verses by Christian authors as prophesies of the Sibyl of Erithrea, and puts them on the same level as the utterances of the prophets of the Old Testament. During the Middle Ages the Sibylline Oracles were highly regarded. Theologians like Thomas Aquinas as well as poets like Dante and Calderon were influenced by them, and artists like Raffael and Michelangelo (Sistine Chapel) received inspiration from their content. The Dies Irae cites the Sibyl side by side with the prophet David as a witness for its description of the Last Judgment.

Edition: J. GEFFCKEN, Oracula Sibyllina (GCS 8). Leipzig, 1902.

Translations: English: M. S. TERRY, The Sibylline Oracles. 2nd ed. 1899. — H. N. BATE, The Jewish Sibylline Oracles. London, 1918. — German: E. KAUTZSCH, Die Apokryphen und Pseudepigraphen des AT 2, 1900, 177ff. — J. GEFFCKEN in: E. HENNECKE, Neutestamentliche Apokryphen. 2nd ed. Tübingen, 1924, 399–422. — Italian: A. PINCHERLE, Gli Oraculi sibillini giudaici (Orac. Sibyl. III–V). Rome, 1922.

Studies: J. GEFFCKEN, Komposition und Entstehungszeit der Oracula Sibyllina (TU 8,1). Leipzig, 1902. — RZACH, PWK II, 2, 2117ff. — T. HALUSA, Die Sibylle und ihre Prophezeiungen. 1923. — K. PRÜMM, Das Prophetenamt der Sibyllen in kirchlicher Literatur mit besonderer Rücksicht auf die Deutung der vierten Ekloge Virgils: Schol 4 (1929) 54–77; 221–246; 498–533. — K. HOLZINGER, Erklärungen zu einigen der umstrittensten Stellen der Offenbarung Johannis und der Sibyllinischen Orakel mit einem Anhang über Martial XI, 33 (SAW, Phil-Hist. KL. 216, 3). Vienna, 1936. — H. JEANMAIRE, Le règne de la femme et la rajeunissement du monde: quelques remarques sur le texte des Oracula Sibyllina VIII, 190-212: Mélanges Cumont. Brussels, 1936, 297-304. — K. KERENYI, Das persische Millenium im Mahabharata, bei der Sibylle und Vergil: Klio 11 (1936) 1-35. — L. MARIES, Strophes et poèmes dans les Livres Sibyllins: RPh (1936) 5-19. — A. KURFESS, Sibyllinische Weissagungen. Eine literar-historische Plauderei: ThQ 117 (1936) 351-366; *idem*, Kaiser Konstantin und die Sibylle: ThQ 117 (1936) 11-27; *idem*, Zu den Oracula Sibyllina: Hermes (1938) 357-360; *idem*, Zu den Oracula Sibyllina: Mnem 7 (1938) 48; *idem*, Der Brand Roms (Oracula Sibyllina V 512): Mnem 7 (1938) 261-272; *idem*, Ad Oracula Sibyllina: Symbolae Osloenses (1939) 99-105; *idem*, Mnem 8 (1939) 319f. — A. CAUSSE, L'appel de la troisième Sibylle à la Grèce et la vision du grand pélerinage à Jerusalem: Actes du Congrès G. Budé à Strasbourg. Paris, 1939, 248-253. — E. M. SANFORD, The Influence of the Sibylline Books: HTP (1940) 50f. — A. KURFESS, Zum IV. Buch der Oracula Sibyllina: PhW 46 (1940) 287-288; *idem*, Zum III. Buch der Oracula Sibyllina: PhW 47 (1941) 524-528; *idem*, Die Sibylle über sich selbst, (Or. Sib. II, 339-345; VII, 151-162): Mnem 9 (1941) 195-198; *idem*, Oracula Sibyllina I–II: ZNTW (1941) 151-165; *idem*, Zu den Oracula Sibyllina: PhW 48 (1942) 138-142; *idem*, Zum III. Buch der Oracula Sibyllina: PhW 49 (1943) 313-317; *idem*, Zum VIII. Buch der Oracula Sibyllina: PhW 49 (1943) 318-319; *idem*, Textkritisches zum XI. Buch der Oracula Sibyllina: PhW 49 (1943) 191-192; 215-216; *idem*, Textkritisches zum XII. Buch der O.S.: PhW 50 (1944) 47-48; Textkr. zum XIII Buch der O.S.: *ibidem* 143-144; Textkr. zum XIV. Buch der O.S.: *ibidem* 215-216.

4. THE SAYINGS OF SEXTUS

The so-called *Sayings of Sextus* are a collection of pagan moral sentences and rules of life, which were attributed to the Pythagorean philosopher Sextus. At the end of the second century, a Christian author (of Alexandria?) revised them. Origen is the first to mention these Sayings. In his *Contra Celsum* (8,30) he recalls 'a beautiful saying in the writings of Sextus, which is known to most Christians: The eating of animals, says he, is a matter of indifference; but to abstain from them is more agreeable to reason'. Rufinus translated 451 of these sayings from the Greek into Latin. In the preface of this Latin version, he identifies without grounds the Pythagorean philosopher Sextus with the Roman Bishop and martyr Sixtus II (257–58). But Jerome (*Comm. in Ez. ad* 18,5ff., *Comm. in Jr. ad* 22,24ff., *Ep.* 133, *ad Ctesiph.*, 3) protested strongly against this blunder.

Platonic ideas regarding purification, illumination and deification, and the Platonic concept of God inspire the majority of these sayings. Temperance in food, drink, and sleep are counseled. Marriage is not recommended. Many of these sayings remind us of the philosophy of life of Clement of Alexandria. It is possible that he is the Christian author who revised them.

A. ELTER, Gnomica I, 1892. — *English translation:* F. C. CONYBEARE, The Ring of Pope Xystus. London, 1910. — *German:* J. KROLL, in: E. HENNECKE, Neutestamentliche Apokryphen. 2nd ed. Tübingen, 1924, 625–643, — *Italian:* F. DE PAOLO, Le Sentenze di Sesto, con introd., testo e versione. Milan, 1937. — TH. HERMANN, Die armenische Ueberlieferung der Sextussentenzen: ZKG 57 (1938) 217–226. — F. X. MURPHY, Rufinus of Aquileia. His Life and His Works. Washington, 1945, 19–23.

5. CHRISTIAN POETRY ON TOMBSTONES

At an early time Christian poetry was used in epitaphs. Two such are outstanding for their antiquity and for their importance.

A. *The Inscription of Abercius*

The queen of all ancient Christian inscriptions is the epitaph of Abercius. In 1883 the archeologist W. Ramsay of the University of Aberdeen in Scotland discovered, near Hieropolis in Phrygia Salutaris, two fragments of this inscription, which are now in the Lateran Museum. A year before he had found a Christian epitaph of Alexander, dated 216, which was merely an imitation of the inscription of Abercius. With the help of this epitaph of Alexander and a Greek biography of Abercius from the fourth century published by Boissonade in 1838, it was possible to restore the entire text of the inscription. It consists of 22 verses, a distichon, and 20 hexameters. In content it is a summary of the life and deeds of Abercius. The text was composed at the end of the second century, certainly before the year 216, the date of the epitaph of Alexander. The author of the inscription is Abercius, Bishop of Hieropolis, who composed it at the age of 72 years. The great event of his life was his journey to Rome, of which he gives an account. The inscription is written in a mystical and symbolical style, according to the discipline of the secret, to conceal its Christian character from the uninitiated. The metaphorical phraseology is responsible for the sharp controversy which followed the discovery of this monument. Several scholars, like G. Ficker and A. Dieterich, tried to prove that Abercius was not a Christian, but a venerator of the Phrygian goddess Cybele, while A. Harnack called Abercius a syncretist. However, De Rossi, Duchesne, Cumont, Dölger and Abel have successfully demonstrated that the content as well as the language proves beyond doubt its Christian origin. Translated into English, the text is as follows:

1. The citizen of an eminent city, I made this (tomb)
2. In my lifetime, that I might have here a resting-place for my body.
3. Abercius by name, I am a disciple of the chaste shepherd,
4. Who feedeth His flocks of sheep on mountains and plains,
5. Who hath great eyes that look on all sides.
6. He taught me. . . faithful writings.
7. He sent me to Rome, to behold a kingdom
8. And to see a queen with golden robe and golden shoes.
9. There I saw a people bearing the splendid seal.
10. And I saw the plain of Syria and all the cities, even Nisibis,
11. Having crossed the Euphrates. And everywhere I had associates
12. Having Paul as a companion, everywhere faith led the way
13. And set before me for food the fish from the spring
14. Mighty and pure, whom a spotless Virgin caught,
15. And gave this to friends to eat, always
16. Having sweet wine and giving the mixed cup with bread.
17. These words, I, Abercius, standing by, ordered to be inscribed.
18. In truth, I was in the course of my seventy-second year.
19. Let him who understands and believes this pray for Abercius.
20. But no man shall place another tomb upon mine.
21. If one do so, he shall pay to the treasury of the Romans two thousand pieces of gold,
22. And to my beloved fatherland Hieropolis, one thousand pieces of gold.

The theological importance of this text is evident. It is the oldest monument of stone mentioning the Eucharist. The chaste shepherd, of whom Abercius calls himself a disciple, is Christ. He has sent him to Rome to see the Church, 'the queen with golden robe and golden shoes', and the Christians, the 'people with the splendid seal'. The term seal ($\sigma\phi\rho\alpha\gamma\iota\varsigma$) for Baptism was well known in the second century. Everywhere on his trip to Rome, he met coreligionists, who offered him the Eucharist under both species, bread and wine. The fish from the spring, mighty and pure, is Christ, according to the acrostic $IX\Theta Y\Sigma$. The spotless Virgin who caught the fish is, according to the language of the time, the Virgin Mary, who conceived the Savior.

G. B. DE ROSSI, Inscriptiones Christianae urbis Romae 2,1. Rome, 1888, XII–XIX. — TH. ZAHN, Avercius Marcellus von Hieropolis (Forschungen zur Geschichte des neutestamentlichen Kanons 5,1). Erlangen, 1895. — G. FICKER, Der heidnische Charakter der Abercius-Inschrift (SAB). Berlin, 1894, 187–212. — A. HARNACK, Zur Abercius-Inschrift (TU 12,4b). Leipzig, 1895. — J. WILPERT, Fractio panis. Freiburg i.B., 1895. — L. DUCHESNE, L'épitaphe d'Abercius: Mélanges d'archéologie et d'histoire 15 (1895) 155–182. — A. DIETERICH, Die Grabinschrift des Aberkios. Leipzig, 1896. — TH. W. WEHOFER, Philologische Bemerkungen zur Aberkios-Inschrift: RQ 10 (1896) 61–84; idem, Eine neue Aberkios-Hypothese: RQ 10 (1896) 351–378. — G. DE SANCTIS, Die Grabinschrift des Aberkios: ZkTh 21 (1897) 673–695. — H. LECLERCQ, Abercius: DAL 1,1 (1907) 66–87. — W. LÜDTKE und TH. NISSEN, Die Grabinschrift des Aberkios, ihre Ueberlieferung und ihr Text. Leipzig, 1910. — TH. NISSEN, St. Abercii vita. Leipzig, 1912. — F. J. DÖLGER, $IX\Theta Y\Sigma$ I. Rome, 1910, 8ff.; 87ff., 136ff.; idem, $IX\Theta Y\Sigma$ II. Münster, 1922, 454–507. — A. GREIFF, Zum Verständnis der Aberkios-inschrift: ThGl 18 (1926) 78–88; idem, Zur Aberkiosinschrift: ThQ 110 (1929) 242–261; 447–474. — A. ABEL, Etude sur l'inscription d'Abercius: Byz 3 (1926) 321–405 with a complete bibliography. — H. GRÉGOIRE Encore l'inscription d'Abercius: Byz 8 (1933) 89–91. — J. QUASTEN, Monumenta eucharistica et liturgica vetustissima. Bonn, 1935-37, 21–24. — H. STRATHMANN and TH. KLAUSER, Aberkios: RAC 1 (1942) 12–17. — G. BARDY, La Théologie de l'Eglise de saint Clément de Rome à saint Irénée (Unam Sanctam 13). Paris, 1945, 72–76.

B. *The Inscription of Pectorius*

The Inscription of Pectorius was found in seven fragments in 1830 in an ancient Christian cemetery not far from Autun in southern France. Cardinal J. P. Pitra was the first to publish it. He and G. B. De Rossi attributed it to the beginning of the second century, while E. Le Blant and J. Wilpert thought the end of the third century the time of its origin. The form and style of the letters point to the period between 350 and 400. But the phraseology is exactly that of the inscription of Abercius from the end of the second century.

The inscription is a beautiful poem of three distichs and five hexameters. The first five verses are bound together by the acrostic *IXΘYΣ*. As to content, it consists of two parts. The first part, comprising verses one to seven, is of doctrinal character and addresses the reader. Here Baptism is called 'the immortal fountain of divine waters'. The Eucharist is referred to as 'the honeysweet food of the Redeemer of the saints'. The ancient Christian ritual of receiving communion into the hands explains the words 'holding the fish in thy hands'. Christ is called the light of the dead. The second part, consisting of the last four verses, is more personal. Here Pectorius prays for his mother and asks his deceased parents and his brothers to remember him in 'the peace of the fish'. It is quite possible that the first part is a quotation from a much older poem. That would explain why the language resembles that of the inscription of Abercius. The text of the inscription is as follows:

(Thou) the divine child of the heavenly Fish,
Keep pure thy soul among the mortals.
Because thou receivest the immortal
Fountain of divine water
Refresh thy soul, friend, with the
Ever flowing water of wealth-giving wisdom.
Take from the Redeemer of the saints
The food as sweet as honey:
Eat with joy and desire, holding the Fish
In thy hands.
I pray, give as food the Fish, Lord and Savior.
May she rest peacefully, my mother,
So I pray to thee, (thou) light of the dead.
Aschandius, father, my heart's beloved,
With my sweet mother and my brothers
In the peace of the Fish remember thy Pectorius.

J. Pitra De inscriptione graeca et christiana in coemeterio sancti Petria via strata reperta, infra urbem Augustodunensem, illustrata variorum notis et dissertationibus, iisque partim ineditis: Spicilegium Solesmense I. Paris, 1852, 534–564; *idem*, *ΙΧΘΥΣ* sive de pisce allegorico et symbolico: Spicilegium Solesmense III. Paris, 1855, 499–543. — F. Lenormant, Mémoire sur l'inscription d'Autun: Mélanges d'archéologie, d'histoire et de littérature, ed. C. Cahier et A. Martin. Paris, 1853, 115f. — E. le Blant, Inscriptions chrétiennes de la Gaul antérieure au VIIIe siècle. I. Paris, 1856, 8–14. — O. Pohl, Das Ichthysmonument von Autun. Berlin, 1880. — G. B. de Rossi, Inscriptiones christianae urbis Romae 2, 1. Rome, 1888, 18–24. — J. Wilpert, Prinzipienfragen der christlichen Archäologie. Freiburg i.B., 56–62. — G. A. van den Bergh van Eysinga, Altchristliches und Orientalisches: ZDMG 60 (1906) 210–212. — K. M. Kaufmann, Handbuch der altchristlichen Epigraphik. Freiburg i.B., 1917, 178–180. — F. J. Dölger, *ΙΧΘΥΣ* I. Rome, 1910, 12–15; 177–183; *idem*, *ΙΧΘΥΣ* II. Münster, 1922, 507–515. — J. Quasten, Monumenta eucharistica et liturgica vetustissima. Bonn, 1935–37, 24–27.

CHAPTER V

THE FIRST ACTS OF THE MARTYRS

Among the most valuable sources of information for the time of the persecutions are the accounts of the suffering of the martyrs which used to be read to the Christian communities at the liturgical services on the anniversary of the martyr's death. From the historical point of view they may be divided into three groups:

I. The first group comprises official court proceedings. These contain nothing but the questions addressed to the martyrs by the authorities, the answers of the martyrs as they were taken down by the notaries public or the clerks of the court, and the sentences imposed. These documents were placed in the public archives and occasionally the Christians succeeded in obtaining copies of them. The term *acts of the martyrs* (*acta* or *gesta martyrum*) should be reserved to this group, because only here do we have immediate and absolutely reliable sources of history, which give merely the data.

II. The second category comprises the reports of eyewitnesses or contemporaries. These accounts are called *passiones* or *martyria*.

III. The third group consists of the legends of the martyrs which were composed for the purpose of edification long after the martyrdom took place. In some cases they are a fantastic admixture of some truth with purely imaginary material. Others are simply fiction with no historical foundation whatever.

Editions: J. BOLLANDUS ET SOCII, Acta Sanctorum. The first two volumes were published at Antwerp, 1643. The latest issue is vol. 65: Acta Sanctorum Novembris. Collecta, digesta, illustrata ab Hippolyto Delehaye et Paulo Peeters. Tomus IV, Quo dies nonus et decimus continentur. Brussels, 1925. Additions are published in: Analecta Bollandiana. Brussels, 1882ff. A survey of the whole work of the Bollandists is given by H. DELEHAYE, A travers trois siècles. L'oeuvre des Bollandistes 1615–1915. Brussels, 1920. — TH. RUINART, Acta primorum martyrum sincera. Paris, 1689, 2nd ed. Amsterdam, 1713. Latest edition: Regensburg, 1859. Cf. E. LE BLANT, Les actes des martyrs. Supplément aux Acta sincera de Dom Ruinart (Mémoires de l'Institut nat. de France Acad. des Inscr. et Belles Lettres 30,2,57–347). Paris, 1883, new ed. Paris, 1923. — O. v. GEBHARDT, Ausgewählte Märtyrerakten. Berlin, 1902. — R. KNOPF, Ausgewählte Märtyrerakten, 3rd ed. revised by G. KRÜGER (SQ 3). Tübingen, 1929. — F. RÜTTEN, Lateinische Martyrerakten und Martyrerbriefe. Münster, 1931. — F. K. LUKMAN. Martyres Christi. Celje, 1934. — Oriental Acts of the Martyrs: *Syriac:* St. E. ASSEMANI. Acta Sanctorum Martyrum orientalium et occid., 2 vols. Rome, 1748. — P. BEDJAN, Acta martyrum et sanctorum, 7 vols. Paris, 1890–1897. — *Coptic:* J. BALESTRI et H. HYVERNAT, Acta martyrum (CSCO, Script. coptici). Paris, 1907ff. with a Latin translation. — AMÉLINEAU, Les actes des martyrs de l'église copte. Paris, 1890. — W. TILL, Koptische Heiligen und Märtyrerlegenden I (Orientalia christiana analecta, Fasc. 102). Rome, 1935; II (Orientalia chr. an., Fasc. 108). Rome, 1936. — *Ethiopic:* M. E. PEREIRA, Acta Martyrum (CSCO, Series Aethiopica II, t. 28).

Translations: English: E. C. E. OWEN, Some Authentic Acts of the Early Martyrs. Translated with notes and introductions. Oxford, 1927. — *French:* H. LECLERCQ, Les Martyrs 2. Paris, 1903; 1–3. Paris, 1921. — P. MONCEAUX, La vraie légende dorée. Relations du martyre. Paris, 1928. — P. HANOZIN, La geste des martyrs. Paris, 1935. — *Italian:* S. COLOMBO, Atti dei martiri. Turin, 1928. — *German:* G. RAUSCHEN, Echte alte Märtyrerakten (BKV 14). Kempten, 1913, 289–369. — O. BRAUN, Ausgewählte Akten persischer Märtyrer (BKV 22). Kempten, 1915. — H. RAHNER, Die Märtyrerakten des zweiten Jahrhunderts. Freiburg i. B., 1941. — *Dutch:* L. HAGEN, Keus van enkele martelaarsakten uit de eerste eeuwen des Christendoms. Utrecht, 1910. — M. F. SCHURMANS, Bloedgetuigen van Christus. Martelaars-documenten uit de eerste eeuwen der Kerk. 3rd. ed. Roermond, 1947.

Studies: H. LECLERCQ, Actes des martyrs: DAL 1, 373–446; *idem*, Martyr: DAL 10, 2359–2512. — E. LUCIUS, Die Anfänge des Heiligenkults in der christlichen Kirche. Tübingen, 1904. — H. GÜNTER, Legendenstudien. Cologne, 1906; *idem*, Die christliche Legende des Abendlandes. Heidelberg, 1910. — A. EHRHARD, Die griechischen Martyrien. Strasbourg, 1907. — P. ALLARD, Ten Lectures on the Martyrs. London, 1907. — H. DELEHAYE, Les légendes grecques des saints militaires. 1909. — A. HARNACK, Das ursprüngliche Motiv der Abfassung von Märtyrer- und Heilungsakten in der Kirche: SAB (1910) 106–215. — W. HELLMANNS, Wertschätzung des Martyriums als eines Rechtfertigungsmittels in der altchristlichen Kirche bis zum Ausgang des vierten Jahrhunderts. Breslau, 1912. — L. H. CANFIELD, The Early Persecutions of the Christians. New York, 1913. — P. DÖRFLER, Die Anfänge der Heiligenverehrung nach den römischen Inschriften und Bildwerken. Munich, 1913. — CALLEGARI, Alessandro Severo e gli Acta martyrum. 1919. — F. GROSSI-GONDI, Principi e problemi di critica agiographia: Atti e spoglie dei martiri. 1919. — O. SILD, Das altchristliche Martyrium. Dorpat, 1920. — H. DELEHAYE, Les passions des martyrs et les genres littéraires. Brussels, 1921; *idem*, Martyr et confesseur: AB 39 (1921) 20–49. — A. PRIESNIG, Die biographischen Formen der griechischen Heiligenlegenden in ihrer geschichtlichen Entwicklung (Diss. Munich). Münnerstadt, 1924. — S. COLOMBO, Gli Acta martyrum e la loro origine: SC (1924) 30–38; 109–122; 189–203. — K. MÜLLER, Die Reden der Martyrer: ZNW (1924) 225f. — M. VILLER, Les martyrs et l'esprit: RSR 14 (1924) 544–551; *idem*, Martyre et perfection: RAM 6 (1925) 3–25; *idem*, Le martyre et l'ascèse: RAM 6 (1925) 105-142. — L. DE REGIBUS, Storia et diritto romano negli Acta martyrum: Did (1926), fasc. 2, 127-187. — E. LOHMEYER, Die Idee des Martyriums im Judentum und Urchristentum: ZST 5 (1927) 232-249. — H. DELEHAYE, Les légendes hagiographiques. 3rd ed. 1927; idem, Sanctus. Essai sur le culte des Saints dans l'antiquité (Subsidia hagiographica 7). Brussels, 1927; idem, La méthode historique et l'hagiographie: Académie Royale Belgique, Classe des Lettres, 1930, n. 7. — O. MICHEL, Prophet und Martyrer. Gütersloh, 1932. — J. QUASTEN, Die Reform des Martyrerkultes durch Augustinus: ThGl 25 (1933) 318-331. — H. DELEHAYE, Les origines du culte des martyrs. 2nd ed. Brussels, 1933. — J. MADOZ, El amor a Jesucristo en la Iglesia de los mártires: EE 12 (1933) 313-344. — J. L. JANSEN, Over het getal der martelaren in het Romeinsche Rijk van 64-313: Nederlandsche Katholieke Stemmen 33 (1933) 311-314. — F. J. DÖLGER, Christophoros als Ehrentitel für Martyrer und Heilige im christlichen Altertum: AC 4 (1934) 73-80. — H. DELEHAYE, Cinq leçons sur la méthode hagiographique. 1934. — H. V. CAMPENHAUSEN, Die Idee des Martyriums in der alten Kirche. Göttingen, 1936. Cf J. DE GHELLINCK, NRTh 64 (1937) 416-417. — E. PETERSON, Der Märtyrer und die Kirche: Hochland 34 (1936) 385-394; idem, Zeuge der Wahrheit. Leipzig, 1937. — H. W. SURKAU, Martyrien in jüdischer und frühchristlicher Zeit. Göttingen, 1938. — J. VERGOTE, Eculeus, Rad- und Pressefolter in den ägyptischen Märtyrerakten: ZNW 37 (1938) 239-250. — J. DE MAYOL DE LUPE, Les actes des martyrs comme source de renseignements pour le langage et les usages des IIe et IIIe siècles: RELA 17 (1939) 90-104. — J. QUASTEN, Vetus superstitio et nova religio: HThR (1940) 253-266. — E. GUENTHER, Martys. Hamburg, 1941. — H. HUMMEL, The Concept of Martyrdom in Cyprian of Carthage (SCA 9). Washington, 1946.

I. To the first group belong:

1. *The Acts of St. Justin and his Companions.* These acts are very valuable, because they contain the official court proceedings against the most important of the Greek apologists, the famous philosopher Justin. Together with six other Christians, he was cast into prison by order of the Roman prefect, Q. Junius Rusticus, during the reign of the Emperor Marcus Aurelius Antoninus, the Stoic philosopher. The acts consist of a very brief introduction, the interrogation and sentence, and a short conclusion. The sentence which the prefect pronounces is: 'Let those who will not sacrifice to the gods and yield to the command of the Emperor be scourged and led away to be beheaded in accordance with the law.' The martyrdom took place probably in 165 A.D. at Rome.

2. *The Acts of the Martyrs of Scilli in Africa.* They constitute the

oldest document in African Church history, and at the same time the oldest dated Christian document in Latin which we possess of North Africa. In content, they are the official record of the trial of Namphano of Madaura, Miggin, Sanam, and six other Christians of Numidia, who were sentenced to death by the proconsul Saturninus and beheaded on July 17, 180. In addition to the Latin original, we have a Greek translation of these Acts.

B. Aubé, Etude sur un nouveau texte des actes des martyrs Scillitains. Paris, 1881; AB 8 (1889) 5ff.; 16 (1897) 64f. — J. A. Robinson, The Passion of Perpetua with an Appendix on the Scillitan Martyrdom (Texts and Studies, 1,2). Cambridge, 1891, 104–121: The original Latin text together with the Greek version and the Latin recensions. — K. J. Neumann, Der römische Staat und die allgemeine Kirche bis auf Diokletian, vol. 1. Leipzig, 1890, 71–74; 284–286. — P. Monceaux, Histoire litt. de l'Afrique chrét. 1. Paris, 1901, 61–70. — P. Franchi de Cavallieri, Le reliquie dei martiri Scillitani: RQ 17 (1903) 209–221. — A. Aclais, Figures et récits de Carthage chrétienne. Etudes sur le christianisme africain aux IIe et IIIe siècles. Paris, 1908. — L. Saltet, BLE (1914) 108–123. — G. Rauschen, FP 3. Bonn, 1915, 104–106. — H. Delehaye, Les passions des martyrs et les genres littéraires. Brussels, 1921, 60–63. — J. H. Baxter, The Martyrs of Madaura, A.D. 180: JThSt 26 (1925) 21ff.

3. *The Proconsular Acts of St. Cyprian*, the bishop of Carthage, who was executed September 14, 258, are founded on officia reports which have been connected by a few phrases of the editor. They consist of three separate documents containing: (1) The first trial which sends Cyprian into exile to Curubis, (2) the arrest and second trial, and (3) the execution. The martyrdom took place under the Emperors Valerian and Gallienus.

G. Hartel, Cypriani opera (CSEL 3,3). Wien, 1871, CX–CXIV. — A. F. Gregg, Decian Persecution. Edinburgh, 1897, 115–152; 274–280. — P. Monceaux, Histoire litt. de l'Afrique chrét. 2. Paris, 1902, 179–197. — R. Reitzenstein, Die Nachrichten über den Tod Cyprians (Sitzungsberichte der Heidelberger Akademie der Wissenschaften). Heidelberg, 1913; idem, Bemerkungen zur Martyrerliteratur II: Nachträge zu den Akten Cyprians: NGWG (1919) 177–219. — P. Franchi de Cavallieri, Studi Romani. Rome, 1914, 189–215. — P. Corssen, Das Martyrium des Bischofs Cyprian: ZNW 15 (1914) 221–233; 285–316; 16 (1915) 54–92; 198–230; 17 (1916) 189–206; 18 (1917) 118–139; 202–233. — H. Delehaye, Cyprien d'Antioche et Cyprien de Carthage: AB 39 (1921) 314–332. — F. C. Conybeare, The Armenian Acts of Cyprian: ZNW 21 (1922) 269–277. — S. Colombo, Gli Acta Proconsularia del martirio di S. Cipriano e alcuni sermoni di S. Agostino: Didascaleion 3 (1925) 101–108.

II. To the second category belong:

1. The *Martyrium Polycarpi*, from the year 156 A.D. (see above p. 77f.)

2. *The Letter of the Churches of Vienne and Lyons to the Churches of Asia and Phrygia*, which gives a moving account of the sufferings of the martyrs who died in the severe persecution of the Church of Lyons in 177, or 178, and which is preserved by Eusebius (*Hist. eccl.* 5,1,1–2,8), is one of the most interesting documents of the persecutions. It does not conceal the apostasy of some members of the community. Among the courageous martyrs we see Bishop Photinus 'being over ninety years of age and very sick in body, scarcely breathing from the sickness, but strengthened by zeal of the spirit from his vehement desire for martyrdom'; the admirable Blandina, a frail and delicate female slave, who upheld the courage of her companions by her example and words; Maturus, a neophyte of amazing fortitude; Sanctus, a deacon of Vienne; Alexander, the physician; and Ponticus, a boy of fifteen years of age. Of Blandina the Acts report: 'The blessed Blandina, last of all, like a noble mother that has encouraged her children and sent them before her, crowned with victory, to the King, retracing herself also all her children's battles, hastened towards them, rejoicing and triumphant in her departure, as though she were called to a marriage supper, instead of being cast to the beasts. After the whips, after the beasts, after the burning, she was thrown at last into a net and cast before a bull. And after being tossed for some long time by the beast, having no further sense of what was happening because of her hope and hold on the things she had believed, and because of her communing with Christ, she was herself offered up also, the very pagans confessing that they had never known a woman endure so many and so great sufferings.'

Translations: B. P. PRATTEN, ANF 8, 778–784. — T. H. BINDLEY, The Epistle of the Gallican Churches: Lugdunum and Vienna (SPCK). London, 1900. — For other translations see above, p. 177.

Studies: O. HIRSCHFELD, Zur Geschichte des Christentums in Lugdunum vor Konstantin: SAB (1895) 381–409. — C. JULLIAN, Quelques remarques sur la lettre des chrétiens de Lyon: Rétanc. 13 (1913) 317ff. — J. W. THOMPSON, The Alleged Persecution of the Christians at Lyons in 177: The American Journal of Theology 16 (1912) 359–384. Against Thompson, who doubted the authenticity of the Epistle, cf. A. Harnack, ThLZ (1913) 74-77; P. Allard, RQH 93 (1913) 53-67; 95 (1914) 83-89. — U. Kahrstedt, Die Märtyrerakten von Lugdunum 177: RhM 68 (1913) 395-412. — P. de Labriolle, Le style de la lettre des chrétiens de Lyon: Bulletin d'anc. litt. et d'archéol. chrét. 3 (1913) 198f. — H. Quentin, La liste des martyrs de Lyon: AB 39 (1921) 113-138. — K. Müller, ZNW 1924, 215ff. — J. Pourrat, Les saint martyrs de Lyon. Lyon, 1926. — G. Bardy, La vie spirituelle d'après les Pères des trois premiers siècles. Paris, 1935, 160-173. — A. Chagny, Les martyrs de Lyon de 177. Lyon, 1936. — P. Prime, The Lyon Martyrs of A.D. 177: IER 77 (1941) 182-189. — J. C. Plumpe, Mater Ecclesia (SCA 5). Washington, 1943, 36-41.

3. *The Passion of Perpetua and Felicitas* gives an account of the martyrdom of the three catechumens Saturus, Saturninus and Revocatus, and two young women, Vibia Perpetua, 22 years of age, 'well born, liberally educated, honorably married, having father and mother and two brothers, one like herself a catechumen, and an infant son at the breast', and her slave Felicitas, who was pregnant at the time of her arrest and gave birth to a girl shortly before her death in the arena. They suffered martyrdom on March 7, 202, at Carthage. The account is one of the most beautiful pieces of ancient Christian literature. It is unique as far as its authorship is concerned. The largest part of the account (ch. 3-10) is Perpetua's own diary: 'the whole story of her martyrdom is from this point onwards told by herself as she left it written by her own hand and with her own mind' (ch. 2). Chapters 11 to 13 were written by Saturus. There is reason to believe that the author of the other chapters and the editor of the entire Passion was no less a person than Tertullian, the contemporary of Perpetua and the greatest writer of the African Church at that time. The resemblance in phrase and syntax and in words and ideas between Tertullian's works *Ad Martyres* and *De Patientia* and the *Passion of Perpetua and Felicitas* is striking. At St. Augustine's time, the Acts were still held in such esteem that he has to warn his listeners not to put them on a level with the canonical Scriptures (*De anima et eius origine* 1, 10, 12).

These Acts are extant in both a Latin and a Greek text. It seems that the Latin text is the original, because the Greek has modified passages and spoils the conclusion. C. van Beek thinks that the same author edited the Passion in Latin as well as in Greek, but passages like chapters 21, 2 and 16, 3 prove that the

Latin text must be the original, and that the Greek text is only a later translation, because the play upon words found in these passages can be understood only in Latin.

The content of this Passion is of considerable importance for the history of Christian thought. Especially the visions which Perpetua had during her imprisonment and which she wrote down are of high value for the knowledge of the eschatological views of early Christians. Dinocrates' vision and the vision of the ladder and the dragon are striking examples. Martyrdom is twice called a second Baptism (18, 3 and 21,2). The ritual of receiving communion appears in her vision of the Good Shepherd.

Separate editions: J. A. Robinson, The Passion of S. Perpetua (Texts and Studies, 1,2). Cambridge, 1891. — P. Franchi de Cavallieri, La Passio SS. Perpetuae et Felicitatis (RQ Suppl. 5). Freiburg i. B., 1896, 104–148. — W. H. Shewring, The Passion of SS. Perpetua and Felicity. New edition and translation of the Latin text, together with the Sermons of St. Augustine upon these saints. London, 1931. — C. J. M. J. van Beek, Passio sanctarum Perpetuae et Felicitatis. T. I. Nijmegen, 1936; *idem,* Passio Sanctarum Perpetuae et Felicitatis, latine et graece (FP 43). Bonn, 1938.

Translations: English: R. E. Wallis, ANF 3, 697–706. — E. C. E. Owen, Some Authentic Acts of the Early Martyrs. Oxford, 1927, 78–92. — W.H. Shewring, l.c. *German:* G. Rauschen, Echte alte Martyrerakten (BKV 14). Kempten, 1913, 328ff. — O. Hagemeyer, Die Passion der hl. Perpetua und Felizitas, aus dem Lateinischen übertragen. Klosterneuburg bei Wien, 1938. *Italian:* G. Sola. Rome, 1920.

Studies: A. de Waal, Der leidende Dinokrates in der Vision der hl. Perpetua : RQ 17 (1903) 839–847. — A. d'Alès, L'auteur de la Passio Perpetuae: RHE 8 (1907) 1–18. — P. de Labriolle, Tertullien, auteur du prologue et de la conclusion de la passion de Perpétue et de Félicité: Bull. anc. litt. arch. chrét. 3 (1913) 126–132; *idem,* La crise montaniste. Paris, 1913, 338–353. — A. H. Salonius, Passio Sanctae Perpetuae. Helsingfors, 1921. — L. Gatti, La Passio SS. Perpetuae et Felicitatis: Did 1 (1923) 31–43. — F. J. Dölger, Gladiatorenblut und Märtyrerblut. Eine Szene der Passio Perpetuae in kultur- und religionsgeschichtlicher Beleuchtung: Vorträge der Bibliothek Warburg (1923/24) 196–214. — J. A. Johnston, The Passion of SS. Perpetua and Felicitas: Month 153 (1929) 216–222. — W. H. Shewring, Prose Rhythm in the Passio Perpetuae: JThSt 30 (1929) 56f. — F. J. Dölger, Antike Parallelen zum leidenden Dinokrates in der Passio Perpetuae: AC 2 (1930) 1–40. — W. H. Shewring, En marge de la passion des saintes Perpétue et Félicité: RB 43 (1931) 15–22. — F. J. Dölger, Der Kampf mit dem Aegypter in der Perpetua-Vision. Das Martyrium als Kampf mit dem Teufel: AC 3 (1932) 177–188. — G. Bardy, La vie spirituelle d'après les Pères des trois premiers siècles. Paris, 1935, 173–180. — J. Quasten, Die

Grabinschrift des Beratius Nikatoras: Mitteilungen des Deutschen Archeo-
logischen Instituts, Römische Abteilung 53 (1938) 66-68. — A. FERRUA,
S. Saturnino martire Cartaginese-Romano: CC 90 (1939) 436-445. —
H. LECLERCQ, DAL 5, 1259-1298. — J. STEIN, Tertullian. Christliches Be-
wusstsein und sittliche Forderungen. Düsseldorf, 1940, 274-313: Tertullians
theologische Ethik als Kommentar zur Passio Perpetuae. — J. QUASTEN,
A Coptic Counterpart of a Vision in the Acts of Perpetua and Felicitas:
Byz 15 (1940/41) 1-9. — E. RUPPRECHT, Bemerkungen zur Passio SS. Perpetuae et Felicitatis: RhM 90 (1941) 177-192. — J. QUASTEN, A Roman Law
of Egyptian Origin in the Passio SS. Perpetuae et Felicitatis: The Jurist 1
(1941) 193-198.

4. *The Acts of St. Carpus, Papylus and Agathonice* are a genuine,
eye-witness account of the martyrdom of Carpus and Papylus,
who died at the stake in the amphitheatre of Pergamon, and of
Agathonice, a Christian woman, who threw herself into the
flames. It seems that the Acts in their present form are incomplete.
Agathonice had been condemned like the other two. This part
of the text is missing, so that she appears to have committed
suicide. The martyrdoms took place in the time of Marcus Aurelius and Lucius Verus (161-169). The Acts were still in circulation at Eusebius' time (*Hist. eccl.* 4, 15, 48).

A. HARNACK, Die Akten des Karpus, des Papylus und der Agathonike. Eine
Urkunde aus der Zeit Mark Aurels (TU 3,3-4). Leipzig, 1888. — A. EHRHARD,
Die altchristliche Literatur und ihre Erforschung von 1884-1900. Erste Ab-
teilung: Die vornicänische Literatur. Freiburg i. B., 1900, 577-579. — G.
RAUSCHEN, FP 3. Bonn, 1915, 313-317. — H. LIETZMANN, Die älteste Ge-
stalt der Passio SS. Carpi, Papylae et Agathonicis: Festgabe für K. MÜLLER.
Tübingen, 1922, 46-57. — H. LECLERCQ, DAL 8, 680-685. — A. M.
SCHNEIDER, Das Martyrium der heiligen Karpos und Papylos zu Konstan-
tinopel: Jahrbuch des Deutschen Archäologischen Instituts 49 (1934) 416-
418. Cf. J. QUASTEN, JL 14 (1938) 412.

5. *The Acts of Apollonius.* In his *Eccl. Hist.* 5, 21, 2-5, Eusebius
gives a summary of these Acts, which he had included in his collection of ancient martyrdoms. Apollonius was a learned philosopher. Judged by Perennis, the Prefect of the Praetorium in Rome,
he was beheaded during the reign of the Emperor Commodus
(180-185). The speeches with which Apollonius defends his faith
before Perennis resemble in their argumentation the writings of
the Apologists. They are most probably based on the answers
which the philosopher gave according to the official *Acta Praefec-
toria.* A. Harnack has called them 'the noblest apology of Chris-

tianity which came down to us from antiquity'. Two versions of
these acts have been published, one in Armenian by Conybeare
in 1893, the other in Greek by the Bollandists in 1895.

For editions and translations see above, p. 176 f.
Studies: F. C. CONYBEARE, The Armenian Apology and Acts of Apollonius
and Other Monuments of Early Christianity. London, 1894, gives an English
translation of the Armenian version. — MAX, PRINZ VON SACHSEN, Der
heilige Märtyrer Apollonius von Rom. Eine historisch-kritische Studie.
Mainz, 1913, gives a new Latin translation of the Armenian Acts. — A. HAR-
NACK, Der Prozess des Christen Apollonius vor dem praefectus praetorii
Perennis und dem römischen Senat: SAB (1893) 721–746. — R. SEEBERG,
Das Martyrium des Apollonius: NKZ 4 (1893) 836–872. — A. HILGENFELD,
Apollonius von Rom: Zeitschrift für wiss. Theologie 37 (1894) 58–91. —
TH. MOMMSEN, Der Prozess des Christen Apollonius und Commodus: SAB
(1894) 497-503. — KLETTE, Der Prozess und die Acta S. Apollonii (TU15,2).
Leipzig, 1897. — A. HILGENFELD, Die Apologie des Apollonius von Rom:
Zeitschrift f. wiss. Theol. 41 (1898) 185–210. — A. PATIN, Apollonius Martyr,
der Skoteinologe; ein Beitrag zu Heraklit und Euemerus: Archiv für Ge-
schichte der Philosophie 12 (1899) 147–158. — O. HEINE, Die Apologie des
Apollonius: Deutsch-evangelische Blätter 27 (1902) 97–108. — J. GEFFCKEN,
Die Acta Apollonii (Nachrichten der Gesellsch. der Wiss. zu Göttingen,
Phil.-hist. Kl. 1904) 262–284. — C. CALLEWAERT, Questions de droit con-
cernant le procès du martyr Apollonius: RQH 77 (1905) 353–375. — C.
ERBES, Das Todesjahr des römischen Märtyrers Apollonius: ZNW 13 (1912)
269ff.

III. To the third group belong the Acts of the Roman martyrs,
St. Agnes, St. Cecilia, St. Felicitas and her seven sons, St. Hippolytus, St. Lawrence, St. Sixtus, St. Sebastian, Sts. John and Paul,
Cosmas and Damian; also the *Martyrium Sancti Clementis* (see
above p. 43) and the *Martyrium Sancti Ignatii*. The fact that these
Acts are unauthentic by no means indicates that these martyrs
did not exist, as some scholars have concluded. The authenticity
or spuriousness of Acts does not prove the existence or non-
existence of martyrs, but merely indicates that these documents
can not be used as sources for history.

Collections. A collection of Acts of the Martyrs was made by
Eusebius in his work *On the Ancient Martyrs*. Unfortunately this
valuable source has been lost. But in his *Ecclesiastical History* he
summarizes most of these Acts. We possess however his treatise
on the martyrs of Palestine, a report of the victims of the persecutions from 303 to 311 which he witnessed as Bishop of Caesarea.

An anonymous author collected Acts of Persian martyrs who died under Sapor II, 339–79. They are extant in Syriac, in which they were composed. The trials and interrogatories are given here in a way similar to the reports of the authentic Acts of the first martyrs. The Syriac Acts of the martyrs of Edessa are legends.

CHAPTER VI

THE GREEK APOLOGISTS

Whereas the works of the Apostolic Fathers and of early Christianity were directed to the guidance and edification of the faithful, with the Greek Apologists the literature of the Church addresses itself for the first time to the outside world and enters the domain of culture and science. In the face of the aggressive attitude of paganism, the missionary type of sermon, which was only occasionally apologetic, was displaced in favor of that predominantly apologetic exposition which gives to the writing of the second century its distinctive character. Not only were vile rumors rampant among the populace, not only did the State regard the profession of Christianity as a capital crime against the official cult and the majesty of the emperor, but even the enlightened judgment of scholars and the weight of opinion among the more cultivated classes of society condemned the new religion as an ever increasing threat to Rome's world-wide dominion. Among the prominent opponents of Christianity in the second century may be mentioned the satirist Lucian of Samosata, whose *De morte peregrini* of 170 A.D. derided the faithful for their brotherly love and contempt of death; the philosopher Fronto of Cirta, teacher of the emperor Marcus Aurelius, in his *Oration*; and, foremost of all, the Platonist Celsus, who issued his attack, *The True Discourse*, $'A\lambda\eta\vartheta\grave{\eta}s$ $\varLambda\acute{o}\gamma os$, in 178 A.D. The numerous excerpts from this last-named work preserved in Origen's refutation enable us readily to appreciate how resourceful and dangerous an antagonist was its author. For Celsus Christianity was but a hodgepodge of superstition and fanaticism.

Such insults to a cause that was step by step becoming an influential factor in history, and that won daily to its service men distinguished for their education, could not be suffered in silence. Consequently, the Apologists set before themselves three objectives:

1) They challenged the widely current calumnies and were at particular pains to answer the charge that the Church was a peril to the State. Pointing to the earnest, strict, chaste and honorable lives of their coreligionists, they insisted that the faith was

a dominant force for the maintenance and welfare of the world, not only emperor and State but civilization itself.

2) They exposed the absurdities and immoralities of paganism and the myths of its divinities, at the same time demonstrating that the Christian alone has a correct understanding of God and the universe. Hence they defended the dogmas concerned with the unity of God, monotheism, the divinity of Christ and the resurrection of the body.

3) Not content with merely rebutting the arguments of the philosophers, they went on to show that this very philosophy, because it had only human reason to rely upon, had either never attained truth, or that the truth it had attained was but fragmentary and mingled with numerous errors, the 'spawn of the demons'. Christianity, they asserted on the other hand, possesses absolute truth, since the Logos, Divine Reason itself, comes down through Christ upon earth. It must thence follow that Christianity is immeasurably above Greek philosophy — is, in fact, divine philosophy.

In making this demonstration of the faith the Apologists laid the foundation of the science of God. They are therefore the Church's first theologians — a fact that adds to their importance. Naturally, we find in their work only the beginnings of a formal study of theological doctrine, since they neither aimed at scientific organization nor attempted to bring the whole body of revelation within their scope. To label their effort a Hellenization of Christianity, however, would be wrong. It is, of course, to be expected that the habits of thought so ingrained in them before their conversion should exert an influence upon their religious outlook; in their theology, also, the Greek Apologists are children of their age. This is particularly evident in the terminology to which they have recourse and in their approach to the interpretation of dogma. It is apparent, too, in the form which their writings take — treatment predominantly dialectic or dialogue in accordance with the norms of Greek rhetoric. The content, however, of the theology of the Apologists has been far less influenced by pagan philosophy than is sometimes asserted. It has been affected only in minor details. We may speak therefore of a Christianization of Hellenism but hardly of a Hellenization of Christianity, particularly if we attempt to appreciate as a whole the intellectual achievement of the Apologists.

In vindicating their religion, these authors did not address themselves solely to pagans and Jews. Most of them wrote anti-heretical treatises also. These, much to our regret, have been lost; they would have been of inestimable value for a complete understanding of the Apologists' theology. In dealing with their extant works, then, we must exercise proper caution. Though the evidences of intimate contact with Catholic ideals and thought are much fewer than might have been expected, the comparative scantiness of such indications must not be interpreted as a tendency towards rationalism. We cannot be at all sure that the readers of the apologies possessed either a sufficiently broad sympathy with the Catholic outlook or an adequate understanding of it. The shortcomings of the audience are the reason why the person of the Savior and the efficacy of grace, for instance, recede into the background. Christianity is portrayed primarily, though not exclusively, as the religion of truth. Hence its claims are seldom substantiated by adducing as proof the miracles of Christ, while its antiquity is an often reiterated motive of credibility. The Church is presented as a neither new nor recent institution. The New Testament is bound up with the Old by a close inner union, an inherent relationship constituted by the prophecies of the Redeemer to come, and since Moses lived long before the Greek thinkers and philosophers, Christianity is the oldest and most venerable of religions and philosophies.

The Apologists attain, perhaps, their greatest stature in our eyes when they proclaim themselves the champions of freedom of conscience as the root and source of all real religion, as the element without which religion cannot survive.

TEXT TRADITION

Most manuscripts of the Greek Apologists may be traced back to the Arethas Codex of the Bibliothèque Nationale (*Codex Parisinus* gr. 451), which was copied at the request of Archbishop Arethas of Caesarea in 914 and was designed to be a *Corpus Apologetarum* from primitive times down to Eusebius. But the writings of St. Justin, the three books of Theophilus *Ad Autolycum*, the *Irrisio* of Hermias and the *Epistle of Diognetus* are not contained therein.

Editions: MG 6. — J. C. Th. Otto, Corpus apologetarum christianorum saeculi secundi. 9 vols. Jena, 1847–1872. The first five volumes containing the works of St. Justin had been published in a separate edition in 1842–1843. A third edition of these five volumes was published 1876–1881. — The best edition is E. J. Goodspeed, Die ältesten Apologeten. Göttingen, 1914; it includes all the second-century Apologists except Theophilus. — A complete edition will be published in GCS of the Berlin Academy.

Index : E. J. Goodspeed, Index apologeticus sive clavis Justini martyris operum aliorumque apologetarum pristinorum. Leipzig, 1912.

Studies: J. Donaldson, A Critical History of Christian Literature and Doctrine from the Death of the Apostles to the Nicene Council. Vols. 2–3: The Apologists. London, 1866. — A. Harnack, Die Überlieferung der griechischen Apologeten des zweiten Jahrhunderts (TU 1,1-2). Leipzig, 1882. — O. v. Gebhardt, Zur handschriftlichen Überlieferung der griechischen Apologeten (TU 1,3). Leipzig, 1883. — G. Schmitt, Die Apologie der drei ersten Jahrhunderte in historisch-systematischer Darstellung. Mainz, 1890. — J. Zahn, Die apologetischen Grundgedanken in der Literatur der ersten drei Jahrhunderte systematisch dargestellt. Würzburg, 1890. — M. Friedländer, Geschichte der jüdischen Apologetik als Vorgeschichte des Christentums. Zürich, 1903. — A. Harnack, Der Vorwurf des Atheismus in den drei ersten Jahrhunderten (TU 28,4). Leipzig, 1905. — L. Laguier, La méthode apologétique des Pères dans les trois premiers siècles. Paris, 1905. — J. Geffcken, Die altchristliche Apologetik: Neue Jahrbücher für das klassische Altertum 15 (1905) 625–666; *idem,* Altchristliche Apologetik und griechische Philosophie: Zeitschrift für das Gymnasialwesen 60 (1906) 1–13; *idem,* Zwei griechische Apologeten. Leipzig-Berlin, 1907. — O. Zöckler, Geschichte der Apologie des Christentums. Gütersloh, 1907. — W. Koch, Die altkirchliche Apologetik des Christentums: ThQ 90 (1908) 7–33. — W. H. Carslaw, The Early Christian Apologists. London, 1911. — M. Freimann, Die Wortführer des Judentums in den ältesten Kontroversen zwischen Juden und Christen: Monatschrift für Geschichte und Wissenschaft des Judentums 55 (1911) 555–585. — A. Puech, Les apologistes grecs du 2e siècle de notre ère. Paris, 1912. — G. Bareille, DTC 1, 1580–1602. — F. Andres, Die Engellehre der griechischen Apologeten des zweiten Jahrhunderts und ihr Verhältnis zur griechisch-römischen Dämonologie (FLDG 12,3). Paderborn, 1914. — A. Waibel, Die natürliche Gotteserkenntnis in der apologetischen Literatur des zweiten Jahrhunderts. Kempten, 1916. — A. Hauck, Die Apologetik in der alten Kirche. Leipzig, 1918. — Marmorstein, Jews and Judaism in the Earliest Christian Apologists: Expositor (1919) 73–80; 100–116. — Corbière, Quid de Graecis saeculi secundi senserint christ. apol. Cahors, 1919. — J. Geffcken, Das Christentum im Kampf und Ausgleich mit der griechisch-römischen Welt. 3rd ed. Leipzig-Berlin, 1920. — C. N. Moody, The Mind of the Early Converts. London, 1920. — Ph. Carrington, Christian Apologists of the Second Century in their Relation to Modern Thought. 1921. — K. Gronau, Das Theodizeeproblem in der altchristlichen Auffassung. Tübingen, 1922. — Corbière, Le christianisme et la fin de la philosophie antique. 1921. — M. FERMI, S. Paolo negli apologetici greci del II⁰ sec.: Rivista trimestrale di studi filosofici e religiosi (1922) 299–306. — J. LORTZ, Das Christentum als Monotheismus in den Apologien des zweiten Jahrhunderts: Festgabe für A. Ehrhard. Bonn, 1922, 301–327. — M. CARENA, La critica della mitologia pagana negli Apologetici greci del II⁰ secolo: Didascaleion 1 (1923) fasc. 2, 23–55; fasc. 3, 1–42. — J. P. WALTZING, Le crime rituel reproché aux chrétiens du deuxième siècle: Bulletin de l'Académie royale d'archéologie de Belgique (1925) n. 5. — J. LEBRETON, Ἀγέννητος dans la tradition philosophique et dans la littérature chrétienne du IIe siècle: RSR 16 (1926) 431–443. — M. FERMI, La morale degli apologisti: RR 2 (1926) 218–235. — F. J. DÖLGER, Sonne und Sonnenstrahl als Gleichnis in de Logostheologie des christlichen Altertums: AC 1 (1929) 271–290. — I. GIORDANI, La prima polemica cristiana, gli apologetici greci del II⁰ secolo. Turin, 1930. — J. RIVIÈRE, Le démon dans l'économie rédemptrice d'après les apologistes et les premiers alexandrins: BLE 31 (1930) 5–20. — E. MERSCH, Le corps mystique du Christ. Louvain, 1933, I, 245–249. — F. J. DÖLGER, Sacramentum infanticidii: AC 4 (1934) 188–228. — V. A. S. LITTLE, The Christology of the Apologists. Doctrinal Introduction. London, 1934. — W. VAN ES, De grond van het Schriftgeloof bij de Apologeten van de tweede eeuw: GTT 35 (1934) 113–142; 282–310; 38 (1937) 305–330; 385–396. — A. L. WILLIAMS, Adversus Judaeos. A Bird's-eye View of Christian Apology until the Renaissance. Cambridge, 1935. Cf. J. DE GHELLINCK, NRTh 63 (1936) 937. — B. CRITTERIO, La polemica anticristiana nei primi sei secoli della Chiesa: SC 64 (1936) 51–63. — G. L. PRESTIGE, God in Patristic Thought. London, 1936. — H. ROSSBACHER, Die Apologeten als politisch-wissenschaftliche Schriftsteller. 1937. — M. H. SHEPHERD, The Early Apologists and Christian Worship: JR 18 (1938) 60–79. — H. LEWY, Aristotle and the Jewish Sage according to Clearchus of Soli: HThR 31 (1938) 205–235. — I. GIORDANI, Il messagio sociale dei primi Padri della Chiesa. Turin, 1938. English translation by A. I. ZIZZAMIA. Patterson, 1944. — J. L. ALLIE, L'argument de prescription dans le droit romain, en apologétique et en théologie dogmatique. Ottawa, 1940. — A. S. PEASE, Caeli enarrant: HThR 34 (1941) 163–300. — E. SCHARL, Recapitulatio mundi. Freiburg i.B., 1941, 120–131. — M. PELLEGRINO, L'elemento propagandistico e protettico negli apologeti greci del II⁰ secolo: RFIC (1941) 1–18; 97–109. — P. PALAZZINI, Il monoteismo nei padri apostolici e negli apologistici del II⁰ secolo. Rome, 1945. — M. PELLEGRINO, Studi sull 'antica apologetica. Rome, 1947.

QUADRATUS

Quadratus is the oldest apologist of Christianity. We are indebted to Eusebius for all we know of him. Eusebius says of Quadratus in his *Ecclesiastical History* (4,3,1-2): 'When Trajan had reigned for nineteen and a half years Aelius Hadrian succeeded to the sovereignty. To him Quadratus addressed a treatise, composing an apology for our religion because some wicked men were trying to trouble the Christians. It is still extant among many of the brethren and we have a copy ourselves. From it can be seen the clear proof of his intellect and his apostolic orthodoxy. He shows his early date by what he says as follows in his own words: *But the works of our Savior were always present, for they were true: those that were healed, and those that rose from the dead who were seen not only when they were healed and when they were raised but were constantly present; and not only while the Savior was living, but even after he had gone they were alive for a long time, so that some of them survived even to our own time.*' The words quoted by Eusebius as coming from the lips of Quadratus are the one and only fragment extant of his apology. For Harris' hypothesis, that the Pseudo-Clementines, the Acts of Saint Catherine of Sinai, the Chronicle of John Malalas and the romance of Barlaam and Joasaph have interwoven fragments of Quadratus' apology, has been proven false. Quadratus most likely presented his apology to the Emperor Hadrian during his stay in Asia Minor in the year 123–124 or in the year 129. It is difficult to prove that he is identical with the prophet and disciple of the Apostles whom Eusebius mentions (*Hist. Eccles.* 3,37,1; 5,17,2). It is definitely incorrect to identify him, as did St. Jerome (*Vir. ill.* 19; *Ep.* 70,4), with Bishop Quadratus of Athens who lived in the reign of Marcus Aurelius.

J. C. Th. Otto, Corpus apol. christ. IX 333ff. — A. Harnack, Die Ueberlieferung der griechischen Apologeten (TU I, 1–2). Leipzig, 1882, 100–109. — Th. Zahn, Der älteste Apologet des Christentums: NKZ 2 (1891) 281–287. *idem*, Forschungen zur Geschichte des neutestamentlichen Kanons 6; Erlangen, 1900, 41–53. — Amann, DTC 13, 1429–31.; ANF 8, 749; EP 109. — J. R. Harris, The Apology of Quadratus: ExpT 8th ser. 21 (1921) 147–160; *idem*, A New Christian Apology: Bull. John Rylands Library 7 (1923) 384–397; *idem*, The Quest for Quadratus: *ibidem* 8 (1924) 384–397. Cf. G. Krüger, ThLZ 48 (1923) 431ff. — E. Klostermann und E. Seeberg, Die Apologie der hl. Katharina. 1924. — Robinson, JThSt 25 (1924) 246–253.

ARISTIDES OF ATHENS

The earliest apology which has been preserved to us is that of Aristides of Athens. Eusebius says after his remarks on Quadratus: 'Aristides also, a man of faith and devoted to our religion, has like Quadratus, left an Apology of the faith addressed to

Hadrian. His writing, too, has been preserved by many ' (*Eccles. Hist.* 4,3,2). From another passage of Eusebius we gather that Aristides was a philosopher of the city of Athens. His work was long considered lost. But to the glad surprise of scholars the Mechitarists of San Lazzaro in Venice published in 1878 a manuscript of the tenth century, an Armenian fragment of an apology bearing the title, 'To Imperator Adrianus Caesar from the Athenian Philosopher Aristides'. The majority of scholars accepted the fragment as the remains of an Armenian translation of Aristides' Apology mentioned by Eusebius. This opinion was to find unexpected substantiation. In the year 1889 the American scholar, Rendel Harris, discovered in the Monastery of St. Catherine on Mount Sinai, a complete Syriac translation of the Apology. This Syriac version enabled J. A. Robinson to prove that a Greek text of the Apology was not only extant but had been edited for some time in the form of a religious novel dealing with Barlaam and Joasaph. The author of this novel, a monk of the Monastery of St. Saba in Palestine in the seventh century, presents the Apology as made by a pagan philosopher in favor of Christianity. The text has come down to us in three forms. The legend of Barlaam and Joasaph, which we have in Greek, was composed about the year 630 A.D. The manuscript of the Monastery of St. Catherine containing the Syriac translation was most likely written between the sixth and seventh centuries, but the translation itself dates from about 350 A.D. Just when the Armenian translation was made has not, as yet, been definitely established. Two large portions of the original Greek text (chapters 5 and 6 and 15,6–16,1) have lately been published from the papyri of the British Museum. Aided by this material it is possible to reconstruct the text in its main lines.

CONTENT

The introduction describes the Divine Being in terms of Stoic formularies and tells us also that Aristides came to a knowledge of a Creator and Preserver of the universe through his meditations upon the world and the harmony existing therein. Even though all speculation and disputation concerning the Divine Being are of small value, it is possible, nevertheless, to determine the attributes of the Godhead negatively to some extent at least.

The one and only correct concept thus gained will then serve as a touchstone for testing the old religions. The author divides human beings into four categories according to the individual's religion: barbarians, Greeks, Jews and Christians. The barbarians worshipped the four elements; but heaven, earth, water fire, winds, sun and moon and finally man himself are all works of God and hence they were never entitled to divine honor. The Greeks worship gods, who through the weaknesses and infamies attributed to them prove themselves anything but divine. The Jews deserve to be respected because of their purer conception of the divine nature, and also because of their superior standards of morality. But they paid more homage to the angels than to God and laid greater importance upon the externals of worship such as circumcision, fasting, the observance of feast days than upon genuine adoration. The Christians alone have the only true idea of God and 'they above all the nations of the world have found the truth. For they acknowledge God the Creator and Maker of all things in the only begotten Son and in the Holy Spirit; and besides him they worship no other' (15). That the Christians worship the one true God manifests itself particularly in their purity of life which Aristides accords the highest praise:

They have the commandments of the Lord Jesus Christ himself graven upon their hearts and these they observe, looking for the resurrection of the dead and for the life in the world to come. They do not commit adultery nor fornication, nor do they bear false witness, nor covet the things of others; they honor father and mother, and love their neighbors; they give right judgment and they never do to others what they would not wish to happen to themselves. They comfort such as wrong them and make friends of them. They are eager to do good to their enemies. They are meek and gentle. They refrain themselves from all unlawful intercourse and all impurity. They despise not the widow and oppress not the orphan. He that has gives ungrudgingly to him that has not. If they see a stranger they take him under their roof and rejoice over him, as it were their own brother. For they call themselves brethren not after the flesh but after the spirit. They are ready to lay down their own lives for the sake of Christ. They keep his commandments without swerving, living righteous and holy lives as the Lord their God commanded them. And they give thanks unto him every hour for all meat and drink and other blessings. Verily then this is the way of truth which leads those who travel therein to the eternal kingdom promised by Christ in the life to come (15).

The apology of Aristides is limited in scope, its style unaffected and its thought and disposition artless. Nevertheless for all its simplicity, its tone is lofty. Aristides, as if upon an eminence, surveys mankind as a composite unit and he is profoundly impressed by the high importance and mission of the new religion. With confident Christian self-assurance he sees in the small flock of the faithful the new people, the new race which is to lead the corrupt world forth from the morass of immorality:

All other nations go astray and deceive themselves. Walking in darkness they stagger one against another like drunken men (16). — I do not hesitate to say that the world continues to exist only because of the prayers of supplication of the Christians.

Editions: J. R. HARRIS, The Apology of Aristides on Behalf of the Christians from a Syriac Ms. Preserved on Mount Sinai Edited with an Introduction and Translation. With an Appendix Containing the Main Portion of the Original Greek Text by J. A. ROBINSON (Texts and Studies, 1,1). 2nd ed. Cambridge, 1893. — E. HENNECKE, Die Apologie des Aristides. Rezension und Rekonstruktion des Textes (TU 4,3). Leipzig, 1893. — R. SEEBERG, Der Apologet Aristides. Der Text seiner uns erhaltenen Schriften nebst einleitenden Untersuchungen über dieselben. Erlangen, 1894. — For the new Greek fragments see GRENFELL and HUNT, The Oxyrhynchus Papyri XV. London, 1922, n. 1778, and H. J. M. MILNE, A New Fragment of the Apology of Aristides: JThSt 25 (1924) 73–77. — A. N. MODONA, L'Apologia di Aristide ed il nuovo frammento d'Ossirinco: Bilychnis 19 (1922) I, 317–327. — J. DE ZWAAN, A Gap in the Recently Discovered Greek of the Apology of Aristides: HThR 18 (1925) 112–114. Cf. G. KRÜGER, ThLZ 1924, 47f. — A. D'ALÈS, RQH 100 (1924) 354–359.

Translations: D. M. KAY, The Apology of Aristides the Philosopher, Translated from the Greek and from the Syriac Version: ANF 9, 263–279. — *German:* R. RAABE, Die Apologie des Aristides, aus dem Syrischen übersetzt und mit Beiträgen zur Textvergleichung und Anmerkungen herausgegeben (TU 9,1). Leipzig, 1892. — J. SCHÖNFELDER, Die Apologie des Aristides übersetzt: ThQ 74 (1892) 531–557. — K. JULIUS, BKV 12. Kempten, 1913.

Studies: J. R. HARRIS, The Newly Recovered Apology of Aristides: its Doctrine and Ethics. London, 1891. — M. PICARD, L'apologie d'Aristide. Paris,

1892. — L. Lemme, Die Apologie des Aristides: Neue Jahrbücher für deutsche Theologie 2 (1893) 303–340. — Pape, Die Predigt und das Brieffragment des Aristides (TU 12,2). Leipzig, 1894. — F. Lauchert, Über die Apologie des Aristides: Internationale Theologische Zeitschrift 2 (1894) 278–299. — E. Hora, Untersuchungen über die Apologie des Aristides (Gymnasialprogramm). Karlsbad, 1904. — J. Geffcken, Zwei griechischen Apologeten. Leipzig-Berlin, 1907. — F. Haase, Der Adressat der Aristidesapologie: ThQ (1917/18) 422–429. — Ph. Friedrich: ZkTh (1919) 31–77. — M. Fermi, L'apologia di Aristide e la lettera a Diogneto: PR 1 (1925) 541–545. — I. P. Bock, Quibus rationibus suadeatur identitas apologetae Aristidis et auctoris Epistolae ad Diognetum: BS 19 (1931) 1–16. — R. L. Wolff, The Apology of Aristides. A Re-examination: HThR 30 (1937) 233–248. — G. Lazzati, Ellenismo e cristianesimo. Il primo capitolo dell' Apologia di Aristide: SC 66 (1938) 35–61. — B. Altaner, Aristides: RAC (1943) 652–654.

ARISTO OF PELLA

The first Christian apologist who defended Christianity in a written tract against *Judaism* seems to have been Aristo of Pella. He composed a *Discussion between Jason and Papiscus concerning Christ*, which unfortunately has been lost. Jason is a Judaeo-Christian and Papiscus a Jew of Alexandria in Egypt. Origen tells us that this apology was attacked by the pagan philosopher Celsus in his work, *The True Discourse*, because the author of the apology manifested a predilection for allegorical interpretation of the Old Testament. Origen defends the short treatise. He points out that the tract was intended for the people at large and hence ought not to have provoked unfavorable comment from any open-minded person. According to Origen (*Contra Cels.* 4,52), this apology describes, 'how a Christian supported by Jewish writings (the Old Testament) carries on a disputation with a Jew and goes on to prove that the prophecies pertaining to Christ find fulfillment in Jesus, while the opponent in a plucky and not unskilled fashion takes the part of the Jew in the controversy'. The discussion ends with the Jew Papiscus acknowledging Christ as the Son of God and asking for Baptism. The fragment of a Latin translation of the dialogue, likewise lost, gives the same story. This fragment, falsely attributed to Cyprian under the title, *Ad Vigilium episcopum de judaica incredulitate*, was in reality the preface to the Latin translation. Aristo must have composed his work about 140 A.D. The allegorical exegesis and the fact that Papiscus was an Alexandrian point to Alexandria as the city of origin.

OTTO IX, 349–363. — B. P. PRATTEN, Aristo of Pella: ANF 8, 749–750. — A. C. McGIFFERT, A Dialogue between a Christian and a Jew, Entitled ἀντιβολὴ Παπίσκου καὶ Φίλωνος Ἰουδαίων πρὸς μοναχόν (Diss.). New York, 1889. — E. J. GOODSPEED, Papiscus and Philo: The American Journal of Theology 4 (1900) 796–802. — F. C. CONYBEARE, The Dialogues of Athanasius and Zacchaeus and of Timothy and Aquila (Anecdota Oxoniensia, Classical Series 8). Oxford, 1898. — D. TAMILIA, De Timothei Christiani et Aquilae Iudaei dialogo. Rome, 1901. — E. J. GOODSPEED, The Dialogue of Timothy and Aquila. Two Unpublished Manuscripts: JBL 24 (1905) 28–78. — A. B. HULEN, The Dialogues with the Jews as Sources for Early Jewish Argument against Christianity: JBL 51 (1932) 58–70. — A. L. WILLIAMS, Adversus Judaeos. A Bird's-eye View of Christian Apology until the Renaissance. Cambridge, 1935, 28–30.

ST. JUSTIN

The most important of the Greek apologists of the second century and one of the noblest personalities of early Christian literature is Justin the Martyr. He was born in Flavia Neapolis, formerly Sichem in Palestine. His parents were pagan. He himself tells us (*Dialog.* 2–8) that he tried first the school of a Stoic, then that of a Peripatetic and finally that of a Pythagorean. None of these philosophers convinced or satisfied him. The Stoic failed because he gave him no explanation concerning God's being. The Peripatetic insisted most importunely that Justin pay him the tuition immediately, which Justin answered by avoiding his lectures. The Pythagorean demanded of him that he must first study music, astronomy and geometry. Justin had no inclination to do so. Platonism, on the other hand, appealed to him for a time, until as he walked along the sea-shore an old man convinced him that the Platonic philosophy could not satisfy the heart of man and called his attention to the 'prophets who alone announced the truth'. 'When he had spoken', relates Justin, 'these and many other things, which there is no time for mentioning at present, he went away, bidding me attend to them; and I have not seen him since. But straightway a flame was kindled in my soul; and a love of the prophets, and of those men who are friends of Christ, possessed me. And whilst revolving his words in my mind, I found this philosophy alone to be safe and profitable. Thus and for this reason I became a philosopher, and I could wish that all men were of the same mind as myself, not to turn from the doctrines of the Savior' (*Dial.* 8). The quest for truth led him to Christianity. We also learn from him that the heroic contempt which Christians entertained for death played no small role in his conversion: 'I myself used to rejoice in the teaching of Plato and to hear evil spoken of Christians. But, as I saw that they showed no fear in face of death and of all other things which inspire horror, I reflected that they could not be vicious and pleasure-loving' (*Apol.* 2,12). Honest searching after truth and humble prayer brought him finally to accept the faith of Christ: 'When I discovered the wicked disguise which the evil spirits had thrown around the divine doctrines of the Christians to deter others from joining them, I laughed both at the authors of these falsehoods and their disguise and at the popular opinion. And I confess that I both prayed and strove with all my might to be found a Christian' (*Apol.* 2,13). After his conversion, which occurred most likely in Ephesus, he devoted his entire life to the defense of the Christian faith. Clothed in the *pallium*, a cloak worn by Greek philosophers, he travelled about, an itinerant teacher. He arrived in Rome during the reign of Antoninus Pius (138–161) and founded a school there; one of his pupils was Tatian, destined later to become an apologist. Here he also met a vehement opponent in the person of the Cynic philosopher Crescens, whom he had charged with ignorance. We possess an authentic account of his death in the *Martyrium S. Justini et Sociorum*, which is based upon an official court report. According to this document St. Justin and six companions were beheaded probably in 165, while Prefect Junius Rusticus (163–167) was in office (cf. above p. 178).

WRITINGS

Justin was a prolific writer. Only three of his works, which were known to Eusebius (*Hist.* 4, 18), have come down to us. These are contained in a single manuscript of poor quality copied in 1364 (Paris, No. 450). They are his two *Apologies* against the pagans and his *Dialogue with the Jew Trypho*. The style of these works is far from pleasant. Not accustomed to adhere to a well-defined plan, Justin follows the inspiration of the moment. He digresses, his thought is disjointed, he has a failing for long-spun sentences. His whole manner of expression lacks force and seldom attains to eloquence or warmth of feeling. Yet, for all their shortcomings, his writings hold for us an unlimited attraction. They reveal an open and honest character, which tries to reach an understanding with the opponent. Justin was convinced 'that everyone who can speak the truth and does not speak it shall be judged by God' (*Dial.* 82). He is the first ecclesiastical writer who attempts to build a bridge between Christianity and pagan philosophy.

C. SEMISCH, Justin der Märtyrer. Eine kirchen- und dogmengeschichtliche Monographie. Breslau, 1840–42. — B. AUBÉ, Essai de critique religieuse. De l'apologétique chrétienne au 2e siècle. St. Justin philosophe et martyr. Paris, 1861. — K. v. WEIZSÄCKER, Die Theologie des Märtyrers Justinus: Jahrbücher für deutsche Theologie 12 (1867) 60–119. — M. v. ENGELHARDT, Das Christentum Justins des Märtyrers. Erlangen, 1878. — A. STÄHLIN, Justin der Märtyrer und sein neuester Beurteiler. Leipzig, 1880. — CH. E. v. FREPPEL, Les Apologistes chrétiens au 2e siècle. Saint Justin. 3d ed. Paris, 1886. — H. SCOTT, Justin: Dictionary of Christian Biography 3 (1882) 560–587. — W. FLEMMING, Zur Beurteilung des Christentums Justins des Märtyrers. Leipzig, 1893. — G. T. PURVES, The Testimony of Justin Martyr to Early Christianity. New York, 1889. — J. WOLNY, Das christliche Leben nach dem hl. Justin (em Märtyrer (Progr.). Vienna, 1897. — A. FEDER, Justin der Märtyrer und die altchristliche Bussdisziplin: ZKTh 29 (1905) 758–761. — J. RIVIÈRE, St. Justin et les apologistes du second siècle. Paris, 1907. — J. GEFFCKEN, Zwei griechische Apologeten. Leipzig-Berlin, 1907, 97–104. — A. BÉRY, St. Justin, sa vie et sa doctrine. Paris, 1911. — M. J. LAGRANGE, Saint Justin. 3rd ed. Paris, 1914. — C. C. MARTINDALE, St. Justin the Martyr. London, 1921. — E. R. GOODENOUGH, The Theology of Justin Martyr. Jena, 1923. Cf. A. FEDER, ThR 23 (1924) 209f. — G. BARDY, Justin: DTC 8 (1925) 2228–2277. — J. LEBRETON, Histoire du dogme de la Trinité II. Paris, 1928. — E. SEEBERG, Die Geschichtstheologie Justins des Martyrers. Diss. Kiel, 1939. — E. SEEBERG, Geschichte und Geschichtsanschauung dargestellt in altchristlichen Geschichtsvorstellungen: ZKG 40 (1941) 309–331. — G. BARDY, La conversion dans les premiers siècles chrétiens: Année théologique 2 (1941) 89–106; 206–232.

I. THE APOLOGIES OF ST. JUSTIN

Justin's most important writings are his two Apologies. Eusebius (*Hist. Eccles.* 4, 18) comments on them:

Justin has left us treatises of an educated intelligence trained in theology which are full of helpfulness, and to them we will refer students, indicating what has come usefully to our knowledge. There is a treatise by him on behalf of our opinions addressed to Antoninus, surnamed Pius, and his children, and to the Roman Senate another, containing a second apology for our defense, which he made to the successor and namesake of the above-mentioned emperor, Antoninus Verus.

We have, indeed, two Apologies of St. Justin. In the manuscript, the longer, of sixty-eight chapters, is addressed to Antoninus Pius; the shorter, of fifteen chapters, to the Roman Senate. But E. Schwartz regards the latter as merely the conclusion of the former. The fact that Eusebius speaks of two apologies was probably the reason why the whole work was divided in the manuscript, and the concluding part was placed in front as an independent writing. Today most scholars agree that the so-called second Apology originally formed an appendix or later addition to the first. Most probably it was occasioned by the incidents which took place under the Prefect Urbicus and with an account of which it begins. Both works are addressed to the emperor Antoninus Pius (138–161). It seems that St. Justin composed them between the years 148 and 161, because he remarks (*Apology* 1, 46): 'Christ was born one hundred and fifty years ago under Quirinius.' The place of composition was Rome.

1. *The First Apology*

A. In the introduction (Chapters 1–3) Justin, in the name of the Christians, requests the emperor to take up their case personally, and to form his own judgment without being misled by bias or the hatred of the mob.

B. The main part has two sections.

I. The first section (Chapters 4–12) is a censure of the official attitude toward the Christians. Here the author criticizes the judicial procedure regularly followed by the government against his coreligionists and the false accusations made against them. He protests against the senseless action of the authorities in punishing the mere acknowledgment of Christianity; the name 'Christian', like the name 'philosopher', does not prove the guilt or innocence of a man. Punishment can be imposed only for crimes of which the defendent has been convicted, but the crimes of which the Christians have been accused are mere calumnies. They are not atheists. If they refuse to worship the gods, they do so because the veneration of such divinities is silly. Their eschatological beliefs and their dread of eternal punishment preserve them from wrong-doing, and make them the best supporters of the government.

II. The second section (Chapters 13–67) turns to a justification of the Christian religion, giving a detailed description particularly of its doctrine and worship, and the basis in history and reason for subscribing to it.

1. *The dogmatic and moral doctrine of the Christians*

It can be proved from divine prophecies that Jesus Christ is the Son of God and the Founder of the Christian religion. He founded it according to God's will in order to transform and repair mankind. The demons imitated and aped the prophecies of the Old Testament in the pagan mystery cults. This explains many similarities and resemblances between the Christian religion and pagan forms of worship. Similarly, the philosophers, like Plato, borrowed from the Old Testament. For this reason we cannot be surprised to find Christian ideas in Platonism.

2. *The Christian Worship*

The author gives here a description of the sacrament of baptism, the eucharistic service and the social life of the Christians.

C. The conclusion (Chapter 68) is a serious admonition to the emperor. At the end of the first apology is added the rescript which the emperor Hadrian, about the year 125, sent to Minucius Fundanus, the proconsul of Asia. This document is of the greatest importance for the history of the Church. It issues four regulations for a more just and correct court procedure in the trials against the Christians:

1. The Christians should be sentenced through a regular procedure before a criminal court;
2. A condemnation can take place only if there is proof that the defendants committed an offense against the Roman laws;
3. The punishment must be proportionate to the nature and the degree of their crimes;
4. Every false accusation must be punished severely.

According to Eusebius (*Hist. Eccles.* 4,8,8) Justin embodied this document, in its original Latin text, into his Apology. Eusebius translated it into Greek, and incorporated it into his *Ecclesiastical History* (4,9).

2. The Second Apology

This writing begins with a recent incident. The prefect of Rome, Urbicus, had had three Christians beheaded only because they confessed to being Christians. Justin appeals directly to Roman public opinion, protesting anew against unjustifiable severities, and replying to various criticisms. He answers, for instance, the sarcastic question of the heathen why the Christians do not permit suicide in order to reach their God as fast as possible. Justin replies: 'We shall, if we so act, be ourselves acting in opposition to the will of God. But when we are examined, we make no denial, because we are not conscious of any evil, but count it impious not to speak the truth in all things' (*Apol.* 2,4). The persecutions of the Christians are instigated by the hatred of the demons against truth and virtue. The same agencies had harried the just of the Old Testament and of the pagan world. But they would have no power over the Christians if God did not intend to lead his followers through trials and troubles to virtue and reward, through death and destruction to eternal life and happiness. At the same time, the persecutions give the Christians opportunity to demonstrate in an impressive way the superiority of their religion over paganism. At the end, he also asks the emperor, in judging the Christians, to be led only by justice, piety, and love of truth.

Separate Editions: A. W. F. BLUNT, The Apologies of Justin Martyr. Cambridge, 1891. — B. L. GILDERSLEEVE, The Apologies of Justin Martyr. New York, 1904. — G. RAUSCHEN, S. Justini Apologiae duae (FP 2). 2nd ed. Bonn, 1911. — J. M. PFÄTTISCH, Justinus des Philosophen und Märtyrers Apologien. Teil 1: Text; Teil II: Kommentar. Münster, 1912. — G. KRÜGER, Die Apologien Justins des Märtyrers (SQ 1). 4th ed. Freiburg. i. B., 1915. — S. FRASCA, S. Justinus, Apologie. Testo, versione, introd. (Corona patrum salesiana, Ser. greca T. III). Turin, 1938.

Translations: English: ANF 1, 159-193. *French:* L. PAUTIGNY, Les Apologies (Textes et Documents 1). Paris, 1904. *Italian:* J. GIORDANI, La prima polemica cristiana. Florence, 1929. — S. FRASCA, l.c. *German:* H. VEIL, Justinus des Philosophen und Märtyrers Rechtfertigung des Christentums, Strasbourg, 1904. — G. RAUSCHEN, BKV² 13. Kempten, 1913.

Studies: G. BARDY, DTC 8, 2228-2277. — E. SCHWARTZ, Observationes prof. et sacrae: Index lectionum von Rostock f. das S.-Sem. 1888, 10-16. — B. GRUNDL, De interpolationi busex S. Justini phil. et mart. Apologia secunda expungendis (progr.). Vienna. 1891. — F. EMMERICH, De Justini phil. et mart. Apologia altera (Diss.). Münster, 1896. — TH. W. WEHOFER, Die Apologie Justins des Phil. und Märt. in literarhistorischer Beziehung zum erstenmal untersucht. (RQ Suppl. 6). Rome, 1897. — P. WILLM, Justin Martyr et son apologétique (Thèse). Montauban, 1897. — G. RAUSCHEN, Die formale Seite der Apologien Justins: ThQ 81 (1889) 188-206. — K. HUBIK, Die Apologien des hl. Justinus des Philosophen und Märtyrers. Wien, 1912. — W. JEHNE, Die Apologie Justins des Philosophen und Märtyrers (Diss.). Leipzig, 1914. — R. GANSZYNIEC, De Justini M. Ap. II: Eos 23 (1918) 55-65; Cf. H. KOCH, ThLZ 1921, 276. — A. FEDER, PhW (1918) 597ff. — J. P. ARENDZEN, Apol. I 15 (Divorce, etc.): JThSt 20 (1919) 231ff. — RAHLFS, ZNW (1921) 191ff. — F. H. COLSON, Notes on Justin Martyr's Apology I: JThSt 23 (1922) 161-171. — R. GANSZYNIEC, Die Apologie und der Libellus Justins des Märtyrers: OC 10/11 (1923) 56-76. — B. CAPELLE, Le rescrit d'Hadrien et saint Justin: RB 39 (1927) 365-368. — P. DEBOUXTHAY, Note sur St. Justin: RBPh 8 (1929) 1193-1195. — J. MOFFAT, Two Notes on Ignatius and Justin Martyr: HThR 23 (1930) 155ff. — W. v. LOEWENICH, Das Johannesverständnis des zweiten Jahrhunderts. Giessen, 1932, 39-50. — B. ANTONIADES, The Anthropology of St. Justin. Archivum philosophiae (1933) 207 ff.— U. HÜNTEMANN, Zur Kompositionstechnik Justins. Analyse seiner ersten Apologie: ThGl 25 (1933) 410-428. — P. PANTALEO, Dogma e disciplina: Religio 11 (1935) 231-238. — R. STAHLER, Justin Martyr et l'apologétique (Thèse). Geneva, 1935. — E. R. BUCKLEY, Justin Martyr's Quotations from the Synoptic Tradition: JThSt 36 (1935) 173-176. — C. C. RICHARDSON, The Meaning of πολιτευαί in Justin I Apol. 65,1: HThR 29 (1936) 89-91. — W. A. VAN ES, De grond van het schriftgeloof bij de apologeten van de tweede eeuw. Justinus Martyr, de beide Apologieën: Gereformeerd Theol. Tijdschrift 34 (1933) 194-226; 35 (1934) 282-310; 37 (1936) 113-142. — W. SCHMIDT, Die Textüberlieferung der Apologie Justins: ZNW (1941) 87-138. — M. PELLEGRINO, L'attualità dell' apologetica di S. Giustino: SC (1942) 130-140.

II.   THE DIALOGUE WITH TRYPHO

The *Dialogue with Trypho* is the oldest Christian apology against the Jews which is extant. Unfortunately, we do not have its complete text. The introduction, and a large part of Chapter 74, have been lost. The Dialogue must have been composed after the Apologies, because there is a reference to the first Apology in Chapter 120. It contains a two-day discussion with a learned Jew, most likely the very Rabbi Tarphon that is mentioned in the Mishna. Eusebius (*Hist. Eccles.* 4, 18, 6) held Ephesus as the place where this conversation was held. St. Justin dedicated his work to a certain Marcus Pompeius. Of considerable length, it runs to one hundred and forty-two chapters. The introduction (Chapters 2–8), contains a detailed narrative by Justin of his intellectual development and his conversion. The first part of the main section (Chapters 9–47) explains the Christian viewpoint regarding the Old Testament. The Mosaic law had only temporary jurisdiction. Christianity is the new and eternal law for all mankind. The second part (Chapters 48–108) justifies the adoration of Christ as God. The third part (Chapters 109–142) proves that the nations who believe in Christ and follow His law represent the new Israel, and the true chosen people of God.

The apologetic method of the Dialogue differs from that of the Apologies because it was addressed to an entirely different type of reader. In his *Dialogue with the Jew Trypho* St. Justin stresses the Old Testament, and quotes the prophets as proof that Christian truth existed even before Christ. Examining carefully his quotations from the Old Testament, one finds that Justin gives preference to passages which speak of the rejection of Israel and the election of the heathens. It is evident that the Dialogue is by no means an exact reproduction of a stenographic report of a real disputation. On the other hand, its form is not altogether a literary convention. Real conversations and discussions seem to have preceded the composition of this work. It is possible that these exchanges took place at Ephesus at the time of the war of Bar Kochba, mentioned in Chapters 1 and 9.

Edition: G. Archambault, Justin, Dialogue avec Tryphon. Texte grec, traduction française, introduction, notes et index (Textes et Documents 8,11) 2 vols. Paris, 1909. Cf. A. L. Feder, ThR (1911) 178ff.

Translations: English: A. C. Coxe, Dialogue of Justin, Philosopher and Martyr, with Trypho, a Jew: ANF 1,194–270. — A. L. Williams, Justin Martyr, The Dialogue with Trypho (SPCK). London, 1931. *French:* G. Archambault, l.c. *German:* Ph. Häuser, BKV 33. Kempten, 1917, 1ff.

Studies: Th. Zahn, Dichtung und Wahrheit in Justins Dialog mit dem Juden Tryphon: ZKG 8 (1886) 37–66. — M. Freimann, Die Wortführer des Judentums in den ältesten Kontroversen zwischen Juden und Christen: Monatschrift für Geschichte und Wissenschaft des Judentums 55 (1911) 565–585. — A. Harnack, Judentum und Judenchristentum in Justins Dialog mit Trypho, nebst einer Kollation der Pariser Handschrift Nr. 450 (TU 39,1b). Leipzig, 1913. — E. Preuschen, Die Einheit von Justins Dialog gegen Trypho: ZNW 19 (1919-20) 102–127. — L. Fonck, Die Echtheit von Justins

Dialog gegen Trypho: Bibl 2 (1921) 342–347. — G. SCHLAEGER, Die Un-
echtheit des Dialogus cum Tryphone: NTT 13 (1924) 117–143. — P. KESELING,
Justins 'Dialog gegen Trypho' (cap. 1–10) und Platons 'Protagoras': RhM 75
(1926) 223–229. — F. C. BURKITT, Justin Martyr and Jeremiah XI, 19:
JThSt 33 (1932) 371–374. — A. B. HULEN, The Dialogues with the Jews as
Sources for Early Jewish Argument against Christianity: JBL 51 (1932)
58–70. — M. SIMON, Sur deux hérésies juives mentionnées par Justin Martyr:
RHPR (1938) 54–58. — Z. K. VYSOKY, Un prétendu souvenir autobiogra-
phique de S. Justin: Listy Filologicke (1938) 435–440. — G. MERCATI,
Note bibliche, Bibl. (1941) 339–366: Un frammento nuovo del Dialogo di
S. Giustino.

III.   LOST WRITINGS

In addition to the Apologies and the Dialogue, Justin is the
author of a number of other writings which have been lost. Of
these, no more than the title, or small fragments, are preserved.
One is mentioned by Justin himself, one quoted by Irenaeus, very
many given in Eusebius' list, still others cited by later ecclesiastical authors. Thus the following writings are known today:

A. *Liber contra Omnes Haereses*, to which Justin refers himself, cf.
Apologia, 1, 26.

B. *Against Marcion*, which St. Irenaeus used (*Adv. Haer.* 4,6,2)
and which Eusebius mentions (*Hist. Eccl.* 4,11,8ff)

F. LOOFS, Theophilus von Antiochien Adv. Marcionem und die andern
theologischen Quellen bei Irenäus. Leipzig, 1930, 225ff.; 339–374. — J. A.
ROBINSON, On a Quotation from Justin Martyr in Irenaeus: JThSt 31 (1930)
374–378. — M. MÜLLER, Untersuchungen zum Carmen adv. Marcionitas.
Diss. Würzburg, 1936, 74–87. — E. BARNIKOL, Verfasste oder benutzte Justin
das um 140 entstandene, erste antimarcionitische Syntagma gegen die
Häresien?: ThJ 6 (1938) 17–19.

C. *Discourse against the Greeks*, in which, according to Eusebius
(4,18,3), 'after a long and expanded argument about many things
inquired into by both the Christians and the philosophers, St.
Justin discourses on the nature of the demons'.

D. *A Confutation*, another treatise which was according to Eusebius (4,18,4) addressed to the Greeks.

E. *On the Sovereignty of God*, 'which he compiled not only from
our own scriptures, but also from the books of the Greeks' (*ibid.*).

F. *On the Soul*. Eusebius (4,18,5) describes its content thus: 'He
propounds various questions concerning the problem under discussion and adduces the opinion of the Greek philosophers; these
he promises to refute and to give his own opinion in another book.'

G. *Psalter.*

H. In the *Sacra Parallela* of St. John Damascene three large fragments of his treatise *On the Resurrection* are preserved. But their authenticity has been questioned.

G. Archambault, Le témoignage de l'ancienne littérature chrétienne sur l'authenticité d'un περὶ ἀναστάσεως attribué à Justin l'apologiste: RPh 29 (1905) 73–93. — A. Puech, Les apologistes grecs du 2e siècle de notre ère. Paris, 1912, 267–275; 339–342. — F. Loofs, Theophilus von Antiochien Adv. Marcionem und die andern theologischen Quellen bei Irenäus. Leipzig, 1930, 211–257; 281–299. — F. R. M. Hitchcock, Loofs' Asiatic Source (IQA) and the Ps.-Justin De Resurrectione: ZNW 36 (1938) 35–60.

Whereas all these writings have been lost, the manuscripts contain a number of pseudo-Justinian works. It is remarkable, however, that three of these have titles which resemble the titles of lost authentic works of St. Justin.

a. The *Cohortatio ad Graecos* tries to convince the Greeks of the true religion in the form of an oration. The ideas which the Greek poets had regarding the gods are objectionable, and the doctrines of the philosophers concerning religious problems are full of contradictions. The truth is to be found with Moses and the prophets, who are earlier than the Greek philosophers. Vestiges, however, of the true knowledge of God can be found even in the Greek poets and philosophers. But the small amount of good they contain was borrowed from the books of the Jews. In his attitude toward Greek philosophy, the author of the *Cohortatio* differs markedly from St. Justin. If only for this reason the work cannot be ascribed to the latter. But, besides, it is much superior in style and uses a distinctive vocabulary. All this together is enough to prove the treatise nonauthentic. The *Cohortatio* most probably originated in the third century, has thirty-eight chapters and is the longest of the writings falsely attributed to St. Justin.

L. Alfonsi, Traces du jeune Aristote dans la 'Cohortatio ad Gentiles' faussement attribuée à Justin: VC 2 (1948) 65–88.

b. Much shorter is the *Oratio ad Graecos*, which counts five chapters only. It is lively and energetic in style, condensed and attractive in arrangement. As is clear from the contents, it is a Greek convert's justification of himself, an *Apologia pro vita sua*.

The author attacks the immorality of the gods as pictured by Homer and Hesiod. He concludes with an enthusiastic appeal for conversion to Christianity. Both the rhetorical style and the excellent knowledge of Greek mythology exclude the authorship of St. Justin. The *Oratio* dates most probably from the first half of the third century. There are two recensions extant. The shorter one is preserved in Greek. Of the longer, compiled by a certain Ambrosius, we have only a Syriac version.

C. BONNER, The Sibyl and Bottle Imps: Quantalacumque. Studies presented to K. Lake. London, 1937, 1–8.

c. *De Monarchia* (6 chapters) is a treatise which endeavors to prove monotheism with the help of quotations from the most famous poets of Greece. The difference of style speaks against St. Justin as author. Moreover, Eusebius gives a description of the authentic work *De Monarchia*, which does not correspond to the content of this treatise.

Besides these three writings there are a number of others which the manuscript ascribes to Justin. Four of them are so similar in language and theological doctrine that they must be by the same author. The latter seems to have lived about 400, and to have had relations with Syria. The four treatises are:

a. *Quaestiones et Responsiones ad Orthodoxos*, a work which contains one hundred and sixty-one questions and answers concerning historical, dogmatical, ethical, and exegetical problems.

b. *Quaestiones Christianorum ad Gentiles*. In this treatise there are five theological questions which Christians address to pagans and which pagans answer. But the answers are refuted as being full of contradictions.

c. *Quaestiones Graecorum ad Christianos*. This treatise contains fifteen questions by the pagans and the same number of answers by the Christians regarding the essence of God, the resurrection of the dead, and other Christian dogmas.

d. *Confutatio Dogmatum Quorumdam Aristotelicorum*. This work refutes in sixty-five paragraphs doctrines of Aristotle regarding God and the universe.

Up to the present day it has been impossible to discover the real author of these four writings. A. Harnack attributed them to Diodorus of Tarsus. Others thought of Theodoret of Cyrus, to whom a manuscript of Constantinople ascribes the *Quaestiones et Responsiones ad Orthodoxos*. But we cannot with any security hold either of them as the author.

Besides these four the manuscripts ascribe the following tracts to Justin:

a. *Expositio Fidei seu De Trinitate*, an explanation of the doctrine of the Trinity. The author of this writing is not known, but it does not seem to antedate the fifth century.

b. *Epistola ad Zenam et Serenum*, a detailed guide to Christian ascetical conduct with instructions about the virtues of meekness and tranquillity, which reminds one of the ethical doctrine of Stoic philosophy. P. Batiffol thinks that Sisinnius of Constantinople is the author, and that the *Epistola* originated about the year four hundred.

THE THEOLOGY OF ST. JUSTIN

Analyzing the theology of St. Justin, we must remember that we do not possess a complete and exhaustive description of the Christian faith from his pen. We must take into consideration that his genuinely theological works like *On the Sovereignty of God, On the Soul, On the Resurrection, Confutation of all Heresies* and *Against Marcion* have been lost. The *Apologies* and the *Dialogue with Trypho* do not give a well-rounded picture of Justin as a divine. In the lost antiheretical writings he had much more occasion to delve into questions of doctrine, whereas, when he is defending the faith against unbelievers, he emphasizes rather its appeal to reason. He endeavors to indicate the similarities existing between the teaching of the Church and that of the Greek thinkers and poets, in order to demonstrate that Christianity is the only safe and profitable philosophy. For this reason, it is not surprising that Justin's theology reveals the influence of Plato; it was his, among all the pagan systems, that Justin valued most highly.

1. *The Concept of God*

In Justin's concept of God there is already evident a leaning to Platonic philosophy. God is without origin (ἄρρητος). From this fact the conclusion must be drawn that God is nameless:

> But to the Father of all, who is unbegotten, there is no

name given. For by whatever name he be called, he has as his elder the person who gives him the name. But these words, Father and God and Creator and Master, are not names, but appellations derived from his good deeds and functions . . . the appellation 'God' is not a name, but an opinion implanted in the nature of men of a thing that can hardly be explained (2,6).

The best name for him is Father, because, being the Creator, he is really the Father of all (πατὴρ τῶν ὅλων, ὁ πάντων πατήρ). Justin denies the substantial omnipresence of God. God the Father dwells, according to him, in the regions above the sky. He cannot leave his place, and therefore he is unable to appear in the world:

He who has but the smallest intelligence will not venture to assert that the Creator and Father of all things, having left all supercelestial matters, was visible on a little portion of the earth (*Dial.* 60). — For the ineffable Father and Lord of all neither has come to any place, nor walks, nor sleeps, nor rises up, but remains in his own place, wherever that is, quick to behold and quick to hear, having neither eyes nor ears, but being of indescribable might; and he knows all things, and none of us escapes his observation. And he is not moved or confined to a spot in the whole world, for he existed before the world was made. How then could he talk to anyone, or be seen by anyone, or appear on the smallest portion of the earth, when the people at Sinai were not able to look even on the glory of him who was sent from him (*Dial.* 127).

But since God is transcendent and beyond all human beings, it is necessary to bridge the abyss which opens up between God and man. This is done by the Logos. He is the mediator between God the Father and the world. God communicates with the world only through the Logos. And he reveals himself exclusively through the Logos. The Logos is therefore the guide to God and the instructor of man. Originally he dwelt as a power in God. But shortly before the creation of the world he emanated and proceeded from him and he himself created the world. In his *Dialogue* Justin explains the generation of the Logos with two pictures:

Just as we see happening in the case of a fire, which is not lessened when it has been kindled but remains the same, and that which has been kindled by it likewise appears to exist by itself, not diminishing that from which it was kindled (*Dial.* 61).

Or just as a work proceeds from man without lessening his substance, so the generation of the Logos, the Divine Word, must be understood as a process within God.

It seems that Justin tends to subordinationism as far as the relation between the Logos and the Father is concerned. This is evident from *Apology* 2, 6:

His Son who alone is properly called Son, the Logos, who alone was with him and was begotten before the works, when at first he created and arranged all things by him, is called Christ, in reference to his being anointed and God's ordering all things through him.

Accordingly, Justin seems to suppose that the Logos became externally independent only in order to create and govern the world. The personal function gave him personal existence. He became a divine person, but subordinated to the Father (cf. *Dial.* 61).

The doctrine of the Logos is the most important doctrine of Justin, because it forms a bridge between pagan philosophy and Christianity. For Justin teaches, that although the Divine Logos appeared in his fulness only in Christ, 'a seed of the Logos' was scattered among the whole of mankind long before Christ. For every human being possesses in his reason a seed (σπέρμα) of the Logos. Thus, not only the prophets of the Old Testament, but even the pagan philosophers carried a germinating seed of the Logos in their souls, as for instance, Heraclitus, Socrates, and the Stoic philosopher, Musonius, who lived according to the directions of the Logos, the Divine Word. In fact, they were truly Christians:

We have been taught that Christ is the firstborn of God, and we have declared that he is the Logos, of whom every race of man were partakers, and those who lived according to the Logos are Christians, even though they have been thought atheists, as among the Greeks, Socrates and Heraclitus, and men like them (*Apology* 1,46).

Hence there can be no opposition between Christianity and philosophy because:

Whatever all men have uttered aright is the property of us Christians. For we worship and love next to God the Logos, which is from the unbegotten and ineffable God, since it was even for us that he became man, that he might be a partaker of our sufferings and bring us healing. For all writers through the implanted seed of the Logos which was engrafted in them, were able to see the truth darkly, for the seed and imitation of a thing which is given according to the capacity of him who receives it is one thing, and quite a different one is the thing itself of which the communication and the imitation are received according to the grace from God (*Apologia*, 2, 13). — For whatever either lawgivers or philosophers uttered well, they elaborated by finding and contemplating some part of the Logos. But since they did not know the entire Logos, which is Christ, they often contradicted themselves. And those who by human birth were more ancient than Christ, when they tried to consider and prove things by reason, were brought before the tribunals, as impious persons and busybodies. And Socrates, who was more zealous in this direction than all of them, was accused of the very same crimes as ourselves. For they said that he was introducing new divinity and did not consider those to be gods whom the state recognized. . . But these things our Christ did through his own power. For no one trusted in Socrates so as to die for this doctrine but in Christ who was partially known even by Socrates, for he was and is the Logos who is in every man (*Apologia*, 2, 10.)

L. Duncker, Zur Geschichte der christlichen Logoslehre in den ersten Jahrhunderten. Die Logoslehre Justins des Martyrers. Göttingen, 1848. — D. H. Waubert de Puiseau, De Christologie van Justinus Martyr (Academisch proefschrift). Leiden, 1864. — L. Paul, Über die Logoslehre bei Justinus Martyr: Jahrbücher für protestantische Theologie 12 (1886) 661–690; 16 (1890) 550–578; 17 (1891) 124–148. — F. Bosse, Der präexistente Christus des Justinus Martyr (Diss.). Greifswald, 1891. — J. A. Cramer, Die Logosstellen in Justins Apologien kritisch untersucht: ZNW 2 (1901) 300–330; *idem*, De Logosleer in de pleitreden van Justinus: Theol. Tijdschr. (1902) 114–159. — J. Leblanc, Le logos de S. Justin: Annales de philos. chrét. 148 (1904) 191–197. — A. L. Feder, Justins des Märtyrers Lehre von Jesus Christus. Freiburg i. B., 1906. — J. Rivière, Le dogme de la rédemption.

Etudes critiques et doctrinales. Louvain, 1931, 79–86. — J. BARBEL, Christos Angelos. Bonn, 1941, 50–63. — J. LECLERCQ, L'idée de la royauté du Christ dans l'oeuvre de S. Justin: Année théologique 7 (1946) 83–95.

Thus Justin gives a metaphysical proof for the existence of elements of truth in pagan philosophy. But in addition he has an historical proof. The pagan philosophers made many true statements because they borrowed them from the literature of the Jews, from the Old Testament:

> Moses is more ancient than all the Greek writers. And whatever both philosophers and poets have asserted concerning the immortality of the soul or punishment after death, or contemplation of heavenly things, or doctrines of similar kind, they have received such suggestions from the prophets, as have enabled them to understand and interpret these things, and hence there seem to be seeds of truth among all men (*Apologia*, 1,44).

But the Christians alone possess the entire truth, because in Christ appeared to them Truth itself.

For the relation of Justin to Greek philosophy see: C. CLEMEN, Die religions-philosophische Bedeutung des stoisch-christlichen Eudämonismus in Justins Apologie. Leipzig, 1890. — E. DE FAYE, De l'influence du Timée de Platon sur la théologie de Justin Martyr: Bibliothèque de l'Ecole des Hautes Etudes, Sciences religieuses 7 (1896) 169–187. — W. LIESE, Justinus Martyr in seiner Stellung zum Glauben und zur Philosophie: ZKTh 26 (1902) 560–570. — J. M. PFÄTTISCH, Christus und Sokrates bei Justin: ThQ 90 (1908) 503–523; *idem*, Platons Einfluss auf die Theologie Justins: Der Katholik 89 (1909) 401–419; *idem*, Der Einfluss Platos auf die Theologie Justins des Märtyrers. Eine dogmengeschichtliche Untersuchung (FLDG 10,1). Paderborn, 1910. — G. BARDY, Saint Justin et la philosophie stoicienne: RSR 13 (1923) 491–510; 14 (1924) 33–45. — P. KESELING, Justins 'Dialog gegen Trypho' c. 1–10 und Platons 'Protagoras': RhM 75 (1926) 223–229. — V. STEGMANN, Christentum und Stoizismus im Kampf um die geistigen Lebenswerte: Die Welt als Geschichte (1941) 295–330.

2. *Mary and Eve*

Justin is the first Christian author who adds a counterpart to the Pauline parallel, Christ-Adam, by contrasting Mary with Eve. In his *Dialogue* (100) he says:

> Christ became man by the virgin in order that the disobedience which proceded from the serpent's might receive its destruction in the same manner in which it derived its

origin. For Eve, who was a virgin and undefiled, having conceived the word of the serpent, brought forth disobedience and death. But the Virgin Mary received faith and joy when the Angel Gabriel announced the good tidings to her, that the spirit of the Lord would come upon her, and the power of the highest would overshadow her; wherefore the Holy Thing begotten of her is the Son of God; and she replied, 'Be it done unto me according to thy word'. And by her has he been born, to whom we have proved so many scriptures refer, and by whom God destroys both the serpent and those angels and men who are like him.

W. STAERK, Eva-Maria. Ein Beitrag zur Denk- und Sprechweise der altkirchlichen Christologie: ZNW 33 (1934) 97–104.

3. *Angels and Demons*

Justin is one of the first authors who testifies to the cult of the angels: 'The host of the other good angels who follow and are made like him and the prophetic spirit we worship and adore' (*Apol.* 1,6).

From heaven they take care of all human beings: 'He committed the care of man and of all things under heaven to angels whom he appointed over them' (*Apol.* 2,5).

Justin attributes to the angels in spite of their spiritual nature a body which is similar to the human body: 'It is evident to us that they are nourished in the heavens even though they are not nourished by food similar to that which mortals use; for concerning the sustenance of manna which supported your fathers in the desert scripture says that they ate angels' food' (*Dial.* 57).

The fact that St. Justin attributes a body to the angels is indicated by his opinion of the fall of the angels. Their sin consisted in sexual intercourse with human women: 'The angels transgressed this appointment and were captivated by love of women and begot children who are those that are called demons' (*Apol.* 2,5).

The punishment of the demons in eternal fire will take place after Christ's return (*Apol.* 1, 28). Therefore, they now are still able to mislead and seduce man. Their whole endeavor after Christ's coming is to prevent the conversion of man to God and to the Logos (*Apol.* 1,26,54,57,62). That is proved by the

heretics, who are tools of the demons, because they teach a god
other than the Father and his Son. The demons blinded and
instigated the Jews to inflict all these sufferings on the Logos who
appeared in Jesus. But knowing that Christ would find most of his
followers among the pagans, they were especially eager to ruin
his chances among them. Interesting in this connection is what
Justin says about the effect of the name of Jesus on the demons:
We call him helper and savior, the power of whose name
even the demons fear, and today, when they are exorcized
in the name of Jesus Christ, crucified under Pontius Pilate,
Governor of Judea, they are overcome. And thus is manifested to all that his Father has given him so great power, by
virtue of which demons are subdued to his name (*Dial.* 30).

F. ANDRES, Die Engellehre der griechischen Apologeten des zweiten Jahrhunderts und ihr Verhältnis zur griechisch-römischen Dämonologie (FLDG 12,3).
Paderborn, 1914, 1–35.

4. *Original Sin and Deification*

Justin is convinced that every human being is capable of deification. At least, this was the case at the beginning of creation.
But the first parents sinned and brought death upon themselves.
But now every man has regained the power of becoming God:
They were made like God, free from suffering and death,
provided that they kept his commandments and were deemed
deserving of the name of his sons, and yet they, becoming
like Adam and Eve, work out death for themselves: let the
interpretation of the psalm (81) be held just as you wish,
yet thereby it is demonstrated that all men are deemed
worthy of becoming gods and having power to become sons
of the Highest and shall be each by himself judged and condemned like Adam and Eve (*Dial.* 124).

L. DUNCKER, Apologetarum secundi saeculi de essentialibus naturae humanae
partibus placita. Part I (Justinus Martyr). Göttingen, 1884. — B. ANTONIA-
DES, 'Ιουστίνου τοῦ φιλοσόφου ἀνθρωπολογία: 'Ἀρχεῖον φιλοσοφίας (1930)
207ff.

5. *Baptism and Eucharist*

Of exceptional value is the description of the liturgy of Baptism and the Eucharist, which Justin gives at the end of his first Apology. About Baptism he remarks:

I will also relate the manner in which we dedicate ourselves to God, when we have been made new through Christ, lest if we omit this we seem to be unfair in the explanation we are making. As many as are persuaded and believe that what we teach and say is true, and undertake to be able to live accordingly, are instructed to pray and to entreat God with fasting for the remission of their sins that are past, we praying and fasting with them. Then they are brought by us where there is water, and are regenerated in the same manner in which we ourselves were regenerated. For in the name of God the Father and Lord of the universe, and of our Savior Jesus Christ, and of the Holy Spirit they then receive the washing with water . . . And for this we have learned from the Apostles this reason. Since at our first birth we were born without our knowledge and our choice by our parents' coming together and were brought up in bad habits and wicked training, in order that we may not remain the children of necessity and of ignorance, but may become the children of choice and knowledge, and may obtain in the water the remission of sins formerly committed, there is pronounced over him who chooses to be born again, and has repented of his sins, the name of God the Father and Lord of the universe, he who leads to the laver the person that is to be washed calling him by this name alone. And this washing is called illumination, because they who learn these things are illuminated spiritually. But also in the name of Jesus Christ, who was crucified under Pontius Pilate, and in the name of the Holy Spirit, who through the prophets foretold all things about Jesus, he who is illuminated is washed (*Apol.* 1,61).

There are two descriptions of the Eucharistic service in Justin's Apology. In the first (Ch. 65) he pictures the Eucharistic liturgy of the newly baptized. In the second (Ch. 67) he gives the details of the regular Sunday service. On Sundays the Liturgy began with a reading taken from the canonical gospels, which here are called explicitly 'Memoirs of the Apostles', or from the books of the prophets. There followed a sermon with a moral application of

the readings. After this the community prayed for the Christians
and for all men in the whole world. At the conclusion of the
prayers all members of the community exchanged the kiss of
peace. Thereupon, bread, wine, and water were brought to the
president. He recited a prayer of consecration over them. The
consecrated gifts were distributed by the deacons to those present
and were brought by them to those absent. Justin explicitly adds,
however, that this is no common bread and no common drink
but the flesh and blood of the incarnate Jesus. As a proof he
quotes the words of institution. The phrasing of the Eucharistic
prayer was left to the celebrating president, but Justin remarks
that the Eucharistic food is consecrated by a prayer containing
Christ's own words. Therefore, it seems that not only the very
words of institution, but most probably the entire account of
the institution was a regular part of the prayer of consecration.
For this reason, one may speak of a semirigid type of Liturgy,
because there are regular elements in it, but there is also still
room for the personal composition of the consecrating priest. It
is interesting that in his account of the Eucharistic service which
followed the reception of the Sacrament of Baptism Justin does
not mention the reading from Scripture and the sermon of the
president. It seems that they were omitted because of the preceding baptismal ceremony. His description of the Mass for the
newly baptized is as follows:

But we, after we have thus washed him who has been
convinced and has given his assent, bring him to those who
are called brethren, where they are assembled together, in
order that we may offer prayer in common both for ourselves and for the person who has received illumination and
for all others in every place with all our hearts that we may
be counted worthy, now that we have learned the truth, by
our works also to be found good citizens and keepers of the
commandment, so that we may obtain everlasting salvation.
Having ended the prayers, we salute one another with a
kiss. Then is brought to the president of the brethren bread
and a cup of water and wine, which he accepts; and he,
taking them, gives praise and glory to the Father of all
things through the name of his Son and of the Holy Spirit;
and he offers thanks at considerable length for our being

counted worthy to receive these things at his hands. When he has concluded the prayers and thanksgiving, all the people who are present express their assent by saying 'Amen'. This word 'Amen' in the Aramaic language means 'so be it'. And when the president has celebrated the Eucharist, and all the people have expressed their assent, they whom we call deacons give to each of those who are present a portion of the Eucharistic bread and wine and water, and to those who are absent, they carry away a portion. And this food is called by us the Eucharist. Of which no one is allowed to partake but he who believes that the things which we teach are true, and who has been washed in the bath for the forgiveness of sins and to regeneration, and who so lives as Christ has directed. For not as ordinary bread and ordinary drink do we receive these, but in like manner as by the word of God Jesus Christ our Savior was made flesh and had both flesh and blood for our salvation, so also the food, which is blessed by the prayer of the Word which proceeded from him and from which our flesh and blood by transmutation are nourished, is, we are taught, the flesh and blood of that Jesus who was made flesh. For the apostles in the memoirs which they composed and which are called gospels have declared that they were commanded to do as follows: that Jesus took bread and gave thanks and said, 'this do in remembrance of me, this is my body', and in like manner he gave thanks and said 'this is my blood' and gave it to them alone (*Apology*, 1,62).

A description of the regular Sunday Mass is given by St. Justin in chapter 67. He explains the fact that this day was chosen for the regular liturgical meeting of the Christian congregation with the statement that it was sanctified in a special way because God created the world and Christ rose from the dead on that day:

And on the day which is called Sunday, all who live in the cities or in the country gather together to one place and the memoirs of the apostles and the writings of the prophets are read as long as time permits. Then the reader concludes, and the president verbally instructs and exhorts us to the imitation of these excellent things, then we all rise together and offer up our prayers; and as I said before when we have ended our prayer, bread is brought and wine and water; and the president in like manner offers up prayers and thanksgivings according to his ability and the people give their assent by saying 'Amen'; and there is a distribution and a partaking by everyone of the Eucharist and to those who are absent a portion is brought by the deacons. And those who are well-to-do and willing give as they choose, each as he himself purposes; the collection is then deposited with the president who supports orphans, widows, those who are in want owing to sickness or any other cause, those who are in prison and strangers who are on a journey and in a word takes care of all who are in need. But Sunday is the day on which we hold our common assembly because it is the first day on which God, when he changed darkness and matter, made the world, and Jesus Christ our Savior on the same day rose from the dead (*Apology*, 1,67).

A lively discussion arose and still continues concerning the question whether St. Justin considered the Eucharist a sacrifice. The decisive passage is found in his *Dialogue with the Jew Tryphon* (Ch. 41):

I have no pleasure in you, says the Lord; and I will not accept your sacrifices at your hands: for from the rising of of the sun to the going down of the same my name has been glorified among the gentiles, and in every place incense is offered to my name, and a pure offering: for my name is great among the gentiles says the Lord, but you profane it. He then speaks of those gentiles, namely us, who in every place offer sacrifices to him, i.e., the bread of the Eucharist and also the cup of the Eucharist, affirming both that we glorify his name and that you profane it.

There can be no doubt that Justin here clearly identifies the Eucharist with the sacrifice which was prophesied by Malachy. However, other passages can be found in which Justin apparently rejects all sacrifice. Thus he says in his *Dialogue* (Ch. 117):

Now that prayers and giving of thanks, when offered by worthy men, are the only perfect and well pleasing sacrifices to God, I admit.

In his first *Apology*, chapter 13, he has a similar thought:

The only honor that is worthy of him is not to consume by fire what he has brought into being for our sustenance, but to use it for ourselves and those who need, and with gratitude to him to offer thanks by praises and hymns for our creation.

From these remarks the conclusion was drawn that Justin rejects every sacrifice and approves only of prayer, especially the Eucharistic prayer. But such an interpretation does not do justice to his ideas. No one will be able to understand his concept of sacrifice unless he takes into account his doctrine of the Logos. What Justin really rejects is the material sacrifice of creatures as practised by the Jews and pagans. By means of his concept of sacrifice he attempts to bridge the gap between pagan philosophy and Christianity just as he uses his concept of the Logos for that same end. His ideal is the λογικὴ θυσία, the *oblatio rationabilis*, the spiritual sacrifice which the Greek philosophers declared to be the only veneration worthy of God. Here, as in the case of the Logos, Christianity represents the fulfillment of a philosophic ideal because it possesses such a spiritual sacrifice. For this reason Justin agrees with the pagan philosophers as well as with the prophets of the Old Testament, that external sacrifices must be abolished. There is no longer any room for bloody material sacrifices. The Eucharist is the long desired spiritual sacrifice, the λογικὴ θυσία, because the Logos himself, Jesus Christ, is here the victim. Justin's identification of the λογικὴ θυσία with the Eucharist proved extremely happy. By incorporating this idea into the Christian doctrine he appropriated for Christianity the highest achievements of Greek philosophy, and stressed at the same time the new and unique character of Christian worship. He retained an objective sacrifice while on the other hand he emphasized the spiritual character of Christian worship, by reason of which it excelled all pagan and Jewish sacrifices. Thus the term, *oblatio rationabilis*, in the canon of the Roman Mass expresses better than any other word Justin's concept of sacrifice.

A. HARNACK, Brot und Wasser die eucharistischen Elemente bei Justin (TU 7,2). Leipzig, 1891. — Γ. X. FUNK, Die Abendmahlselemente der Eucharistie in den ersten drei Jahrhunderten (FLDG 3,4). Mainz, 1903. —

M. Goguel, L'Eucharistie des origines à Justin Martyr. Paris, 1909. —
S. Salaville, La Liturgie décrit par saint Justin et l'épiclèse: EO 12 (1909)
129–136; 222–227. — F. Wieland, Der vorirenäische Opferbegriff. München,
1909. — E. Dorsch, Der Opfercharakter der Eucharistie einst und jetzt,
2nd ed. Innsbruck, 1911. — O. Casel, Die Eucharistielehre des hl. Justinus
Martyr: Der Katholik 94 (1914) I, 153–176; 243–263; 331–355; 414–436. —
J. Brinktrine, Der Messopferbegriff in den ersten zwei Jahrhunderten (Frei-
burger Theologische Studien 21). Freiburg i. B., 1918, 85–105. — J. B.
Thibaut, La Liturgie Romaine. Paris, 1924, 38–56. — P. Batiffol, L'Eucharistie. La présence réelle et la transsubstantiation (Etudes d'histoire et de
théologie positive 2e sér.). 9th ed. Paris, 1930, 6–32. — J. N. Greiff, Brot,
Wasser und Mischwein die Elemente der Taufmesse: ThQ 113 (1932) 11–34.
— J. Quasten, Monumenta eucharistica et liturgica vetustissima. Bonn,
1935–37, 13–21; 337–339. — J. Beran, Quo sensu intelligenda sint verba
S. Justini Martyris ὅση δύναμις αὐτῷ in I Apologia, n. 67: DTP 39 (1936)
46–55. — O. Perler, Logos und Eucharistie nach Justinus I Apol. c. 66:
DT 18 (1940) 296–316. — St. Morson, St. Justin and the Eucharist: IER
79 (1943) 323–328. — J. A. Jungmann, Missarum Sollemnia. Vienna, 1948,
I, 30–34.

6. Eschatological Ideas

In his eschatological ideas Justin shares the views of the Chili-
asts concerning the millenium: 'But I and others are right-minded
Christians in all points and are assured that there will be a
resurrection of the dead and a thousand years in Jerusalem,
which will then be built, adorned and enlarged.' But he feels
bound to admit that not all Christians hold this Chiliastic view:
'I signify to you that many who belong to the pure and pious
faith and are true Christians think otherwise' (Dialogue, ch.80).
According to Justin the souls of the departed enter first into
Hades where they remain until the world comes to an end. The
only exceptions are the martyrs. Their souls are immediately
received into heaven. But even in Hades the good souls are
separated from the bad ones. The good souls rejoice, expecting
their eternal salvation, whereas the bad souls are unhappy because of their impending punishment (Dialogue, 5;80).

J. Daniélou, La typologie millénariste de la semaine dans le christianisme
primitif: VC 2 (1948) 1–16.

TATIAN THE SYRIAN

Tatian, a Syrian by birth, was of pagan parentage, and as mentioned above, was a pupil of Justin Martyr. He has this in common with his master that after much wandering he found the Christian doctrine to be the only true philosophy. He gives us the following information regarding the reason for his conversion:

> Wherefore having seen these things, and moreover also having been admitted to the Mysteries, and having everywhere examined the religious rites performed by the effeminate and the pathic, and having found among the Romans the Latiarian Jupiter delighting in human gore and the blood of slaughtered men, and Artemis not far from the great city sanctioning acts of the same kind, and one demon here another there instigating to the perpetration of evil, retiring by myself, I sought how I might be able to discover the truth. And while I was giving my most earnest attention to the matter, I happened to meet with certain barbaric writings too old to be compared with the opinions of the Greeks, and too divine to be compared with their errors; and I was led to put faith in these by the unpretending cast of the language, the unartificial character of the writers, the foreknowledge displayed of future events, the excellent quality of the precepts, and the declaration of the government of the universe as centered in one Being. And my soul being taught by God, I discovered that the former class of writings lead to condemnation, but that these put an end to the slavery that is in the world and rescue us from a multiplicity of rulers and ten thousand tyrants, while they give us not indeed what we had not before received, but what we had received but were prevented by error from retaining (*Orat.* 29).

It seems that Tatian's conversion took place in Rome. There he frequented Justin's school. Although Justin was Tatian's teacher, we notice sharp contrasts between them as soon as we compare their writings. This is especially evident in the evaluation which they place on non-Christian philosophy and culture. Whereas Justin attempts to find at least elements of truth in the

writings of some Greek thinkers, Tatian teaches complete renunciation of all Greek philosophy on principle. Justin in his
defense of Christianity paid high respect to non-Christian philosophy. Tatian betrays a determined hatred of all that belongs
to Greek civilization, art, science and language. His character
was so inclined to extremes that in his mind Christianity did not
go far enough in its rejection of contemporary education and
culture. He returned to the East, about the year 172, where he
became the founder of the sect of the Encratites, i.e., the Absti-
nents, which belongs to the group of Christian Gnostics. This
heresy rejected matrimony as adultery, condemned the use of
meat in any form, the drinking of wine, and went so far as to
substitute water for wine in the Eucharistic service. For this
reason the adherents of this sect were called the *Aquarii*. We know
nothing about Tatian's death.

I. *The Discourse to the Greeks*

Only two of Tatian's works are extant, *The Discourse to the Greeks*
and the *Diatessaron*. The time of composition of his *Discourse to
the Greeks* and the purpose of this oration are controverted.
Most probably it was written after the death of St. Justin, but
apparently not at Rome. Whether Tatian composed it before
or after his apostasy remains uncertain. Some scholars think that
the oration is not an apology intended to defend Christianity or
to justify the conversion of the author, but a dedicatory speech,
containing an invitation to attend the school of the author. But
even if it was delivered as an oration at the opening of a school
there is no doubt that from the beginning it was thought to be
an address to the public. It remains true, however, that the speech
is not so much an apology for Christianity as it is a vehement,
immoderate polemic treatise which rejects and belittles the whole
culture of the Greeks. The philosophy, religion and achievements
of the Greeks are all in his mind foolish, deceitful and immoral,
and without value. In the introduction Tatian states that everything that seems to be of any value in Greek civilization has
been borrowed from the barbarians. But most of it is without

value, or promotes immorality, as do their poetry, philosophy and rhetoric.

The main part of this work has four sections:

I.   The first section (Ch. 4,3–7,6) contains a Christian cosmology.

1. The author gives a definition of the Christian concept of God (Ch. 4,3–5).
2. He then treats of the relation of the Logos to the Father, the formation of matter and the creation of the world (Ch. 5).
3. There follows a description of the creation of man, of the resurrection, and of the last judgment (Ch. 6–7,1).
4. At the end of this section (Ch. 7, 2–8) Tatian deals with the creation of the angels, the freedom of the will, the fall of the angels, the sin of Adam and Eve, bad angels and demons. This matter ushers in the second section.

II.   A Christian demonology (Ch. 8–20).

1. Astrology is an invention of the demons. Man misused his freedom of will and thus became a slave of the demons. But there is a possibility of freeing oneself from this bondage by an entire renunciation of all worldly things (Ch. 8–11).
2. In order to gain strength for this renunciation, and thus escape the power of the demons, we must endeavor to reunite our soul with the *pneuma*, the heavenly spirit. Originally this pneuma lived in the bosom of the first man, but was expelled by the first sin, which was the work of the demons (Ch. 12––15,1).
3. The demons are images of matter and iniquity. They are not able to do penance, but men are images of God and are thus able to attain immortality by self-mortification (Ch. 15, 2–16, 6).
4. Man must not fear death because he is obliged to reject all matter in order to gain immortality (Ch. 16, 7–20).

III.   Greek civilization in the light of the Christian attitude toward life (Ch. 21–30) is the content of the third section.

1. The foolishness of all Greek theology forms a sharp contrast to the sublimity of the mystery of the incarnation (Ch. 21).
2. The Greek theatres are schools of vice. The arena resembles a slaughter house. Dancing, music and poetry are sinful and without value (Ch. 22–24).

3. Greek philosophy and law are contradictory and deceitful (Ch. 25–28).
4. Against this dark background of Greek civilization the superiority of the Christian religion shines forth the brighter (Ch. 29–30).
IV. The age and moral value of Christianity (Ch. 31–41).
1. The Christian religion is older than all others because Moses lived before Homer, long before all the lawgivers of Greece, and even before the seven wise men (Ch. 31, 1–6, 36–41).
2. Christian philosophy and Christian conduct of life are free from all envy and ill-will and for this reason differ from the wisdom of the Greek writers. The accusations of immorality and cannibalism made falsely against the Christians fall back on their authors, the venerators of the Greek gods, because such crimes are frequent and well known in the cult of the Greeks. The morality and the purity of the Christians cannot be stained by such calumnies (Ch. 31,7–35).

At the end Tatian presents himself for any criticism:
'These things, O Greeks, I, Tatian, a disciple of the barbarian philosophy, have composed for you. I was born in the land of the Assyrians, having been first instructed in your doctrines, and afterwards in those which I now undertake to proclaim. Henceforward, knowing who God is and what is His work, I present myself to you prepared for an examination concerning my doctrines while I adhere immovably to that mode of life which is according to God' (Chapter 42 ANF 2, 81/2).

Separate Edition: E. Schwartz, Tatiani Oratio ad Graecos (TU 4,1). Leipzig, 1888.

Translations: English: J. E. Ryland, ANF 2, 65–83. — *French:* A. Puech, Recherches sur le Discours aux Grecs de Tatien, suivies d'une traduction française du Discours avec notes. Paris, 1903, 107–158. — *Italian:* P. Ubaldi. Turin, 1921. — M. Fermi, Taziano, Discorso ai Greci. Rome, 1924. — *German:* A. Harnack, Giessener Universitätsprogramm,1884.—R. C. Kukula, Tatians Rede an die Bekenner des Griechentums (BKV 12). Kempten, 1913.

Studies: H. Dembowski, Die Quellen der christlichen Apologetik des zweiten Jahrhunderts. Teil 1: Die Apologie Tatians. Leipzig, 1878. — F. X. Funk, Zur Chronologie Tatians: ThQ 65 (1883) 219-233; *idem*, Kirchengeschichtliche Abhandlungen und Untersuchungen 2 (1899) 142-152. — J. M. Fuller, Tatianus: Dictionary of Christian Biography 4 (1887) 783-804. —

A. Kalkmann, Tatians Nachrichten über Kunstwerke: RhM 42 (1887) 489–524. — W. Steuer, Die Gottes- und Logoslehre des Tatian mit ihren Berührungen in der griechischen Philosophie. Leipzig, 1893. — B. Ponschab, Tatians Rede an die Griechen (Progr.). Metten, 1895. — J. Dräseke, Zu Tatians 'Rede an die Griechen': Zeitschrift für wissenschaftliche Theologie 43 (1900) 603–612. — R. C. Kukula, Tatians sogenannte Apologie. Exegetisch-chronologische Studie. Leipzig, 1900; idem, 'Altersbeweis' und 'Künstlerkatolog' in Tatians Rede an die Griechen (Progr.). Vienna, 1900. — P. Fiebig, Zur Frage nach der Disposition des λόγος πρὸς ''Ελληνας des Tatian: ZKG 21 (1901) 149–159. — H. U. Meyboom, Tatianus en zijne Apologie: Theol. Tijdschrift 37 (1903) 193–247. — A. Puech, Recherches sur le Discours aux Grecs de Tatien. Paris, 1903; idem, Les Apologistes grecs du 2e siècle de notre ère. Paris, 1912, 148–171. — J. Leblanc, Le Logos de Tatien, Athénagore et Théophile: Annales de philosophie chrét. 149 (1905) 634–639. — J. Feuerstein, Die Anthropologie Tatians und der übrigen griechischen Apologeten des zweiten Jahrhunderts mit einleitender Gottes- und Schöpfungslehre (Diss.). Münster, 1906. — J. Geffcken, Zwei griechische Apologeten. Leipzig-Berlin, 1907, 105–113. — J. van Beek, Athenagoras' geschrift de resurrectione (Diss.). Leyden, 1908. — C. L. Heiler, De Tatiani apologetae dicendi genere (Diss.). Marburg, 1909. — F. Andres, Die Engellehre der griechischen Apologeten des zweiten Jahrhunderts. Paderborn, 1914, 36–65. — M. Zappalà, Taziano e lo gnosticismo: RSFR 3 (1922) 307–338. — J. de Zwaan, Ad quosdam Tatiani adversus Graecos orationis locos: Mnem 48 (1920) 313–320. — W. Bornstein, Beiträge zu Tatians Rede an die Griechen (Diss.). Rostock, 1923; idem, Zu Tatians λόγος πρὸς ''Ελληνας ZKG 44 (1925) 62. — G. Botti, Il fattore personale nel λόγος πρὸς ''Ελληνας di Taziano: Studi dedicati alla memoria di Paolo Ubaldi. Milan, 1937, 87–97. — C. Bonner, Rhetologia or aretologia: HThR 33 (1940) 317–319. — H. J. Rose, Aretalogia or teralogia?: HThR 34 (1941) 217. — A. Casamassa, L'accusa di 'hesterni' e gli scrittori cristiani del II secolo: Angelicum 20 (1943) 184–194.

2.   The Diatessaron

Tatians' most important work is his Diatessaron (Τὸ διὰ τεσσάρων εὐαγγέλιον). Actually, it is a harmony of the Gospels. Tatian called it 'out of four' because it ranges sections of all four Gospels into a continuous Gospel story. This book was for a long time officially used in the liturgy of the Syrian Church, and not before the fifth century was it displaced by the four canonical Gospels. The Diatessaron was probably composed after Tatian returned to the Orient. The original has been lost, and it remains a question whether it was put together in Greek or Syriac. There are reasons to assume that Tatian composed it in Greek, and afterwards translated it into Syriac. Only recently American archaeologists discovered a fragment of the Greek text. This fragment of fourteen lines was found during the excavations conducted by Johns Hopkins University at Dura Europos in Syria, in the year 1934, and was evidently written before the year 254. A Greek text of such an early date seems to favor the opinion of a Greek origin of the Diatessaron. The entire text can be reconstructed from extant translations. Preserved are Arabic, Latin, and Middle Low Franconian versions. Moreover, between 360 and 370, Ephrem Syrus composed a commentary to the Diatessaron, of which we possess, not the original Syriac text, but an Armenian version from the sixth century. All these versions of the Diatessaron suggest that it influenced the Gospel text of the whole Church in a high degree. The Latin translation originated at an early date, and comprises the first attempt to present the Gospel in the Latin language.

All other writings of Tatian have been lost. Three of them are mentioned by the author himself in his *Apology*. Chapter fifteen of this work presupposes that Tatian had previously written a treatise *On Animals* (περὶ ζῴων). In Chapter sixteen he declares that on another occasion he had composed a work *On Demons*. Chapter fourteen announces a future writing *Against Those Who Have Treated of Divine Things*. Clement of Alexandria quotes (*Stromat.* 3,81,1f.) a passage from Tatian's treatise *On Perfection According to the Precepts of the Savior*. Rhodon reports (Eusebius, *Hist. Eccl.* 5,13,8) that his teacher Tatian 'had prepared a book *On Problems* in which he undertook to set out what was unclear and hidden in the divine scriptures'. In addition, Eusebius states that Tatian 'ventures to paraphrase some words of the Apostle (Paul), as though correcting their style' (*Hist. Eccl.* 4,29,6).

H. Leclercq, DAL 4, 747-770. — Th. Zahn, Tatians Diatessaron. Erlangen, 1881. — P. A. Ciasca, Tatiani Evangeliorum harmoniae arabice. Nunc primum ex duplici codice edidit et translatione latina donavit. Rome, 1888. 2nd ed. 1934. — J. R. Harris, The Diatessaron of Tatian. A Preliminary Study. London, 1890. — M. Maher, Recent Evidence for the Authenticity of the Gospels: Tatian's Diatessaron. London, 1893. — J. H. Hill, The Earliest Life of Christ Ever Compiled from the Four Gospels: Being the Diatessaron of Tatian (circa 160). Literally Translated from the Arabic Version. Edinburgh, 1894. 2nd ed. 1910. — J. R. Harris, Fragments of the

Commentary of Ephrem Syrus upon the Diatessaron. London, 1895. — H. W. HOGG, Ante-Nicene Library, addit. vol., Edinburgh, 1897, 33–138. — A. HJELT, Die altsyrische Evangelienübersetzung und Tatians Diatessaron. Leipzig, 1903. — A. A. HOBSON, The Diatessaron of Tatian and the Synoptic Problem. Chicago, 1904. — F. C. BURKITT, Evangelion da Mepharreshe, The Curetonian Version of the Four Gospels, with the Reading of the Sinai Palimpsest and the Early Syriac Patristic Evidence. 2 vols. Cambridge, 1904. — H. GRESSMANN, Studien zum syrischen Tetraevangelium I: ZNW (1904) 248–252. — J. F. STENNING, Diatessaron: Hastings, Dictionary of the Bible, extra vol. (1904) 451–461. — G. A. BARTON and H. H. SPOER, Traces of the Diatessaron of Tatian in Harclean Syriac Lectionaries: JBL 24 (1906) 179–195.— R. H. CONNOLLY, 1. The Diatessaron in the Syriac Acts of John; 2. Jacob of Serug and the Diatessaron: JThSt 8 (1907) 571–590. — J. HONTHEIM, Die Abfolge der evangelischen Perikopen im Diatessaron Tatians: ThQ 90 (1908) 204–255; 339–376. — R. H. CONNOLLY, A Side-light on the Methods of Tatian: JThSt 12 (1911) 268–273. — H. J. VOGELS, Die altsyrischen Evangelien in ihrem Verhältnis zu Tatians Diatessaron. Freiburg i. B., 1911. — S. EURINGER, Die Überlieferung der arabischen Übersetzung des Diatessarons. Mit einer Textbeilage: Die Beiruter Fragmente, herausgegeben und übersetzt von G. Graf. Freiburg i. B., 1912. — J. SCHÄFERS, Eine altsyrische antimarkionitische Erklärung von Parabeln des Herrn. Mit Beiträgen zu Tatians Diatessaron und Markions NT. Münster, 1917. — E. PREUSCHEN, Untersuchungen zum Diatessaron Tatians (SB Heidelberg. Akadem. 9,15). Heidelberg, 1918. — H. J. VOGELS, Beiträge zur Geschichte des Diatessaron im Abendland. Münster, 1919. — D. PLOOIJ, A Primitive Text of the Diatessaron. The Liège Manuscript of a Mediaeval Dutch Translation. A Preliminary Study with an Introductory Note by J. R. HARRIS. Leyden, 1923. Cf. H. J. VOGELS, ThR 22 (1923) 81–84. — H. LIETZMANN, ZNW 22 (1923) 150–153. — J. R. HARRIS, Muhammed and the Diatessaron: ExpT 34 (1923) 377 f. — F. C. CONYBEARE, An Armenian Diatessaron?: JThSt 25 (1924) 232–245. — A. JÜLICHER, Der echte Tatiantext: JBL 43 (1924) 132–171. — J. R. HARRIS, Some Diatessaron Readings from Sinai: ExpT 35 (1924) 296–298. — F. C. BURKITT, Tatian's Diatessaron and the Dutch Harmonies: JThSt 25 (1924) 113ff. — D. PLOOIJ, A Further Study of the Liège Diatessaron. Leyden, 1925. — J. R. HARRIS, Was the Diatessaron anti-Judaic?: HThR 18 (1925) 103–109. — E. PREUSCHEN, Tatiani Diatessaron, aus dem Arabischen übersetzt. Edited by A. POTT. Heidelberg, 1926. — F. C. BURKITT, St. Luke IX 54,56 and the Western Diatessaron: JThSt 28 (1927) 48ff. — D. DE BRUYNE, La préface du Diatessaron latin avant Victor de Capoue: RB 39 (1927) 5–11. — D. PLOOIJ, Die heutige Lage des Diatessaronproblems: OC 3rd ser. 1 (1927) 201–22. — Q. CATAUDELLA, Note d'interpretazione sopra il testo di Tatiano: Didascaleion 8 (1929) 197–202. — A. BAUMSTARK, Die Evangelienzitate Novatians und das Diatessaron: OC (1930) 1–14; idem, Tatianismen im römischen Antiphonar; ibidem 165–174. — A. VACCARI, Propaggine del Diatessaron in Occidente: Bibl 12 (1931) 326–354. — A. RÜCKER, Die Zitate aus dem Matthäusevangelium im syrischen 'Buche der Stufen': Biblische Zeitschrift 20 (1932) 342–354. — G. DIX, Didache and Diatessaron: JThSt 34 (1933)

242-250. — R. H. CONNOLLY, Didache and Diatessaron: JThSt 34 (1933) 342-349. — A. BAUMSTARK, Zur Geschichte des Tatiantextes vor Aphrem: OC 8 (1933) 1-12; *idem,* Arabische Übersetzung eines altsyrischen Evangelientextes und die Sure 21,105 zitierte Psalmenübersetzung: OC 9 (1934) 165-180; *idem,* Markus 2 in der arabischen Übersetzung des Isaak Velasquez. Veröffentlicht und unter dem Gesichtspunkt des Zusammenhangs mit dem Diatessaron gewürdigt: OC 9 (1934) 226-239. — R. H. CONNOLLY, A Negative Form of the Golden Rule in the Diatessaron?: JThSt 35 (1934) 351-357. — C. H. KRAELING, A Greek Fragment of Tatian's Diatessaron from Dura (Studies and Documents 3). London, 1935. — D. PLOOIJ, A Fragment of Tatian's Diatessaron in Greek: ExpT 46 (1935) 471-476. — F. C. BURKITT, The Dura Fragment of Tatian: JThSt 36 (1935) 255-259. — PH. H. MENOUD, Un fragment grec du Diatessaron de Tatien: RTP 23 (1935) 379-382. — A. BAUMSTARK, Forschungen und Funde: Das griechische Diatessaron-Fragment von Dura-Europos: OC 11 (1935) 244-251; *idem,* Die syrische Übersetzung des Titus von Bostra und das Diatessaron: Bibl 16 (1935) 257-299. — W. HEFFENING und C. PETERS, Spuren des Diatessaron in liturgischer Überlieferung. Ein türkischer und ein Karsuni-Text: OC 10 (1935) 225-238. — C. PETERS, Nachtrag zu 'Spuren des Diatessaron in liturgischer Überlieferung': OC 11 (1936) 96-97. — D. PLOOIJ - C. A. PHILLIPS - A. J. BARNOUW, The Liège Diatessaron Edited with a Textual Apparatus and an English Translation. Amsterdam, 1929-1935. — L. CERFAUX, Un fragment du Diatessaron grec: ETL 13 (1936) 98-100. — A. MERK, Ein griechisches Bruchstück des Diatessaron Tatians: Bibl 17 (1936) 234-241. — A. S. MARMARDJI, Diatessaron de Tatien. Texte arabe établi, traduit en français, collationné avec les anciennes versions syriaques, suivi d'un évangéliaire diatessarique syrique. Beyrouth, 1935. — L. KHALIL, Le Diatessaron dans sa récente édition. Notes critiques: Al-Machriq. 34 (1936) 269-276. — P. JOUON, La nouvelle édition du Diatessaron arabe de Tatien: RSR 27 (1927) 91-96. — A. BAUMSTARK, OC 11 (1936) 235-252. — P. ESSABALIAN, Le Diatessaron de Tatien et la première traduction des évangiles arméniens. Appendice: résumé français. Vienna, 1937. — M. J. LAGRANGE, Deux nouveaux textes relatifs à l'Evangile. I. Un fragment grec du Diatessaron de Tatien. II. Un nouveau papyrus évangelique: RBibl 44 (1938) 321-343. — O. STEGMÜLLER, Ein Bruchstück aus dem griechischen Diatessaron (P. 16388): ZNW 37 (1938) 223-230. — R. P. CASEY, The Armenian Marcionites and the Diatessaron: JBL 57 (1938) 185-194. — V. TODESCO, A. VACCARI e M. VATTASSO, Il Diatessaron in volgare italiano. Testi inediti dei secoli XIII-XIV (ST 81). Vatican City, 1938. — C. PETERS, Das Diatessaron Tatians. Seine Überlieferung und sein Nachwirken im Morgen - und Abendland, sowie der heutige Stand seiner Erforschung (Orientalia Christiana Analecta 123). Rome, 1939. — A. BAUMSTARK, Der Tatiantext von Luc. 24,13: OC 35 (1939) 19-37; *idem,* Zwei italienische Diatessaron-Texte: OC 35 (1939) 225-242. — A. MERK, Tatian in italienischem Gewand: Bibl 20 (1939) 294-305. — C. PETERS, Daniel Plooij und die Diatessaronforschung: NTT 28 (1939) 233-241. — A. F. L. BESTON, The Arabic Version of Tatian's Diatessaron: Journal of the Royal Asiatic Society of Great Britain and Ireland (1939)

608–610. — C. Peters, Ein neues Fragment des griechischen Diatessaron?: Bibl 21(1940) 51–55; *idem*, Zum Problem der Stilistik in Tatians Diatessaron: OCP 6 (1940) 508–517. — M. Black, The Palestinian Syriac Gospel and the Diatessaron: OC 35 (1939) 101—111. — C. S. C. William, Tatian and the Text of Mark and Matthew: JThSt 43 (1942) 37–42. — C. Peters, Neue Funde und Forschungen zum Diatessaron-problem: Bibl 23 (1942) 68–77; *idem*, Der Diatessarontext von Mt. II,9 und die westsächsische Evangelienversion: Bibl 23 (1942) 323–332. — G. Messina, Un Diatessaron persiano del secolo XIII tradotto dal siriaco: Bibl 23 (1942) 268–305; 24 (1943) 59–106.— B. M. Metzger, Recently Published Greek Papyri of the New Testament: Biblical Archaeologist 10 (1947) 25–44.

MILTIADES

Miltiades, the rhetorician, was born in Asia Minor. A contemporary of Tatian, he was, most probably, also a pupil of Justin. Unfortunately, all his writings have been lost; but Tertullian (*Adv. Valent.* 5) and Hippolytus (Eusebius, *Hist. Eccl.* 5,28,4) report that he defended Christianity against the pagans as well as against the heretics. According to Eusebius (*Hist. Eccl.* 5,17,5) he wrote an *Apology for Christian Philosophy* which he addressed to 'temporal rulers'. The 'rulers' were most likely the emperor Marcus Aurelius (161–180) and his co-regent Lucius Verus (161–169). Of a similar apologetic nature were his work, *Against the Greeks*, in two books, and another work *Against the Jews*, also in two books. The treatise which he composed against the Montanists dealt with the question *That a Prophet Should not Speak in Ecstasy*, and explains that the Montanistic prophets were pseudo-prophets. Another anti-heretical treatise of Miltiades was directed against the Valentinian Gnostics.

APOLLINARIS OF HIERAPOLIS

Claudius Apollinaris was Bishop of Hierapolis, the city of Papias, during the time of Marcus Aurelius (161–180). Eusebius reports about him (*Hist. Eccl.* 4,27):

'Of the many writings of Apollinaris which have been widely preserved, the following have reached us: A treatise to the above-mentioned emperor (Marcus Aurelius), five books *Against the Greeks* (πρὸς Ἕλληνας), two books *On the Truth* (περὶ ἀληθείας), two books *Against the Jews* (πρὸς Ἰουδαίους), and after this the treatises which he wrote against the heresy of the Phrygians (Montanists) which had begun its innovations not long before, and was then, as it were, beginning to sprout, while Montanus with his false prophecies was making the beginnings of the error.'

None of the books which Eusebius mentions is extant. The same is true of another work of Apollinaris, not mentioned by Eusebius, but known to the author of the *Chronicon paschale*. The title was *On Easter* (περὶ τοῦ πάσχα). The two quotations which the author of the *Chronicon* cites seem to suggest that Apollinaris was against the quartodeciman dating of Easter.

ATHENAGORAS OF ATHENS

Athenagoras was a contemporary of Tatian, but he differs from him as well as from Justin. His judgment regarding the philosophy and culture of the Greeks was much kinder than Tatian's. On the other hand, he shows far more ability in language and style and in the arrangement of his material than Justin. Indeed, he is unquestionably the most eloquent of the early Christian apologists. He likes quotations taken from poets and philosophers, and uses philosophical expressions and sentences. His style and rhythm prove that he attended a school of rhetoric, and that he intended to write according to the pattern of the Atticists. Almost nothing is known about his life, because he is mentioned only once in ancient Christian literature (Methodius, *De resurrectione* 1,36,6–37,1). Th. Zahn was of the opinion that he is the same Athenagoras to whom Boethos, the Platonist, dedicated his work *On Difficult Expressions in Plato*, as Photius (*Bibl. Cod.* 154f.) reports. In the title of his *Supplication for the Christians* he is called a 'Christian philosopher of Athens'. In addition to this writing he composed a treatise *On the Resurrection of the Dead*.

WRITINGS

1. *The Supplication for the Christians*

The *Supplication for the Christians* (πρεσβεία περὶ τῶν χριστιανῶν) was written about the year 177, and addressed to the Emperors Marcus Aurelius Antoninus and Lucius Aurelius Commodus. The latter was the son of Marcus Aurelius to whom the imperial title was granted in 176. This supplication is written in a calm tone and is well arranged. The introduction (Chapter 1–3) contains the address and states the purpose plainly: 'You will learn from this discourse that we suffer unjustly and contrary to all law and reason and that it will devolve upon the sovereigns to remove by law this despiteful treatment.' Then Athenagoras refutes (Chapter 4–36) the three accusations of atheism, cannibalism, and Oedipean incest, which the pagans made against the Christians.

1. The Christians are no atheists. Although they do not believe in gods, they believe in God. They are monotheists. Monotheistic tendencies can be found even in some of the pagan poets and philosophers. But nobody ever accused these men of atheism, although they gave only weak proofs of their ideas. The Christians, however, received a divine revelation and instruction on this point from their prophets, who were inspired by the Holy Ghost. In addition, they have proofs from reason for their faith. The Christian concept of God is purer and more perfect than that of all philosophers. This is a fact which is demonstrated by the Christians, not only by words, but by deeds: 'Who of them (the pagan philosophers) have so purged their souls as, instead of hating their enemies, to love them; and, instead of speaking ill of those who have reviled them, to bless them; and to pray for those who plot against their lives? . . . . But among us you will find uneducated persons and artisans and old women, who if they are unable to prove in words the benefit of our doctrine, yet by their deeds exhibit the benefit arising from their possession of its truth' (*Apol.* 11). For the same reason, in being monotheists, the Christians are not polytheists. Therefore they do not have sacrifices like the pagans, and they do not believe in gods. Moreover, they do not even adore the world, which is a greater piece of art than any idol, but they venerate their Creator.

2. The Christians are not guilty of cannibalism. They do not kill anybody. What is more, they do not look on while murder is committed, though this is a special pleasure of the pagans, as the shows of the gladiators indicate. The Christians have more respect for human life than the pagans. For this reason they condemn the exposition of children. Their belief in the resurrection of the body alone would make them refrain from eating human flesh.

3. The accusation of Oedipean incest is nothing but the outgrowth of hate. History shows that virtue has always been persecuted by vice. The Christians are so far from committing such crimes that they do not even permit a sin against purity in thought. The Christian ideas regarding marriage and virginity indicate how high their esteem of chastity is.

The closing of the *Apology* (Chapter 37) is an entreaty to be judged fairly:

'Now that I have disposed of the several accusations, and proved that we are pious, and gentle, and temperate in spirit, bend your royal head in approval. For who are more deserving to obtain the things they ask, than those who, like us, pray for your government, that you may, as is most equitable, receive the kingdom, son from father, and that your empire may receive increase and addition, all men becoming subject to your sway? And this is also for your advantage, that we may lead a peaceable and quiet life, and may ourselves readily perform all that is commanded us.'

2. *On the Resurrection of the Dead*

At the end of the *Apology* (Chapter 36) Athenagoras announces a discourse concerning the resurrection. This writing is preserved under the title *On the Resurrection of the Dead* (περὶ ἀναστάσεως νεκρῶν). In the Arethas Codex of 914, it is expressly stated that it is a work of Athenagoras, and it follows immediately after his *Apology*. The treatise on the resurrection has a decidedly philosophical character and proves the doctrine of the resurrection from reason. It has two parts. The first (Chapter 1–10) deals with God and the resurrection. It shows that God's wisdom, omnipotence, and justice do not interfere with the resurrection of the dead, but are in harmony with it. The second part (Chapter 11–25) deals with man and the resurrection. The resurrection is necessary on account of human nature, for first of all, man is created for eternity (Chapter 12–13), and secondly, he consists of body and soul. This unity, which is destroyed by death, must be restored by the resurrection in order to enable man to live on forever (Chapter 14–17). Thirdly, body as well as soul is to be rewarded, because both of them are subject to the moral order. It would be unjust to let the soul alone do penance for what she did instigated by the body, and it would be equally unjust not to reward the body for the good deeds which were performed by its cooperation (Chapter 18–23). Fourthly, man is destined for happiness, which cannot be achieved in this terrestrial life, but must be found in another life (Chapter 24–25).

ASPECTS OF ATHENAGORAS' THEOLOGY

1. Athenagoras was the first to attempt to prove monotheism scientifically. For this purpose, he tries to establish by speculative reasoning the oneness of God to which the prophets testify. He does this by a study of the relation of the existence of God to place:

> As regards, then, the doctrine that there was from the beginning one God, the Creator of this universe, consider it in this wise that you may be acquainted with the argumentative grounds of our faith. If there were from the beginning two or more gods, they were either in one and the same place, or each of them separately in his own. In one and the same place they could not be. For, if they are gods, they are not alike; but because they are uncreated they are unlike: for created things are like their patterns; but the uncreated are unlike, being neither produced from anyone, nor formed after the pattern of any one . . . . But if, on the contrary, each of them exists separately, since he that made the world is above the things created, and about the things he has made and set in order, where can the other or the rest be? For if the world, being made spherical, is confined within the circles of heaven, and the Creator of the world is above the things created, managing it by his providential care of these, what place is there for the second god, or for the other gods? (*Apol.* 8, ANF 2, 132).

2. Athenagoras is much clearer and less reserved than St. Justin in defining the divinity of the Logos and his essential unity with the Father. He avoids the subordinationism of the other Greek apologists, as can be seen from the following passage:

> But if, in your surpassing intelligence, it occurs to you to inquire what is meant by the Son, I will state briefly that he

is the product of the Father, not as having been brought
into existence — for from the beginning, God, who is the
eternal mind (νοῦς), had the Logos in Himself, being from
eternity instinct with Logos (λογικός) — but inasmuch as he
came forth to be the idea and energizing power of all material things, which lay like a nature without attributes, and an
inactive earth, the grosser particles being mixed up with the
lighter. The prophetic Spirit also agrees with our statements:
'The Lord', it says, 'made me the beginning of his ways to
his works' (Apol. 10, ANF 2,133).

3. Regarding the Holy Spirit, Athenagoras states:

The Holy Spirit also, which operates in the prophets, we
assert to be an effluence of God, flowing from him, and re-
turning back again like a beam of the sun (Apol. 10, ibidem).

4. One of the finest theological passages of the Apology is the
ingenious, and for the ante-Nicean time, surprisingly well-devel-
oped definition of the Christian doctrine of the Trinity:

That we are not atheists, seeing that we acknowledge one
God, I have sufficiently demonstrated. Who, then, would
not be astonished to hear men who speak of God the Father,
and of God the Son, and of the Holy Spirit, and declare
both their power in union and their distinction in order,
called atheists? (Apol. 10, ibidem).

5. About the existence of angels he says in the same chapter:

We recognize also a multitude of angels and ministers,
whom God the Maker and Framer of the world distributed
and appointed to their several posts by his Logos, to occupy
themselves about the elements, and the heavens, and the
world, and the things in it, and the goodly ordering of
them all.

6. Athenagoras is an excellent witness to the doctrine of inspiration:

For poets and philosophers, as to other subjects, so also
to this, have applied themselves in the way of conjecture,
moved, by reason of their affinity with the afflatus from God,
each one by his own soul, to try whether he could find out
and apprehend the truth; but they have not been found
competent fully to apprehend it, because they thought fit to
learn, not from God concerning God, but each one from

himself; hence they came each to his own conclusion respecting God, matter and form, and the world. But we have for witnesses of the things we apprehend and believe, prophets, men, who have pronounced concerning God and the things of God, guided by the Spirit of God. And you too will admit . . . that it would be irrational for us to cease to believe in the Spirit from God, who moved the mouths of the prophets like musical instruments, and to give heed to mere human opinions (*Apol.* 7, ANF 2,132).

7. He praises virginity as one of the most beautiful fruits of Christian ethics:

You will find among us both men and women growing old unmarried in the hope of living in closer communion with God (*Apol.* 33).

With these words the positive goal of Christian virginity is very well defined.

8. About the Christian idea of marriage he says in the same chapter:

Having the hope of eternal life, we despise the things of this life, even the pleasures of the soul, each of us reckoning her his wife whom he has married according to the laws laid down by us, and that only for the purpose of having children. For as the husbandman throwing seed into the ground awaits the harvest, not sowing more upon it, so to us the procreation of children is the measure of our indulgence in appetite.

Athenagoras' words indicate clearly that the child is the first and ultimate goal in matrimony. Similarly, another passage shows the struggle that primitive Christianity had to defend the right to life of the unborn. When the pagans accused the Christians of committing murder in their services, Athenagoras answered this accusation in the following way:

When we say that those women who use drugs to bring on abortion commit murder and will have to give an account to God for the abortion, on what principle should we commit murder? For it does not belong to the same person to regard the very fetus in the womb as a created being, and therefore an object of God's care, and when it has passed into life, to kill it; and not expose an infant because those who expose them are chargeable with child-murder, and on the other hand, when it has been reared, to destroy it. But we are in all things always alike and the same, submitting ourselves to reason and not ruling over it (*Apol.* 35, ANF 2, 147). It is very important that Athenagoras refers here to the fetus as a created being. According to Roman law of that time it was not considered a being at all, and had no right to existence.

9. Athenagoras is so convinced of the indissolubility of marriage that, according to him, even death can not dissolve the marital bond. He goes so far as to call a second marriage a 'decent adultery':

A person should either remain as he was born or be content with one marriage; for a second marriage is only a decent adultery. . . . For he who deprives himself of his first wife, even though she be dead, is a cloaked adulterer, resisting the hand of God, because in the beginning God made one man and one woman (*Apology*, 33, ANF 2, 146 f.).

Separate Editions: E. SCHWARTZ, Athenagorae libellus pro Christianis. Oratio de resurrectione cadaverum (TU 4,2). Leipzig, 1891. - W. B. OWEN, Athenagoras, with Explanatory Notes. New York, 1904. A separate edition of the Apology was published by J. GEFFCKEN, Zwei griechische Apologeten. Leipzig, 1907, 115-154 and P. UBALDI, Turin, 1920. — P. UBALDI e M. PELLEGRINO, Atenagora (with text, introduction, Italian translation and notes). Turin, 1947.

Translations: English: B. P. PRATTEN, ANL 2 (1870) 371-456; idem, ANF 2 (1885) 129-162. *French:* G. BARDY, SC 3 (Supplique). Paris, 1943. *Italian:* P. UBALDI, Turin, 1913. — P. UBALDI e M. PELLEGRINO, l.c. *German:* A. EBERHARD, BKV 23. Kempten, 1913, 259-375.

Studies: C. H. HEFELE, Lehre des Athenagoras und Analyse seiner Schriften: Beiträge zur Kirchengeschichte, Archäologie und Liturgik 1. Tübingen, 1864, 60-86. — F. SCHUBRING, Die Philosophie des Athenagoras (Progr.). Berlin, 1882. — A. JOANNIDES, Πραγματεία περὶ τῆς παρ' Ἀθηναγόρᾳ φιλοσοφικῆς γνώσεως (Diss.). Jena, 1883. — J. LEHMANN, Die Auferstehungslehre des Athenagoras (Diss.). Leipzig, 1890. — P. LOGOTHETES, Ἡ θεολογία τοῦ Ἀθηναγόρου. Leipzig, 1893. — G. SCHEURER, Das Auferstehungsdogma in der vornicänischen Zeit. Würzburg, 1896, 26-43. — L. ARNOULD, De Apologia Athenagorae, Patris Graeci secundo saeculo florentis, Πρεσβεία περὶ χριστιανῶν inscripta. Paris, 1898. — K. F. BAUER, Die Lehre des Athenagoras von Gottes Einheit und Dreieinigkeit. (Diss.). Bamberg, 1902. — A. POMMRICH, Des Apologeten Theophilus von Antiochia Gottes- und Logoslehre, dargestellt unter Berücksichtigung der gleichen Lehre des Athenagoras von Athen. (Diss.). Leipzig, 1904. — L. RICHTER, Philosophisches in der Gottes- und Logoslehre des Apologeten Athenagoras aus Athen (Diss.). Meissen, 1905. — L. CHAUDOUARD, La philosophie du dogme de la résurrection de la chair au 2e siècle. Etude sur le Περὶ ἀναστάσεως d'Athénagore (Thèse). Lyon, 1905. — J. LEBLANC, Le logos chez Tatien, Athénagore et Théophile: Annales de philosophie chrét. 149 (1905) 634–639. — J. GEFFCKEN, Zwei griechische Apologeten. Leipzig, 1907, 155–238. — J. VAN BEEK, Athenagoras' geschrift 'De resurrectione mortuorum' (Proefschrift). Leyden, 1908. — F. WALLINGER, Athenagoras und die ihm zugeeigneten Schriften (Progr.). Kalksburg, 1909. — F. ANDRES, Die Engellehre der griechischen Apologeten des zweiten Jahrhunderts (FLDG 12,3). Paderborn, 1914, 66–95. — J. P. ARENDZEN, Ante-Nicene Interpretations on the Sayings on Divorce: JThSt 20 (1919) 232ff. — S. PAPPALARDO, Il monoteismo e la dottrina del Logos in Atenagora: Didascaleion 2 (1924) 11–40; idem, La teoria degli angeli e dei demoni e la dottrina della providenza in Atenagora: ibidem, 67–180. — K. PREYSING, Ehezweck und zweite Ehe bei Athenagoras: ThQ 110 (1929) 85–110. — H. A. LUCKS, The Philosophy of Athenagoras: Its Sources and Value (Diss.). Washington, 1936. — G. LAZZATI, L'Aristotele perdutto e gli scrittori cristiani. Milan, 1938, 69–72. — M. PELLEGRINO, Studi sull' antica apologetica. Rome, 1947, 65–79.

THEOPHILUS OF ANTIOCH

Theophilus was, according to Eusebius (*Hist. Eccl.* 4, 20), the sixth bishop of Antioch in Syria. It is evident from his writings that he was born near the Euphrates, was of pagan parentage and received a Hellenistic education. Not until he had reached maturity and even then only after long consideration and a study of scripture, did he become a convert to Christianity. He gives the following account of his conversion:

Do not be sceptical but believe; for I myself also used to disbelieve that this (the resurrection of the dead) would take place; but now, having taken these things into consideration, I believe. At the same time, I met with the sacred scriptures of the holy prophets, who also by the spirit of God foretold the things that have already happened, just as they came to pass, and the things now occurring as they are now happening, and things future in the order in which they shall be accomplished. Admitting, therefore, the proof which events happening as predicted afford, I do not disbelieve but I believe, obedient to God (1,14).

WRITINGS

1. Of his works only the three books *Ad Autolycum* are extant. They must have been composed shortly after the year 180, because the third book contains a chronology of the history of the world which reaches down to the death of Marcus Aurelius (March 17, 180 A.D.). In three books the author defends Christianity against the objections of his pagan friend Autolycus. In the first book he speaks of the essence of God, who can be seen only by the eyes of the soul:

> God is seen by those who are enabled to see him, when they have the eyes of their soul opened; for all have eyes; but in some they are overspread, and do not see the light of the sun. Yet it does not follow because the blind do not see, that the light of the sun does not shine; but let the blind blame themselves and their own eyes. . . as a burnished mirror, so ought man to have his soul pure. When there is rust on the mirror, it is not possible that a man's face be seen in the mirror; so also when there is sin in a man, such a man can not behold God (1,2).

The first book deals, furthermore, with the absurdities of idolatry and with the difference between the honor paid to the emperor and the worship due to God:

> I will rather honor the emperor, not indeed worshipping him, but praying for him. But God, the living and true God I worship, knowing that the emperor is made by him (1,11).

At the end Theophilus treats of the meaning and importance of the name Christian, which has been scoffed at by his adversary. After an explanation of the belief in the resurrection he closes with the words:

> Since you said, 'Show me thy God', this is my God and I counsel you to fear him and to trust him (1,14).

The second book contrasts the teachings of the prophets, who were inspired by the Holy Ghost, with the foolishness of the pagan religion and the contradictory sayings of the Greek poets, like Homer and Hesiod, concerning the gods and the origin of the world. The account of Genesis regarding the creation of the world and mankind, paradise and the fall, is analyzed in detail and explained allegorically. At the end the author quotes some of the instructions of the prophets on the manner of venerating God rightly and on the proper conduct of life. It is interesting to note that Theophilus refers for these instructions even to the authority of the Sibyl. Thus he preserves for us two extensive fragments of the Sibyl which are not contained in any of the manuscripts of the *Oracula Sibyllina*. These two fragments comprise eighty-four verses and praise in beautiful words the belief in one God.

The third book demonstrates the superiority of Christianity from the moral point of view. It refutes the calumnies of the pagans and the accusations of immorality made against the Christians. On the other hand, it proves the immorality of the pagan religion from the wickedness attributed to the gods by pagan writers. Finally in order to show that the Christian doctrine is older than all other religions, Theophilus uses the chronology of the world to prove that Moses and the prophets are older than all philosophers.

2. *Lost Writings*. In addition to the three books *Ad Autolycum* Theophilus composed, according to Eusebius (*Hist. Eccl.* 4,24), a treatise *Against the Heresy of Hermogenes*, a work *Against Marcion*, and 'some catechetical writings'. Jerome (*De Viris Illustribus*, 25) mentions besides the catechetical treatises two other works of Theophilus, his *Commentaries on the Gospel*, and *On the Proverbs of Solomon*. In another passage Jerome (*Epistula* 121,6,15) speaks of a gospel harmony. Theophilus himself refers several times to a work περὶ ἱστοριῶν which he wrote before he composed the three books *Ad Autolycum*. From his words it appears it was a history of mankind, for he says (2,30):

'To those who desire to be informed regarding all generations it is easy to give explanations by means of the holy scriptures. For, as we have already mentioned, this subject, the order of the genealogy of man, has partly been handled by us in another discourse in the first book of *The History*.'

All his writings except the three books *Ad Autolycum* were lost. Attempts have been made to reconstruct them, but up to the present time they have failed. Zahn thought that he had discovered the *Commentary on the Gospels* in a Latin commentary on the four gospels which M. de la Bigne edited under the name of Theophilus in the *Bibliotheca SS. Patrum*, Paris, 1575, 5, 169–192.

But it has been found that this commentary is merely a compilation from Cyprian, Ambrose, Jerome, Pseudo-Arnobius Junior, and Augustine, composed towards the end of the fifth century. Similarly, Loofs failed when he attempted to prove that Theophilus' treatise *Against Marcion* could be partly reconstructed from Irenaeus' *Adversus Haereses*. Though Theophilus calls himself 'not educated to the art of speaking' (2,1), he shows himself to be well acquainted with rhetoric. It is true he writes in an easy and graceful manner full of vitality and vigor. But he is familiar also with such devices of rhetoric as antithesis and anaphora. His work is made most attractive by an abundance of pointed metaphors. He shows himself well versed in contemporary literature and philosophy. This suggests that he had a comprehensive education and knowledge. Although he draws, on the whole, from the same sources as the other Greek apologists, he makes far more use of the writings of the New Testament than they did. To him the evangelists are not less inspired by the Holy Ghost than the prophets of the Old Testament: 'Confirmatory utterances are found both with the prophets and in the gospels, because they all spoke inspired by one spirit of God' (3,12). The gospels are to him 'holy word' and the Epistles of St. Paul are introduced by him with a constant formula, 'The divine word teaches us, διδάσκει ἡμᾶς ὁ θεῖος λόγος' (3,14).

St. John is explicit numbered among the spirit-bearing men: 'And hence the holy writings teach us, and all the spirit-bearing men, one of whom, John, says, 'In the beginning was the Word' ' (2,22). Theophilus is therefore the first who clearly teaches the inspiration of the New Testament.

ASPECTS OF THEOPHILUS' THEOLOGY

1. Theophilus is the first to use the word τριάς (trinitas) for the union of the three divine persons in God. He calls the first three days before the creation of the sun and moon images of the Trinity:

> The three days which were before the luminaries, are types of the Trinity of God, and his word, and his wisdom (2,15).

2. Theophilus is the first Christian author to distinguish

between the Logos ἐνδιάθετος and the Logos προφορικός, the Word internal or immanent in God and the Word emitted or uttered by God. Concerning the origin of the Logos he states:

> God, then, having his own Word internal (λόγον ἐνδιάθετον), within his own bowels begot him, emitting him along with wisdom before all things. He had this Word as a helper in the things that were created by him, and by him he made all things (2,10).

This Logos spoke to Adam in Paradise:

> The God and Father of all, indeed, cannot be contained, and is not found in a place, for there is no place of his rest: but his Word, through whom he made all things, being his power and his wisdom, assuming the person of the Father and Lord of all, went to the garden in the person of God, and conversed with Adam. For the divine writing itself teaches us that Adam said that he had heard the voice. But what else is this voice but the word of God, who is also his son? Not as the poets and writers of myths talk of the sons of gods from intercourse, but as truth expounds, the Word, that always exists, residing within the heart of God. For before anything came into being he had him as a counsellor, being his own mind and thought. But when God wished to make all that he determined on, he begot his Word, uttered (προφορικόν) the firstborn of all creation, not himself being emptied of the Word, but having begotten Reason, and always conversing with Reason (2,22).

3. Like Justin (*Dial.* 5) and Irenaeus (*Adv. Haer.* 4,4,3) Theophilus regards the immortality of the soul not as belonging to its nature but as a reward for keeping the commandments of God. The human soul is in itself neither mortal nor immortal, but capable of mortality as well as immortality:

> Was man made by nature mortal? Certainly not. Was he then immortal? Neither do we affirm this. But one will say, was he then nothing? Not even this hits the mark. He was by nature neither mortal nor immortal, for if he had made him mortal, God would seem to be the cause of his death. Neither then immortal nor yet mortal did he make him, but as we have said above, capable of both; so that if he should incline to the things of immortality keeping the

commandment of God, he should receive as reward from him immortality, and should become God; but if, on the other hand, he should turn to the things of death disobeying God, he should himself be the cause of death to himself. For God made man free, and with power over himself (2,27).

Editions: See above p. 189. *Separate Editions:* S. FRASCA, Justinus, Apologie: Segue: Theophilus Antiochenus, Gli tre libri ad Autolico. Testo, versione, introd. Turin, 1938.

Translations: English: M. DODS, ANL 3 (1868) 53–133 = ANF 2 (1885) 89–121. — *German:* J. LEITL, Des Theophilus von Antiochien drei Bücher an Autolykus, zweite verbesserte Ausgabe von A. DI Pauli (BKV 14). Kempten, 1913, 12–106. *Italian:* E. RAPISARDA. Turin, 1937. — S. FRASCA, l.c.

Studies: K. OTTO, Gebrauch neutestamentlicher Schriften bei Theophilus von Antiochien: Zeitschrift für historische Theologie 29 (1859) 617–622. — L. PAUL, Der Begriff des Glaubens bei dem Apologeten Theophilus: Jahrbuch für protestantische Theologie 1 (1875) 546–559. — A. HARNACK, Der angebliche Evangelienkommentar des Theophilus von Antiochien (TU 1,4). Leipzig, 1883. — W. SANDAY, A Commentary on the Gospels Attributed to Theophilus of Antioch: Studia Biblica (1885) 98–101. — C. ERBES, Die Lebenszeit des Hippolytus nebst der des Theophilus von Antiochien: Jahrbücher für prot. Theologie 14 (1888) 611–656. — A. HARNACK, Theophilus von Antiochien und das Neue Testament: ZKG 11 (1890) 1–21. — G. KARABANGELES, Ἡ περὶ θεοῦ διδασκαλία Θεοφίλου τοῦ Ἀντιοχέως (Diss.). Leipzig, 1891. — O. GROSS, Die Weltentstehungslehre des Theophilus von Antiochien. Leipzig, 1895; *idem,* Die Gotteslehre des Theophilus von Antiochia (Progr.). Chemnitz, 1895. — O. CLAUSEN, Die Theologie des Theophilus von Antiochien: Zeitschrift für wissenschaftl. Theologie 46 (1903) 81–141; 195–213. — A. POMMRICH, Des Apologeten Theophilus von Antiochien Gottes- und Logos lehre (Diss.). Leipzig, 1904. — J. GEFFCKEN, Zwei griechische Apologeten. Leipzig, 1907, 250–252. — H. QUENTIN, Jean de Jérusalem et le commentaire sur les Evangiles attribué à Théophile d'Antioche: RB 24 (1907) 107–109. — C. H. TURNER, Theophilus of Antioch as Commentator: JThSt 12 (1911) 99ff.—A. PUECH, Les Apologistes grecs du 2e siècle de notre ère. Paris, 1912, 207–227. — J. LEBRETON, Histoire du dogme de la Trinité. Vol. 2, Paris, 1928, 508–513. — F. LOOFS, Theophilus von Antiochien Adversus Marcionem und die andern theologischen Quellen bei Irenaeus (TU 46,2). Leipzig, 1930. Cf. J. LEBON, RHE 26 (1930) 675–679. — J. STIGLMAYR, ThR 29 (1930) 290ff. — F. R. M. HITCHCOCK, JThSt 38 (1937) 130–139; 255–266. — AGUADO, Teófilo y el Canon del N.T.: Estud. Bibl. (1932) 176ff.; 281ff.; (1933) 3ff. — E. RAPISARDA, Teofilo di Antiochia. Turin, 1937; *idem,* Cenni su Teofilo d'Antiochia: Studi dedicati alla memoria di Paolo Ubaldi. Milan, 1937, 381–400. — M. RICHARD, Les fragments exégétiques de Théophile d'Alexandrie et de Théophile d'Antioche: RBibl. 47 (1938) 387–397. — N. TERZAGHI,

Minutiores curae I: A. Teofilo di Antiochia: BPEC (1941) 111–115. — F.
OGARA, Aristidis et epistolae ad Diognetum cum Theophilo Antiocheno
cognatio: Greg (1944) 74–102. — R. M. GRANT, Theophilus of Antioch to
Autolycus: HThR 40 (1947) 227-256.

MELITO OF SARDIS

Melito, bishop of Sardis in Lydia, is one of the most venerable
figures of the second century. In his letter to Pope Victor (189–
199) Polycrates of Ephesus names him among the 'great lumi-
naries' of Asia now gone to their rest and calls him 'Melito, the
eunuch (i.e. unmarried), who lived entirely in the Holy Spirit,
who lies in Sardis, waiting for the visitation from heaven when
he will rise from the dead' (Eusebius, *Hist. Eccl.* 5,24,5). Beyond
what is mentioned in this brief notice, very little is known of his
life. Melito was a prolific writer on a wide variety of subjects in
the second half of the second century.

1. About the year 170 A.D. he addressed an apology for the
Christians to the emperor Marcus Aurelius, of which only frag-
ments are preserved by Eusebius and in the *Chronicon Paschale*.
Among these fragments is a sentence which is of importance for
Melito's idea regarding the relations between Church and State.
He is the first to advocate solidarity of Christianity with the
Empire. The world Empire and the Christian religion are foster
sisters; they form a pair. In addition, the Christian religion means
blessing and welfare to the empire:

Our philosophy became an omen of good to your Empire,
for from that time (of Augustus) the power of Rome has
increased in size and splendor. You are now his happy
successor and shall be so along with your son, if you protect
the philosophy which grew up with the Empire and began
with Augustus. Your ancestors held it in honor together with
other religions. The most convincing proof that the flourishing of our religion has been a boon to the Empire thus
happily inaugurated is the fact that the Empire has suffered
no mishaps since the reign of Augustus, but on the contrary,
everything has increased its splendor and fame in accordance
with the general prayer (Eusebius, *Hist. Eccl.* 4, 26,7–8).

For the fragments of his writings: M. J. ROUTH, Reliquiae Sacrae, ed. alt., 1.
Oxford, 1846, 111–153. — J. C. TH. OTTO, Corpus apol. christ. 9. Jena, 1872,

374-478; 497-512. — A. HARNACK, Marcion, 2nd ed. Leipzig, 1924, 422ff. — For the Syriac fragments see I. RUCKER, Florilegium Edessenum anonymum (SAB). Berlin, 1933, 12-16; 67-73.

Studies: A. HARNACK, Die Überlieferung der griechischen Apologeten (TU 1,1-2). Leipzig, 1882, 240-278. — C. THOMAS, Melito von Sardes. Eine kirchengeschichtliche Studie. Osnabrück, 1893. — A. EHRHARD, Die altchristliche Literatur und ihre Erforschung von 1884 bis 1900. Freiburg, 1900, 258-262. — W. BAUER, Rechtgläubigkeit und Ketzerei im ältesten Christentum. Tübingen, 1934, 155-157. — AMANN, DTC, 10, 540-547. — J. QUASTEN, Melito: LThK 7, 69.

2. Of this *Apology* and of his other works we possessed until recently only small fragments or the titles which Eusebius (*Hist. Eccl.* 4,26,2) and Anastasius Sinaita (*Viae Dux*, 12.13) preserve. For this reason a recent find is all the more interesting. A nearly complete *Homily on the Passion* of Melito was discovered and published by Campbell Bonner. The sermon was hitherto unknown even by title though unidentified scraps of it did exist in Syriac, Coptic, and Greek. The *Homily* occupies the latter part of a papyrus codex of the fourth century containing the last chapters of Enoch, eight leaves of which belong to the collection of Mr. A. Chester Beatty and the British Museum, six to the University of Michigan. As the title εἰς τὸ πάθος indicates, the newly discovered sermon treats of the passion of our Lord. The opening words suggest a sermon at Mass following an Old Testament reading and the subject matter of this homily fits Holy Week so well that Bonner calls it a 'Good Friday sermon'. Since Melito held to the quartodeciman view, to him this day was the Paschal festival. The story of the Exodus and especially of the institution of the Passover is paraphrased and then expounded as a type of the redemptive work of Christ. Both are called μυστήρια in the sense of actions having a supernatural effect beyond their historical setting. Exodus and Passover became the type of what followed when Jesus died and rose again. Jesus' passion and death insure the Christian's escape from sin and mortality just as the slaughtered Passover lamb secured the flight of the Hebrews. The Christians like the Hebrews have been sealed as a sign of their deliverance. But the Jews, as was prophesied, rejected the Lord and killed him, and although his death was foreordained, their responsibility in it was voluntary. They are lost, but the faithful to whom he preached in Hades as

well as those on earth share in the triumph of the resurrection. The language of this sermon reveals a fondness for unusual and poetic words and for set stylistic devices. The style is highly artificial and studied, anaphora and antithesis being especially favored. That explains Tertullian's reference to Melito's *elegans et declamatorium ingenium* (Jerome, *De Viris Illus.* 24).

THEOLOGICAL DOCTRINE OF THE HOMILY

1. *Christology*

    a. The conception of the divinity and preexistence of Christ dominates Melito's entire theology. He calls him: θεός, λόγος, πατήρ, υἱός, ὁ πρωτότοκος τοῦ θεοῦ, δεσπότης, ὁ βασιλεὺς Ἰσραήλ, ὑμῶν βασιλεύς. The title 'Father' for Christ is unusual. It occurs in an important passage describing the various functions of Christ:

    > For born as a son, and led forth as a lamb, sacrificed as a sheep, buried as a man, he rose from the dead as God, being by nature God and man. Who is all things: in that he judges, Law, in that he teaches, Word, in that he saves, Grace, in that he begets, Father, in that he is begotten, Son, in that he suffers, the sacrificial sheep, in that he is buried, Man, in that he arises, God. This is Jesus Christ, to whom belongs the glory to the ages of ages (8–10 Bonner).

    This complete identification of Christ with the Godhead itself could be interpreted in favor of the monarchian modalism of a later period. If that were the case it would explain the neglect and eventual loss of Melito's works.

    b. On the other hand, Melito is very clear regarding the Incarnation:

    > This is he who was made flesh in a virgin, whose (bones) were not broken upon the tree, who in burial was not resolved into earth, who arose from the dead and raised man from the grave below to the heights of the heavens. This is the lamb that was slain, this is the lamb that was dumb, this is he that was born of Mary the fair ewe (70–71 Bonner).

    In a similar way the author calls Christ ἐκεῖνον ἔτι [σαρκωθέντα] διὰ παρθένου Μαρίας (66).

    c. The preexistence of Christ is described in the form of hymnological praises, as in the following passage:

This is the firstborn of God
who was begotten before the morning star
who made the light to rise
who made the day bright
who parted the darkness
who fixed the first mark for creation
who hung the earth in its place
who dried up the abyss
who spread out the firmament
who brought order to the world (82).

d. The function of Christ was to rescue man from sin (54.103) death (102.103) and the devil (67.68.102).

e. Melito's description of Christ's descent into Hades suggests that he may have embodied in his sermon some parts of an older liturgical hymn:

And he arose from the dead and cries to you: 'Who is he that contendeth against me? Let him stand before me. I freed the condemned, I made the dead to live again, I raise him who was buried. Who is he who raises his voice against me? I', he says again, 'am the Christ, I am he who put down death, and triumphed over the enemy, and trod upon Hades, and bound the strong one and brought man safely home to the heights of the heavens; I', he says, 'Christ' (101–102).

2. The doctrine of original sin

This doctrine is clearly expressed by Melito:

Upon every soul sin sets its mark and all alike she devoted to death. These must die. So all flesh fell into the power of sin, everybody into the power of death (54–55).

3. The Church

The Church is called 'the reservoir of truth', ἀποδοχεῖον τῆς ἀληθείας (40).

Edition and translation: C. BONNER, The Homily on the Passion by Melito Bishop of Sardis (SD 12). London, 1940. — French transl. of select passages by J. DANIÉLOU: VS 327 (1948) 262–271.

Studies: C. BONNER, The Homily on the Passion by Melito Bishop of Sardis: Annuaire de l'Institut de philol. et d'hist. orient. et slaves 4 (1936) 108–119;

idem, The Homily on the Passion by Melito, Bishop of Sardis: Mélanges F. Cumont I. Brussels, 1936, 107–119; *idem*, The New Homily of Melito and its Place in Christian literature: Actes du Ve Congrès international de papyrologie. Oxford, 1937, 94–97; *idem*, Two Problems in Melito's Homily on the Passion: HThR 31 (1938) 175–190. — M. RIST, Additional Parallels to the Rending of the Veil in Melito's Homily on the Passion: HThR 31 (1938) 249–250. — C. BONNER, A Coptic Fragment of Melito's Homily on the Passion: HThR 32 (1939) 141–142. — G. ZUNTZ, On the Opening Sentence of Melito's Paschal Homily: HThR 36 (1943) 299–315. — C. BONNER, A Supplementary Note on the Opening of Melito's Homily: HThR 36 (1943) 317–319. — P. KAHLE, Was Melito's Homily on the Passion originally written in Syriac: JThSt 44 (1943) 52–56. — E. J. WELLESZ, Melito's Homily on the Passion. An Investigation into the Sources of Byzantine Hymnography: JThSt 44 (1943) 41–52. — A. WIFSTRAND, The Homily of Melito on the Passion: VC 2 (1948) 201–223. — C. BONNER, The text of Melito's Homily: VC 3 (1949) 184–185.

In addition to the *Apology* and the newly discovered sermon Melito is the author of the following writings:

1. Two books *On the Passover*, in which he defended the so-called quartodeciman usage (composed about 166/67).
2. A treatise *On Christian Life and the Prophets*, of probably anti-Montanistic character.

3.	*On the Church*	11.	*On Baptism*
4.	*On the Lord's Day*	12.	*On Truth*
5.	*On the Faith of Man*	13.	*On Faith and Christ's Birth*
6.	*On Creation*	14.	*On Prophecy*
7.	*On the Obedience of Faith*	15.	*The Key*
8.	*On the Senses*	16.	*On the Devil*
9.	*On the Soul and Body*	17.	*On the Apocalypse of John*
10.	*On Hospitality*	18.	*On God Incarnate*

19. Six books of *Extracts from the Law and the Prophets concerning our Savior and our entire faith*. The preface of this work has been preserved by Eusebius (*Hist. Eccl.* 4,26,13–14). It contains the oldest list of the canonical scriptures of the Old Testament.
20. *On the Incarnation of Christ*.

From all these titles of his lost works it appears that Melito discussed many practical and theological questions of his time in an open-minded way.

For the fragment *On Baptism* see J. B. PITRA, Analecta sacra 2. Paris, 1884, 3-5. — J. M. MERCATI, Symbolae Melitonianae: ThQ 76 (1894) 597–600.

Unauthentic writings:

1. A Syriac manuscript of the British Museum (Add. 14658) contains an apology under Melito's name, which however was not composed by him. The content shows that the author was well acquainted with the apologies of Aristides and Justin. It seems that it was written in Syriac and not translated from the Greek. The time of its composition is most probably during the reign of Caracalla.

Edition and translation: W. CURETON, Spicilegium Syriacum: Containing Remains of Bardesan, Meliton, Ambrose and Mara Bar Serapion. Now First Edited with an English Translation and Notes. London, 1855. — J. C. TH. OTTO, l.c., 9,497–512, Latin translation 419–432.

Studies: TH. ULBRICH, Die pseudomelitonische Apologie (Kirchengeschichtliche Abhandlungen 4). Breslau, 1906. — F. HAASE, Zur Bardesanischen Gnosis. Leipzig, 1910, 68–72; *idem*, Altchristliche Kirchengeschichte nach orientalischen Quellen. Leipzig, 1925, 133f.

2. There is another writing in a Latin version of the fifth century which was wrongly attributed to Melito. Its title is *De Transitu Beatae Mariae Virginis* (ἡ κοίμησις τῆς θεοτόκου).

There are indications that this apocryphal account of the death and assumption of the Blessed Virgin did not originate before the fourth century. It forms a counterpart to the apocryphal infancy gospels. The text is extant in several Greek revisions and in a number of versions.

Edition: C. TISCHENDORF, Apocalypses Apocryphae, 1866, 124–136. For an Old English translation of this text see R. WILLARD, Rev. of English Studies (1936) 5–23.

Studies: F. DIEKAMP, Hippolytos von Theben. Münster, 1898, 91ff. — TH. ZAHN, Die Dormitio sanctae Mariae und das Haus des Johannes Markus: NKZ (1899) 377–429. — A. BAUMSTARK, Die leibliche Himmelfahrt der allerseligsten Jungfrau und die Lokaltradition von Jerusalem: OC 4 (1904) 371–392. — ST. D. SEYMOUR, Irish Versions of the Transitus Mariae: JThSt 22 (1921) 36–43. — F. CAVALLERA, A propos d'une enquête patristique sur l'assomption: BLE 27 (1928) 97–116. — M. JUGIE, La mort et l'assomption de la sainte vierge dans la tradition des cinq premiers siècles: EO 29 (1926) 5–20; 129–143; 281–307; 33 (1930) 271–275. — A. VITTI, Libri Apocryphi de Assumptione Beatae Mariae Virginis: Verbum Domini (1926) 225–234. — A. WILMART, L'ancien récit latin de l'assomption (ST 59). Rome, 1933, 323–362. — J. RIVIÈRE, Le plus vieux 'Transitus' latin et son dérivé grec: RTAM (1936) 5–23. — M. JUGIE, La mort et l'Assomption de la Sainte Vierge (ST 114). Vatican City, 1944. — O. FALLER, De priorum saeculorum silentio circa As-

sumptionem B. Mariae Virginis. Rome, 1946, 59 ff. Cf. B. ALTANER, ThR
44 (1949) 134–137; 45 (1949) 129–142.

3. Another unauthentic work is the *Clavis Scripturae*, a biblical
glossary compiled from Augustine, Gregory the Great, and other
Latin writers. It was edited by Cardinal Pitra in his *Analecta
Sacra*, Vol. 2, 1884.

Editions: J. B. PITRA, Spicilegium Solesmense 2–3, 1. Paris, 1855; *idem*,
Analecta Sacra 2. Paris, 1884.

Studies: O. ROTTMANNER, Ein letztes Wort über die 'Clavis' Melitonis: ThQ
78 (1898) 614–629.

THE EPISTLE TO DIOGNETUS

The *Epistle to Diognetus* is an apology for Christianity composed
in the form of a letter addressed to a high-ranking pagan, Diognetus. Nothing else is known of the author or the addressee.
H. Lietzmann thinks that Diognetus is possibly to be identified
with the tutor of Marcus Aurelius. The time of composition is a
matter of conjecture. The content of the epistle has much in
common with the writings of Aristides. But there seems to be no
direct dependency. On the other hand the author made use of
the works of Irenaeus. Moreover, chapter 7, 1 to 5, reminds one
of Hippolytus' *Philosophoumena*, 10,33, and chapters 11 and 12 are
simply the conclusion of this work. For this reason N. Bonwetsch
and R. H. Connolly thought that Hippolytus of Rome was the
author. This would place its origin at the beginning of the third
century. Another reason for this date is suggested by the author's
remark in the course of the work that Christianity had already
spread through the whole world.

Recently a new suggestion was made regarding the author of
the Epistle. P. Andriessen thinks that Quadratus composed it
and that the Epistle is nothing less than the lost apology of that
author. Although it is true that the only sentence quoted by
Eusebius (*Hist. eccl.* 4,3,2) of that apology does not occur in the
Epistle to Diognetus, there is a gap between the verses 6 and 7
of the seventh chapter in which the fragment of the apology
would fit very well. The additional information we have about
Quadratus from Eusebius, Jerome, Photius, the martyrology of
Bede and the Apocryphal Letter of St. James addressed to him

is in agreement with the contents of the *Epistle to Diognetus*. The impression which we gain of the author from reading the Epistle corresponds to what is known about the apologist Quadratus from tradition, e.g., that he was a disciple of the apostles, that he wrote in the classical style and that he was opposed not only to paganism but also to Judaism. In addition, as we learn from Eusebius, Quadratus addressed his apology to Hadrian, and the facts furnished by the work about its addressee Diognetus would fit that Emperor very well. Finally, if we assume that Quadratus is identical with the author of the *Epistle to Diognetus* the question of the authenticity of the last two chapters (11 and 12) which form a kind of epilogue, is placed in an entirely different light. The author of this epilogue calls himself a disciple of the apostles and a teacher of the pagans. It seems to P. Andriessen that no other ecclesiastical author exists to whom this can be strictly applied. However, the difference of style between the last two chapters and the preceding chapters remains. Thus Andriessen's thesis reopens the discussion of the authorship of the *Epistle to Diognetus*.

Unfortunately, no manuscripts of the epistle are extant today. The only manuscript we possessed of it perished in the year 1870, when during the Franco-Prussian War the library of Strasbourg was burned. This manuscript of the thirteenth or fourteenth century belonged formerly to the Alsatian monastery of Maursmuenster. The epistle was here listed among the writings of Justin martyr. All editions are based on this manuscript.

The epistle was occasioned by the request of Diognetus, who asked his Christian friend for information about his religion. The questions of Diognetus can be gathered from the introduction of the letter:

> I see, Diognetus, that you take exceedingly great pains to investigate the religion of the Christians and are making very exact and careful inquiries concerning them. 'Who is the God in whom they trust', you wonder, 'and what kind of cult is theirs, to enable them, one and all, to disdain the world and despise death, and neither to recognize the gods believed in by the Greeks nor to practice the superstition of the Jews? And what is the secret of that strong affection

they have for one another? And why has this new blood or
spirit come into the world we live in now, and not before?'
The author then (ch. 2–4) depicts in glowing terms the superiority of Christianity over the foolish idolatry of the pagans, and
over the external formalism of the worship of the Jews. In his
criticism of pagan and Jewish religion he makes use of arguments
which may be found already in the writings of the Greek apologists. The best part of the epistle is the account which the author
gives of the supernatural life of the Christians (ch. 5–6):

Christians are not distinguished from the rest of mankind
by either country, speech, or customs; the fact is, they nowhere settle in cities of their own; they use no peculiar language; they cultivate no eccentric mode of life. Certainly,
this creed of theirs is no discovery due to some conceit or
speculation of inquisitive men; nor do they, as some sects
do, champion any doctrine of human origin. Yet while
they settle in both Greek and non-Greek cities, as each one's
lot is cast, and conform to the customs of the country in
dress, diet, and mode of life in general, the whole tenor
of their way of living stamps it as worthy of admiration and
admittedly contrary to expectation. They reside in their
respective countries, but only as aliens; they take part in
everything as citizens, and put up with everything as for-
eigners; every foreign land is their home, and every home a
foreign land. They marry like all others, and beget children;
but they do not expose their offspring. Their board they
spread for all, but not their bed. They find themselves *in
the flesh,* but do *not* live *according to the flesh.* They spend their
days on earth, but hold citizenship in heaven. They obey
the established laws, but in their private lives go beyond
the laws. They love all men, and are persecuted by all.
They are unknown, yet are condemned; they are put to
death, and are restored to life. *They are poor, and enrich many,*
destitute of everything, they abound in everything. They
are dishonored, and in their dishonor find their glory. They
are calumniated, and are vindicated. *They are reviled, and
they bless;* they are insulted, and render honor. Doing good,
they are penalized as evildoers; when penalized, they rejoice
because they are quickened into life. The Jews make war

upon them as men of a different tribe; the Greeks persecute them; and those who hate them can assign no reason
for their enmity.

(6) To say it briefly: what the soul is in the body, that the
Christians are in the world. The soul is spread through all
the members of the body, and the Christians throughout
the cities of the world. The soul dwells in the body, but is
not part and parcel of the body; so Christians dwell in the
world, but are not part and parcel of the world. Itself invisible, the soul is kept shut up in the visible body; so
Christians are known as such in the world, but their religion
remains invisible. The flesh, though not at all wronged by
the soul, yet hates and makes war on it, because it is hindered
from indulging its passions; so, too, the world, though not
at all wronged by the Christians, hates them because they
oppose its pleasures. The soul loves the flesh that hates it,
and its members; so, too, Christians love those that hate
them. The soul is locked up in the body, yet is the very thing
that holds the body together; so, too, Christians are shut
up in the world as in a prison, yet are the very ones that
hold the world together. Immortal, the soul is lodged in a
mortal tenement; so, too, Christians, though residing as
strangers among corruptible things, look forward to the incorruptibility that awaits them in heaven. The soul, when
stinting itself in food and drink, is the better for it; so, too,
Christians, when penalized, increase daily more and more.
Such is the important post to which God has assigned them,
and it is not lawful for them to desert it (ACW 6).

Chapters seven and eight contain a brief instruction regarding
the divine origin of the Christian faith, which was revealed by the
Son of God, for the purpose of manifesting the essence of divinity.
The kingdom appeared so late on earth because God intended
to show mankind its helplessness and its need of redemption (ch. 9).
In conclusion the author exhorts Diognetus to accept the Christian
doctrine (ch. 10). The epistle deserves to rank among the most
brilliant and beautiful works of Christian Greek literature. The
writer is a master of rhetoric, his sentence structure is full of charm
and subtly balanced, his style limpid. The content reveals a man
of fervent faith and wide knowledge, a mind thoroughly imbued

with the principles of Christianity. The diction sparkles with fire and vitality.

For editions and translations see the editions and translations of the Apostolic Fathers by O. GEBHARDT, A. HARNACK, TH. ZAHN, F. X. FUNK, J. B. LIGHTFOOT, K. LAKE, K. BIHLMEYER, etc., above, p. 41 and the edition of the Apologists by J. C. TH. OTTO, above, p. 189. The Epistle is found also in U. v. WILAMOWITZ-MOELLENDORFF, Griechisches Lesebuch. Berlin, 1902, 356-363.

Separate editions: E. BUONAIUTI, Lettera a Diogneto. Testo, traduzione, note (Scrittori cristiani antichi 1). Rome, 1921. — J. GEFFCKEN, Der Brief an Diognetos. Heidelberg, 1928. — E. H. BLAKENEY, The Epistle to Diognetus. London, 1943.

Translations: English: A. ROBERTS and J. DONALDSON, ANL 1 (1868) 303-316 = ANF 1 (1885) 25-30. — J. B. LIGHTFOOT, l. c. — K. LAKE, l. c. — L. B. RADFORD, The Epistle to Diognetus (SPCK). London, 1908. — G. G. WALSH, FC 1 (1947) 355-367. — J. A. KLEIST, ACW 6 (1948) 125-147. — *German:* H. KIHN, Der Ursprung des Briefes an Diognet. Freiburg i.B., 1882, 155-168. — W. HEINZELMANN, Der Brief an Diognet. Erfurt, 1896. — G. RAUSCHEN, BKV 12. Kempten, 1912, 155ff. — J. GEFFCKEN, in: E. HENNECKE, Neutestamentliche Apokryphen, 2nd ed. Tübingen, 1924, 619ff. — *Italian:* E. BUONAIUTI, l.c.

Studies: J. DONALDSON, A Critical History of the Christian Literature and Doctrine from the Death of the Apostles to the Nicene Council 2. London, 1866, 126-142. — F. OVERBECK, Über den pseudo-justinischen Brief an Diognet (Univ.-Progr.). Basel, 1872. — H. DOULCET, L'apologie d'Aristide et l'épître à Diognète: RQH 28 (1880) 601-612. — J. DRÄSEKE, Der Brief an Diognetos. Leipzig, 1881. — H. KIHN, Der Ursprung des Briefes an Diognet. Freiburg i. B., 1882. — G. KRÜGER, Aristides als Verfasser des Briefes an Diognet: Zeitschrift für wissenschaftliche Theologie 37 (1894) 206-223. — N. BONWETSCH, Der Autor der Schlusskapitel des Briefes an Diognet: NGWG, Phil.-Hist. Klasse (1902) 621-634. — H. KIHN, Zum Briefe an Diognet c. 10,3-6: ThQ 84 (1902) 495-498. — F. X. FUNK, Das Schlusskapitel des Diognetenbriefes: ThQ 85 (1903) 638-639. — BECK, Die Sittenlehre des Briefes an Diognet: Philosophisches Jahrbuch 17 (1904) 438-445. — A. DI PAULI, Die Schlusskapitel des Diognetbriefes: ThQ 88 (1906) 28-36. — L. RADFORD, The Epistle to Diognetus. London, 1908. — E. J. KARPATHIOS, Συμπλήρωσις τοῦ χάσματος τῆς πρὸς Διόγνητον ἐπιστολῆς. Saloniki, 1925. — M. FERMI, L'apologia di Aristide e la lettera a Diogneto: RR (1925) 541ff. — A. D. NOCK, A note on Ep. ad Diognetum X 31: JThSt 29 (1927) 40. — P. THOMSEN, PhW (1930) 561-563; (1932) 111f. — E. MOLLAND, Die literatur- und dogmengeschichtliche Stellung des Diognetbriefes: ZNW 33 (1934) 289-312. — P. ROASENDA, Epistula ad Diognetum II, 1 : II, 3; Aevum (1934) 522-523; *idem,* In Epistulae ad Diognetum XI-XII capita adnotatio: Aevum (1935) 248-253; *idem,* Il pensiero paolino nell'Epistola a Diogneto: Aevum (1935) 468-473. — G. BARDY, La vie spirituelle d'après les Pères des trois pre-

miers siècles. Paris, 1935, 88–93. — R. H. CONNOLLY, The Date and Authorship of the Epistle to Diognetus: JThSt 36 (1935) 347–353; *idem*, Ad Diognetum XI–XIII: JThSt 37 (1936) 2–15. — G. GODET, Diognète: DTC
1366–1369. — E. H. BLAKENEY, A Note on the Epistle to Diognetus X § 1:
JThSt 42 (1941) 193–195. — F. OGARA, Aristidis et epistolae ad Diognetum
cum Theophilo Antiocheno cognatio: Greg (1944) 74–102. — P. ANDRIESSEN,
L'apologie de Quadratus conservée sous le nom d'épître à Diognète: RTAM
(1946) 5–39; 125–149; *idem*, The Authorship of the Epistula ad Diognetum:
VC 1 (1947) 129–136.

HERMIAS

There is another work of apologetic nature which must be
mentioned here. It is the *Satire on the Profane Philosophers*, Διασυρμὸς
τῶν ἔξω φιλοσόφων by a certain Hermias. Through the course
of the ten chapters of this book, Hermias attempts to demonstrate
by means of sarcasm the nothingness of pagan philosophy,
showing the contradictions in their doctrines regarding the
essence of God, the world and the soul. Nothing is known about
the person of the author even to the present day. It would be a
mistake to presume that he was a professional philosopher. He
owes his knowledge of philosophy not to an intensive study of
the old philosophers, but has drawn it from the customary com-
pendia of philosophy. His work is primarily satirical and not
didactic. Nowhere in ancient Christian literature is there any
mention of this satire. For this reason it is impossible to establish
the date of composition, especially since the content does not
furnish any evidence that would be of help. Opinions differ from
200 to 600 A.D. but judging from internal evidence, the third
century is the most probable date. The treatise is extant in sixteen manuscripts, only one of which is older than the fifteenth
century, the Codex Patmius 202 of the tenth century.

Editions: MG 6. — H. DIELS, Doxographi. 2nd edit. Berlin, 1929, 651ff. —
E. A. RIZZO, Turin, 1930.

Translations: A. DI PAULI, BKV² 14. Kempten, 1913.

Studies: A. DI PAULI, Die Irrisio des Hermias (FLDG 7,2). Paderborn, 1907:
idem, Die Irrisio des Hermias: ThQ 90 (1908) 523–531.

CHAPTER VII

THE BEGINNINGS OF HERETICAL LITERATURE

Christianity had to defend itself, not only against two enemies from without, Judaism and paganism, but also against two enemies from within, Gnosticism and Montanism. Although the latter both had as their starting-point the Christian religion, they were of entirely different character. While the Gnostics were the protagonists of a Christianity conformed to the world, the Montanists advocated a complete flight from the world. The Gnostics endeavored to create a Christianity which, fitting into the culture of the time, would absorb the religious myths of the Orient and give the dominant role to the religious philosophy of the Greeks, to leave but a small place for revelation as the foundation of all theological knowledge, for faith, and for the Gospel of Christ. The Montanists, awaiting the impending destruction of the world, regarded a religious life in seclusion and complete abandonment of the world and its pleasures as the only true Christian ideal to which all Christians should tend. Both sects devised a successful propaganda, and both gained adherents in Christian communities. The Church, therefore, underwent a two-fold crisis. Gnosticism threatened its spiritual foundation and its religious character, Montanism endangered its world-wide mission and its universal character. Of these two enemies, Gnosticism was by far the most dangerous.

PRE-CHRISTIAN GNOSTICISM

The beginnings of Gnosticism must be sought irf pre-Christian times. Recent investigations have proved that ever since Alexander the Great inaugurated the Hellenistic period with his triumphal conquests of the Orient (334–324 B.C.) there developed this strange mixture of Oriental religion and Greek philosophy which we call Gnosticism. From the Oriental religions, Gnosticism inherited the belief in an absolute dualism between God and the world, between soul and body, the derivation of good and bad from two fundamentally different principles and substances, and the longing for redemption and immortality. From Greek philosophy, Gnosticism received its speculative element. Thus the speculations concerning mediators between God and the world were incorporated from Neo-Platonism; a naturalistic kind of mysticism from Neo-Pythagoreanism; and the appreciation of the individual and his ethical task from Neo-Stoicism.

SIMON MAGUS

The last representative of pre-Christian Gnosticism was Simon Magus. He was a contemporary of the Apostles. When the deacon Philip went to Samaria, Simon Magus was well known there, and had many followers. The Acts of the Apostles report (8, 9–24) that he was called the 'power of God', 'the great'. His name appears together with that of Cerinthus, as a representative of the Gnostic heresy, in the introduction of the so-called *Epistola Apostolorum* (cf. above p. 150). Justin Martyr reports that he was born at Gitton in Samaria, and arrived in Rome in the reign of the Emperor Claudius, where he was venerated as a god. Hippolytus of Rome attributes (*Philosophoumena*, 6, 7–20) to him a work entitled *The Great Tidings*. Apparently it contained an allegorical interpretation of the Mosaic narrative of creation, which suggests the influence of the religious philosophy of Alexandria. But it is very doubtful that this writing, of which we have only some fragments, was composed by Simon Magus.

Texts: W. VÖLKER, Quellen zur Geschichte der christlichen Gnosis. Tübingen, 1932, 1–11.

DOSITHEUS AND MENANDER

There are two other Samaritans who are mentioned as Gnostics in ancient Christian literature. Both of them are related to Simon Magus; Dositheus is his teacher, and Menander his pupil. According to the *Pseudoclementines*, Dositheus was the founder of a school in Samaria. Origen reports that he tried to convince the Samaritans he was the Messias predicted by Moses. Menander was born at Capparetaea in Samaria, as Justin testifies. According to Irenaeus, he told his followers that he was sent by the invisible powers as a redeemer for the salvation of mankind. While he was the pupil of Simon Magus, he was the teacher of Satornil and

Basilides. Thus he represents the link between pre-Christian and Christian Gnosticism.

CHRISTIAN GNOSTICISM

When Christianity entered the great cities of the East, many highly educated men became converts to the new religion. Among them were some belonging to pre-Christian Gnostic sects. Instead of surrendering their former beliefs they only added some Christian doctrines to their Gnostic views. Thus, Christian Gnosticism was born. Pre-Christian Gnosticism differs from Christian Gnosticism in so far as the person Jesus does not have any place in its systems. In Christian Gnosticism the preaching of the one true God, the Father of Jesus Christ, the Redeemer, is one of the basic doctrines. The founders of the different Christian Gnostic sects endeavored to raise Christianity from the state of faith to that of knowledge and in this way make Christianity at home in the Hellenistic world.

The literary output of Gnosticism was tremendous, especially in the second century. The first Christian theological literature and the first Christian poetry were of Gnostic character. Much of this literature is anonymous. To this group belong many apocryphal gospels, apocryphal acts and epistles of the apostles, and apocryphal apocalypses (treated above, p. 106 ff.). This propaganda had a tremendous effect because of its popular content.

The most important part of Gnostic literature consists of theological treatises, composed by the founders of the different sects and their pupils. Most of this literature has been lost.

Texts: W. Völker, Quellen zur Geschichte der christlichen Gnosis. Tübingen, 1932.

Studies: H. L. Mansel, The Gnostic Heresies. London, 1875. — A. Hilgenfeld, Die Ketzergeschichte des Urchristentums urkundlich dargestellt. Leipzig, 1884. — W. Bousset, Hauptprobleme der Gnosis. Göttingen, 1907. — E. Buonaiuti, Lo Gnosticismo. Rome, 1907. — J. P. Steffes, Das Wesen des Gnostizismus und sein Verhältnis zum kath. Dogma. Paderborn, 1922. — L. Fendt, Gnostische Mysterien. Munich, 1922. — E. Buonaiuti, Frammenti gnostici. Rome, 1923. — E. de Faye, Gnostiques et gnosticisme. Etude critique des documents du Gnosticisme chrétien aux IIe et IIIe siècles. 2nd edit. Paris, 1925. — F. C. Burkitt, The Church and Gnosis. Cambridge, 1932. — H. Jonas, Gnosis und spätantiker Geist. Göttingen, 1934. — R. P. Casey,

The Study of Gnosticism: JThSt 36 (1935) 45–59. — H. Leisegang, Die Gnosis. 2nd edit. Leipzig, 1936. — J. Th. Carlyon, The Impact of Gnosticism on Early Christianity: Environmental Factors of Christian History, ed. by J. Th. McNeill. Chicago, 1939. — W. Bousset, PWK 7, 1503–1547. — H. Leclercq, DAL 6, 1327–67. — Bareille, DTC 6, 1434–1467. — E. F. Scott, Gnosticism: Encyclopaedia of Religion and Ethics, 6, 231–242.

BASILIDES

Basilides was, according to Irenaeus (*Adv. Haer.* 1,24,1), a teacher at Alexandria in Egypt. He lived at the time of Hadrian and Antoninus Pius (120–145). He wrote a gospel, of which we have only one fragment (cf. page 128), and a commentary to this gospel, entitled *Exegetica*, of which several fragments remain. Thus Hegemonius (*Acta Archelai*, 67, 4–11 ed. Benson) quotes from the thirteenth book of the *Exegetica* a passage in which the war of light and darkness is described. Clement of Alexandria (*Stromat.* 4,12,81,1 to 88,5) cites several passages from the twenty-third book which dealt with the problem of suffering. However, these fragments do not enable us to get an exact idea of the doctrinal system of Basilides. In addition, he composed psalms and odes, of which nothing remains.

Irenaeus (*Adv. Haer.* 1,24,3–4) gives the following summary of the teaching of Basilides:

Basilides again, that he may appear to have discovered something more sublime and plausible, gives an immense development to his doctrines. He sets forth that Nous was first born of the Unborn Father, that from him again was born Logos, from Logos Phronesis, from Phronesis Sophia and Dynamis and from Dynamis and Sophia the powers and principalities and angels, whom he also calls the first; and by them the first heaven was made. Then other powers, being formed by emanation from these, created another heaven similar to the first; and in like manner when others again had been formed by emanation from them corresponding exactly to those above them, these too framed another heaven; and from this third in downward order there was a fourth succession of descendants; and so on after the same fashion they declared that more and more principalities and angels were formed and three hundred and sixty-five heavens. Wherefore, the year contains the same number of days in conformity with the number of the heavens.

Those angels who occupied the lowest heaven, that namely which is visible to us, formed all the things which are in the world, and made allotments among themselves of the earth and of those nations which are upon it. The chief of them is he who is thought to be the God of the Jews; in as much as he desired to render the other nations subject to his own people, that is the Jews, all the other princes resisted and opposed him. Wherefore all other nations were at enmity with his nation. But the Father without birth and without name, perceiving that they would be destroyed, sent his own first-begotten Nous — he it is who is called Christ — to bestow deliverance on them that believe in him from the power of those who made the world. He appeared then on earth as a man to the nations of these powers and wrought miracles. Wherefore he did not himself suffer death, but Simon, a certain man of Cyrene, being compelled, bore the cross in his stead; so that this latter being transfigured by him that he might be thought to be Jesus, was crucified through ignorance and error while Jesus himself received the form of Simon and standing by laughed at them. For since he was an incorporeal power and the Nous of the unborn Father, he transfigured himself as he pleased and thus ascended to him who had sent him, deriding them in as much as he could not be laid hold of and was invisible to all. Those then who know these things have been freed from the principalities who formed the world; so it is not incumbent on us to confess him who was crucified, but him who came in the form of man and was thought to be crucified and was called Jesus and was sent by the Father, that by this dispensation he might destroy the work of the makers of the world (ANF 1, 349).

From the passage that then follows it appears that Basilides drew the following practical conclusions from his cosmology:

1. Knowledge (Gnosis) delivers from the principalities which form the world.

2. Only a few, one in a thousand, two in ten thousand, are able to possess the true knowledge.

3. Mysteries should be kept secret.

4. Martyrdom is futile.

5. Redemption affects only the souls, and not the body, which is subject to corruption.

6. Every action, even the most heinous sins of lust, is a matter of perfect indifference.

7. The Christian should not confess Christ the crucified but Jesus, who was sent by the Father. Otherwise he remains a slave and under the power of those who formed our bodies.

8. Pagan sacrifices ought to be despised, but can be used without any scruple because they are nothing.

From this summary of Irenaeus it is evident that Basilides did not share dualistic views as some scholars have claimed. The fragment of his *Exegetica* in the *Acta Archelai*, which deals with the war between light and darkness, cannot be quoted as a proof of his dualistic belief, because therewith begins, as it clearly indicates itself, a refutation of the Zoroastrian dualism between light and darkness as the powers of good and bad.

Texts: W. VÖLKER, Quellen zur Geschichte der Gnosis. Tübingen, 1932, 38–57.

Studies: G. UHLHORN, Das basilidianische System. Göttingen, 1855. — A. HILGENFELD, Das System des Gnostikers Basilides: Theol. Jahrbücher (1856) 86ff.; *idem*, Der Basilides des Hippolyt: Zeitschrift für wissenschaftl. Theologie (1875) 288–350. — F. X. FUNK, Der Basilides der Philosophumena kein Pantheist: Kirchengeschichtliche Abhandlungen 1 (Paderborn, 1897) 358–372. — H. STÄHELIN, Die gnostischen Quellen des Hippolyt (TU 6,3). Leipzig, 1899. — S. KENNEDY, Buddhist Gnosticism, the System of Basilides: Journal of the Asiatic Society (1902) 377–415. — H. WINDISCH, Das Evangelium des Basilides: ZNW 7 (1906) 236–246. — SCOTT-MONCRIEFF, Gnosticism and Early Christianity in Egypt: ChQ (1909) 64ff. — P. HENDRIX, De alexandrijnsche haeresiarch Basilides. Diss. Dordrecht, 1926. — S. PETRÉMENT, Le dualisme chez Platon, les gnostiques et les manichéens. Paris, 1947.

ISIDORE

The work of Basilides was continued by his son and pupil Isidore, of whom we know even less than of his father. Clement of Alexandria (*Stromat.* 2,113; 6,53; 3,1–3) has a few quotations from three of his writings. He wrote *An Explanation of the Prophet Parchor*, in which he tried to prove that the Greek philosophers borrowed from the prophets. In addition he composed an *Ethica* and a treatise *On the Attached Soul.* The latter deals with the human passions, which emanate from a second part of the soul. The passage which Clement quotes from the *Ethica* gives an odd interpretation of the Lord's words on the eunuch (Matt. 19,10ff.).

Texts: W. VÖLKER, l. c.

VALENTINUS

By far more important than Basilides and his son Isidore was their contemporary Valentinus. Irenaeus '(*Adv. Haer.* 3,4,3) states of him: 'Valentinus came to Rome in the time of Hyginus (ca. 136 to 140 A.D.), flourished under Pius (ca. 150 to 155) and remained until Anicetus' (ca. 155 to 160). Epiphanius (*Haer.* 31,7 to 12) is the first who reports that he was born in Egypt, educated in Alexandria, and that he spread his doctrine in Egypt before he went to Rome. Epiphanius adds that he later left Rome for Cyprus. Clement of Alexandria has six fragments of his writings incorporated into his *Stromata:* two of them are from his letters, two from his homilies, and two of them do not give any indication from which of his writings they are taken. One of the passages of his letters quoted by Clement (*Stromata*, 2,20,114) is as follows:

There is one good by whose presence is the manifestation which is by the son, and by him alone can the heart become pure by the expulsion of every evil spirit from the heart; for the multitude of spirits dwelling in it do not suffer it to be pure; but each of them performs his own deeds, insulting it often with unseemly lusts. And the heart seems to be treated somewhat like a caravanserai, for the latter has holes and ruts made in it and is often filled with dung, man living filthily in it and taking no care for the place as belonging to others. So fares it with the heart as long as there is no thought taken for it, being unclean and the abode of many demons. But when the only good father visits it, it is sanctified and gleams with light. And he who possesses such a heart is so blessed that he shall see God (ANF 2,372).

Passages like this explain why Valentinus found many believers among the faithful. They throw light on what Irenaeus (*Adv. Haer.* 3,15,2) says of Valentinus and his disciples:

By these words they entrap the more simple and entice

them, imitating our phraseology that these (dupes) may
listen to them the oftener; and then these are asked regarding us how it is that, when their whole doctrine is
similar to ours, we without cause keep ourselves aloof from
their company (ANF 1,439).
Valentinus found many followers both in the East and in the
West. Hippolytus speaks of two schools, an Oriental and an Italian.

Texts: A. HILGENFELD, Die Ketzergeschichte des Urchristentums. Leipzig,
1884, 292-307. — W. VÖLKER, Quellen zur Geschichte der Gnosis. Tübingen,
1932, 57-141.

Studies: A. HILGENFELD, Der Gnostiker Valentinus und seine Schriften: Zeitschrift für wissenschaftl. Theologie 23 (1880) 280-300; *idem,* Valentiniana:
ibidem, 26 (1883) 356-360. — G. HEINRICI, Die Valentinianische Gnosis und
die hl. Schrift. Berlin, 1871. — R. A. LIPSIUS, Valentinus und seine Schule:
Jahrbücher für protestantische Theologie (1887) 585-658. — O. DIBELIUS,
Studien zur Geschichte der Valentinianer: ZNW 9 (1908) 230-247; 329-340.
— C. BARTH, Die Interpretation des Neuen Testamentes in der valentinianischen Gnosis (TU 37,3). Leipzig, 1911. — K. MÜLLER, Beiträge zum
Verständnis der valentinianischen Gnosis: NGWG, Phil.-Hist. Klasse (1920)
179-204. — W. FÖRSTER, Von Valentin zu Herakleon. Giessen, 1928. —
J. QUISPEL, The Original Doctrine of Valentine: VC 1 (1947) 43-73.

PTOLEMY

The most prominent member of the Italian school of Valentinus was Ptolemy. He wrote *A Letter to Flora,* which deals with
the value of the Mosaic Law. It divides the Mosaic law into three
essential parts. The first comes from God, the second from Moses,
and the third from the elders of the Jewish people. The part which
originated from God has again three sections. The first section
contains the pure law, untainted by any evil, in other words the
ten commandments. This is the section of the Mosaic law which
Jesus came to fulfill rather than to suspend. The second section
is the law adulterated with injustice, namely that of retaliation,
which was suspended by the Savior. The third section is the ceremonial law which the Savior spiritualized. The letter is preserved
by Ephipanius, *Haer.* 33,3 to 7. It is the most important piece
of Gnostic literature that is extant today.

A. HILGENFELD, Der Brief des Valentinianers Ptolemaeus an die Flora:
Zeitschrift für wissenschaftl. Theologie 24 (1881) 214-230. — A. HARNACK,

Der Brief des Ptolemaeus an die Flora, eine religiöse Kritik am Pentateuch im 2. Jahrhundert (SAB 1902) 507–545; *idem*, Der Brief des Ptolemaeus an die Flora (KT 9). Bonn, 1912. — G. QUISPEL, La lettre de Ptolémée à Flora: VC 2 (1948), 17–54; *idem*, Lettre à Flora. Texte grec, introduction et traduction (SCH). Paris, 1949.

HERACLEON

According to Clement of Alexandria (*Stromat.* 4,71,1) Heracleon was the most esteemed of the disciples of Valentinus. He belongs to the Italian school, like Ptolemy. He composed a commentary to the Gospel of St. John. Origen quotes not less than forty-eight passages of this work in his own commentary to this Gospel. Clement of Alexandria cites two passages from Heracleon without indicating whether they are from his commentary on St. John or some other writing of his.

Texts: A. E. BROOKE, The Fragments of Heracleon (TSt 1,4). Cambridge, 1891.

Studies: W. FOERSTER, Von Valentin zu Herakleon. Giessen, 1928.

FLORINUS

Another member of the Italian school of Valentinus was the Roman presbyter Florinus. Eusebius is the first to report that Irenaeus addressed a letter to Florinus *On the Sole Sovereignty*, or *That God is not the Author of Evil*; Florinus seems to have been defending the opposite opinion. Eusebius (*Hist. Eccl.* 5,20,4) quotes a passage from this letter in which Irenaeus reminds Florinus:

> These opinions of Florinus, that I may speak sparingly, do not belong to sound doctrine. These opinions are inconsistent with the Church, and bring those who believe in them into the greatest impiety. These opinions not even the heretics outside the Church ever dared to proclaim. These opinions those who were presbyters before us, they who accompanied the apostles, did not hand on to you (LCL 1,497).

Irenaeus then goes on to remind Florinus of Bishop Polycarp of Smyrna, whom Florinus knew personally in his youth.

In addition to this letter Irenaeus wrote a work *On the Ogdoad* against Florinus 'when he was attracted by the Valentinian error' (Eusebius *ibid.* 5,20,1). There is extant a Syriac fragment of a letter which Irenaeus addressed to Pope Victor. In this letter Irenaeus asks the pope to take steps against the writings of a Roman presbyter, because these writings had spread to Gaul and endangered the faith of his Christians. The title of this fragment mentions Florinus as an adherent of the foolishness of Valentinus and as the author of an abominable book.

BARDESANES

On the Oriental school of Valentinus we have less information than on his Italian. One of the most important of his oriental disciples is Bardesanes (Bar Daisan). He was born on July 11, 154 A.D. at Edessa. He came from a noble family and was educated by a pagan priest at Mabug (Hieropolis). His friend was King Abgar IX of Osrhoene. He became a Christian at the age of twenty-five. When Edessa was conquered by Caracalla in 216 to 217, he fled to Armenia. After his return to Syria he died in A.D. 222/3. Eusebius (*Hist. Eccl.* 4,30), who calls Bardesanes 'a most noble man, skilled in Syriac', reports that he had first been a member of the Valentinian school, but that he later condemned this sect and refuted many of its fables. However, as Eusebius puts it, 'He did not completely clean off the filth of his ancient heresy'. According to the same source Bardesanes 'composed dialogues against the Marcionites and other leaders of various opinions, and he issued them in his own language and script, together with many other of his writings. Those who knew them, and they were many, for he was a powerful arguer, have translated them from the Syriac into Greek. Among them is his very powerful dialogue addressed to Antoninus *Concerning Fate*, and they say that he wrote many other works in consequence of the persecution of that time' (LCL 1.399).

While all other writings perished, the dialogue *Concerning Fate* or *Book of the Laws of the Countries*, which Eusebius mentions, survived in its original Syriac. The author, however, is not Bardesanes but his disciple Philip, although Bardesanes is the chief speaker in the dialogue, who answers the questions and problems of his followers regarding the characters of men and the position of the stars. According to Ephrem the Syrian Bardesanes is the creator of Syrian hymnody, because he composed one hundred and fifty hymns in order to spread his doctrine. His success was so tremendous that Ephrem in the second half of the fourth century had to combat this sect of Bardesanes by composing hymns himself. Some scholars were of the opinion that the beautiful poem, *The Hymn of the Soul*, in the apocryphal *Acts of Thomas* (cf. above, page 139) was composed by Bardesanes. But this remains very doubtful, especially since the contents of this famous hymn do not show any sign of Bardesanian Gnosis. The Arab Ibn Abi Jakub in his list of sciences entitled *Fihrist* from the end of the tenth century attributes to Bardesanes three other writings, of which one dealt with *Light and Darkness*, a second with *The Spiritual Nature of Truth*, and a third with *The Movable and the Immovable*.

Editions and Translations: *Syriac text and English translation*: W. CURETON, Spicilegium Syriacum. London, 1855. — *Syriac text and French translation*: F. NAU, Patrologia Syriaca, Pars I, Tom. 2. Paris, 1907, 490–658; *idem*, Bardesane. Le livre des lois des Pays. Paris, 1931. — *Italian translation:* G. LEVI DELLA VIDA, Il dialogo delle leggi dei paesi. Rome, 1921. — *German translations:* A. MERX, Bardesanes von Edessa. Halle, 1863. — H. WIESMANN, in: 75 Jahre Stella Matutina I, 1931, 553–572.

Studies: A. HAHN, Bardesanes gnosticus. Leipzig, 1819. — C. KUEHNER, Astronomiae et astrologiae in doctrinis gnost. vestigia I: Bardesanes Gnost. numina. Hildburghausen, 1833. — A. HILGENFELD, Bardesanes, der letzte Gnostiker. Leipzig, 1864. — F. NAU, Une biographie inédite de Bardesane l'astréopologue. Paris, 1897; *idem*, DTC 2 (1904) 391–401. — TH. NISSEN, Die Petrusakten und ein bardesanitischer Dialog in der Aberkios-Vita: ZNW 9 (1908) 190–203; 315–328. — E. BUONAIUTI, Bardesane l'astreologo: Revista stor.-critica delle scienze teol. 5 (1909) 691–704. — F. HAASE, Zur bardesanischen Gnosis (TU 34,4). Leipzig, 1910; *idem*, OC (1925), 129–140. — O. WEINRICH, Genethliakon W. Schmidt (1929) 398ff. — G. V. WESENDONK, Bardesanes und Mani: Acta Orientalia 10 (1932) 336–363. — W. SCHAEDER, ZKG (1932) 21–73. — L. TONDELLI, Mani. Rapporti con Bardesane. Milan, 1932. — A. BAUMSTARK, OC (1933) 62–71. — J. HUBY, Stoicheia dans Bardesane et dans S. Paul: Bibl (1934) 365–368. — W. BAUER, Rechtgläubigkeit und Ketzerei im ältesten Christentum. Tübingen, 1934, 33–38. — B. REHM, Bardesanes in den Pseudoklementinen: Phil 93 (1938) 218–247.

HARMONIUS

Harmonius was Bardesanes' son, who continued the work of his father. The first to grant us any information about him is the historian Sozomen in the middle of the fifth century. According to him (Sozomen, *Hist. Eccl.* 3,16), Harmonius 'was deeply versed in Grecian erudition and was the first to compose verses in his vernacular language; those verses he delivered to the choirs, and even now the Syrians frequently sing, not the precise verses written by Harmonius, but others of the same meter. For as Harmonius was not altogether free from the errors of his father and entertained various opinions concerning the soul, the generation and destruction of the body, and the doctrine of transmigration, which are taught by the Greek philosophers, he introduced some of these sentiments into the lyrical songs which he composed. When Ephrem perceived that the Syrians were charmed with the elegant diction and melodious versification of Harmonius, he became apprehensive lest they should imbibe the same opinions; and therefore although he was ignorant of Grecian learning he applied himself to the study of the metres of Harmonius and composed similar poems in accordance with the doctrines of the Church, and sacred hymns in praise of holy men. From that period the Syrians sang the odes of Ephrem according to the method indicated by Harmonius.'

In this quotation Harmonius takes completely the place of his father, except that Sozomen states in a previous sentence that Bardesanes originated a heresy designated by his name. But from the fact that Ephrem does not mention Harmonius at all we may conclude that Harmonius did no more than continue the work of his father.

THEODOTUS

Another member of the Oriental school of Valentinus is Theodotus. He is known to us from the so-called *Excerpta ex Scriptis Theodoti*, which forms an appendix to Clement of Alexandria's *Stromata*. Eighty-six of the excerpts contain extracts from the writings of Theodotus although he himself is mentioned in only four of them. The contents speak of the mysteries of Baptism, the Eucharist of bread and water, and anointing, as means to free oneself from the domination of the evil power. In addition, typical Valentinian doctrines regarding the pleroma, the Ogdoas and the three classes of men are found in these excerpts.

Texts: O. Stählin, Klemens von Alexandrien 3 (GCS) 103–133; 135–155. — R. P. Casey, Excerpta ex Theodoto of Clement of Alexandria (SD 1). London, 1940. — F. Sagnard, Clément d'Alexandrie, Extraits de Théodote (SCH). Paris, 1948. Cf. A. J. Festugière, VC 3 (1949) 193–207.

MARCUS

Irenaeus mentions a certain Marcus who taught in Asia Proconsularis as a member of the Oriental school of Valentinus. From the account of Irenaeus it appears that Marcus shared doctrines of Valentinus regarding the aeons, that he celebrated a Eucharist by means of magic and fraud, and that he seduced many women. His disciples preached even in the section near the Rhone in Gaul and Irenaeus knew some of them personally. The latter mentions in *Adv. Haer.* 1,20,1 that they used a great many apocryphal and unauthentic writings which they had composed themselves.

CARPOCRATES

The city of Alexandria in Egypt produced besides Basilides and Valentinus the founder of another Gnostic sect, Carpocrates. According to Irenaeus (*Adv. Haer.* 1,25,1) Carpocrates and his followers maintained 'that the world and the things which are therein were created by angels greatly inferior to the unbegotten Father. They also hold that Jesus was the son of Joseph and was just like other men with the exception that he differed from them in this respect that in as much as his soul was steadfast and pure he remembered perfectly those things which he had witnessed within the sphere of the unbegotten God. On this account a power descended upon him from the Father, that by means of it he might escape from the creators of the world; and they say that it, after passing through them all and remaining in all points free, ascended again to him.'

This position of Jesus was by no means unique because in the same way 'the soul which is like that of Christ can despise those rulers who were the creators of the world, and in like manner receives power for accomplishing the same results. This idea has raised them (the Carpocratians) to such a pitch of pride, that some of them declared themselves similar to Jesus while others still more mighty maintained that they were superior to his disciples, such as Peter and Paul and the rest of the apostles, whom they considered to be in no respect inferior to Jesus' (1,25,2).

A peculiar, syncretistic cult was practiced by these followers of Carpocrates:

'They also possess images some of them painted and others formed from different kinds of material, while they maintain that a likeness of Christ was made by Pilate at that time when Jesus lived among them. They crown these images and set them up along with the images of the philosophers of the world; that is to say with the images of Pythagoras and Plato and Aristotle and the rest. They have also other modes of honoring these images after the same manner of the gentiles' (*Adv. Haer.* 1,25,6, ANF 1,351).

'The Carpocratians also practice magical arts and incantations, philters and love potions, and have recourse to familiar spirits, dreams sending demons and other abominations, declaring that they possess power to rule over even now the princes and formers of this world and not only over them but also things that are in it' (*Adv. Haer.* 1,25,3, ANF 1,350).

For the dating of Carpocrates it is of importance that according to Irenaeus one of his women disciples, Marcellina, went to Rome during the reign of Pope Anicetus (154–165), and seduced many. This proves that Carpocrates was a contemporary of Valentinus.

Texts: W. VÖLKER, Quellen zur Geschichte der Gnosis. Tübingen, 1932, 36–38.

EPIPHANES

While we have no writings of Carpocrates, several passages of the treatise *On Justice* are preserved which his son Epiphanes composed. Epiphanes wrote this treatise as an infant prodigy. He died at the age of seventeen, and was worshipped as a god at Cephalonia, the native island of his mother, Alexandria. The Cephalonians dedicated a temple to him in the town of Same and his followers celebrated his apotheosis with hymns and sacrifices at every new moon. The passages of his treatise *On Justice* which Clement of Alexandria quotes (*Strom.* 3,2,5–9) indicate that Epiphanes advocated a community of goods. He went even so far as to demand that women should like all other property be common to all.

Texts: W. Völker, l.c. 33–36.

MARCION

Marcion was born at Sinope, in Pontus, the present day Sinob, on the Black Sea. His father was a bishop, and his family belonged to the highest social class of this important port and commercial city. He himself had made a fortune as a ship owner. He came to Rome about 140 A.D. in the reign of Antoninus Pius, and associated himself at first with the congregation of the faithful. Soon, however, his teachings caused sharp opposition, so that the leaders of the Church required him to give an account of his faith. The result was that in July 144 A.D. he was excommunicated. There is an important difference between Marcion and the other Gnostics. While the other Gnostics founded only schools, Marcion after his separation from the Church of Rome founded his own church. He established a hierarchy of bishops, priests and deacons. The liturgical meetings were very similar to those of the Roman Church. For this reason he gained more adherents than any other Gnostic. Ten years after his excommunication, Justin reports that his church had spread, 'over the whole of mankind'. Up to the middle of the fifth century there remained many Marcionite communities in the Orient, especially in Syria. Some of them were still in existence at the dawn of the Middle Ages.

It is interesting to note that Marcion had been excommunicated by his father previous to his coming to Rome. Most probably in his native town of Sinope he had met with the same opposition to his doctrine which he met in Rome. For this reason it would be important to know something about his teachings. Unfortunately the only work which he ever wrote, entitled *Antitheses*, which contained his doctrine, has not been preserved. Lost also is his letter addressed to the leaders of the Roman Church, in which he gave an account of his faith. Irenaeus associates Marcion with the Syrian Gnostic, Cerdon, who sojourned in Rome under Hyginus (136–140) 'and taught that the God proclaimed by the Law and the Prophets is not the Father of Our

Lord Jesus Christ, the one being revealed, the other unknown; the one again being just, the other good' (*Adv. Haer.* 1,27,1).

Irenaeus states that Marcion extended Cerdon's school in Rome, 'shamelessly blaspheming him who is called God by the Law and the Prophets; affirming him to be an evil-doer and fond of wars, and inconstant also in his judgments and contrary to Himself; and as for Jesus, that he came from that Father who is above the God who made the world into Judaea in the time of Pontius Pilate, the Governor, who was Tiberius Caesar's Procurator, and was manifest in human form to the inhabitants of Judaea, to do away with the Prophets and the Law and all the works of that God who made the world, whom he also calls Ruler of the World. And moreover mutilating the Gospel according to St. Luke, and taking away all that is written of Our Lord's birth and much also from the doctrine of Our Lord's discourses, wherein it is most plainly written how Our Lord confessed the maker of this world to be his Father; he persuaded his disciples that he was himself more trustworthy than the apostles who wrote the Gospel; while he was putting into their hands not the Gospel but a small portion of it, and in like manner, the Epistles of the Apostle Paul too were mutilated by him, by taking out whatever is plainly spoken by the Apostle of the God who made the world, how that he is the Father of Our Lord Jesus Christ; and whatsoever out of the prophetic writings the Apostle hath quoted in his teachings as predictive of the coming of the Lord. And salvation, he says, will be of our souls only, those souls which have learned his doctrine; but the body, because in truth it is taken from the earth, cannot possibly partake of salvation'.

In another passage (*Adv. Haer.* 3,3,4) Irenaeus reports that Bishop Polycarp of Smyrna on one occasion met Marcion and when Marcion asked him, 'Do you recognize me?' he answered, 'I recognize you as the first-born of Satan'.

Irenaeus like all other anti-heretical writers numbered Marcion among the Gnostics. A. von Harnack, however, is of the opinion that Marcion was no Gnostic at all, but the first Christian reformer and the restorer of Paulinism. Harnack is right in so far as Marcion made no attempt to bridge the distance between the infinite and the finite by a whole series of aeons as the Gnostics did. Neither did he trouble himself with speculations about the cause of the disorder in the visible world. He differs also from the Gnostics in his repudiation of all allegorism in the interpretation of Scripture, but on the other hand, Marcion's theology shows clearly the typical mixture of Christian and pagan ideas which is so characteristic of Gnosticism. His concept of the godhead is Gnostic since he makes a real distinction between the good god who lives in the third heaven and the just god who is inferior to him. The same Gnostic character can be traced in his cosmology. The second god who created the world and man is none other than the demiurge, well known from other Gnostic sects. Gnostic also is Marcion's idea, that this second god did not create the world out of nothingness, but that he formed it out of the eternal matter, the seed of all evil. Marcion identifies this second god with the God of the Jews, the God of the Law and the Prophets. He is just but he has passions; he is irate and revengeful; he is the author of all evil, be it physical or moral. For this reason he is the instigator of all wars. Marcion's Christology shows this same Gnostic tendency. Christ is not the Messias who was prophesied in the Old Testament; he was not born of the Virgin Mary, because he had neither birth nor growth, nor even the semblance of them. In the fifteenth year of the reign of Tiberius he manifests himself suddenly in the synagogue of Capharnaum. Since that moment he had a semblance of humanity which he kept until his death on the cross. By the shedding of his blood he redeemed all souls from the power of the demiurge whose reign he destroyed by his teaching and by his miracles. But here again a Gnostic idea is evident because according to Marcion redemption is limited to the soul whereas the body remains subject to the power of the demiurge and is destined for destruction. The inconsistency and lack of all logic in these doctrines is striking. Marcion did not consider it incumbent on him to explain the origin of his god of justice, nor why the sacrifice on the cross had such value in his eyes when it was only that of a phantom.

A definitely Gnostic tendency appears also in his method of 'purifying' the texts of the New Testament, for he eliminated all passages which indicate that God the Father of Christ is the same as the creator of the world, that Christ is the Son of God who made heaven and earth, that the Father of Jesus Christ is identical with the God of the Jews. All these passages were in striking contrast to Gnostic views. In addition Marcion had something in common with Valentinus, that is, his repudiation of the entire Old Testament. But he differs again from most of the Gnostics in as far as he did not compose any new gospels or holy books, although he did object to a number of New Testament writings and repudiated the Old Testament completely. He was convinced that the Jews had falsified the original gospel of Christ by introducing into it Jewish elements. For this reason Christ called the Apostle Paul to restore the Gospel in its original form. But even St. Paul's epistles had been corrupted by his enemies. Marcion therefore eliminated the Gospels of Mathew, Mark and John, and repudiated all the so-called Jewish interpolations in the Gospel of Luke, which contained substantially the gospel of Christ. From the collection of St. Paul's letters he excluded the pastoral epistles and the Epistle to the Hebrews. In the letters which he retained he omitted some passages. He placed the Letter to the Galatians first, and changed the name of the Epistle to the Ephesians to the Epistle to the Laodiceans. By this redaction he reduced the New Testament to two documents of faith which he called the *Gospel,* and the *Apostle.* To these documents he added his book *Antitheses* in which he justified his repudiation of the Old Testament by accumulating all objectionable passages in order to prove the bad character of the God of the Jews. He also explains his objections to the Gospels and to the Acts of the Apostles.

A. HAHN, Antitheses Marcionis gnostici. Königsberg, 1823; *idem,* De canone Marcionis. Leipzig, 1824; *idem,* Das Evangelium Marcionis in seiner ursprünglichen Gestalt. Leipzig, 1824. — J. C. THILO, Codex apocr. Novi Test. I. Leipzig, 1832, 401–480; Evangelium Marcionis ex auctoritate veterum monumentorum. — RITSCHL, Das Evangelium Marcions. Tübingen, 1846. — A. HILGENFELD, Kritische Untersuchungen über die Evangelien Justins, der klementinischen Homilien und Marcions. Halle, 1850. — G. VOLKMAR, Das Evangelium Marcions. Leipzig, 1852. — A. HILGENFELD, Marcions Apostolikon: Zeitschrift f. histor. Theologie (1855) 426ff. — H. U. MEYBOOM, Marcion en de Marcionieten. Leiden, 1888. — TH. ZAHN, Geschichte des neutestamentl. Kanons I, 2, 585–718; II, 2, 409–529: Marcions Neues Testament. — V. ERMONI, Marcion dans la littérature arménienne: ROChr I (1896) 461ff.; *idem,* Le marcionisme: RQH 82 (1910) 5–33. — H. WAITZ, Das Ps.-Tertullianische Gedicht 'Adv. Marcionem'. Ein Beitrag zur Geschichte der altchristl. Literatur sowie zur Quellen-kritik des Marcionitismus. Darmstadt, 1901. — A. HARNACK, Marcion. Das Evangelium vom fremden Gott (TU 45). Leipzig, 1921; 2nd edit. 1924; *idem*, Neue Studien zu Marcion (TU 44,4). Leipzig, 1923. — E. BOSSHARDT, Essai sur l'originalité et la probité de Tertullien dans son traité contre Marcion. Lausanne, 1921. — A. D'ALÈS, Marcion. La réforme chrétienne au IIe siècle: RSR 13 (1922) 137–168. — H. RASCHKE, Der Römerbrief des Marcion nach Epiphanius: Abhandl. u. Vorträge der Bremer wissenschaftl. Gesellschaft I, 1–2. Bremen, 1926, 128–201. — H. KAYSER, Natur und Gott bei Marcion: ThStKr (1929) 279–296. — F. LOOFS, Theophilus von Antiochien und die andern theologischen Quellen bei Irenaeus. Leipzig, 1930. — E. BARNIKOL, Die Entstehung der Kirche im zweiten Jahrhundert und die Zeit Marcions, 2nd edit. Kiel, 1933; *idem*, Philipper 2. Der marcionitische Ursprung des Mythos-Satzes. Phil. 2, 6f. Kiel, 1932 — R. S. WILSON, Marcion. London, 1933. — W. BAUER, Rechtgläubigkeit und Ketzerei im ältesten Christentum. Tübingen 1934, 135f., 224–227. — A. HOLLARD, Deux hérétiques: Marcion et Montan. Paris, 1935. — COUCHOUD, Is Marcion's Gospel one of the Synoptics?: HJ (1936) 265–277. — A. LOISY, Marcion's Gospel: a Reply: HJ (1936) 378–387. — M. MÜLLER, Untersuchungen zum *Carmen adversus Marcionitas*. Würzburg. Phil. Diss. Ochsenfurt, 1936. — W. F. HOWARD, The anti-Marcionite Prologue to the Gospels: ExpT 47 (1936) 534–538. — E. BARNIKOL, Marcions Paulusbriefprologe: TJHC 6 (1938) 15–16. — H. KAYSER, Zur marcionitischen Taufformel: ThStKr 108 (1938) 370–386. — J. KNOX, On the Vocabulary of Marcion's Gospel: JBL 58 (1939) 193–201. — J. KNOX, Marcion and the New Testament. Chicago, 1942. — B. STEIDLE, Neue Untersuchungen zu Origenes Περὶ ἀρχῶν: ZNW (1941) 239–243. — E. SEEBERG, Geschichte und Geschichtsanschauung dargestellt an altchristlichen Geschichtsauffassungen: ZKG 60 (1941) 309–331. — S. PETRÉMENT, Le dualisme chez Platon, les gnostiques et les manichéens. Paris, 1947. — G. QUISPEL, De Bronnen van Tertullianus' Adversus Marcionem. Leiden, 1943. Cf. J. W. PH. BORLEFFS, VC 1 (1947) 193–198.

APELLES

Marcion's most important disciple was Apelles. According to Tertullian he first lived with Marcion in Rome, but after some friction with his teacher he left for Alexandria in Egypt. Later he returned to Rome. Rhodon, his literary adversary who knew him personally, gives us the following valuable information about the disciples of Marcion and about Apelles in particular:

Therefore they (the followers of Marcion, the Marcionites) have ceased to agree among themselves, maintaining inconsistent opinions. One of their herd is Apelles, who is reverenced for his life and old age. He admits that there is one Principle but says that the prophecies are of an opposing spirit, and he was persuaded by the utterances of a possessed maiden

named Philoumena. But others, such as the captain himself
(Marcion), introduced two Principles. To them belong Po-
titus and Basilicus. These followed the wolf of Pontus (Marcion), not perceiving the division of things, any more than
he, and, turning to a simple solution, announced two Principles boldly and without proof. Others again, passing into
worse error, supposed that there are not only two but even
three natures. Of them the chief and the leader is Syneros,
as those state who represent his school (Eusebius, *Hist. Eccl.*
5,13,2-4 LCL 1, 467-69).

More important is the fact that Rhodon had a discussion with
Apelles which A. Harnack calls 'the most important religious
discussion of Church history'. Rhodon gives the following report
of this discussion:

> For the old man Apelles, when he consorted with us, was
> proved to make many false statements. Hence also he used
> to say that it is not necessary to investigate the argument
> fully, but that each should remain in his own belief, for he
> asserted that those who place their hope in the Crucified
> would be saved, if they persisted in good works. But as we
> have said, the most obscure part of all the doctrines which
> he put forward were about God. For he kept on saying that
> there is only one Principle just as our doctrine states. . . . .
> And when I said to him, 'where is this proof of yours, or
> how can you say that there is one Principle? Tell us', he
> said that the prophecies refute themselves by not having
> spoken the truth at all for they are inconsistent and false
> and contradict themselves, but as to how there is one Prin-
> ciple he said that he did not know it, but merely inclined
> to that view. Then when I adjured him to speak the truth
> he swore that he was speaking the truth, when he said that
> he did not know how the unbegotten God is one, but that
> he believed it. But I laughed at him and condemned him,
> because though he called himself a teacher he did not know
> how to establish what he taught (Eusebius, *Hist. Eccl.*
> 5,13,5-7 LCL 1,469).

From this account it appears that Apelles disagreed with
Marcion in most important questions. First of all, he rejected
his teacher's avowed dualism and endeavored to get back to a

single first Principle. Consequently he presented the demiurge as a creature of God, as an angel who created the world. Secondly, Apelles eliminated Marcion's Docetism. Jesus Christ was no phantom; he had a real body although he did not receive it from the Virgin Mary but borrowed it from the four elements of the stars. When he ascended he restored his body to the elements.

On the other hand Apelles went much farther than Marcion in his rejection of the Old Testament. Marcion regarded the Old Testament as a document of purely historical value without any religious significance. To Apelles it was a lying book, full of contradictions and fables and entirely unreliable. In order to prove the worthlessness of the Old Testament Apelles composed a book entitled *The Syllogisms* which comprised at least thirty-eight books. Ambrose has preserved a large number of passages from this work in his treatise *De Paradiso*. Nothing is extant from the book of *Manifestations* (φανερώσεις) of Apelles in which he published the visions of the prophetess Philoumena.

A. HARNACK, De Apellis gnosi monarchica. Leipzig, 1874; *idem*, Sieben neue Bruchstücke der Syllogismen des Apelles (TU 6,37). Leipzig, 1890; 111–120; *idem*, Unbeachtete und neue Quellen zur Kenntnis des Häretikers Apelles (TU 20). Leipzig, 1900, 93–100.

THE ENCRATITES

Related in doctrine to Marcion are the so-called Encratites. The founder of this sect is Tatian the Syrian (cf. above, p. 221). According to Irenaeus the Encratites agreed with Marcion in rejecting marriage. The fact that the genealogies of Jesus were lacking in Tatian's Diatessaron is also an indication that he had something in common with Marcion.

JULIUS CASSIANUS

Another representative of the Encratites is Julius Cassianus. Clement of Alexandria mentions two of his writings in *Stromat*. 3,13,92. The first of these was entitled *Exegetica*. We learn from Clement that the first book of this work dealt with the age of Moses. The title of the second work was *Concerning Abstinence or*

Eunuchry, Περὶ ἐγκρατείας ἤ περὶ εὐνουχίας. Two passages which Clement quotes from this work reject all sexual intercourse, and a third makes use of the Gnostic *Gospel of the Egyptians* (cf. above, p. 113). On account of his Docetism Clement associates him with Valentinus and Marcion. It would appear that Julius Cassianus taught in Egypt about the year 170 A.D.

OTHER GNOSTIC WRITINGS

Besides the Gnostic writings mentioned by ecclesiastical authors, there are other Gnostic writings extant in Coptic translations.

I. Codex Askewianus, a parchment manuscript formerly owned by A. Askew, now in the British Museum (Add. 5114), contains four books which usually bear the title *Pistis Sophia*. But these four books are by no means one writing. The fourth book consists of revelations which Jesus is supposed to have made to his disciples immediately after his resurrection. It is older than the first three books, which contain revelations of the same kind from the twelfth year after the resurrection. The fourth book must have been composed in the first half of the third century, and the first three books in the second half of that century. All four of them originated most probably in Egypt in Barbelo-Gnostic circles. *Pistis Sophia* is mentioned only in the first three books in which Jesus gives instructions about the fate and the fall and redemption of *Pistis Sophia*. The latter is a spiritual being of the world of aeons, which suffers the same fate as mankind in general. Since the text contains many Greek words the original must have been Greek. According to Carl Schmidt the manuscript is from the second half of the fourth century.

II. Codex Brucianus, formerly owned by James Bruce, now in the Bodleian of Oxford, is a papyrus from the fifth or sixth century, which consists of two different manuscripts. The first contains the two books of the *Mystery of the Great Logos* (λόγος κατὰ μυστήριον), which Carl Schmidt identified with the two books of Jeû cited in Pistis Sophia. They contain revelations of Jesus about 'the treasures through which the soul must pass'. The treasures are indicated in mystic diagrams, numbers, and meaningless collections of letters. The second treatise of the Codex Brucianus is mutilated. It contains speculations about the origin and evolution of the transcendental world, which seem to have originated in the circles of the Gnostic Seth. III. A third manuscript is preserved at Berlin. It contains three treatises. The first is entitled the *Gospel of Mary*, and gives revelations conveyed by Mary. The second entitled *Apocryphon of John* is the translation of a Greek work refuted by Irenaeus at the end of the first book of his *Against Heresies* (1,29). Jesus appears in a vision and reveals himself to John the Apostle as 'The Father, the Mother and the Son'. The third treatise is entitled *Sophia Jesu Christi*. According to C. Schmidt this *Sophia* is identical with the *Sophia* attributed to Valentinus.

Editions and translations: J. H. PETERMANN, Pistis Sophia. Opus gnosticum Valentino adjudicatum e codice manuscripto coptico Londinensi descripsit et latine vertit M. G. Schwartze. Berlin, 1851. — C. SCHMIDT, Koptisch-gnostische Schriften. 1. Bd. (GCS). Berlin, 1905 (German translation). The Coptic text was edited in a revised edition by C. SCHMIDT, Pistis Sophia. Neu herausgegeben. Copenhagen, 1925. A revised German translation was published by C. SCHMIDT, Pistis Sophia. Ein gnostisches Originalwerk des dritten Jahrhunderts aus dem Koptischen übersetzt; in neuer Bearbeitung mit einleitenden Untersuchungen und Indices. Leipzig, 1925. — *English translation:* G. HORNER, Pistis Sophia. Literally Translated from the Coptic. With an introduction by F. Legge. London, 1924. — H. R. S. MEAD, Pistis Sophia. English translation, with introduction, notes, bibliography. London, 1947. — *French translation:* E. AMÉLINEAU, Paris, 1895. — Codex Brucianus was edited with a French translation by E. AMÉLINEAU, Notices et extraits des manuscripts de la Bibliothèque Nationale et autres bibliothèques. Paris, 1891. A year later a new edition with a German translation appeared by C. SCHMIDT, Gnostische Schriften in koptischer Sprache, aus dem Codex Brucianus herausgegeben, übersetzt und bearbeitet (TU 8,1–2). Leipzig, 1892. A new German translation is given in C. SCHMIDT, Koptisch-gnostische Schriften, vol. 1 (GCS). Leipzig, 1905. The second treatise in Codex Brucianus was edited with an English translation by A. CH. BAYNES, A Coptic Gnostic Treatise in the Codex Brucianus. Cambridge, 1933. For the Greek text of the *Gospel of Mary* cf. C. H. ROBERTS, Catalogue of the Greek and Latin Papyri in the John Rylands Library, III. Theological and Literary Texts (Nos. 457–551). Manchester, 1938, Nr. 463.

Studies: K. R. KÖSTLIN, Das gnostische System des Buches Pistis Sophia: Theologische Jahrbücher 13 (1854) 1–104; 137–196. — A. HARNACK, Über das gnostische Buch Pistis Sophia (TU 7,2). Leipzig, 1891. — C. SCHMIDT, Die in dem koptisch-gnostischen Codex Brucianus enthaltenen beiden Bücher Jeû in ihrem Verhältnis zu der Pistis Sophia untersucht: Zeitschrift für wissensch. Theologie 37 (1894) 555–585. — R. LIECHTENHAU, Untersuchungen zur koptisch-gnostischen Literatur: Zeitschrift für wissensch. Theologie 44 (1901) 236–253. — LIEBLEIN, Pistis Sophia. L'antimimom gnostique est-il le ka égyptien?

Christiania, 1908; *idem*, Pistis Sophia. Les conceptions égyptiennes dans le gnosticisme. Christiania, 1909. — F. C. BURKITT, Pistis Sophia: JThSt 23 (1922) 271ff.; *idem*, Pistis Sophia Again: JThSt 26 (1924/25) 391-399; *idem*, Pistis Sophia and the Coptic Language: JThSt 27 (1925/26) 148-157. — C. SCHMIDT, Die Urschrift der Pistis Sophia: ZNTW 24 (1925) 218-240. — CASEY, JThSt 27 (1926) 374ff. — EISLER, Angelos (1930) 93ff. — SCHOLEM, ZNW (1931) 170-176. — F. LEXA, Egyptian Religion. New York, 1933, 106-116. — PUECH, AIPh (1936) 935-962. — E. AMANN, Ophites: DTC 11, 1063-1075.

In 1946 a great collection of Gnostic texts was discovered in Egypt consisting of twelve volumes or more than one thousand pages in the Coptic language. They were found in a jar near Nag-Hammadi, in the vicinity of the ancient Chénoboskion, thirty miles north of Luxor on the east bank of the Nile. The thousand pages contain thirty-seven complete works and five in a fragmentary condition. All of these works had been lost. Some of them have been identified as those from which Irenaeus, Hippolytus, Origen and Epiphanius quote in their polemical anti-Gnostic writings. Others are altogether unknown and many are described as secret works not to be known to unbelievers so that the ecclesiastical writers who write against the Gnostics probably never saw them. Five of the works are attributed to "thricegreat" Hermes. Others bear such titles as *The Ascension of Paul the First, Second Apocalypse of James, The Gospel According to Thomas and Philip, The Secret Book of John, The Five Revelations According to Seth, The Gospel of the Egyptians, The Traditions of Matthias, The Wisdom of Jesus, The Epistle of Blessed Eugnostos* and *The Dialogue of the Savior*. Several titles are identical with those of known apocryphal gospels, but the works bearing them do not appear to be the same. The recovered papyri will cast a flood of light on the history of Gnosticism and on the centuries when Christian theology was crystallizing.

Studies: TOGO MINA, Le papyrus gnostique du musée copte: VC 2 (1948) 129-136. — J. DORESSE, Trois livres gnostiques inédits: VC 2 (1948) 137-160. — H. PUECH-J. DORESSE, Nouveaux écrits gnostiques découverts en Egypte: Comptes-rendues de l'Académie des Inscriptions, séance du février 1948, 89ff. — J. DORESSE, Nouveaux textes gnostiques coptes découverts en Egypte. Le Livre Secret de Jean: Communication faite au VIIe Congrès International des Études Byzantines. Brussels, 1948. — J. DORESSE-TOGO MINA, Nouveaux textes gnostiques coptes découverts en Haute-Egypte. La bibliothèque de Chénoboskion: VC 3 (1949) 129-141.

CHAPTER VIII

THE BEGINNINGS OF
ANTI-HERETICAL LITERATURE

There were two ways in which the Church encountered the danger emanating from the propaganda of Gnostic literature. The ecclesiastical authorities reacted by excommunicating the heresiarchs and their adherents and issuing pastoral letters in order to warn the faithful. This defensive procedure was effectively supported by theological writers, who took upon themselves the task of exposing the errors of the heretics by explaining the true doctrine of the Church from Scripture and tradition. Thus was created the so-called anti-heretical literature, of which only very few treatises are extant today.

I. PAPAL AND EPISCOPAL WRITINGS OF THE SECOND CENTURY AGAINST HERESIES AND SCHISMS

SOTER (166-174)

Eusebius (*Hist. Eccl.* 4,23,9–10) has preserved a fragment of a letter which Bishop Dionysius of Corinth addressed to Pope Soter (166–174). The text of this fragment is as follows:

> This has been your custom from the beginning, to do good in manifold ways to all Christians, and to send contributions to the many Churches in every city, in some places relieving the poverty of the needy, in ministering to the Christians in the mines, by the contribution which you have sent from the beginning, preserving the ancestral custom of the Romans, true Romans as you are. Your blessed Bishop, Soter, has not only carried on this habit, but has even increased it, by administering the bounty distributed to the saints, and by exhorting with his blessed words the brethren who come to Rome as a loving father would his children (LCL 1,381–383).

From *Hist. Eccl.* 4,23,11 it appears that Pope Soter wrote a letter to the Christians of Corinth which he accompanied with a contribution. A. Harnack's view that this letter is actually the so-called *Second Epistle of Clement* has been dealt with above (p. 54).

According to the *Praedestinatus* (1,26), Soter also wrote a work against the Montanists, but this report is absolutely unreliable.

ELEUTHERUS (174–189)

Recent investigations have proved that it was Eleutherus and not Soter who first rejected the Montanistic heresy in a written statement. The *Auctoritates* mentioned by Tertullian (*Adv. Prax.* 1) seem to refer to this document. According to Eusebius (*Hist. eccl.* 5,3,4–4,2 and 5,1,2–3) he received in 177 or 178 Irenaeus, who brought him two letters concerning Montanism. The first was from the Christian community of Lyons, the second from several martyrs of Lyons. It seems that both letters tried to intervene in favor of a milder handling of the Montanists.

VICTOR I (189–198)

Victor wrote several letters which dealt with the paschal controversy, and are of importance for the history of the Roman primacy (Euseb., *Hist. eccl.* 5,23–25). St. Jerome (*De viris illustr.* 34) seems to refer to these letters when he states that Victor composed 'super quaestione paschae et alia quaedam opuscula'. There must have been another document by Victor because, according to Eusebius (*Hist. eccl.* 5,28,6–9), Victor excommunicated Theodotus, the currier from Byzantium, who taught that Jesus except for his miraculous birth was a man like all other men, and that he became God only after his resurrection. It remains very doubtful whether Victor was the first ecclesiastical author to write in Latin, as Jerome suggests (*De viris illustr.* 53).

ZEPHYRINUS (198–217)

According to Optatus of Milevis (*Contra Parm.* 1,9) Zephyrinus defended in his writings the Catholic faith against the heretics. Since there is no other source which verifies this report it remains doubtful. Hippolytus of Rome reports, however, that Zephyrinus gave a definition against the doctrine of Sabellius in which he declared 'I know one God only, Jesus Christ, and beside him no other who was begotten and who could suffer' (Hippolytus,

Ref. 9,11,3). A. Harnack calls this statement 'the oldest dogmatic definition of a Roman bishop which is known to us in its text.' He gives it an interpretation which makes Pope Zephyrinus a modalist who does not know God the Father and preaches Jesus Christ, the only God of the Christians. But this interpretation is not justified. The fact that Zephyrinus calls Jesus Christ the 'begotten God' presupposes that he acknowledged the 'begetting God' who cannot be identified with the begotten.

Text: The Papal documents are found in: P. COUSTANT, Epistolae Romanorum Pontificum 1. Paris, 1721. — P. COUSTANT-SCHOENEMANN, Romanorum Pontif. Epistolae. Göttingen, 1796.

Translations: German: S. WENZLOWSKY, Die Briefe der Päpste 1 (BKV). Kempten, 1875.

Studies: C. SILVA TAROUCA, Le antiche lettere dei Papi e le loro edizioni: CC 72 (1921) 13–22; 323–336. — H. GETZENY, Stil und Form der ältesten Papstbriefe bis auf Leo den Grossen. Tübingen Diss. Günzburg, 1922. — G. BARDY, L'autorité du Siège Romain et les controverses du 3e siècle: RSR (1924) 255ff. — G. LA PIANA, The Roman Church at the End of the Second Century: HThR 18 (1925) 201–277. — E. LACOSTE, Les Papes à travers les âges 2: De s. Pie I à s. Fabien. Paris, 1929. — E. CASPAR, Geschichte des Papsttums 1. Tübingen, 1930, 22ff. — C. SILVA TAROUCA, Nuovi studi sulle antiche lettere dei papi. 2nd part: Greg 12 (1931) 349–425. — G. BUONCUORE, Da S. Pio I a S. Vittore I. Siena, 1932.

DIONYSIUS OF CORINTH

An outstanding writer among the non-Roman bishops is Dionysius of Corinth who corresponded with Pope Soter about the year 170 A.D. Eusebius (*Hist. eccl.* 4,23) gives a description of his eight letters. Since none of his writings are extant the report of Eusebius is important. It runs as follows:

Concerning Dionysius, it must be first said that he was appointed to the throne of the episcopate of the diocese of Corinth, and that he communicated his divine industry ungrudgingly not only to those under him but also to those at a distance, rendering himself most useful to all in the general epistles which he drew up for the churches. Among them the letter to Lacedaemonians is an instruction in orthodoxy on the subject of peace and unity. And the letter to

the Athenians is a call to faith and to life according to the
Gospel, and for despising this he rebukes them as all but
apostates from the truth since the martyrdom of Publius,
their leader in the persecution of that time. He mentions
that Quadratus was appointed their bishop after the martyrdom of Publius, and testifies that through his zeal they had
been brought together and received the revival of their
faith. Moreover, he mentions that Dionysius the Areopagite
was converted by the Apostle Paul to the faith according to
the narrative in the Acts and was the first to be appointed
to the bishopric of the diocese of Athens.

There is another extant letter of his to the Nicomedians in
which he combats the heresy of Marcion and compares it
with the rule of the truth. He also wrote to the Church
sojourning in Gortyna together with the other Cretan dioceses
and welcomes their bishop Philip for the reputation of the
Church in his charge for many noble acts, and he enjoins
care against heretical error. He also wrote to the Church sojourning in Amastris, together with the churches in Pontus,
and mentioned that Bacchylides and Elpistus had urged
him to write; he adduces interpretations of the divine scriptures and mentions by name their bishop Palmas. He gives
them many exhortations about marriage and chastity and
orders them to receive those who are converted from any
backsliding, whether of conduct or of heretical error.

To this list has been added another epistle to Gnossus in
which he exhorts Pinytos, the bishop of the diocese, not to
put on the brethren a heavy compulsory burden concerning
chastity, and to consider the weaknesses of the many.

There is, moreover, extant a letter of Dionysius to the
Romans addressed to Soter, who was then bishop, and there
is nothing better than to quote the words in which he welcomes the custom of the Romans, which was observed down
to the persecutions in our own time (cf. above, p. 279).

In this same letter he also quotes the letter of Clement to
the Corinthians, showing that from the beginning it had
been the custom to read it in the church. 'Today we observed the holy day of the Lord and read out your letter
which we shall continue to read out from time to time for

our admonition, as we do with that which was formerly sent to us through Clement. . . '

Besides these there is extant another letter of Dionysius to Chrysophora, a most faithful Christian, in which he writes to her suitably imparting to her the proper spiritual food. Such are the facts about Dionysius (LCL).

From this passage it appears almost certain that the letters of Bishop Dionysius, except for the last one, were collected into a volume, perhaps during his lifetime. Eusebius must have known them in this form. The letters of Dionysius to the different Christian communities were held in universal esteem, because he himself reports that the heretics tried to falsify them:

When Christians asked me to write new letters I wrote them, and the apostles of the devil have filled them with tares, by leaving out some things and by putting in others. But woe awaits them. Therefore it is no wonder that some have gone about to falsify even the scriptures of the Lord, when they have plotted against writings so inferior (Eusebius, *Hist. eccl.* 4, 23,12, LCL).

The heretics to whom he refers must be the disciples of Marcion and Montanus, because in the third letter which was addressed to the Nicomedians he refuted the heresy of Marcion, while the letter to the Christians of Amastris and the one to those of Gnossus dealt with problems which resulted from the Montanistic movement.

W. BAUER, Rechtgläubigkeit und Ketzerei im ältesten Christentum. Tübingen, 1934, 128–131. — J. HOH, Die kirchliche Busse im zweiten Jahrhundert. Breslau, 1932, 87–89.

PINYTUS OF GNOSSUS

One of the letters of Bishop Dionysius of Corinth was addressed to Pinytus of Gnossus in Crete. The letter with which Pinytus answered was evidently embodied in the corpus of the letters of Dionysius. Eusebius after he has mentioned the letter of Dionysius to Pinytos continues:

'To this Pinytus replied that he admired and welcomed Dionysius, but exhorted him in turn to provide at some time more solid food, and to nourish the people under him with another

more advanced letter, so that they might not be fed continually
on milky words and be caught unaware by old age while still
treated as children. In this letter the orthodoxy of Pinytus in the
faith, his care for those under him, his learning and theological
understanding, are shown as in a most accurate image' (Eusebius,
Hist. eccl. 4,23,8 LCL).

St. Jerome lists Pinytus in his *De viris illustribus*, 28.

SERAPION OF ANTIOCH

Serapion was the eighth bishop of Antioch. His episcopate
corresponds more or less with the reign of Septimius Severus. His
letter to Pontius and Caricus deals with the Montanistic heresy,
and states that 'the so-called new prophecy of this false order is
abominated in the whole of Christendom, throughout the world'
(Eusebius, *Hist. eccl.* 5,19,2, LCL). Another letter was addressed
to the church of Rhossus in Cilicia on the Syrian coast of the
gulf of Issus. Eusebius quotes a passage from this letter (*ibid.*
6,12,3–6) which deals with the apocryphal *Gospel of St. Peter*:

> For our part, brethren, we receive both Peter and the
> other apostles as Christ, but the writings which falsely bear
> their names we reject, as men of experience, knowing that
> such were not handed down to us. For I myself, when I
> came among you, imagined that all of you clung to the true
> faith; and without going through the Gospels put forward
> by them in the name of Peter, I said: 'If this is the only
> thing that seemingly causes captious feelings among you,
> let it be read.' But since I have now learnt, from what has been
> told me, that their mind was lurking in some hole of heresy,
> I shall give diligence to come again to you; wherefore,
> brethren, expect me quickly. But we, brethren, gathering
> to what kind of heresy Marcianus belonged, were enabled
> by others to study this very Gospel, that is, by the succes-
> sors of those who began it, whom we call Docetae (for most
> of the ideas belong to their teaching) – using the material
> supplied by them, we were enabled to go through it, and
> discover that the most part indeed was in accordance with
> the true teaching of the Savior, but that some things were
> added, which also we place below for your benefit.

It is interesting that a large tragment of this Gospel, discovered at Akhmim in 1886, corresponds exactly to Serapion's
description. It is on the whole orthodox but contains strange ideas
inspired by Docetism. (For the date and editions of this Gospel
cf. above, p. 114).

Eusebius knew of a third letter of Serapion which was addressed
to a certain Domnus, 'who had fallen away from the faith of
Christ, at the time of the persecution, to Jewish will-worship'
(*Hist. eccl.* 6,12,1, LCL). Eusebius adds that it is likely that other
writings of Serapion existed and were preserved by other persons.

2. THE THEOLOGICAL REFUTATION OF THE HERESIES

In order to destroy the influence of the heretical doctrines on
the members of the Church the theological refutation of the
heresiarchs had as its purpose to expose their errors and to describe correctly the teaching of the Apostles and their rightly appointed successors regarding God, the creation of the world and
of man, incarnation and redemption. The majority of the numerous treatises issued during this campaign were lost. Of the many
anti-Gnostic works of the second century and their authors we
know only what Eusebius reports in his *Ecclesiastical History*. He
mentions (4,24) two anti-Gnostic writings of Bishop Theophilus
of Antioch, one against Hermogenes, the other against Marcion.
Bishop Philip of Gortyna composed an 'excellent treatise against
Marcion' (4,25). Agrippa Castor wrote against Basilides (4,7,
6-8); Modestus against Marcion (4,25), and Rhodon against
Marcion and Apelles (5,13). Maximus treated the problem of
evil and the creation of matter (5,27). Musanus refuted the Encratites (4,28). In addition, the treatises of Candidus and Apion
on Genesis, of Sextus on the resurrection and of Heraclitus 'On
the Apostle' which Eusebius mentions (5,27) were written against
the Gnostic heresies. However, all of these treatises are lost. One
of whose work we have fragments is Hegesippus.

HEGESIPPUS

Hegesippus was born in the Orient. Eusebius (*Hist. eccl.* 4,22,8)
reports that he (Hegesippus) made 'extracts from the Gospel ac-

cording to the Hebrews, and from the Syriac and particularly from the Hebrew languages, showing that he had been converted from among the Hebrews, and mentions points as coming from the unwritten tradition of the Jews.'

There are reasons for supposing that he was a Hellenistic Jew. He made a journey which took him to Corinth and Rome and of which he gives the following account:

'And the Church of the Corinthians remained in the true doctrine until Primus was bishop of Corinth, and I conversed with them on my voyage to Rome and spent some days with the Corinthians, during which we were refreshed by the true word. When I was in Rome I covered the list of the succession until Anicetus whose deacon was Eleutherus; Soter succeeded Anicetus, and after him came Eleutherus. In each list and in each city things are as the law, the prophets, and the Lord preach' (Euseb., *Hist. eccl.* 4, 22,2–3).

From these words it appears that Hegesippus visited Rome during the pontificate of Pope Anicetus (155–156) and remained there up to the time of Pope Eleutherus (174–189). The reason for his journey was the alarming spread of the Gnostic heresy. He intended to collect information regarding the true doctrine from several of the most important Churches, and above all to hear about the doctrine of Rome. After his return to the Orient he published an account of his journey in his 'memoirs', ὑπομνήματα. This work, which is no longer extant, comprised five books. It was a polemic against Gnosticism. Eusebius, who has preserved a number of fragments, testifies (*ibidem* 4,7,15–8,2) to the controversial character of this work in the following words: 'At the time spoken of, the truth again brought forward for itself more champions who campaigned against the godless heresies not only by unwritten arguments but also in written demonstrations. Among these Hegesippus was famous and of his words we have already made much use; for from his tradition we have quoted details as to the apostolic age. He collected his material in five books, giving in the simplest style of writing the unerring tradition of the Apostolic preaching (τὴν ἀπλανῆ παράδοσιν τοῦ ἀποστολικοῦ κηρύγματος).'

Most of the fragments preserved by Eusebius deal with the early history of the Church of Jerusalem, e.g., with the legend

286   THE BEGINNINGS OF ANTI-HERETICAL LITERATURE

of the death of St. James, the brother of the Lord, with Simeon, the second bishop of that city and with the relatives of Jesus. The question of Hegesippus' list of the popes has remained controversial. According to C. H. Turner and E. Caspar, Eusebius' words γενόμενος δὲ ἐν ʿΡώμῃ διαδοχὴν ἐποιησάμην μέχρις Ἀνικήτου do not indicate that Hegesippus compiled a list of the bishops of Rome in order of their succession but that he in his crusade against the heresies of his time visited Corinth, Rome and other metropolitan cities in order to ascertain the διαδοχή, that is, the tradition or preservation of the true doctrine.

Editions: MG 5, 1307-1328. — TH. ZAHN, Forschungen zur Geschichte des neutestamentlichen Kanons und der altkirchlichen Literatur 6. Erlangen, 1900, 228-273. — E. PREUSCHEN, Antilegomena. 2nd edit. Tübingen, 1905, 107-113. — H. J. LAWLOR, Eusebiana: Essays on the Ecclesiastical History of Eusebius. Oxford, 1912, 1-107.

Studies: C. ALLEMAND-LAVIGERIE, De Hegesippo disquisitio historica. Paris 1850. — TH. JESS, Hegesippos nach seiner kirchengeschichtlichen Bedeutung: Zeitschrift für die historische Theologie 35 (1865) 3-95. — F. NÖSGEN, Der kirchliche Standpunkt Hegesipps: ZKG 2 (1878) 193-233. — A. HILGEN-FELD, Hegesippus und die Apostelgeschichte: Zeitschrift für wissenschaftl. Theologie 21 (1878) 297-330. — H. DANNREUTHER, Du témoignage d'Hégé-sippe sur l'Eglise chrétienne aux deux premiers siècles. Nancy, 1878. — H. J. LAWLOR, Two Notes on Eusebius: Hermathena 11 (1901) 10-49; idem, Hegesippus and the Apocalypse: JThSt 8 (1907) 436-444. For Hegesippus' catalogue of the popes see: J. B. LIGHTFOOT, The Apostolic Fathers. Pt. I, Vol. I, 327-333. — F. X. FUNK, Der Papstkatalog Hegesipps: HJG 9 (1888) 674-677; idem, Zum angeblichen Papstkatalog Hegesipps: HJG 11 (1890) 77-80; idem, Zur Frage nach dem Papstkatalog Hegesipps: Kirchengeschicht-liche Abhandlungen und Untersuchungen 1. Paderborn, 1897, 373-390. — J. CHAPMAN, La chronologie des premières listes épiscopales de Rome: RB 18 (1901) 399-417; 19 (1902) 13-37; 145-170. — C. H. TURNER in: H. B. SWETE, Essays on the Early History of the Church (1918) 297ff. — E. CASPAR, Die älteste römische Bischofsliste. Berlin, 1926, 233ff., 443ff. — H. LECLERCQ, DAL 9, 1207-1236. — J. RANFT, Der Ursprung des kathol. Traditionsprin-zips.Würzburg, 1931, 33ff.; E. CASPAR, Geschichte des Papsttums 1. Tübingen, 1930, 8ff. — J. T. SHOTWELL, and L. R. LOOMIS, The See of Peter. New York, 1927, 248-251. — TH. KLAUSER, Die Anfänge der römischen Bischofsliste: BoZ (1931) 193-213. — E. KOHLMEYER, Zur Ideologie des ältesten Papst-tums: Succession und Tradition: ThStKr 103 (1931) 230-243. — W. BAUER, Rechtgläubigkeit und Ketzerei im ältesten Christentum. Tübingen, 1934, 199f., 216f. — H. J. BARDSLEY, Reconstructions of Early Christian Docu-ments, vol. I, 1935. — G. BARDY, La Théologie de l'Eglise de saint Clément de Rome à saint Irénée. Paris, 1945, 196-198. — E. BUONAIUTI, Marcione ed Egesippo: Religio (1936) 401-413. — L. HERRMANN, La famille du Christ

d'après Hégésippe: Rev. de l'univ. de Bruxelles 42 (1937) 387-394. — H.
SUHLIN, Noch einmal Jacobus 'Oblias': Bibl 28 (1947) 152-53.

IRENAEUS OF LYONS

Irenaeus of Lyons is by far the most important of the theologians of the second century. The exact year of his birth is not known, but it was probably between the year 140 and 160. His native city was in Asia Minor, and most probably it was Smyrna, because in his letter to the Roman presbyter Florinus, he tells us that in his early youth he had listened to the sermons of Bishop Polycarp of Smyrna. His letter reveals such an accurate knowledge of this martyr and bishop that it could not have been gained except through personal acquaintance:

For, when I was still a boy, I knew you (Florinus) in lower Asia, in Polycarp's house, when you were a man of rank in the royal hall, and endeavoring to stand well with him. I remember the events of those days more clearly than those which happened recently, for what we learn as children grows up with the soul and is united to it, so that I can speak even of the place in which the blessed Polycarp sat and disputed, how he came in and went out, the character of his life, the appearance of his body, the discourses which he made to the people, how he reported his intercourse with John and with the others who had seen the Lord, how he remembered their words, and what were the things concerning the Lord which he had heard from them, and about their miracles, and about their teachings, and how Polycarp had received them from the eye-witnesses of the Word of Life, and reported all things in agreement with the Scriptures. I listened eagerly even then to these things through the mercy of God which was given me, and made notes of them, not on paper, but in my heart, and ever by the grace of God do I truly ruminate on them (Euseb. *Hist. eccl.* 5,20,5-7).

From these words it is evident that through Polycarp Irenaeus was in touch with the Apostolic age. For reasons unknown Irenaeus left Asia Minor and went to Gaul. In the year 177 (178) as presbyter of the Church of Lugdunum he was sent by the martyrs of that city to Pope Eleutherus in Rome to mediate in a question of Montanism. The letter which on this occasion he carried to the Pope gave him an excellent recommendation: 'We have asked our brother and companion Irenaeus to bring this letter to you, and we beg you to hold him in esteem, for he is zealous for the covenant of Christ. For had we known that rank can confer righteousness on anyone, we should first of all have recommended him as being a presbyter of that church (i.e. Lugdunum) for that is his position' (Euseb. *Hist. eccl.* 5,4,2). When Irenaeus returned from Rome, the old bishop, Photinus, had died a martyr, and Irenaeus became his successor. Later, Pope Victor I having excommunicated the Asiatics in the Paschal controversy, Irenaeus wrote to a number of these bishops and to Victor himself exhorting them to make peace. For this reason Eusebius (5,24,17) states that Irenaeus lived up to his name, because he proved himself to be a real peacemaker, εἰρηνοποιός. After this incident he drops completely out of sight, and even the year of his death is unknown. Not before the time of Gregory of Tours (*Historia Francorum*, 1,27) do we find any mention of his having died as a martyr. Since Eusebius gives no hint of such a martyrdom, this late testimony seems to be very questionable.

THE WRITINGS OF IRENAEUS

In addition to the administration of his diocese, Irenaeus dedicated himself to the task of refuting the Gnostic heresies by means of his extensive writings. In these works he gives an excellent refutation and critical analysis of the fantastic speculations of the Gnostics. With a comprehensive knowledge of sources he combines moral seriousness and religious enthusiasm. His thorough acquaintance with ecclesiastical tradition, which he owed to his friendship with Polycarp and with other disciples of the Apostles, was a great asset in his fight against heresy. Unfortunately his writings were lost at an early time. Only two of the many works which he composed in his native Greek are extant. One of these two is his most important work, and is preserved not in the Greek original but in a Latin translation, which is very literal. Regarding the date of this translation, critics differ widely.

I. This main work of Irenaeus bears the title Ἔλεγχος καὶ

ἀνατροπὴ τῆς ψευδονόμου γνώσεως, *Detection and Overthrow of the Pretended but False Gnosis*. It is usually called *Adversus Haereses*. As the original title indicates, the work is composed of two parts. The first part deals with the detection of Gnostic heresy. Although this part is confined to the first book, it is invaluable for the history of Gnosticism. Irenaeus starts with a detailed description of the doctrine of the Valentinians, which he intersperses with polemic. Only when he has done this does he take up the beginnings of Gnosticism. He speaks of Simon Magus and Menander, and then cites the other leaders of Gnostic schools and sects in the following order: Satornil, Basilides, Carpocrates, Cerinthus, the Ebionites, the Nicolaites, Cerdon, Marcion, Tatian, and the Encratites. But he emphasizes the fact that with these names the number of those who in one way or another departed from the truth is not exhausted. The second part, the 'Overthrow', comprises the four books which follow:

Book II refutes the gnosis of the Valentinians and the Marcionites from reason;

Book III, from the doctrine of the Church on God and Christ;

Book IV, from the sayings of the Lord.

Book V treats almost exclusively of the resurrection of the flesh, which was denied by all the Gnostics. In conclusion he speaks of the millenium, and it is here that Irenaeus proves himself to be a chiliast. The whole work suffers from a lack of clear arrangement and unity of thought. Prolixity and frequent repetition make its perusal wearisome. The reason for this defect is most probably that the author wrote the work intermittently. According to the preface of the third book, he had already sent the first two books together to the friend at whose request they had been composed; the other three followed one by one. But it seems that the project was designed from the beginning, because the author refers already in the third book to his later remarks about the Apostle Paul, which follow only in the fifth book. Moreover, at the end of the third book he announces the fourth and at the the end of the fourth the fifth. But it would appear that Irenaeus inserted additions and enlargements from time to time. Evidently he did not have the ability to shape his materials into a homogeneous whole. The defects of form which offend the reader are the result of this lack of synthesis. Nevertheless Irenaeus knows how to give a simple, clear, and convincing description of the doctrines of the Church. His work remains therefore of the greatest importance for the knowledge of the Gnostic systems and the theology of the early Church. Irenaeus makes no pretensions to producing a piece of artistic literature. 'Thou wilt not expect from me, who am resident among the Celts, and am accustomed for the most part to use a barbarous dialect, any display of rhetoric, which I have never learned, or any excellence of composition, which I have never practiced, or any beauty and persuasiveness of style, to which I make no pretensions. But thou wilt accept in a kindly spirit what I in a like spirit write to thee simply, truthfully, and in my own homely way' (*Adv. Haer. I*, Praef. 3).

For his description of the Gnostic doctrine Irenaeus relies on his own extensive reading of Gnostic treatises, but he also made use of older anti-heretical writers.

It is extremely difficult to identify these sources, since almost all of them have been lost, even some of those which Irenaeus mentions specifically by name, such as 'The Sayings of Papias of Hieropolis', 'The Sayings of the Elders of Asia Minor', and the 'Treatise Against Marcion' by Justin Martyr. We definitely know that Irenaeus used these works, but it is impossible to determine the extent of his dependence because all of these works have been lost. According to F. Loofs, the writings of Bishop Theophilus of Antioch were one of the main sources of Irenaeus. But unfortunately the two anti-Gnostic treatises, one *Against Hermogenes*, the other *Against Marcion*, which Theophilus wrote are no longer extant. Only their titles are preserved by Eusebius. We have of course Theophilus' *Discourse to Autolycus*, but Loofs himself must admit that none of the parallels which he established in comparing this work with the writings of Irenaeus are sufficient proof that Irenaeus made use of the book. Moreover, it is not even certain that Theophilus' treatise *Against Marcion* existed at the time when Irenaeus wrote his main work against the Gnostics.

THE TRADITION OF THE TEXT

1. The Latin version, in which the complete text is extant, is preserved in a number of manuscripts. H. Jordan and A.

Souter think that this translation was made in North Africa
between the years 370 and 420. According to H. Koch, however, it must have originated before 250, because Cyprian made
use of it. W. Sanday goes beyond this, and assigns it to the
date 200.

2. Quite a number of fragments from the lost Greek original
are preserved by Hippolytus, Eusebius, and especially by Epiphanius. Additional fragments are found in some *catenae* and
papyri. From these fragments almost the whole of the complete
text can be reconstructed.

3. A literal translation in Armenian of the fourth and fifth
books was discovered and edited by E. Ter-Minassiantz.

4. Twenty-three fragments are extant in Syriac translations.

Editions: R. Massuet, Paris, 1710; Venice, 1734. Reprinted in MG 7. —
A. Stieren, 1-2. London, 1848/53. — W. W. Harvey, Sancti Irenaei ep.
Lugdunensis libros quinque adversus haereses. 2 vols. Cambridge, 1857. The
Armenian translation of Books IV and V was published by E. Ter-Minas-
siantz, TU 35. 1910.

Translations: J. Keble, A Library of Fathers of the Holy Catholic Church,
vol. 42. Oxford, 1872. — A. Roberts and W. H. Rambaut, The Ante-Nicene
Christian Library, vol. 5 (Edinburgh, 1868), 1-480, vol. 9 (1869) 1-187. —
ANF 1, 315-578. — A translation of the principal passages by F. R. Montgom-
ery Hitchcock, The Treatise of Irenaeus of Lugdunum Against the Heresies
(SPCK). 2 vols. London, 1916. *German:* E. Klebba, BKV² 3-4. Kempten,
1912. — Selected passages: H. U. von Balthasar, Geduld des Reifens.
Basel, 1944. *Dutch:* H. U. Meyboom, Ireneus, Weerlegging en afwending der
valschelijk dusgenaamde wetenschap. Leyden, 1920.

Studies: For the Greek text see Diobouniotis and Harnack, TU 38,3. 1911.
For the Latin version cf. W. Sanday and C. H. Turner, Novum Testamentum sancti Irenaei. Oxford, 1923. Souter, *ibidem* LXVff. Turner, *ibidem*,
CLXXff. — H. Koch, I rapporti di Cipriano con Ireneo e altri scrittori greci:
RR 5 (1929) 137-163; *idem*, Ancora Cipriano e la letteratura cristiana greca:
RR 5 (1929) 523-537. — E. Klostermann, Neue Beiträge zur Geschichte der
lateinischen Handschriften des Irenaeus: ZNW 36 (1937) 1-34. — S. Lund-
ström, Studien zur lateinischen Irenaeusübersetzung. Lund, 1943; *idem*, Text-
kritische Beiträge zur lateinischen Irenaeusübersetzung: Eranos Löfstedtianus.
Uppsala, 1945, 285-300. — For the Armenian version see: H. Jordan,
Armenische Irenaeusfragmente (TU 36,3). 1913. — A. Merk, Der armenische
Irenaeus Adversus Haereses: ZKTh 50 (1926) 371-407; 481-514. —
S. Euringer, ThR 27 (1928) 309f. — J. A. Robinson, The Armenian
Capitula of Irenaeus Adv. Haereses, IV: JThSt 32 (1930) 71-74; *idem*, Notes
on the Armenian Version of Irenaeus Adv. Haereses IV-V: JThSt 32 (1931)
153-166, 370-393. — J. Stiglmayr, Irenaeus Adv. Haer. 3,20 und die Dar-

stellung des Jonas auf altchristlichen Denkmälern: ThGl (1916) 294ff. — T. Schneider, Die Amwas-Inschrift und Irenaeus adv. Haer. II, 24,2: ZNW 29 (1930), 155–158. — L. Froidevaux, Une difficulté du texte de S. Irénée (Adv. haer. IV, 14): ROChr 8 (1932), 441–443. — F. Loofs, Theophilus von Antiochien Adversus Marcionem und die anderen theologischen Quellen bei Irenaeus (TU 46,2). 1930. — J. Stiglmayr, ThR 29 (1930) 290ff. — F. R. M. Hitchcock, Loof's Theory of Theophilus of Antioch as a Source of Irenaeus: JThSt 38 (1937) 130–139, 255–265. — B. Reynders, La polémique de S. Irénée: RTAM 7 (1935) 5–27. — R. Forni, Problemi della tradizione. Ireneo di Lione. Milan, 1939.

II. Besides this main work of Irenaeus we possess another Ἐπίδειξις τοῦ ἀποστολικοῦ κηρύγματος, The Demonstration of the Apostolic Teaching. For a long time not more than the title of this work (Euseb. Hist. eccl. 5,26) was known. In 1904 the entire text was discovered in an Armenian version by Ter-Mekerttschian who edited it for the first time in 1907. This work is not a catechesis as some scholars thought, but an apologetic treatise as the title suggests. It is composed of two parts. After some introductory remarks on the motives which led to the writing of this work (ch. 1–3) the first part (ch. 4–42) deals with the essential content of the Christian faith. The Three Divine Persons, the Creation and Fall of Man, the Incarnation and Redemption are treated. Thus the whole guidance accorded to mankind by God, from Adam to Christ, is described. The second (ch. 42–97) adduces proofs for the truth of the Christian revelation from the prophecies of the Old Testament, and presents Jesus as the Son of David and the Messias. The author argues that:

if the prophets thus predicted that the Son of God would appear on earth, if they announced where on earth, how and in what manner he would manifest himself, and if the Lord took upon himself all that had been foretold of him, our belief in him is firmly established and the tradition of our preaching must be true, i.e., true is the testimony of the Apostles who were sent by God, and who preached all over the world about the sacrifice which the Son of God made by suffering death and resurrection (ch. 86).

In conclusion the author exhorts his readers to a life in accordance with the faith and warns them against heresy and its godlessness. This outline of the contents shows that the Apology has no polemical part. It is limited to a positive proof of the true doctrine and refers the reader for a refutation of the Gnostics to the main work of Irenaeus.

Editions and Translations: The Armenian version was published by K. TER-MEKERTTSCHIAN and E. TER-MINASSIANTZ, TU 31,3. 1907, with German translation. Latin translation by S. WEBER, Freiburg i. B., 1917. Republished with English and French translations by E. TER-MINASSIANTZ, PO 12,5. Paris, 1919. *English translation:* J. A. ROBINSON, St. Irenaeus, The Demonstration of the Apostolic Preaching, Translated from the Armenian (SPCK). London, 1920. *German:* S. WEBER, BKV² 4, 1912. — *Italian:* U. FALDATI. Rome, 1923. *Dutch:* H. U. MEYBOOM. Leyden, 1920.

Studies: A. NUSSBAUMER, Das Ursymbolum nach der Epideixis des hl. Irenaeus. Paderborn, 1921. — F. LOOFS, l.c., 434ff.

III. Of the other works of Irenaeus we have only a few fragments or the titles.

1. Irenaeus addressed a letter to the Roman presbyter Florinus *On the Sole Sovereignty* or *That God is Not the Author of Evil.* Eusebius in his *Historia ecclesiastica* (5,20,4–8) quotes a long passage from this letter.

2. After Florinus had renounced his faith, Irenaeus wrote *On the Ogdoad.* Eusebius gives the closing words of this treatise (*Hist. eccl.* 5,20,2).

3. Irenaeus addressed another letter *On Schism* to Blastus, who lived in Rome, and who, like Florinus, was bent on making innovations. Only the title of this letter has been preserved by Eusebius (*Hist. eccl.* 5,20,1).

4. A fragment of a letter which Irenaeus sent to Pope Victor is extant in Syriac. In this letter he petitions the Pope to proceed against Florinus and to suppress his writings.

5. Eusebius gives (*Hist. eccl.* 5,23,3; 24,11–17) excerpts from the letter which Irenaeus wrote to Pope Victor concerning the computation of Easter (cf. above, p. 280).

6. In addition Eusebius (*Hist. eccl.* 5,26) was familiar with his treatise *Concerning Knowledge,* and with 'a little book of various discourses in which he mentions the *Epistle to the Hebrews* and the so-called *Wisdom of Solomon,* quoting certain passages from them.' Most probably the latter was a collection of sermons.

7. The fragments which Ch. M. Pfaff published in 1715, allegedly from manuscripts in Turin, were proved to be forgeries by A. Harnack (TU 20,3. Leipzig, 1900).

THE THEOLOGY OF IRENAEUS

As a theologian Irenaeus is important for two reasons. He unmasked the pseudo-Christian character of the gnosis, and thereby accelerated the elimination of the adherents of this heresy from the Church. Secondly, so succesfully did he defend the articles of faith of the Catholic Church which the Gnostics had denied or misinterpreted that he deserves to be called the founder of Christian theology. His mind was not given to theorizing nor did he make any new theological discoveries. On the contrary he was always inclined to be suspicious of any science which aimed at speculation:

It is better that one should have no knowledge whatever of any one reason why a single thing in creation has been made but should believe in God and continue in his love than that, puffed up through knowledge of this kind, he should fall away from that love which is the life of man; and that he should search after no other knowledge except Jesus Christ, the Son of God, who was crucified for us, than that by subtle questions and hairsplitting expressions, he should fall into impiety (*Adv. Haer.* 2,26,1).

In spite of his suspicious attitude toward speculative theology, Irenaeus deserves great credit for having been the first to formulate in dogmatic terms the entire Christian doctrine.

1. *Trinity*

Although his contemporary Theophilus of Antioch had already employed the term τριάς, Irenaeus does not make use of it in defining the one God in three Persons. He prefers rather to emphasize another aspect of the Divinity in his battle with the Gnostics: the identity of the one true God with the creator of the world, with the God of the Old Testament, and with the Father of the Logos. Although Irenaeus does not discuss the relationships of the three Divine Persons within God, he is convinced that the existence of the Father, Son and Holy Ghost is clearly proved in the history of mankind. They existed before the creation of man, because the words, 'Let us make man after our image and likeness' are addressed by the Father to the Son and the Holy Spirit, whom St. Irenaeus allegorically calls the 'hands of God'

(*Adv. Haer.* 5,1,3; 5,5,1; 5,28,1). Again and again Irenaeus explains how the Holy Ghost in the service of the Logos fills the prophets with the chrism of inspiration, and how the Father gave the orders for all this. Thus the whole economy of salvation in the Old Testament is an excellent instruction regarding the three Persons in the one God.

A. MARMORSTEIN, Zur Erklärung der Gottesnamen bei Irenaeus: ZNW 25 (1926) 253–258. — J. LEBRETON, La connaissance de Dieu chez S. Irénée: RSR 16 (1926) 385–406; *idem*, Histoire du dogme de la Trinité II: de S. Clément à S. Irénée. 2nd ed., 1928. — G. L. PRESTIGE, Περιχωρέω and Περιχώρησις in the Fathers: JThSt 29 (1928) 242ff.

2. Christology

a) Concerning the relation of the Son to the Father Irenaeus says clearly and plainly:

If anyone says to us 'how then was the Son produced by the Father?' we reply to him, that no man understands that production or generation or calling or by whatever name one may describe his generation, which is in fact altogether indescribable... but the Father only who begat, and the Son who was begotten. Since, therefore, his generation is unspeakable, those who strive to set forth generations and productions cannot be right in their mind, inasmuch as they undertake to describe things which are indescribable (2,28,6).

Moreover, we find in Irenaeus the first attempt to grasp the relationship between the Father and the Son in a speculative manner: 'God has been declared through the Son, who is in the Father and has the Father in himself' (3,6,2).

With these words Irenaeus teaches the *perichoresis* or *circumincessio*. Just as he defends the identity of the Father with the creator of the world against the Gnostics, so he teaches that there is only one Christ, although we give him different names. Therefore Christ is identical with the Son of God, with the Logos, with the God-man Jesus, with our Savior and our Lord.

b) *Recapitulation:* The heart of Irenaeus' Christology and indeed of his entire theology is his theory of recapitulation (ἀνακεφαλαίωσις). Although he borrowed this idea from the Apostle Paul, he developed it considerably. Recapitulation is for

Irenaeus a taking up in Christ of all since the beginning. God rehabilitates the earlier divine plan for the salvation of mankind which was interrupted by the fall of Adam, and gathers up his entire work from the beginning to renew, to restore, to reorganize it in his incarnate Son, who in this way becomes for us a second Adam. Since by the fall of man the whole human race was lost, the Son of God had to become man in order to effect as such the re-creation of mankind:

The things which had perished possessed flesh and blood. For the Lord, taking dust from the earth, moulded man; and it was upon his behalf that all the dispensations of the Lord's advent took place. He had himself, therefore, flesh and blood, recapitulating in himself not a certain other, but that original handiwork of the Father, seeking out that thing which had perished (5,14,2).

By this recapitulation of the original man, not only Adam personally but the whole human race was renovated and restored:

When he became incarnate and was made man, he recapitulated in himself the long history of man, summing up and giving us salvation in order that we might receive again in Christ Jesus what we had lost in Adam, that is, the image and likeness of God (3,18,1).

At the same time the evil effects of the disobedience of the first Adam are destroyed: 'God recapitulated in himself the ancient formation of man, that he might kill sin, deprive death of its power and vivify man' (3,18,7). In this manner the second Adam had renewed the ancient conflict against the devil, and conquered him.

Now the Lord would not have recapitulated in himself that ancient and primary enmity against the serpent, fulfilling the promise of the creator, if he had come from another Father. But as he is one and the same who formed us at the beginning and sent his Son at the end, the Lord did perform his command, being made of a woman, by both destroying our adversary and perfecting man after the image and likeness of God (5,21,2).

Thus Christ renewed everything by this recapitulation.

What then did the Lord bring at his coming? Know that he brought all newness, by bringing himself, who had been foretold. For this was announced, that a newness would come, to renew and give life to man (4,34,1).

F. R. M. HITCHCOCK, Irenaeus of Lugdunum. A Study of his Teaching. Cambridge, 1914. — A. D'ALÈS, La doctrine de la récapitulation en saint Irénée: RSR 6 (1916) 185–211. — G. N. BONWETSCH, Die Theologie des Irenaeus. Gütersloh, 1925. — J. LEBRETON, La connaissance de Dieu chez S. Irénée: RSR 16 (1926) 385–406. — L. CRISTIANI, S. Irénée, évêque de Lyon. Paris, 1927. — E. MERSCH, Le corps mystique du Christ I. Louvain, 1933, 250–281. — J. RIVIÈRE, Le dogme de la rédemption. Louvain, 1931, 95–145. — P. GÄCHTER, Unsere Einheit mit Christus nach dem hl. Irenaeus: ZkTh 58 (1934) 503–534. — A. VERRIELE, Le plan du salut d'après S. Irénée: RSR 14 (1934) 493–524. — B. REYNDERS, Optimisme et théocentrisme chez S. Irénée: RTAM 8 (1936) 225–252. — K. PRÜMM, Göttliche Planung und menschliche Entwicklung nach Irenaeus Adversus haereses: Schol 13 (1938) 206–224, 342–366. — M. VILLAIN, Une vive conscience de l'unité du corps mystique: S. Ignace d'Antioche et S. Irénée: RAp 66 (1938) 257–271. — W. GERICKE, Irenaeus und die Hohepriestervorstellung von Hebr. 6 und 7: Theologische Jahrbücher 7 (1939) 69–71. — K. PRÜMM, Zur Terminologie und zum Wesen der christlichen Neuheit bei Irenaeus: Pisciculi (1939) 192–219. — L. ESCOULA, Le verbe sauveur et illuminateur chez saint Irénée: NRTh (1939) 385–400; 551–567. — J. BARBEL, Christos Angelos. Bonn, 1941, 63–68. — E. SCHARL, Recapitulatio mundi. Der Rekapitulationsbegriff des hl. Irenaeus und seine Anwendung auf die Körperwelt. Freiburg i. B., 1941. — W. HUNGER, Der Gedanke der Weltplaneinheit und Adameinheit in der Theologie des hl. Irenaeus: Schol (1942) 161–177. — CH. MARTIN, Saint Irénée et son correspondant, le diacre Démètre de Vienne: RHE 38 (1942) 143–152. — TH. A. AUDET, Orientations théologiques chez saint Irénée: Traditio I (1943) 15–54. — J. DANIÉLOU, Saint Irénée et les origines de la théologie de l'histoire: RSR 34 (1947) 227–231.

3. Mariology

This idea of recapitulation has strongly influenced Irenaeus' doctrine regarding Mary. Justin was the first to show the parallelism between Eve and Mary, as Paul had done between Adam and Christ. Irenaeus extends this parallelism:

In accordance with this design, Mary the Virgin is found obedient, saying 'Behold the handmaid of the Lord, be it done unto me according to thy word.' But Eve was disobedient; for she did not obey when as yet she was a virgin. And even as she, having indeed a husband, Adam, but being nevertheless as yet a virgin, having become disobedient, was made the cause of death both to herself and the whole human race; so also did Mary, having a man betrothed (to her) and being nevertheless a virgin, by yielding obedience, become *the cause of salvation*, both to herself and the whole human race. And on this account does the law term a woman betrothed to a man the wife of him who had betrothed her, although she was as yet a virgin; thus indicating the back reference from Mary to Eve, because what is joined together could not otherwise be put asunder than by inversion of the process by which these bonds of union had arisen, so that the former knots be cancelled by the latter, that the latter set the former again at liberty. And it has in fact happened, that the first compact looses from the second tie, but that the second tie takes the position of the first, which had been cancelled. For this reason did the Lord declare that the first should in truth be the last, and the last first. And the prophet too indicates the same, saying, 'Instead of fathers, children have been born unto thee.' For the Lord, having been born 'the First-begotten of the dead' and receiving into his bosom the ancient Fathers, has regenerated them unto the life of God, he having been made himself the beginning of those that live, as Adam became the beginning of those who die. Wherefore also Luke, commencing the genealogy with the Lord, carried it back to Adam, indicating that it was he who regenerated them into the gospel of life, and not they him. And thus also it was that the knot of Eve's disobedience was loosed by the obedience of Mary. For what the virgin Eve had bound fast through unbelief, this did the virgin Mary set free through faith (3,22,4).

According to Irenaeus, therefore, the procedure of redemption follows exactly the course of events of the fall of man. For every faulty step which man took, having been seduced by Satan, God exacts from him a compensation in order to make his victory over the seducer complete. Mankind receives a new progenitor in place of the first Adam. But since the first woman was also implicated in the fall by her disobedience, the healing process starts also by the obedience of a woman. Giving life to the New Adam, she becomes the true Eve, the true mother of the living, and the *causa salutis*. In this way Mary becomes the *advocata Evae*:

And if the former (Eve) did disobey God, yet the latter (Mary) was persuaded to be obedient to God, in order that the Virgin Mary might become the advocate of the virgin

Eve. And thus, as the human race fell into bondage to death by means of a virgin, so it is rescued by a virgin; virginal disobedience having been balanced in the opposite scale by virginal obedience (5,19,1). Moreover, Irenaeus extends the parallelism between Eve and Mary even further. He is so convinced that Mary is the new mother of mankind that he calls her the womb of mankind. Thus he teaches the universal motherhood of Mary. He speaks of the birth of Christ as 'the pure one opening purely that pure womb which regenerates men unto God' (4,33,11).

P. GALTIER, La vierge qui nous régénère: RSR 5 (1914) 136–145. — J.M. BOVER, La mediación universal de la 'Segunda Eva' en la tradición patrística: EE 2 (1923) 321–350. — W. SCHERER, Zur Mariologie des hl. Irenäus: ZkTh 47 (1923) 119–129. — H. KOCH, Adhuc virgo. Mariens Jungfrauschaft und Ehe in der altkirchlichen Überlieferung bis zum Ende des vierten Jahrhunderts (Beiträge zur histor. Theologie 2). Tübingen, 1929. — O. BARDENHEWER, Zur Mariologie des hl. Irenäus: ZkTh 55 (1931) 600–604. — J. JOUASSARD, Le premier-né de la Vierge chez S. Irénée et S. Hippolyte: RSRUS (1932) 509–532; (1933) 25–37. — J. GARÇON, La Mariologie de S. Irénée. Lyons, 1932. — M. A. GENEVOIS, La maternité universelle de Marie selon S. Irénée: RT 41 (1936) 26–51. — H. D. SIMONIN, La figure providentielle de la Vierge Marie: RJ (1936) 601ff. — H. KOCH, Virgo Eva-Virgo Maria. Neue Untersuchungen über die Lehre von der Jungfrauschaft und der Ehe Mariens in der ältesten Kirche. Berlin, 1937, 17–60. — K. ADAM, Theologische Bemerkungen zu Hugo Kochs Schrift: Virgo Eva-Virgo Maria: ThQ 119 (1938) 171–189. — B. PRZYBYLSKI, De Mariologia sancti Irenaei Lugdunensis. Rome, 1937. Cf. H. D. SIMONIN: RSPT 27 (1938) 261–262.

4. *Ecclesiology*

a) Even the ecclesiology of Irenaeus is linked up with his theory of recapitulation. God sums up in Christ not only the past but also the future. Therefore he made him the head of the entire Church, in order to perpetuate through her his work of renovation until the end of the world:

Thus there is one God the Father, as we have shown, and one Christ Jesus our Lord, who comes by a universal dispensation and recapitulates all things in himself. But in 'all things' man also is comprised, a creature of God; therefore he recapitulates man in himself. The invisible is become visible, the incomprehensible is become comprehensible, and the impassible possible; and the Logos is become man, recapitulating all things in himself. Thus, just as he is the first among heavenly and spiritual and invisible things, so also is he the first among visible and corporal things. He takes the primacy to himself and by making himself the head of the Church, he will draw all things to himself at the appointed time (*Adv. Haer.* 3,16,6).

b) Irenaeus is firmly convinced that the teaching of the Apostles continues to live on unaltered. This tradition is the source and the norm of the faith. It is the canon of truth. For Irenaeus this canon of truth seems to be the baptismal creed, for he says that we receive it in baptism (*Adv. Haer.* 1,9,4). He gives a description of the faith of the Church which follows exactly the Apostolic Symbol.

The Church, although scattered over the whole world even to its extremities, received from the Apostles and their disciples the faith in one God, the Father Almighty, Maker of heaven and earth, the seas and all that is in them, and in one Christ Jesus, the Son of God, who became incarnate for our salvation, and in the Holy Spirit, who by the prophets proclaimed the dispensation, the advent, the virgin birth, the passion and resurrection from the dead, the bodily ascension of the well-beloved Christ Jesus Our Lord into heaven, and his parousia (advent) from the heavens in the glory of the Father to gather up all things in himself and to raise the flesh of all mankind to life, in order that everything in heaven and in earth and under the earth should bow the knee to Christ Jesus our Lord and God, our Savior and our King, according to the will of the invisible Father, and that every tongue should confess to him, and that he should pronounce a just judgment upon all and dismiss the spirits of wickedness and the angels who transgressed and became apostates, and the ungodly, unrighteous, lawless and profane, into everlasting fire, but in his graciousness should confer life and the reward of incorruption and eternal glory upon those who have kept his commandments and have abided in his love either from the beginning of their life or since their repentance.

This preaching and this faith the Church, although scattered over the whole world, diligently observes, as if it occupied but one house, and believes as if it had but one mind, and preaches and teaches as if it had but one mouth. And although there are many dialects in the world, the meaning of the tradition is one and the same. For the same faith is held and handed down by the Churches established in the Germanies, the Spains, among the Celtic tribes, in the East, in Lybia, and in the central portions of the world. But as the sun, the creation of God, is one and the same in all the world, so is the light of the preaching of the truth, which shines on all who desire to come to the knowledge of the truth (*Adv. Haer.* 1,10,1–2 Hitchcock).

c) Only the Churches founded by the Apostles can be relied upon for the correct teaching of the faith and for the truth, because the uninterrupted succession of bishops in these churches guarantees the truth of their doctrine:

Anyone who wishes to discern the truth may see in every church in the whole world the Apostolic tradition clear and manifest. We can enumerate those who were appointed as bishops in the churches by the Apostles and their successors to our own day, who never knew and never taught anything resembling their (that is, the Gnostics') foolish doctrine. Had the Apostles known any such mysteries, which they taught privately and sub rosa to the perfect, they would surely have entrusted this teaching to the men in whose charge they placed the Churches. For they wished them to be without blame and reproach to whom they handed over their own position of authority (3,3,1, Hitchcock).

For this reason the heretics lack an essential qualification; they are not the successors of the Apostles and they do not have the charism of truth:

Wherefore it is incumbent to obey the presbyters who are in the Church, those who as I have shown possess the succession from the Apostles; those who, together with the succession of the episcopate, have received the certain gift of truth, according to the good pleasure of the Father (4,26,2 ANF).

P. BATIFFOL, L'Eglise naissante et le catholicisme. Paris, 1909, 195–276. — L. SPIKOWSKI, La doctrine de l'Eglise dans Irénée. Diss. Strassbourg, 1926. — W. SCHMIDT, Die Kirche bei Irenaeus. Helsingfors, 1934. — H. RAHNER, Flumina de ventre Christi. Die patristische Auslegung von Joh. 7,37–38:

Bibl (1940) 269–302; 367–403. — J. C. PLUMPE, Mater Ecclesia (SCA 5). Washington, 1943, 41–44. — G. BARDY, La Théologie de l'Eglise de saint Clément de Rome à saint Irénée. Paris, 1945, 167–169; 184–186; 186–198; 204–210. — H. HOLSTEIN, Les formules du symbole dans l'oeuvre de saint Irénée: RSR 34 (1947) 454–461. — M. S. ENSLIN, Irenaeus, Mostly Prolegomena: HThR 40 (1947) 137–165.

5. The Primacy of Rome

Irenaeus, after he has declared that he is fortunately in a position to enumerate the bishops appointed by the Apostles and their successors down to his own time, remarks that it would lead him too far afield were he to give the lists of succession of the bishops of all the churches founded by the Apostles. For this reason he wishes to limit himself to the list of bishops of the greatest of these churches (*Adv. Haer.* 3,3,2):

> But it would be very long in a book of this kind, to enumerate the episcopal lists in all the churches, but by pointing out the apostolic tradition and creed which has been brought down to us by a succession of bishops in the greatest, most ancient, and well known Church, founded by the two most glorious Apostles Peter and Paul at Rome, we can confute all those who in any other way, either for self-pleasing or for vainglory or blindness or badness, hold unauthorized meetings.

And then follows a very important statement. Unfortunately we do not possess the original Greek text of this sentence but only a Latin translation, which, however, is very slavish:

> *Ad hanc enim ecclesiam propter potentiorem principalitatem necesse est omnem convenire ecclesiam, hoc est eos qui sunt undique fideles, in qua semper ab his qui sunt undique, conservata est ea quae est ab apostolis traditio.*

The question arises: what is the meaning of the word *principalitas*? Unfortunately, the Latin words *principalitas*, *principalis*, *principaliter* can be used to translate quite a number of Greek words which differ considerably from one another, e.g. αὐθεντία, ἐξουσία, καθολικός, ἡγεμονικός, προηγουμένως, πρωτεύειν. Van den Eynde and Bardy suggest translating *principalitas* by ἀρχή, ἀρχαῖον or ἀρχαιότης. In that case Irenaeus would assign a higher place to the Church of Rome because of its 'superior origin', founded, as it was, by the two princes of the Apostles.

Ehrhard translated *propter potentiorem principalitatem* 'because of its more efficient leadership'. The entire passage would then read: For with this Church, because of its more efficient leadership, all Churches must agree, that is to say, the faithful of all places, because in it the apostolic tradition has been always preserved by the (faithful) of all places. Most probably the words 'must agree' are not to be understood in the sense of an obligation but of a fact. This is proved by the context because Irenaeus intends to demonstrate that the fables and fictions of the Gnostics are foreign to the Apostolic tradition. Accordingly, this passage we have cited does not refer to the ecclesiastical constitution but to the faith which is common to all individual churches, which is in sharp opposition to Gnosis and its speculations. Nevertheless this whole passage is of great importance for the history of the primacy, because Irenaeus attributes to the Church of Rome, 'a more efficient leadership' than to any other Church. Moreover, he states that this Church of Rome, by being founded by Peter and Paul, by her episcopal succession, and by her doctrine, is a conclusive proof of the Christian faith. The only possible intrinsic reason for the recognition of this preeminence of the Church of Rome is of course the dogma of the primacy. It is typical that Irenaeus after this passage enumerates the Roman bishops up to Eleutherus (174–189) and then continues:

In this order and by this succession, the ecclesiastical tradition from the Apostles and the preaching of the truth have come down to us. And this is most abundant proof that there is one and the same vivifying faith which the Church has received from the Apostles, preserved until now, and handed down in truth (3,3,3).

H. HAGMANN, Die römische Kirche und ihr Einfluss auf Disziplin und Dogma in den ersten drei Jahrhunderten. Freiburg i. B., 1864, 598–627: Irenaeus über den Primat der römischen Kirche. — A. HARNACK, Das Zeugnis des Irenaeus über das Ansehen der römischen Kirche: SAB (1893) 939–955. — J. CHAPMAN, Le témoignage de S. Irénée en faveur de la primauté romaine: RB 12 (1895) 49–64. — F. X. FUNK, Der Primat der römischen Kirche nach Ignatius und Irenaeus: Kirchengeschichtliche Abhandlungen und Untersuchungen 1 (Paderborn, 1897) 1–23. — H. BOEHMER, Zu dem Zeugnisse des Irenaeus von dem Ansehen der römischen Kirche: ZNW 7 (1906) 193–201. — C. A. KNELLER, Der hl. Irenaeus und die römische Kirche: Stimmen

11

aus Maria Laach 76 (1909) 402–421. — L. SALVATORELLI, La 'principalitas' della Chiesa Romana in Ireneo ed in Cipriano. Rome, 1910. — G. ESSER, Das Irenaeuszeugnis für den Primat der römischen Kirche: Katholik (1917) 1, 289–315; 2, 16–34. — A. D'ALÈS, RSR (1921) 374–380. — H. KOCH, Irenaeus über den Vorzug der römischen Kirche: ThStKr (1921) 54–72. — G. ESSER, ThGl (1922) 244–362. — FORGET, Le témoignage de saint Irénée en faveur de la primauté romaine: ETL (1928) 437–461. — H. PRECHT, Die Begründung des römischen Primats auf dem vatikanischen Konzil nach Irenaeus und dem Florentinum. Diss. Göttingen, 1923. — G. LA PIANA, The Roman Church at the End of the Second Century: HThR (1925) 251–253. — E. CASPAR, Die älteste römische Bischofsliste. Berlin, 1926. — K. ADAM, ThQ (1928) 196–203. — M. O'BOYLE, St. Irenaeus and the See of Rome: CHR (1930/31) 413ff. — A. EHRHARD, Die Kirche der Märtyrer. Munich, 1932, 277f. — D. VAN DEN EYNDE, Les normes de l'enseignement chrétien dans la littérature patristique des trois premiers siècles. Paris,. 1933, 171–179. — J. MADOZ, El primado Romano. Madrid, 1936. — B. J. KIDD, The Roman Primacy to A.D. 461. London, 1936. — A. D. DOYLE, St. Irenaeus on the Pope and the Early Heretics: IER 54 (1939) 298–306. — G. BARDY, La Théologie de l'Eglise de saint Clément de Rome à saint Irénée. Paris, 1945, 204–210. — W. L. KNOX, Irenaeus, Adv. Haer. 3.3.2: JThSt 47 (1946) 180–184. — R. JACQUIN, Le témoignage de S. Irénée sur l'Eglise de Rome: AT 9 (1948) 95–99. — C. MOHRMANN, A propos de Irenaeus, Adv. Haer. 3. 3. 1: VC 3 (1949) 57–61. — P. GALTIER, 'ab his qui sunt undique' — Irénée 3. 3. 2: RHE 44 (1949) 411–428.

6. The Eucharis t

Irenaeus is so convinced of the real presence of the body and blood of the Lord in the Eucharist, that he derives the resurrection of the human body from the fact that this body has been nourished by the body and blood of Christ:

When, therefore, the mingled cup and the manufactured bread receives the Word of God ($\epsilon\pi\iota\delta\epsilon\chi\epsilon\tau\alpha\iota\ \tau\grave{o}\nu\ \lambda\acute{o}\gamma o\nu\ \tau o\hat{v}\ \vartheta\epsilon o\hat{v}$) and the Eucharist becomes the blood and body of Christ, from which things the substance of our flesh is increased and supported, how can they affirm that the flesh is incapable of receiving the gift of God, which is life eternal, which is nourished from the body and blood of the Lord and is a member of him? . . . that flesh which is nourished by the cup which is his blood and receives increase from the bread which is his body. And just as a cutting from the vine planted in the ground fructifies in its season, or, as a grain of wheat falling into the earth and becoming decomposed rises with manifold increase by the Spirit of God, and becomes the Eucharist, which is the body and blood of Christ, so also our bodies, being nourished by it, and deposited in the earth, and suffering decomposition there, shall rise at their appointed time (5,2,3, ANF). — And how say they that the flesh passes into corruption and partakes not of life, which is nourished by the Lord's body and blood. Either let them change their opinion, or decline to make the offerings which I have mentioned. But our opinion is in harmony with the Eucharist, and the Eucharist again confirms our opinion. And we offer to him the things which are his own, showing forth accordingly our communion and union, and professing a resurrection of flesh and spirit. For as bread from the earth, receiving the invocation of God (προσλαβόμενος τὴν ἐπίκλησιν τοῦ θεοῦ) is no longer common bread but a Eucharist composed of two things, both an earthly and a heavenly one, so also our bodies, partaking of the Eucharist, are no longer corruptible, having the hope of eternal resurrection (4,18,5). From these words it appears that Irenaeus thinks bread and wine are consecrated by an epiclesis. The sacrificial character of the Eucharist is evident to Irenaeus, because he sees in it the new sacrifice which was prophesied by Malachy:

Giving directions to his disciples to offer to God the first-fruits of his own created things – not as if he stood in need of them, but that they might be themselves neither unfruitful nor ungrateful – he took that created thing, bread, and gave thanks, and said: 'This is my body.' And the cup likewise, which is part of that creation to which we belong, he confessed to be his blood, and taught the new oblation of the new covenant, which the Church, receiving from the Apostles, offers to God throughout all the world, to him who gives us as the means of subsistence the first-fruits of his own gifts in the New Testament, concerning which Malachy, among the twelve prophets, thus spoke beforehand: 'I have no pleasure in you, saith the Lord omnipotent, and I will not accept sacrifice at your hands. For from the rising of the sun unto the going down, my name is glorified among the gentiles, and in every place incense is offered to my name and a pure sacrifice; for great is my name among the gentiles, saith the Lord omnipotent,' indicating in the plainest manner by these words, that the former people (the Jews) shall indeed cease to make offerings to God, but that in every place sacrifice shall be offered to him, and that a pure one; and his name is glorified among the gentiles (4,17,5 ANF).

Texts: J. QUASTEN, Monumenta eucharistica et liturgica vetustissima. Bonn, 1935–37, 346–348.

Studies: J. W. F. HÖFLING, Die Lehre des Irenäus vom Opfer im christlichen Kultus (Progr.). Erlangen, 1860. — L. HOPFENMÜLLER, S. Irenaeus de eucharistia (Diss.). Bamberg, 1867. — J. WATTERICH, Der Konsekrationsmoment im heiligen Abendmahl und seine Geschichte. Heidelberg, 1896, 47–60. — F. S. RENZ, Die Geschichte des Messopferbegriffs I. Freising, 1901, 179–196. — A. STRUCKMANN, Die Gegenwart Christi in der hl. Eucharistie nach den schriftlichen Quellen der vornicänischen Zeit. Vienna, 1905, 63–89. — J. BRINKTRINE, Der Messopferbegriff in den ersten zwei Jahrhunderten. Freiburg i. B., 1918, 127–135. — A. D'ALÈS, La doctrine eucharistique de saint Irénée: RSR 13 (1923) 24–46. — P. BATIFFOL, L'Eucharistie. La présence réelle et la transsubstantiation. 9th ed. Paris, 1930, 167–183. — H. D. SIMONIN, A propos d'un texte eucharistique de S. Irénée: RSPT 23 (1934) 281–292. — J. L. KOOLE, De avondmaalsbeschouwing van den kerkvader Irenaeus. GTT 37 (1936) 295–303; 39 (1938) 412–417. — D. VAN DEN EYNDE, Eucharistia ex duabus rebus constans: S. Irénée, Adv. haer. IV, 18,5: Ant 15 (1940) 13–28. — F. R. M. HITCHCOCK, The Doctrine of the Holy Communion in Irenaeus: ChQ 129 (1939/40) 206–225.

7. Scripture

The New Testament Canon of Irenaeus comprises the four Gospels, the Epistles of St. Paul, the Acts of the Apostles, the Epistles of St. John and the Apocalypse, the First Epistle of St. Peter, and the recent prophetic writing of the Shepherd of Hermas, but not the Epistle to the Hebrews. He does not yet have a definite designation for the whole complex of these writings, although he regards them as a complete collection. Irenaeus calls the books of the New Testament *Scripture* (γραφή) because they have the same character of inspiration as the writings of the Old Testament. Concerning the origin of the four Gospels, he states:

> Matthew issued a written Gospel among the Hebrews in their own dialect, while Peter and Paul were preaching at Rome and laying the foundations of the Church. After their departure, Mark, the disciple and interpreter of Peter, did also hand down to us in writing what had been preached by Peter. Luke also, the companion of Paul, recorded in a book

the Gospel preached by him. Afterwards, John, the disciple
of the Lord, who also had leaned upon his breast, did himself publish a Gospel during his residence at Ephesus in
Asia (3,1,1).
Irenaeus explains that there are exactly four Gospels, no more
and no less, thus:

> For it is impossible that the Gospels should be in number
> either more or fewer than these. For since there are four
> regions of the world wherein they are, and four principal
> winds, and the Church is a seed sown in the whole earth, and
> the Gospel is the Church's pillar and ground, and the breath
> of life: it is natural that it should have four pillars, from all
> quarters breathing incorruption, and kindling men into life.
> Wherefore it is evident that the Artificer of all things, the
> Word, who sitteth upon the Cherubim, and keepeth all to-
> gether, when He was made manifest unto men, gave us his
> Gospel in four forms, kept together by one Spirit (3,11,8).

It is of importance for the history of Christian art that, in the
sentences which follow, Irenaeus derives the number four of the
Gospels from the number of the Cherubim:

> The Cherubim had four faces, and their faces are images
> of the dispensation of the Son of God. For 'the first living
> creature' it saith, 'was like a lion' (St. John), denoting his
> real efficiency, his guiding power, his royalty; 'and the
> second like a calf' (St. Luke), signifying his station as a Sac-
> rificer and Priest; 'and the third having the face of a man'
> (St. Matthew), most evidently depicting his presence as man;
> 'and the fourth like an eagle in flight' (St. Mark), declaring
> the gift of the Spirit flying down upon the Church (*ibid.*).

Differently from the later development of symbolism, the lion
is here attributed to John, and the eagle to Mark.

In determining the canonicity of a writing, Irenaeus insists
that not only apostolicity but also ecclesiastical tradition must
be considered. The Church has the decisive voice also in the
interpretation of Scripture, for the individual writings of the Old
and the New Testament are like trees in the garden of the Church.
She nourishes us with their fruits:

> It behooves us, therefore, to avoid their (heretical) doc-
> trines, and to take careful heed lest we suffer injury from

them; but to flee to the Church, and be brought up in her bosom, and be nourished with the Lord's Scripture. For the Church has been planted as a paradise in this world; therefore says the Spirit of God, 'Thou mayest freely eat from every tree of the garden', that is, Eat you may from every Scripture of the Lord; but you shall not eat with an uplifted mind, nor touch any heretical discord (5,20,2).

J. WERNER, Der Paulinismus des Irenaeus. Eine kirchen- und dogmenge-schichtliche Untersuchung über das Verhältnis des Irenaeus zu der paulini-schen Briefsammlung und Theologie (TU 6,2). Leipzig, 1889. — A. CAMER-LIJNK, S. Irénée et le canon du Nouveau Testament. Louvain, 1896. — F. S. GUTJAHR, Die Glaubwürdigkeit des irenäischen Zeugnisses über die Abfassung des vierten kanonischen Evangeliums aufs neue untersucht: Festschrift der k.k. Karl-Franzens-Universität in Graz. Graz, 1904. — J. CHAPMAN, St. Irenaeus on the Dates of the Gospels: JThSt 6 (1905) 563ff. — F. G. LEWIS, The Irenaeus Testimony to the Fourth Gospel, its Extent, Meaning and Value. Chicago, 1908. — REILLY, L'Inspiration de l'Ancien Testament chez S. Irénée: RBibl (1917) 489–507. — J. HOH, Zur Herkunft der vier Evange-listensymbole: Biblische Zeitschrift (1918/21) 229–234. — J. HOH, Die Lehre des hl. Irenäus über das Neue Testament. Münster, 1920. — S. HERRERA, S. Irénée de Lyon exégète (Diss.). Freibourg i. B., 1920. — W. SANDAY and C. H. TURNER, Novum Testamentum Sancti Irenaei, Being the New Testa-ment Quotations in the Old-Latin Version of the ἔλεγχος. Edited with Intro-duction, Apparatus, Notes and Appendices (Old Latin Texts 7). Oxford, 1923. Cf. H. J. VOGELS, ThR 23 (1924) 9–14; A. MERK, ZKTh 49 (1925), 302–315; J. DE GHELLINCK, RHE 20 (1924) 119f. — F. C. BURKITT, Dr. Sanday's New Testament of Irenaeus: JThSt 25 (1924) 56–67. — H. J. VOGELS, Der Evangelientext des hl. Irenaeus: RB (1924) 21–23. — J. CHAP-MAN, Did the Translation of S. Irenaeus Use a Latin New Testament: RB (1924) 34–57. — B. KRAFT, Die Evangelienzitate des heiligen Irenaeus (BS 21,4). Freiburg i. B., 1924. — W. V. LOEWENICH, Das Johannesverständnis im zweiten Jahrhundert. Gieben, 1932, 130–137. — J. T. CURRAN, St. Irenaeus and the Dates of the Synoptics: CBQ 5 (1943) 34–46; 160–178; 301–310.

8. *Anthropology*

Following the Platonic idea that man consists of φύσις, ψυχή and νοῦς, Irenaeus teaches that man is composed of body, soul, and spirit:

Everyone will allow that we are composed of a body taken from the earth, and a soul which receives the spirit from God (3,22,1).

Therefore, a human body which is animated by a natural soul

only is not a complete and perfect man. It seems that most of the time Irenaeus, like St. Paul, considers the third essential part, πνεῦμα, which completes and crowns human nature, to be the personal Spirit of God. Christ had promised this Spirit as a gift to his Apostles and believers, and St. Paul admonishes the Christians again and again that they carry this Spirit in themselves as in a temple; but in some passages it is difficult to decide whether Irenaeus understands the third essential part of man to be the spirit of man or the Spirit of God. That seems to be evident from the passage in which he describes the perfect man who is created after the image of God:

For by the hands of the Father, that is, by the Son and the Spirit, man, and not merely a part of man, was made in the likeness of God. Now the soul and the spirit are certainly a part of the man, but certainly not the man; for the perfect man consists in the commingling and the union of the soul receiving the Spirit of the Father, and the mixture of that fleshly nature which was also moulded after the image of God. . . For if anyone take away the substance of flesh, that is, of the handiwork of God, and consider the spirit only, such then would not be a spiritual man but would be the spirit of man, or the Spirit of God. But when the spirit here blended with the soul is united to the body, the man becomes spiritual and perfect because of the outpouring of the Spirit, and this is he who was made in the image and likeness of God. But if the spirit be wanting to the soul, he who is such indeed is of an animal nature, and being left carnal, shall be an imperfect being, possessing indeed the image of God in his formation, but not receiving the similitude through the Spirit; and thus is this being imperfect. Thus also, if any one take away the image and set aside the body, he cannot then understand this as being a man, as I have already said, or as something else than a man. For that flesh which has been moulded is not a perfect man in itself, but the body of a man and the part of a man. Neither is the soul itself, considered apart by itself, the man; but it is the soul of a man and part of a man. Neither is the spirit a man, for it is called the spirit, and not a man; but the commingling and union of all three constitutes the per-

fect man (5,6,1 ANF). — There are three things out of
which, as I have shown, the complete man is composed
— flesh, soul, and spirit. One of these does indeed save and
form — this is the spirit; while as to another it is united and
formed — that is the flesh; that which is between those two
— that is the soul, which sometimes indeed, when it follows
the spirit, is raised up by it, but sometimes it sympathizes
with the flesh and falls into carnal lusts. Those then, as many
as they be, who have not that which saves and forms, nor
unity, shall be flesh and blood and shall be called thus
(5,9,1).

The reception and the preservation of the third part, the spirit,
on which the essential perfection of man depends, is conditioned
by actions of the will and by moral conduct. Even the eternal
existence of the soul depends on her conduct here on earth, because she is not immortal by nature. Her immortality is a matter
of moral development. She is able to become immortal if she is
grateful to her Creator:

For as the heaven which is above us, the firmament, the
sun, the moon, the rest of the stars and all their grandeur,
although they had no previous existence, were called into
being, and continue throughout a long course of time according to the will of God, so also anyone who thinks thus respecting souls and spirits, and, in fact, respecting all created
things, will not by any means go far astray, inasmuch as all
things that have been made had a beginning when they were
formed, but endure as long as God wills that they should
have an existence and continuance... For life does not
arise from us, nor from our own nature; but is bestowed
according to the grace of God. And therefore he who shall
preserve the life bestowed upon him, and give thanks to him
who imparted it, shall receive also length of days forever
and ever. But he who shall reject it, and prove himself ungrateful to his Maker, inasmuch as he has been created, and
has not recognized him who bestowed, deprives himself of
the continuance forever and ever (2,34,3).

Irenaeus thought it necessary to refute the assertion of the
Gnostics that the soul is immortal by nature independently of
her moral conduct, and thus he was led to these false ideas.

9. *Soteriology*

The pivot of Irenaeus' doctrine of redemption is the fact that every man has need of redemption and is capable of redemption. This follows from the fall of the first parents, through which all their descendants are subject to sin and death and have lost the image of God. The redemption brought by the Son of God has liberated mankind from the slavery of Satan, sin, and death. Moreover, it has summed up the whole of mankind in Christ. It has effected the reunion with God, the adoption by God, and the assimilation to God. But Irenaeus avoids the word 'deification' θεοποίησις in this connection. He uses the terms 'to be attached to God', 'to adhere to God', '*participare gloriae Dei*', but he avoids effacing the boundaries between God and man, as was customary in the pagan religions and in the Gnostic heresies. Irenaeus makes a distinction between *imago Dei* and *similitudo Dei*. Man is by nature, by his immaterial soul, an image of God. The *similitudo Dei* is the similarity to God of a supernatural kind which Adam possessed by a voluntary act of God's goodness. This *similitudo Dei* is effected by the divine Pneuma.

The redemption of the individual is effected by the Church and her sacraments in the name of Christ. The sacrament is to nature what the new Adam is to the old. A creature receives its perfection in the sacraments. The sacrament is the climax of the recapitulation of creation in Christ. By baptism man is born again to God. On this occasion Irenaeus testifies for the first time in ancient Christian literature to infant baptism:

For He came to save all through means of himself — all, I say, who through Him are born again to God — infants, and children, and boys, and youths, and old men (2,22,4).

E. KLEBBA, Die Anthropologie des hl. Irenaeus. Münster, 1894. — F. STOLL, Die Lehre des hl. Irenaeus von der Erlösung und Heiligung: Katholik 85, 1 (1905) 46–71; 46–109; 181–201; 264–289; 349–353. — L. BAUR, Untersuchungen über die Vergöttlichungslehre der griechischen Väter: ThQ 101 (1920) 28–64; 155–186. — A. D'ALÈS, La doctrine de l'Esprit en S. Irénée: RSR 14 (1924) 497–538. — H. KOCH, Zur Lehre vom Urstand und von der Erlösung bei Irenaeus: ThStKr (1925) 183–214. — J. LEBRETON, La connaissance de Dieu chez S. Irénée: RSR 16 (1926) 385–406. — J. N. VAN DEN BRINK, Incarnatie en Verlossing bij Irenaeus. The Hague, 1934. — L. ESCOULA, Saint Irénée et la connaissance naturelle de Dieu: RSRUS (1940) 252–270. — B. POSCHMANN, Paenitentia secunda. Bonn, 1940, 211–229. —

A. HEITMANN, Imitatio Dei. Rome, 1940, 96–101. — E. PETERSON, L'immagine di Dio in S. Ireneo: SC (1941) 46–54.

10. *Eschatology*

Even in his eschatology the influence of Irenaeus' theory of recapitulation is clearly visible. The anti-Christ is the demoniac counterpart of Christ, because he is the summing up of all apostasy, injustice, malice, false prophecy, and treachery, from the the beginning of the world to its end:

> And there is therefore, in this beast, when he comes, a recapitulation, made of all sorts of iniquity and of every deceit, in order that all apostate power, flowing into and being shut up in him, may be sent into the furnace of fire. Fittingly, therefore, shall his name possess the number six hundred and sixty-six, since he sums up in his own person all the commixture of wickedness which took place previous to the deluge due to the apostasy of the angels. . . Thus then the six hundred years. . . do indicate the number of the name of that man in whom is concentrated the whole apostasy of six thousand years, and unrighteousness, and wickedness, and false prophecy, and deception, for which things' sake a cataclysm of fire shall also come (5,29,2).

Irenaeus demonstrates even his chiliastic view by his theory of the rehabilitation of the world:

> They are both ignorant of God's dispensations and of the mystery of the resurrection of the just and of the kingdom which is the commencement of incorruption, by means of which kingdom those who shall be worthy are accustomed gradually to comprehend God; and it is necessary to tell them respecting those things that it behooves the righteous first to receive the promise of the inheritance which God promised to the fathers, and to reign in it when they rise again to behold God in this creation which is renovated, and that the judgment should take place afterwards. For it is just that in that very creation in which they toiled or were afflicted, being proved in every way by suffering, they should receive the reward of their suffering; and that in the creation in which they were slain because of their love to God, in that they should be revived again; and that in the creation

in which they endured servitude, in that they should reign.
For God is rich in all things and all things are his. It is fitting,
therefore, that the creation itself, being restored to its prime-
val condition, should be without restraint under the dominion of the righteous (5,32,1 ANF).

M. GERHARDT, Die Bedeutung der Eschatologie bei Irenäus. Berlin, 1922. —
V. CREMERS, Het millenarisme van Irenaeus: Bijdragen van de Philosophische
en Theologische Faculteiten der Nederlandsche Jezuieten 1 (1938) 28–80. —
O. CULLMANN, Christus und die Zeit. Die urchristliche Zeit- und Geschichts-
auffassung. Zollikon-Zürich, 1946, 48f.; 173f. — J. DANIÉLOU, La typologie
millénariste de la semaine dans le Christianisme primitif: VC 2 (1948) 1–16.

INDEXES

I. REFERENCES

1. OLD AND NEW TESTAMENT

2. APOCRYPHA

3. ANCIENT CHRISTIAN WRITERS

(Brackets enclosing the name = Pseudo-)

12

4. MODERN AUTHORS

Chase, F. H., 115
Chaudouard, L., 236
Chavasse, C., 58
Chawner, W., 62
Choppin, L., 42
Christ, W., 159
Ciasca, P. A. 225
Cladder, H. J., 153
Clarke, W. K. L., 51, 168
Clarke, C. P. S., 75, 81
Clausen, O., 241
Clemen, C., 211
Cloin, G., 76
Coan, A. J., 28
Colmann, O., 52
Colombie, F., 41, 57
Colombo, S., 41, 177, 179
Colson, F. H., 202
Connolly, R. H., 28, 38, 39, 82, 92, 137, 140, 167, 220, 226, 227, 248, 253
Conybeare, F. C., 122, 133, 171, 179, 184, 196
Cooper, C. M., 267
Corbière, Ch., 189
Corssen, P., 179
Costas, P. S., 21
Cotelier, J. B., 40
Cotter, A. C., 12
Couard, L., 111
Couchoud, P. L., 272
Coustant, P., 280
Coxe, A. C., 16, 41, 203
Crafer, T. W., 57
Cramer, J. A., 210
Creed, J. M., 39
Cremers, V., 313
Creusen, J., 13
Creyghton, J., 29
Cristiani, L., 297
Critterio, B., 190
Crombie, F., 41, 57
Crone, P. G., 74
Crozier, W. P., 118
Cruttwell, Ch. Th., 5
Cullmann, O., 29, 63, 313
Cumont, F., 143, 172f, 246
Cureton, W., 74, 142, 247, 264
Curran, J. T., 308
Czapla, B., 3

Dahlmann, J., 140
Daniélou, J., 15, 17, 219, 245, 297, 313

Dannenbauer, H., 52, 135
Dannreuther, H., 286
Davies, A. L., 110
Deblavy, J., 42
Debouxthay, P., 202
Deeleman, C. F. M., 133, 135
Deemter, R. van, 105
Deferrari, R. J., 22
Deissmann, A., 21
Deissner, K., 156
Delafosse, H., 52, 74, 75
Delazer, J., 153
Delehaye, H., 82, 176, 177, 178, 179
Dembowski, H., 223
Deneffe, A., 12
Denzinger, H., 19
Dibelius, M., 6, 39, 53, 105, 111, 261
Diekamp, F., 3, 41, 59, 247
Diels, H., 253
Dieterich, A., 145, 172, 173
Diettrich, G., 167
Diobouniotis, C., 291
Dix, G., 39, 85, 226
Dobschütz, E. von, 28, 118, 143
Dodd, J. T., 112
Dods, M., 241
Dölger, F. J., 28, 75, 76, 133, 137, 153, 159, 172f, 175, 178, 182, 190
Donaldson, J., 16, 41, 57, 62, 189, 252
Donckel, E., 63
Donovan, J., 84
Doren, R. van, 148
Doresse, J., 277
Dörfler, P., 177
Dörholt, B., 27
Dorsch, E., 219
Doulcet, H., 252
Doyle, A. D., 304
Dräseke, J., 224, 252
Dressel, A. R. M., 62
Drexl, F., 20
Du Cange, C., 18
Duchesne, L., 29, 172f
Duckett, E. S., 7
Duensing, H., 145, 153
Duncker, L., 210, 213
Duriez, G., 122
Dürr, L., 12
Dutilleul, J., 19
Duval, R., 8
Dzialowski, G. V., 3, 4

Eberhard, A., 235
Edsman, C. M., 146

Grande, C. del, 159, 160
Grant, R. M., 85, 168, 242
Grébaut, S., 109, 145, 153
Gregg, A. F., 179
Grégoire, H., 173
Greiff, A., 39, 173
Greiff, J. N., 219
Grenfell, B. P., 110, 160, 194
Gressmann, H., 226
Grimme, H., 167
Gronau, K., 189
Groot, J. F. de, 13
Gross, O., 241
Grossi-Gondi, F., 177
Grossouw, W., 108
Grundl, B., 202
Gry, L., 153
Gudemann, A., 7
Guenther, E., 178
Guerrier, L., 109, 153
Guibert, J. de, 19
Guidi, J., 8, 15, 130
Guillon, N. S., 17
Gunkel, H., 18, 159
Günter, H., 177
Gutjahr, F. S., 308
Gwyn, J., 133

Haase, F., 111, 122, 125, 127, 130,
    140, 195, 247, 264
Hagen, L., 177
Hagemeyer, O., 182
Hagmann, H., 303
Hahn, A., 27, 264, 271
Hallock, F. H., 108
Halusa, T., 169
Handmann, R., 112
Hanozin, P., 177
Harden, J. M., 8
Harmer, J. R., 38, 41
Harnack, A. v., 5, 13, 15, 27, 38, 41,
    51, 52, 59, 73, 75, 90, 108, 115,
    133, 145, 154, 155, 157, 167, 172f,
    177, 181, 183, 184, 189, 191, 203,
    206, 218, 223, 241, 243, 252, 261f,
    269, 272, 273, 274, 276, 278, 280,
    291, 293, 303
Harris, J. R., 38, 54, 57, 75, 105, 160,
    161, 162, 167, 168, 191, 192, 194,
    225, 226
Harrison, P. N., 76, 79f, 81
Hartel, G., 179
Harvey, W. W., 291
Hastings, J., 18, 110, 118, 159

Hauck, A., 18, 189
Hauler, E., 149
Häuser, Ph., 92, 203
Hayes, W., 124
Hefele, C. H., 235
Hefenning, W., 227
Heiler, C. L., 224
Heilmann, A., 19
Heine, O., 184
Heinrici, G., 261
Heintze, W., 62
Heinzelmann, W., 252
Heitmann, A., 76, 312
Hellmanns, W., 177
Hemmer, H., 16, 17, 38, 41
Hendrix, P., 259
Hennecke, E., 27, 38, 41, 57, 62, 108,
    110, 122, 124, 133, 135, 137, 138,
    140, 145, 153, 154, 159, 167, 169,
    171, 194, 252
Henschel, G. A. L., 18
Herding, G., 2, 3
Hermann, Th., 171
Herrmann, L., 52, 286
Hermes, J. J., 4
Herrera, S., 308
Hertling, L., 52
Heussi, K., 52
Higgins, M. J., 21
Hilgenfeld, A., 62, 108, 184, 256,
    259, 261, 264, 271, 286
Hill, J. H., 225
Hirsch, S., 4
Hirschfeld, O., 180
Hitchcock, F. R. M., 29, 38, 205, 241,
    291, 292, 297, 306
Hjelt, A., 226
Hobson, A. A., 226
Hödum, A., 52, 76
Hoffmann, G., 29, 140
Höfling, J. W. F., 306
Hofmann, R., 111
Hogg, H. W., 226
Hoh, J., 39, 58, 75, 105, 153, 282, 308
Holl, K., 27
Hollard, A., 272
Holstein, H., 302
Holzhey, C., 133
Holzinger, K., 169
Hommes, N. J., 85
Hontheim, J., 226
Hopfenmüller, L., 306
Hopfner, Th., 15
Hoppe, H., 63

Kutsch, W., 8

Labourt, J., 167
Labriolle, P. de, 7, 156, 181, 182
Lacoste, A., 280
Lagarde, P. de, 62
Lagrange, M. J., 112, 122, 149, 198, 227
Laguier, L., 189
Laistner, L. W., 7
Lake, K., 15, 28, 38, 41, 57, 104, 118, 153, 252
Lake, S., 15
Lambot, C., 84
Landgraf, A., 148
La Piana, G. 281, 305
Larfeld, W., 84
Lauchert, F., 195
Laurent, A., 41
Lawlor, H. J., 84, 286
Lazzati, G., 195, 236
Leblanc, J., 210, 224, 236
Lebon, J., 29, 241
Lebreton, J., 28, 51, 75, 105, 159, 190, 198, 241, 295, 297, 311
Leclercq, J., 211
Leclercq, H., 8, 18, 173, 177, 183, 225, 257, 286
Lefort, L. Th., 59, 105, 108
Lehmann, J., 62, 235
Leigh-Bennet, E., 6
Leipoldt, J., 8
Leisegang, H., 257
Leitl, J., 241
Lejay, P., 16, 17
Lelong, A., 41, 74
Lemarchand, L., 52
Lemm, O. von, 130
Lemme, L., 122, 195
Lenormant, F., 175
Levi della Vida, G., 264
Lewis, A. S., 122, 130, 140
Lewis, F. G., 308
Lewy, H., 168, 190
Lexa, F., 277
Liberty, S., 29
Liddell, H. G., 19
Lieblein, J. D. C., 276
Liechtenhau, H., 276
Liénard, E., 156
Liese, W., 211
Lietzmann, H., 6, 16, 27, 28, 38, 39, 41, 52, 57, 76, 90, 92, 137, 140, 153, 183, 220, 248

Lightfoot, J. B., 38, 41, 54, 57, 73, 81, 154, 252, 286
Lilje, H., 38
Lipsius, R. A., 118, 130, 132, 134, 137, 138, 139, 142, 143, 261
Little, V. A. S., 190
Littmann, E., 8
Ljungvik, H., 130
Loewenich, W. von, 42, 81, 168, 202, 308
Löfstedt, E., 22
Logothetes, P., 235
Lohmeyer, E., 178
Loisy, A., 38, 272
Loofs, F., 13, 28, 75, 85, 133, 204, 205, 239, 241, 272, 290, 292, 293
Loomis, L. R., 19, 52, 57, 110, 135, 286
Lorimer, W. L., 51, 52
Lortz, J., 190
Lösch, St., 52
Lowe, J., 63
Lubac, H. de, 15, 17
Lucius, E., 177
Lucks, H. A., 236
Lüdtke, W., 125, 173
Lukman, F. K., 177
Lumbroso, G., 160
Lundström, S. 291

Mabillon, J., 14
MacDonald, A., 28
McGiffert, A. C., 13, 196
MacKnight, W. J., 155
MacLean, A. J., 38, 159
MacMunn, V. C., 137
Macke, K., 140
Mackenzie, F. S., 104
Madoz, J., 12, 19, 20, 29, 52, 178, 304
Magnin, E., 18
Maher, M., 225
Mai, A., 168
Manacorda, G., 16, 17
Mangenot, E., 18
Manoir, H. du, 12, 28
Mansel, H. L., 256
Manucci, U., 6
Maran, P., 14
Margoliouth, D. S., 140
Marin-Sola, F., 13
Marique, J. M. F., 41
Marmardji, A. S., 227
Marmiet, 14
Marmorstein, A., 145, 189, 295

Palazzini, P., 190
Pangerl, Fr., 20
Pantaleo, P., 202
Pantelakis, E. G., 140, 159
Paolo, F. de, 171
Pape, P., 195
Pappalardo, S., 236
Paranikas, M., 159
Parpal, C., 17
Patin, A., 184
Paul, L., 210, 241
Pauli, A. di, 241, 252, 253
Pauly, A. F. von, 18
Pautigny, L., 201
Pease, A. S., 190
Peeters, P., 110, 124, 176
Peitz, W. M., 29
Pellegrino, M., 190, 202, 230, 235, 236
Peradze, G., 8, 39
Pereira, M. E., 177
Pérez, P. J. de, 29
Perler, O., 76, 219
Perrella, G., 85
Petavius, D., 12
Petermann, J. H., 276
Peters, C., 227, 228
Peterson, E., 39, 133, 143, 178, 312
Peterson, P., 62
Petrément, S., 259, 272
Pfaff, Ch. M., 293
Pfättisch, J. M., 201, 211
Phillips, C. A., 227
Phillips, G., 142
Piana, G. la, 280, 304
Picard, M., 194
Pichon, R., 7
Pick, B., 110, 130, 133, 134, 137, 138, 140
Pighi, G. B., 22, 160
Pieper, K., 63
Pincherle, A., 169
Piontek, F., 130
Pistelli, E., 122
Pitra, J. P., 174, 175, 246, 248
Plooij, D., 226, 227
Plummer, Ch., 111
Plumpe, J. C., 16, 58, 105, 181, 302
Pohl, O., 175
Pommrich, A., 235, 241
Ponschab, B., 224
Poschmann, B., 39, 52, 58, 105, 153, 311
Postel, G., 118

Pott, A., 226
Pourrat, J., 181
Prada, M. dal., 38
Pratten, B. P., 59, 143, 180, 196, 235
Precht, H., 304
Preisigke, F., 18
Preiss, Th., 76
Prestige, G. L., 190, 295
Preuschen, E., 110, 145, 203, 226, 286
Preysing, K., 236
Priesnig, A., 117
Prime, P., 181
Proctor, W. C., 108
Prümm, K., 29, 76, 146, 169, 297
Przybylski, B., 299
Puech, A., 7, 63, 105, 189, 205, 223, 224, 241, 277
Purves, G. T., 198
Pusey, E., 16

Quasten, J., 8, 12, 16, 19, 39, 53, 76, 135, 137, 140, 153, 159, 160, 173, 175, 178, 182, 183, 219, 243, 306
Quentin, H., 181, 241
Quispel, G., 261, 262, 272

Raabe, R., 194
Rackl, M., 75
Rademacher, L., 21, 138
Radford, L., 252
Raemers, S. A., 6
Ragg, L., 127
Rahlfs, A., 202
Rahmani, J. E., 118
Rahner, H., 53, 82, 177, 301
Rahner, K., 42, 76
Rambaut, W. H., 291
Ramsay, W. M., 75, 82, 133, 171, 173
Rand, E. K., 8
Ranft, J., 12, 286
Rapisarda, E., 241, 242
Raschke, H., 272
Rauschen, G., 38, 81, 82, 104, 115, 122, 177, 179, 182, 183, 201, 202, 252
Reagan, J. N., 135
Regibus, L. de, 178
Rehm, B., 62, 63, 264
Reilly, Th., 308
Reinach, S., 75
Reinach, Th., 160
Reinhold, H., 21

Schwartz, E., 28, 63, 143, 199, 223, 235
Schwartze, M. G., 277
Schweitzer, V., 104
Schwyzer, E., 21
Scott, E. F., 257
Scott, H., 198
Scott, R., 19
Sdralek, M., 3
Sedgwick, S. N., 108
Sedlacek, J., 118
Seeberg, E., 191, 198, 272
Seeberg, R., 13, 28, 184, 194
Segala, L., 17
Segur Vidal, G., 149
Seitz, O. J. F., 105
Semisch, C., 198
Sepp, B., 82
Serruys, D., 148
Seymour, St. D., 148, 247
Shahan, J. J., 6
Shepherd, M. H., 76, 190
Shewring, W. H., 182
Shotwell, J. T., 19, 52, 57, 110, 135, 286
Shrawley, J. H., 74
Silbernagl, J., 4
Sild, O., 177
Silva Tarouca, C., 280
Silverstein, Th., 148, 149
Simon, M., 204
Simonin, H. D., 42, 299, 306
Siouville, A., 62, 63
Sizoo, A., 22
Skeat, T. C., 111
Skutsch, F., 7
Slee, H. M., 168
Smital, O., 28
Smith, Th., 62
Smith, W., 18
Smothers, E. R., 159
Snell, B. J., 108
Söder, R., 130
Sola, G., 182
Sophocles, E. A., 18
Souter, A., 133, 291
Sparrow-Simpson, W. J., 16
Speranskij, M. N., 138
Spikowski, L., 301
Spitta, F., 145
Spoer, H. H., 226
Spörri, R., 76
Staerk, W., 167, 212
Stähelin, H., 259

Stahler, R., 202
Stäh. lin, O., 7, 126, 198, 266
Stanton, V. H., 115
Staufer, E., 53
Stearns, W. N., 6
Steffes, J. P., 256
Stegmann, V., 211
Stegmüller, O., 227
Steidle, B., 6, 12, 272
Stein, J., 183
Stenning, J. F., 226
Stephanus, H., 18
Steuer, W., 224
Stieren, A., 291
Stiglmayr, J., 22, 241, 291, 292
Stoll, F., 311
Stölten, W., 167
Strathmann, H., 173
Streeter, H., 39, 54, 58, 137
Ström, A. V., 105
Strucker, A., 41
Struckmann, A., 135, 137, 306
Stuhlfaut, G., 135
Suhlin, H., 287
Surkau, H. W., 82, 178
Svennung, J., 63, 105
Swete, H. B., 6, 115, 286
Sychowski, St. v., 2
Sykutris, J., 84

Tamilia, D., 196
Taylor, C., 104
Telfer, W., 39
Ter-Mekerttschian, K., 292, 293
Ter-Minassiantz, E., 291, 293
Terry, M. S., 169
Terzaghi, N., 7, 160, 241
Teuffel, W. S., 7
Thalhofer, V., 16
Thiele, J., 69, 75
Thieme, K., 92
Thierry, A., 14
Thilo, J. C., 108, 271
Thomas, C., 243
Thomas, J., 63
Thompson, J. W., 180
Thomsen, P., 252
Thornell, G., 22
Thumb, A., 21
Thibaut, J. B., 219
Till, W., 177
Tischendorf, C., 110, 111, 118, 122, 124, 132, 148, 150, 247
Tisserant, E., 110, 127

Youtie, H. C., 143

Zahn, Th., 41, 73, 75, 115, 137, 173, 189, 191, 203, 225, 229, 238, 247, 252, 271, 286
Zappalà, M., 133, 224
Zeller, F., 38, 41
Zellinger, J., 15, 17
Ziegler, J., 168

Zingerle, P., 59, 148
Zizzamia, A. I., 42
Zob, J. N., 12
Zöckler, O., 189
Zscharnack, L., 18
Zuntz, G., 246
Zwaan, J. de, 133, 153, 168, 194, 224

5. GREEK WORDS

II. GENERAL INDEX

IMPRIMATUR
Driebergen, d. 11 m. dec. A. D. 1949
J. A. M. PREIN, cens. a.h.d.